If there were ever a book that can cry in the wilderness, it is this one.  of disaster. We are in the midst of it trying to sort out relics of decency and compassion in an ever-growing entitled, apathetic and oblivious American culture that wants to ignore and purchase around and beyond the suffering of others we induce. Gruba-McCallister's work here is a call to arms, but to arms that once again welcome those who suffer, and with a renewed wisdom that such suffering is due to oppression. This book is the sine qua non example of the public scholar—the engaged practitioner and postmodern advocate who offers decades of therapeutic and educational wisdom for various interprofessional and transdisciplinary contexts. *Embracing Disillusionment* demystifies tranquilizing ideologies embedded in deceptive discourses about who suffers, why, and to what ends. Gruba-McCallister writes in the tradition of Foucault's challenges to institutional hegemony, but more on the ground, accessible, and from the heart—but with nonetheless scholarly soundness and provocation. This is a "read it or else face the consequences" book in true prophetic form. It is imperative that a copy of this book be sent via express mail to the White House!

Todd DuBose, PhD,
Full Professor in the Clinical Psychology Department
at the Chicago School of Professional Psychology—Chicago Campus

This fascinating book is a rigorous examination of what it means to be human in the 21st century. The author challenges dominant assumptions that neoliberalism is the only possible way to be human. With great skill and knowledge, Gruba-McCallister shows how the ideology of neoliberalism becomes hegemonic, and how we can resist its noxious effects. The book combines science with humanity, theory with practice. The result is an essential contribution toward achieving wellness and fairness for all.

Isaac Prilleltensky, PhD, Professor,
Vice Provost for Institutional Culture, Erwin
and Barbara Mautner Chair in Community Well-Being,
University of Miami

Frank Gruba-McCallister has given us a brilliant and penetrating analysis of the ways in which our human vulnerability to self-deception and ideological conditioning maintain power and wealth of the few. The book has extraordinary breadth, drawing on psychological theory, political and economic theory, religious writings about suffering, and Frank's personal experience of disillusionment in our current crisis. I am deeply and sincerely impressed by this original, powerful explication of the interplay of practices maintaining our collective suffering and by this prophetic call for liberation from oppression.

Marge Witty, PhD, Professor,
Illinois School of Professional Psychology
and Past President of the Association for the Development
of the Person-Centered Approach (ADPCA)

With *Embracing Disillusionment: Achieving Liberation Through the Demystification of Suffering*, Dr. Gruba-McCallister has written a book that is extremely relevant in today's social and political climate.

One only has to look at the extreme political polarization and social/financial disparity that continues to worsen throughout the world. I have seen first-hand as a former educator of students with emotional/behavioral problems, a former school administrator, a current College Trustee, attorney and elected official how too many in our country are oppressed and yet deny their status. By mentally altering their reality, they refuse to confront what is happening to them and thus, the "haves" get stronger while the "have nots" become more dehumanized.

This book is especially relevant to educators, attorneys, politicians and those in mental health fields. Dr. Gruba-McCallister pulls together ideologies of multiple theorists and explains how fear, suspension of disbelief, and creating one's own reality causes and/or supports suffering and oppression. It provides an in-depth discussion of psychological, spiritual, and ideological theories that work in tandem in trying to explain why humans often do not confront the realities of oppression, suffering, and social injustice. It also provides a guideline for steps one can use to pursue "liberation" from suffering.

Amanda. D. Howland, MA, MS, JD, Elected Trustee,
College of Lake County

Frank Gruba-McCallister has written a magnum opus which draws together a lifetime of his wisdom and love for helping to empower people to learn from and transcend their experiences with suffering. This book is a fantastic integration of his wisdom about the nature of suffering from the viewpoints of many powerful traditions of wisdom and love, including Buddhism, critical psychology, existentialism, humanistic counseling, liberation pedagogy, social justice, and even

Taoism. His approach to understanding the nature of suffering is fully embodied as he writes with great compassion, emotion, and transparency about his own struggles with the suffering of his own life. His transparency really helps one to understand the personal grounding of his lofty and impressive intellectual insights into the causes of human suffering. This book functions like a manual for achieving liberation through gaining insights into the nature of the suffering that we all face and encounter in intrapersonal, interpersonal, institutional, environmental, and societal contexts and then taking some action with ourselves and others.

This book is very unique in that it joins up deeply intrapersonal and interpersonal insights into why we suffer with powerful political and societal insights stemming from our reigning obsessions with denying the reality of suffering and the exploitation of individuals caused by a shared focus on neo-liberalism ideologies. Frank Gruba-McCallister discusses how we can gain a critical consciousness of our own lives and roles in maintaining the matrix of self-deception and mystification in which we come to view suffering so erroneously that we come to oppress ourselves and others even while believing that we are doing the right thing. Frank weaves together a powerful book that encourages you to transcend the illusions that we have about ourselves that cause us to suffer needlessly and to oppress others. *If there was one book that you could read to learn how to exit the matrix of the suffering of suffering, this is it!* His words encourage you to gain liberation from these personal and neo-liberal illusions and in so doing to open yourself up to new insights about what we can do together to save our societies and the planet itself from the needless suffering of neoliberal-inspired oppression. His writing masterfully inspires curiosity, wonder, and awe to take up our part in transforming our cultures and our planet into a place where we can turn to our suffering as a guide rather than as an enemy while simultaneously combatting oppression to create compassion and justice for all.

Ian E. Wickramasekera II, PsyD, Assistant Professor,
Core Faculty, Naropa University

In his well-written book, Dr. Gruba-McCallister calls on those of us who struggle for social justice to critically examine how our world enables an oppression that somehow seems invisible. An illusion has been created, that the poor will always be with us — and those who end up impoverished in the land of opportunity have only themselves to blame. The market is there to respond to our needs, and if the so-called market can't offer the fix—did people really have needs in the first place? Through this book we are reminded that the illusion that oppression is not real harms both the oppressed and the oppressor. People who experience oppression and those who render it become disillusioned by the suffering that is created. We isolate ourselves, blame each other, and seek to buy the perfect strategy that will enable each individual their success. Our mutual self-deception, however, may also be leading to our mutual self- destruction.

We must suffer as part of the human condition, Dr. Gruba-McCallister reminds us, but suffering can enrich our humanity, enabling sympathy for ourselves and for others who fail to rise to the standard of success dictated by a neoliberal standard of consumption. This book compellingly makes the case that the powerful have always tried to blame the poor for their poverty. As social and economic disparities create even greater chasms between rich and poor, we must become better at demystifying and critically examining the moral and ethical choices of how we gather ourselves as a society.

We can challenge this deception, however. Dr. Gruba-McCallister offers a path for us to engage with each other, to challenge the hegemonic frame of individualism that neoliberalism has imposed on us. We must stop denying that suffering does not exist. We must acknowledge that we have developed a system that oppresses people for not being powerful. We can recognize that through our understanding of each other's pain, our very humanity is strengthened. We are all co-strugglers sharing a common pursuit of social justice, and we will suffer as humans in our common struggle. As pointed out in this book, our empathy for one another in doing so can help us achieve a common liberation that promotes our common humanity.

Nancy Bothne, PhD, Associate Professor,
Clinical Psychology Doctoral Program,
Chicago School of Professional Psychology

Embracing Disillusionment:

Achieving Liberation Through the Demystification of Suffering

Frank Gruba-McCallister, Ph.D.

University
PROFESSORS PRESS

Colorado Springs, CO
www.universityprofessorspress.com

First Published in 2019, University Professors Press.

Print ISBN: 978-1-939686-50-3
ebook ISBN: 978-1-939686-51-0

University Professors Press
Colorado Springs, CO
www.universityprofessorspress.com

Front Cover Art by Kristyn Beckstrom
Cover Design by Laura Ross

To Jimmy Dore

A blue-collar Chicago boy like me
for his courageous speaking truth to power
and his genuine compassion for the oppressed

Table of Contents

Foreword

Wellness depends on *fairness*, and fairness, in turn, depends on *awareness*. This enlightening book documents the linkages among these three foundational elements of the human experience. By wellness I mean a state of complete well-being in which individuals experience pleasure and purpose, or hedonic and eudaimonic well-being, in various domains of life, including interpersonal, community, occupational, physical, psychological, and economic. The extent to which we experience wellness in these facets of our lives is determined, in large part, by our experiences of fairness in relationships, at work, and in society at large. Fairness, as the practice of justice, consists of experiences in which people and groups are accorded their legitimate due. People are due respect, voice, and choice in decisions affecting their lives. This is typically called *procedural justice*. In addition, individuals and groups are due resources to lead a full and meaningful life. This is a form of *distributive justice* in which people receive the resources required to thrive. There are other subtypes of justice, such as *retributive, informational, and restorative.*

It is not hard to see how levels of wellness are impacted by levels of fairness. In families and relationships, when dominant figures make decisions without consulting other members, a violation of procedural and possibly distributive justice is taking place. In workplaces, when employees are exploited, the sense of fairness evaporates and the worker suffers. At the social level, when people living in poverty are deprived of medical care due to lack of universal health care, we are facing a pretty fundamental violation of distributive justice: access to a fundamental right. In contrast, in families, workplaces, and societies where fairness prevails, people are happier and report higher levels of life satisfaction and physical and mental health. As societies improve their levels of economic and political fairness, so does the well-being of the population. Fairness at levels from the microcosm of relationships to the macrocosm of environmental and health policy has a tremendous impact on levels of wellness. The work of British epidemiologists

Embracing Disillusionment

Richard Wilkinson and Kate Pickett in particular document the deleterious effects of injustice on psychological and mental health. In the United States, psychologist Keith Payne has recently documented the pernicious effects of inequality on our psyche. These facts are well known. What is less known, and by far less articulated, is the role of awareness in challenging the perpetuation of injustice and illegitimate inequality. This is where Gruba-McCallister makes a brilliant contribution to our understanding of our culture and its psychological effects.

According to the author of this important and timely book, supporters of the status quo are invested in obfuscating the role of oppression and injustice in personal and collective suffering. Through well-crafted stratagems, media consultants and spin doctors create myths that perpetuate the status quo. Their approach entails redefining social problems such as oppression and injustice into intrapsychic maladies. An entire lexicon of maladaptive behaviors has been created to induce people to believe that society is best the way it is, and it is only the self that requires transformation. This is an astute approach to deflect blame from social injustice to personal inadequacy. How this neoliberal ideology becomes embodied in all of us is the main contribution of this magnificent volume. The author deciphers the ways in which neoliberalism becomes hegemonic and dominates internal life. Gruba-McCallister illuminates the dark path where neoliberalism traffics in dogma.

Without awareness of how ideology becomes the regnant psychology, there is no chance to contest the rules of the game, which is why the captains of industry are invested in obfuscation. Consumerism cannot work without a supportive ideology, just as inequality cannot survive without a justificatory discourse. As a result, illusions are created that we all have the power to overcome adversity and acquire the goods that will fill our void. The author shows us how to get disillusioned and how to get the power to challenge stories of self-blame and fatalistic suffering.

This book is an antidote to ignorance. It seeks to educate about our most precious resource: ourselves. It is an education as well as a wake-up call. Gruba-McCallister calls on us to question not only hegemonic conceptions of the good life, but also the cultural workers who perpetuated distorted images of happiness and well-being. These workers include psychologists, psychiatrists, social workers, counselors, consultants, and coaches who want us to focus inward and not outward. Ironically, many of these healers decry the mind–body dualism while perpetuating the internal–external split. They propagate images of human beings as isolated and decontextualized. These atomistic views disconnect us from reality. Gruba-McCallister is invested in reconnecting us to reality and to ourselves. In that regard, this book is a work of enlightenment and protest at the same time. It deconstructs at the same time that it reconstructs. It is a profoundly humane work. It seeks to recapture what is essential about human beings while contesting toxic versions of ourselves. The book combines science with humanity, rigorous critique with inspirational hope. I highly recommend it as one of the very best volumes that connect the political with the psychological.

Isaac Prilleltensky, Miami, March 2019

References

Payne, K. (2017). *The broken ladder: How inequality affects the way we think, live, and die.* New York, NY: Penguin.

Pickett, K., & Wilkinson, R. (2010). *The spirit level: Why greater equality makes societies stronger.* New York, NY: Bloomsbury.

Wilkinson, R., & Pickett, K. (2018). *The inner level: How more equal societies reduce stress, restore sanity and improve everyone's well-being.* London, UK: Penguin.

Preface

Suffering is a fact of life! How often have we heard this assertion made and wished this harsh fact wasn't so? It seems almost incomprehensible that anyone could deny the irrefutable reality of suffering. Its impact on life is pervasive. Every person whose life is touched by suffering—large or small—provides categorical testimony to its reality. Through the course of human history, it has been the source of incalculable physical damage, mental anguish, and spiritual agony. The devastation it has wrought is incomprehensible. In the face of this evidence how can anyone genuinely act as if these facts are subject to dispute? How can they choose to turn a blind eye or deaf ear to the afflicted? Where can they retreat in order to evade personal encounters with suffering? Though these questions sound rhetorical, tragically they are not. Just as suffering is a fact, it is equally a fact that the effort exerted by human beings to reject and escape its reality is staggering. People spend an immense amount of time and energy engaging in all manner of evasions and ploys to close themselves off from any encounter with suffering—whether theirs or others.

Understanding this paradox and the often-tragic consequences that follow from how human beings negotiate it is the subject I will be tackling in this book. In doing so I will be calling upon many years of study, personal reflection, clinical practice, and teaching that I have devoted to understanding suffering and trying in whatever modest ways I could to alleviate its impact on others. Suffering comes in many forms and arises from different causes. The suffering that I will be focusing on is that caused by oppression. This is because of the substantial role that oppression plays in causing suffering. It is also because I perceive a troubling decline in a commitment to the values of compassion and justice necessary to ending oppression not only in our country but throughout the world. The rise of oppression and failing to treat our fellow human beings and the world around us with the respect and dignity owed to them are to my mind inextricably intertwined. And what I see behind this connection is an unwillingness to courageously confront suffering, whether it is suffering over which we have no control or suffering we create by our own actions—most especially actions that are responsible for oppression.

The conundrums posed by this complex and conflictual relationship we have with suffering are considerable. I cannot promise to completely sort out all of them in the pages that follow. However, we cannot afford to delay acting to rectify the destructive ways in which we deal with suffering until all such mysteries have been resolved. The stakes are much too high. Our decline into an abyss from which there may be no escape is an ever more looming peril. The ever-expanding chasm that separates the haves from the have nots cannot be sustained without tearing away at whatever vestiges of the social fabric remain. As social beings, the utter deterioration of our essential interdependency leaves us without social support, opportunities for mutual dialogue, and the bonds of affection necessary to our survival. Similarly dismissing the interdependency of our species with the rest of the natural world has set in motion a climate change disaster that irrefutably threatens our long-term survival. And it is not merely oppression at work in these perils but, more fundamentally, the psychological, social, economic and political processes that sustain that oppression and inure us to the pain and suffering it inflicts.

The very suffering that we so desperately seek to deny, distort and evade is the very thing that provides us with the answer to our quandary. We must recover our ability to meet suffering with open hearts and inquiring minds. No matter how disorienting and discomfiting, we must accept the fear and pain that come with this encounter. We have not been promised a life free of sorrow, frustration, disappointment and even moments of terror—though this seems to be an astonishingly common belief. This belief does not come from nowhere, and it would not persist without influences that foster and maintain it. It arises in part out of some very natural propensities within human beings. It is not surprising that over time human beings have developed certain predispositions and resources to buffer themselves against the painful and disruptive impacts of suffering. But, far more important, this illusion of a suffering-free life is carefully cultivated from the moment we are born by a prevailing ideology called neoliberalism.

This ideology employs this illusion about how suffering is unnecessary and easily dispensed with to maintain existing power relationships within the capitalist status quo. These same deceptions keep subordinated members of society passive, compliant, and even fatalistic about the suffering inflicted on them through abuses of power and privilege. I will look at the natural processes that foster our self-defeating responses to suffering as they provide an important foundation to our resistance. However, I will be devoting far more attention to the ideological bases of resistance to the necessity of suffering and the ways in which this defeats any recognition of the potentially positive possibilities of suffering to challenge the status quo and create a more just society. This greater focus on the role of ideology is essential to any hope we might have to unveil the role of oppression in causing suffering while also obscuring the very suffering it creates.

Any examination of the lack of compassion shown by those who engage in oppressive practices, sometimes leading to an immense degree of suffering, can be both baffling and disturbing. How do we begin to wrap our heads around the most egregious examples of oppression, such as genocide or large-scale violence? How do we explain attitudes that range from indifference to outright contempt shown by the privileged toward people whom they exploit, derogate, dominate, and even destroy? At the time I write this Preface, the issue of gun violence has again attracted greater national attention following another in a series of tragic school shootings at Marjory Stoneman Douglas High School in Parkland, Florida, which killed 17 people. Mass shootings have become a sickening routine linked to unrestricted access to firearms in the United States and the death-affirming culture we have adopted as we expand wars, prey on the disadvantaged and the weak, and submit the environment to unbounded depredations.

Unlike other incidents involving a shooting, many of the students who witnessed the death of their fellow students and teachers courageously spoke out against the easy access to guns and criticized the lack of action on the part of politicians to put an end to the epidemic of gun deaths in the United States. The world they had come to believe in—a world of safety, contentment, and everyday pleasure—had in an instant been violently torn apart. They witnessed with terror the brutality of death and would be haunted with images of violence. There can be no doubt that their world had been turned upside down; they and their families had become disillusioned. The old world they occupied just the day before was left in shreds. But what was most inspiring was that they did not shun their suffering; nor did they allow it to swallow them up and either embitter or deaden them. Instead they turned their anger, sadness and fear to positive social action by starting the Never Again movement aimed at putting pressure on politicians for much needed gun legislation. Just yesterday, March 14, 2018, students throughout the country and in other countries staged a walkout to protest school violence. They embraced a moment of grief and anger as a time to turn the tides against oppression.

However, at the very same time that young people and those they inspired saw in tragedy an opportunity to turn suffering to positive change a very different response was displayed by the powerful and privileged. Rather than being empathic with the anguish of those whose lives were touched by violence, experiencing grief at those who were lost, and recognizing their complicity for those deaths, they adamantly and coldly refused to take decisive action. For example, at a town hall meeting televised by CNN attended by students who survived the shooting and their parents, Senator Marco Rubio was confronted regarding the millions of dollars he had received from the National Rifle Association (and thus from gun manufacturers). When asked whether he would refuse such donations in the future, he blithely said that he would not do so while also trying unconvincingly to assert that this exerted no influence on his stand on gun control.

The president of the National Rifle Association, Wayne Lapierre, spoke to a conference of conservatives condemning these young courageous protesters as a threat to Second Amendment rights. Then behind the scenes they continued to funnel millions of dollars from gun manufacturers to politicians who placed personal greed before saving lives. In still another case of utter madness and craven kowtowing to their corporate donors, legislators in Florida prepared a law approving millions of dollars to buy firearms from the very peddlers of death in order to arm teachers and thus assure even more unnecessary killing. These very same merchants of destruction, not satisfied with blood money tied to mass shootings, reap even greater profits as beneficiaries of a grossly bloated defense budget that enables them to export their instruments of death throughout the world. All the while our elected officials gladly take their share of blood money in order to do the bidding of their bribers.

And yet one can imagine the indignant cries of these betrayers of the public good and perpetrators of injustice if faced with these damning accusations. Those moved by such tragedies might struggle to imagine how people like Senator Rubio and Wayne Lapierre are able to look at themselves in the mirror or sleep at night. Startlingly, they suffer from no such moral scruples or attacks of conscience. Rather than shrug our shoulders in dismay or rail against them, we must step back and examine how this can be the case. Because if we can wrap our heads around how such incorrigible lack of empathy and abandonment of moral responsibility is possible, we can see what is keeping this madness going. Though the cases I describe here may be extreme examples, other less dramatic ones can be found throughout society. They include not only those who actively oppress others but those who do nothing when they witness it happening—even at times victims of oppression themselves. They will have moments when the power of suffering batters down the illusions they have erected. But just when the promise of turning suffering to compassion is offered, their crippling fear, their arrogant pride, and their desperate clinging to the status quo hardens their hearts and closes their minds once again.

Subscribing uncritically to the insidious influence of neoliberal ideology, the powerful and privileged wrap themselves in what they hope is an impervious suit of armor. Though they cannot silence the nagging fear that someone or something will shatter their illusions, they cling to whatever is at hand to protect themselves with a desperate life or death attitude. The deceptions and ruses in which they have so thoroughly immersed themselves have become as invisible as the air that they breathe. They lock themselves into seemingly airtight echo chambers with like-minded companions who mirror back the manufactured beliefs and values they share. Instead of heeding the call of their conscience, they listen to the soothing validation they receive from others that they know best and are on the right side of history. They are unable to perceive the patent contradictions and obvious lies that they peddle because they refuse to take stock, to reflect, to question or to imagine. They make every effort to see no farther than the tip of their noses and to confine their sympathies to those of their own class. They will not suffer to be discomforted, to feel the accusing voices of conscience, or to listen to the better angels of their nature. When all else fails, they project their dark, cynical, pejorative, and untrusting worldview on others and make the world in their own dismal and despicable image. This then justifies the abuse and hatred they hurl at those they consider inferior and dispensable.

Let us make no mistake. This is what we are contending with in our fight to reclaim compassion and restore justice. The challenge is daunting, but we should not be discouraged. Because the alternative is that oppression is victorious. Courage or taking heart is the one thing that will see us through. The courage I speak of is not the hyped version depicted in the media or the pablum mouthed by politicians. As Paul Tillich (1952) observed, the essence of courage is to affirm life in the face of anxiety, pain, and terror. It is to carry forward in spite of whatever suffering and trials we may undergo in the service of a just cause. It may seem to require a Herculean effort to pierce through the armor of the powerful and to keep it open long enough to allow for the potential power of suffering to transform tragedy into transcendence. However, it will not take long to realize that behind the furious and desperate efforts of the powerful to maintain their illusions is the palpable fear they have vainly tried to escape. And behind that fear is a contradiction or fracture that they are trying just as desperately to hold together.

You will recognize the fractures and the fear when you have become familiar with your own. If you can resist the temptation to avoid the encounter with suffering and make peace with it, the deniers will see that power in you. You will be living testimony that someone can be thoroughly disillusioned and choose not to retreat to their old worldview. Perhaps they will be frightened by what they see. Perhaps they will ridicule your courage and resolve. But none of that will matter because your awakening now makes their awakening an imperative. Suffering has seen you through this far and it paves the path that leads to liberation. This is the path that I hope to lay before you in this book.

Frank Gruba-McCallister, Ph.D.
Park Ridge, IL
March 15, 2018

Acknowledgments

This book was a long time in the making. As such, it represents the culmination of decades of thinking, research, clinical work, and teaching. It would not have been possible without the rewarding and meaningful interactions and exchanges with the many colleagues, clients, and students with whom I had the privilege of working over the years. These dialogues played a substantive and invaluable role in shaping my ideas and validating my commitment to opposing oppression and advancing social justice. In addition, I owe a great debt of gratitude to my wife of 45 years, Sandra. She has been a valued fellow activist whose astute observations, steadfast support, and calm reassurance has helped me to clarify, re-examine, and sharpen my thinking. I wish to express particular gratitude to Dr. Isaac Prilleltensky, whose work has been a constant source of inspiration to me, for his kindness in writing a Foreword and endorsement for my book. Also thanks to my colleague Dr. Ian Wickramasekera for directing me to submit my manuscript to University Professors Press, for his enthusiastic endorsement, and for his steadfast support and encouragement throughout the process. Particular acknowledgement is likewise due to those who kindly consented to provide endorsements for my work: Dr. Nancy Bothne, Dr. Todd DuBose. Dr. Marge Witty, and Ms. Amanda Howland, JD. I would like to thank the editor-in-chief of University Professors Press, Dr. Louis Hoffman, and my editor, Lisa Vallejos, for their guidance, feedback, and support. And finally my gratitude for Senator Bernie Sanders, whose visionary leadership helped to lift me from the darkness of my disillusionment and inspired me to continue the fight for social justice, and for Julian Assange and Chelsea Manning for their living embodiment of selfless sacrifice to truth and justice.

Chapter 1

Introduction

A Painful Confrontation

I began this book in what proved to be a tumultuous year for me and, I believe, for many of my fellow Americans. It was 2016. There were many times when I experienced the proverbial emotional roller coaster—moments of exhilaration and hope followed by exasperating frustration and bitter disappointment. My long-dormant hopes for real change in our country rose with the remarkable campaign of Senator Bernie Sanders, but to my dismay they were dashed. In time it became clear to me that the source of these emotions was a string of painful realizations. These realizations arose out of the ferment of the painfully long and utterly maddening campaign for who would run for and eventually be elected to the U.S. Presidency. As these events unfolded, I discovered to my shock and dismay that my pain and despair were only beginning. However, what was beginning to become apparent to me was nothing new to others who had long been acquainted with oppression. My position of privilege had cushioned me from what people of color and members of other historically marginalized groups had known and spoken out against for some time. They had long suffered under the burdens of oppression and—as I found in looking to their experiences, their stories, and their scholarship—had provided eloquent and perceptive critiques of its destructive impact.

No sooner had Trump assumed office, I watched as our country descended ever deeper into a moral abyss. I was not naïve about the sad state of affairs before his inauguration. Unbridled greed, obsession with power, single-minded pursuit of self-interest, and contempt for the poor and marginalized had all been clearly in evidence before the election of President Trump. But now it felt to me as if nothing remained to hold back these destructive forces. Over and over I saw them turned into ever more extreme measures that would have dire and detrimental effects on millions of people—many of whom were already suffering under the brunt of inequality and injustice. There seemed to scarcely be a day when I was not plagued by feelings of shame, outrage, dread, disgust, and—perhaps worse of all—an infuriating sense of helplessness.

Through it all a most disturbing fact became ever clearer to me. And that is the sad realization that the most pernicious force in the world is still very much at work. Day after day it continues to cause unspeakable suffering. And yet very rarely does anyone dare speak its name or recognize the havoc that it wreaks. Evidence for this conspiracy of silence can be found no matter where one turns. Rather than accept their responsibility for unleashing this force upon millions of individuals, our elected officials wrap themselves in garments of a sickening self-righteousness that only thinly veils their love of power and contempt for the powerless. And the servants of power, the mass media, maintains the deception and mystification either through scurrilous and sensationalized titillation designed to divert the attention of the masses or underhanded propaganda designed to manufacture consent to their own undoing. Even those who claim that their desire is to help the afflicted proceed to trivialize their distress and misrepresent the actual cause of their suffering. In these ways and so many more, strenuous effort is exerted to forbid any awareness of the destructive and malicious force that is at work.

It follows that if this problem doesn't exist, then of course there's nothing to be done about it. This abolition of awareness is itself an act of violence committed against a person's experience. It is just the beginning of the harm done and lays the foundation for far greater suffering. The goal is not merely to ensure that people are made to believe that their experience is untrustworthy and so dispensable. Means must also be devised to then sap away their capacity for agency and thus undermine their ability to take action should an inkling of awareness somehow break through. With their sense of being enlivened beings stunted by a diminished capacity of being open to their lived experience, they lapse into numb complacency. With their sense of potency and possibility undermined, they are lulled into mindless compliance.

Those responsible for inflicting these harms are deftly skilled in using all the strategies of creating confusion and obfuscation at their disposal. They have learned how blatant efforts at denying the existence of a problem risk exposing it and so prove to be self-defeating. And so, they recruit an army of those calling themselves experts who have employed their well-honed skills at their behest. When the true source of our anguish cannot be cleverly hidden, they provide some alternative and seemingly plausible explanation for it—an explanation that not coincidentally conveniently advances the agenda of the powerful and meets their needs. If the veil of illusion they have created is lifted, one cannot help but be struck by the perversity of their machinations. For what emerges is not only the immense amount of suffering caused by this force, but the ways in which the subsequent masking of that very suffering is also used to serve their darker purposes. The fact nonetheless remains that so many of those who fancy themselves to be sincerely working on our behalf are more typically actual purveyors of our pain and suffering. And in the most remarkable twist of all, if anyone were to confront them with this ugly truth, they would be utterly dumbstruck, thoroughly offended, and, perhaps most ironically, swift to retaliate against their accuser.

Oppression—The Principal Cause of Suffering

What then is the destructive "force" that I am referring to? It is *oppression*. Thus, this book will first and foremost be about oppression. It will be my argument that the single greatest factor contributing to human suffering, in all its various forms and expressions, is oppression. Even as I make this assertion, I know that some may find it extremely bold, others utterly false, others as gravely unsettling, and perhaps still others as inspired. No matter what the reaction may be, given the uncompromising (and hence in the minds of some, doubtful) nature of this claim, I know that I clearly have my work cut out for me if I hope to make a convincing case for it. What further complicates the task is that any confrontation with oppression brings with it resistance (which I described above). As one becomes more fully aware of its destructive impact, there is the temptation to shut out the accompanying pain. Nonetheless, despite any trepidation I might feel about taking up these challenges, it is more than counterbalanced by an ever-growing sense of urgency I feel about our need to openly confront what is without question the major cause of human suffering.

I understand there clearly are obstacles that must be faced and ultimately surmounted if I am to have any hope of persuading and eventually convincing you—the reader—to experience the same sense of urgency. What sustains me despite these hurdles is a firm commitment, which I believe is informed by my desire to render compassionate service to the suffering, to expose the illusions that blind us to the pernicious impact of oppression on our lives and the lives of countless others. It is only in doing so that we will have any chance of making a concerted effort to put an end to it. And so, no matter how audacious, troubling, or perilous the road ahead of us may be, I believe a serious examination of the role of oppression in our troubles and travails is worth the effort. It is a critical first step in opening a way for us to more fully secure the happiness and well-being that all human beings desire and deserve.

So, permit me to broadly sketch out the path that I will take in this exploration. In the chapters that follow, I plan to consider a number of questions. What is oppression? What factors contribute to producing and maintaining it? In what ways does it exert its toxic influence on virtually every aspect of human life? What can be done to mitigate or, more important, prevent its impact? How can our confrontation with oppression ultimately become the means by which we attain true liberation? Each of these questions can lay claim to being laden with complexity that defies my providing a thorough investigation of any of them. Thus, I am mindful from the outset of the need for modesty when trying to tackle all of them in a single work. I make no claims here to being comprehensive in my treatment of the various issues involved. In addition, my scope will be narrowed by the fact that I will be drawing principally from my training and experience as a psychologist. That said, my scope will be broadened by integrating material from other sources I have identified in my study of the issues when it helps to shed additional light on the topic. Finally, as will become clearer in the pages that follow, I will conduct this examination of oppression, in part, by charting my own personal search for answers to these questions. In the process I will describe how my own ideas and attitudes have evolved over time. I believe that a narrative of this journey will be useful in providing readers with some appreciation for how and why I have chosen to approach the issue of oppression in the ways that I will be advancing in the pages ahead.

Disillusionment—The Possibility of Awakening

But first I must return to what it was about this time that stirred me to embark on this project. On reflection, I cannot truthfully say that many of the reactions I had to recent events were dramatically different from those I have experienced at earlier times. However, what I came to see was that my reactions were far more intense. Gradually, I saw that this intensity was rooted in my experiencing an even more profound sense of disillusionment at what was occurring. This realization became crystal clear when my wife, who shared this sense of disillusionment with me, observed that the string of disturbing events we had witnessed had "caused the scales to fall from our eyes." Suddenly, we were both compelled to see the things unfolding without the benefit of our typical buffers and blinders. Our presumptions, preconceptions and preferences had been so undermined that they no longer kept us insulated from the painful truths facing us. No longer protected by these convenient and comfortable strategies for shielding ourselves from brutal facts, we were confronted with the most unsettling of all fears. The world as we had once believed in and wished it to be had collapsed before our eyes.

Describing what had occurred as becoming "disillusioned" now strikes me as very apt. I find among the definitions of "disillusionment" to become "disenchanted" or "disappointed." These meanings capture the understandably negative and painful aspects of this experience. However, this perspective is too one-sided. The full meaning of the experience of being disabused of one's illusion also needs to capture the positive and potentially transformative aspects as well. What seems to me to really get at the heart of this aspect of the experience is the meaning "to bring down to earth." Let me explain. For all the temporary comfort provided by the cleverly crafted half-truths and seductive distortions that make up our personal illusions, the fact remains that they inevitably carry us off on harmful and dangerous flights of fancy. The more we indulge in evading the truth and allowing ourselves to be deceived, the more we become "ungrounded" from the one place we must keep beneath our feet—earth, our home. The exhilaration of becoming untethered from something firm and secure can seem to be liberating, particularly when it promises to take us to even greater heights. However, it proves to be only temporary and eventually we come to realize that being unanchored is ultimately terrifying. We no longer feel rooted in a place we all need and desire—home. There can be no true freedom to be found in false promises and shrewdly spun lies. In time they vanish into thin air and leave us suspended up there. We must come back to earth.

The most destructive lies are built upon self-deception—a form of evasion that we shall see is ultimately self-defeating. Thus, the tenuous fabric of the veil of illusion that the Hindus call "maya" is doomed to be torn asunder. What immediately follow are the throes of disappointment and the sadness that comes with it. But in time we learn that the short-term relief provided by evading a painful truth is more than outweighed by the long-term cost of our exquisite capacity for self-deception. Regrettably, my years as a psychologist convinced me that this is a lesson that remains difficult for human beings first to learn and then to retain. And so long as this continues to be the case, efforts to unveil the dark power of oppression and to advance human liberation will be greatly hindered.

In recent years I became convinced that the role of oppression in the development of both physical and psychological disorders had been greatly underestimated. Though I did not require any further persuasion, my encounter with an even deeper and more painful sense of disillusionment further highlighted the multiple ways in which oppression was at work. The crises and tragedies that seemed almost daily occurrences—vicious terrorist attacks, ugly reminders of continuing racism and intolerance, deadly mass shootings, growing dire impacts of climate change—progressively took their toll on whatever remaining illusions I stubbornly clung to. One by one my dearest preconceptions were demolished. The hypocrisy of many of those whom I had long mistakenly believed to be proponents of justice was starkly exposed. Many whom I had regarded as my allies in the service of compassion were revealed to be responsible for inflicting suffering on the vulnerable and powerless. Rarely did a week go by in which I did not feel betrayed and bitterly disappointed.

As my worldview collapsed, it was difficult for me to keep at bay feelings of helplessness and despair. From spiritual literature that I had long been acquainted with, I saw that I was undergoing something very much like what John of the Cross called the "dark night of the soul." The attachments, expectations, and beliefs that had propped up my ego or presumed sense of self had been systematically purged and I was left staring into an ever-darkening emptiness. This is a very perilous point on the spiritual path as one can fall into an abyss of an even deeper sense of despair. And there were certainly days like that. However, the shattering of all illusions offers a chance for one to see the unvarnished truth, to glimpse what would have otherwise remained hidden behind the artifices of our own and others' manufacture.

What I saw were things I had already found suspect, but they stood out even more starkly. For example, the differences that I once mistakenly saw between the two political parties in our country completely evaporated. Both had become corrupted by greed and had their hands in creating the crises and tragedies plaguing our country. My disillusionment with the profession that I had chosen to devote my life to was only further confirmed as I saw even greater evidence for its complicity in perpetuating the status quo. However, and most significant, I realized that the neglect and silence shown by the many so-called experts and thought leaders to the real issue of oppression was calculated. Every effort was being made to obscure the toxic economic and political influences on the oppressed to the advantage of the privileged. And it was not until I had come to this conclusion—no matter how painful and disappointing—that I had any hope of rejecting that this was either natural or inevitable. I had to be disillusioned in order to achieve a clarity that brought with it the promise of liberation.

The Seductions of Self-Deception

There were other lessons to be learned from this awakening. I saw just how seductive my illusions were. If, like many others, I had become so thoroughly duped by skillfully crafted distortions, comforting half-truths, and soothing panaceas that made up "common sense," then exploring how this sorry state had come about was clearly essential. What makes illusions like these so alluring? What purposes do they serve—both positive and negative? Why is the confrontation and abandoning of these illusions so painful and yet also so essential to our long-term growth and well-being? And how can we best understand the ways in which such illusions play a pivotal role in oppression and the suffering it causes?

As I raised these questions, I soon realized that they were familiar to me. If there was one certainty that my years of study and practice in psychology had provided to me, it was that human beings possess an incredible capacity for self-deception. Considering this, it is not surprising that an extensive body of theory and research exists regarding the subject of self-deception. It can be legitimately asserted that this is one of psychology's most important and enduring contributions to the study of human beings. The unconscious, defense mechanisms, resistance, persuasion—familiar topics like these abound in this area of study. As this pertains to the subject of oppression, among the challenging questions posed to those who study it is why under certain circumstances individuals are unaware of the impact it has on them and in the most extreme case, why they willingly consent to oppressive practices (Cudd, 2006). These questions are especially vexing considering how pervasive and destructive the impact of oppression is on the lives of these individuals. How could something so harmful be so neglected, and why would people submit themselves to such treatment? This is where the literature on self-deception is particularly useful and relevant. I will be turning to these insights later. For the moment, I want to focus on one prominent theme that consistently emerges in this literature.

When all the various facets and dimensions that form the basis for self-deception are considered, one fundamental fact emerges and that is the central role played by fear. Human beings have a powerful need for control that has been evolutionarily hard-wired into them. This need is expressed in the desire for stability, order, certainty, and predictability. If this need is not met and our sense of control is challenged, we experience fear. This need for control and predictability has been linked with engaging in self-deception (Goleman, 1985) as measures often are taken to deny or distort experiences that challenge our established ways of thinking. The unexpected and unfamiliar may sometimes be met with pleasure and appreciation. Nonetheless, when our need for certainty is more seriously challenged and our most important beliefs exposed to threat, we exert considerable effort to maintain our accustomed worldview no matter how inaccurate it may be. When we resist making changes that are demanded by facts that confront us and are willing to go contrary to what our experience is actually telling us, we are engaging in self-deception. Being right is more important in such situations, even if holding fast to our beliefs may cause us the very suffering we are trying to avoid. In other words, self-deception is ultimately self-defeating.

The very belief that our lives can be totally predictable and thus free of fear and suffering forms the greatest illusion of all—the illusion that is the wellspring from which all other illusions originate. This is often described quite eloquently in existential thought. For example, it is expressed in one of its core concepts, existential anxiety (May, 1958). This view of anxiety does not see it as an emotion in the way that is generally understood. Rather, it is an ontological given—that is, an experience inherent to being alive. The experience of existential anxiety is rooted in another ontological given, our awareness that we are going to die. For human beings, death is both a biological and a psychological reality. While death is the ultimate loss and our greatest fear, the losses large and small that we experience throughout our lives are a reminder of our mortality and evoke a sense of apprehension and dread. In a similar vein, Spinelli (2014) connects the experience of existential anxiety to existential insecurity. Because each human life is lived in an ever-unfolding process of realizing some possibilities but not others, the stability or certainty we may seek is not attainable. Uncertainty is paradoxically the one certainty.

However, the pain and dread that we may experience in response to loss or uncertainty is only part of the story. Existential anxiety also has the capacity to encourage us to live life more fully and with a greater sense of meaning. This point of view is also asserted by Alan Watts (1951) who sagely observes that an important ingredient to living a satisfying and meaningful life is learning the wisdom of insecurity. He writes:

> If, then, we are to be fully human and fully alive and aware, it seems we must be willing to suffer for our pleasures. Without such willingness there can be no growth in the intensity of consciousness. Yet, generally speaking, we are not willing, and it may be thought strange to suppose that we can be. For "nature in us" so rebels against pain that the very notion of "willingness" to put up with it beyond a certain point may appear impossible and meaningless. (pp. 31–32)

Thus, we are faced with a paradox about fear. It will be one of a number of paradoxes that will be uncovered in my analysis of oppression. Fear and the pain it brings are not only necessary—albeit unpleasant—ingredients in making our way through life, but they are also what makes our pleasures possible. We may be dogged by the dread of our eventual death, but awareness of our mortality can also enable us to live our lives with greater passion and purpose. It is in our nature to meet fear with resistance, to try and abolish it from awareness. Therefore, fear inhibits the reflection necessary to achieve a clear awareness of what is giving rise to it. This lack of awareness not only ultimately proves to be ineffective, but it actually compounds our pain and discomfort. However, there is always an alternative response. Our encounter with fear also provides us with an opportunity to first acknowledge and surrender our resistance, to acknowledge the source of our distress, and eventually to discover what enables us to rise above the challenge in a way that promotes our development and well-being.

There is one other paradox that becomes elucidated in an examination of self-deception. Our need for stability and control is very powerful. If permitted to go unchecked, it will render our lives boring, lifeless and ultimately without meaning. Alan Watts again helps us to see this point. While human beings may fancy the idea of being like God and thus able to foresee all events before they happen, in time this kind of omniscience would deprive our lives of any element of surprise or novelty. While some surprises are no doubt unpleasant and at times even frightening, there are others that give us delight and pleasure. Such delights would be utterly lost in a perfectly predictable world. Watts (1951) thus concludes:

> If we are to have intense pleasures, we must also be liable to intense pains. The pleasure we love, and the pain we hate, but it seems impossible to have the former without the latter. Indeed, it looks as if the two must in some way alternate, for continuous pleasure is a stimulus that must either pall or be increased. And the increase will either harden the sense buds with its friction, or turn into pain. A consistent diet of rich food either destroys the appetite or makes one sick. (p. 30)

If the fear that fuels our need for control was all-consuming and capable of going unchecked, efforts to end oppression would be extremely difficult—perhaps even impossible. As we will see, it is our ability to be open to the transient nature of our lives and to embrace the distress and even pain that loss sometimes brings that enable us to oppose injustice and to conceive of a better way of living.

The Perils Posed by Fear

With a brief description of the dynamics of self-deception provided, we can see how the way in which it is at work in oppression poses a very similar paradox. Fear is one of the most powerful tools wielded by those who oppress others. Throughout history it has been effectively used to induce individuals to accept conditions of exploitation, discrimination, and exclusion in order to secure what they believe to be some measure of security and comfort. One way in which this occurs is when the oppressed mistakenly are led to believe that their unfortunate lot is an inescapable necessity based on some higher power or irresistible forces of nature. Another is when they are deceived into believing that they are responsible for their misfortune. They have made their nest and now they must live in it. In either case, though they may find some reassurance in believing that their world is not governed by arbitrary and capricious forces, much of their suffering goes unabated. Believing someone or something is in charge may salve their fear of the unknown, but that also means surrendering themselves to their painful plight. We see that, paradoxically, people are either rendered unaware of their oppression or willingly consent to it. They erroneously believe that an alternative state of affairs—being uncertain and unknown—would be even worse. Better the devil you know than the one you don't know.

Though the dynamics of fear are clearly at work in the oppressed, those who engage in oppressive practices also harbor anxiety about their ability to maintain their status and privilege. While the disadvantages for the privileged are far fewer, they hold similar illusions regarding a life free of uncertainty and the suffering it brings. They are aware of the anger and resentment experienced by those they hold under thumb. They must maintain constant vigilance regarding indications of any threats to their grip on power. History contains ample examples of such often violent reversals of power in which the oppressed heap suffering on their former tormentors.

In the case of both the oppressed and the oppressors, whatever benefits may be derived from maintaining their illusions are short-lived and soon give way to ever-increasingly harmful consequences. In seeking to rid their lives of inevitable pain and distress that come with life, they suffer all the more. More notable, they paradoxically inflict suffering upon themselves that could have been avoided. What this pattern makes apparent is that engaging in self-deception is inevitably self-defeating. And yet it goes on and will continue to do so until we realize the integral role played by self-deception in oppression. *It is only by undoing self-deception that we can hope to end oppression.*

That being said, achieving that goal is compromised by some substantial problems with how psychology typically understands self-deception. Some of the contributions of psychology in helping those who have been victimized by oppression (as well as to a certain degree those who are perpetrators of it) are unquestionable. However, there are ways in which psychology has not only fallen short in these efforts but has also both wittingly and unwittingly contributed to oppressive practices. Similarly, the knowledge that psychologists have acquired on the human capacity for self-deception has been utilized to cultivate a greater awareness of the dangers it poses and finding ways of undoing it. Yet that same knowledge has been sometimes used to induce its victims to willingly accept these deceptions, resist critically examining them, and even consent to their own exploitation and the suffering caused by it. Marketing aimed at promoting over-consumption, political propaganda designed to obfuscate rather than elucidate issues, manipulation of language and images to veil acts of inhumanity, and even guidance provided on forms of torture are all painful examples of the ways in which psychological knowledge has been and continues to be abused.

This realization has been another one of those painful moments of disillusionment for me, but one that I am grateful for. It has helped me to remember the importance of always examining my own profession critically. Nevertheless, I know that I cannot in all fairness level this criticism toward psychology without also taking some ownership for similar errors and misdeeds. Thinking back on mistaken ideas that I have held and the ways in which this has adversely influenced my work as a psychologist makes this painfully clear to me. Simple realization is not enough. Inasmuch as psychology is the science and profession I have devoted my life to, I believe it is my responsibility to act on this realization and do what I can to remedy the problem.

The Political Uses of an Individualist Ideology

While some dramatic examples of psychology's failings regarding oppression are given above, its typical approach to understanding self-deception reveals a subtler and more pervasive way in which psychology's traditional manner of approaching issues has been detrimental to understanding oppression. This can be found in how the problem is described as *self*-deception. Historically, psychology has pursued studying human beings and providing service to them based on what is going on *inside of* them. The drawbacks of this one-sided emphasis in which individual human beings are the focus of study has been the subject of a number of critiques, particularly among critical psychologists. For example, Klaus Holzkamp founder of the German School of Critical Psychology (Schaube & Osterkamp, 2013), described the approach of traditional psychology as the study of the "worldless" individual. By this he meant that by examining the person in isolation and a-contextually, psychology neglects the most distinguishing characteristic of human beings, their societal nature. The evolution of the human species would have been impossible without the ability of humans to rely upon others and organize themselves into networks of relationships that enabled them to ensure their survival. Further, human beings always live under material conditions created by larger sociohistorical factors. As a result, their thoughts and actions are significantly influenced by these conditions.

This does not mean that these material conditions act unilaterally on human beings and that they passively react to them. Critical Psychology argues for a deep appreciation of the mutual and interdependent relationship between the subjectivity and agency possessed by individual persons and their societal nature. Human beings seek to exercise a certain degree of control over their lives and so act upon and influence conditions under which they live. They are not just shaped by history, but also make history. Moreover, because they are social beings, humans do not do this as isolated individuals but exercise this control in communication and coordination with others.

Another way of describing the dangers posed by the over-emphasis on the individual in psychology is provided by the critical psychologist, Isaac Prilleltensky and his colleagues (Prilleltensky, 1989, 1997; Prilleltensky & Nelson, 2002; Prilleltensky & Prilleltensky, 2006). His work is especially pertinent as Prilleltensky has identified oppression as a substantive factor that works against human well-being while also noting that oppression cannot be understood by adopting the usual narrow lens of psychology. He writes:

> At a structural level, a pervasive dichotomy between the individual and society is observed in psychology....The immediate ideological benefit derived from such a dichotomy is that the individual is studied as an asocial and ahistorical being whose life vicissitudes are artificially disconnected from the wider sociopolitical context. Consequently, solutions for human predicaments are to be found, almost exclusively, within the self, leaving the social order conveniently unaffected. (Prilleltensky, 1989, p. 796)

Viewed solely from an individual perspective, only the adverse psychological consequences of oppression, such as feelings of inferiority, shame, helplessness, and pessimism, are revealed. While these effects are extremely important and worthy of efforts to remove or alleviate them, such efforts would ultimately fail because the more significant causal factors at work would, as Prilleltensky states, be neglected. The psychological dimension of oppression must be paired with the role that politics play in creating and maintaining it (Prilleltensky & Gonick, 1996; Prilleltensky, 2008). This becomes particularly apparent when examining the concrete material basis to oppression. Political and economic barriers, exploitation, inequality, and other forms of social injustice all have such material consequences in the form of impoverishment, deprivation, toxic environmental conditions, and a host of other physical harms. Moreover, all these broader ecological and systemic factors operate *outside* of the individual. By failing to give attention and credence to these sociohistorical and economic factors, psychology renders the social order invisible and thus unchallenged. The status quo is defended, and the victims of oppression are blamed for their misfortunes (Ryan, 1971).

By extending the scope of our focus to structural and systemic factors beyond the individual, we gain a fuller picture of the way in which illusions give rise to oppression. The previous quote by Prilleltensky includes mention of that additional element. As he notes, the dichotomizing of the individual and society by psychology serves a useful *ideological* purpose. In examining ideology, we discover the role of external factors in shaping and maintaining dangerous illusions. Our illusions are not merely personal constructions but are also significantly shaped by social forces.

The Role of Ideology in Oppression

The term "ideology" has many meanings and has been understood in multiple ways by different theorists. In his article Hamilton (1987) describes twenty-seven different elements of how ideology is defined. Staying within the framework of the individual, for example, ideology functions as a type of mental map used to explain and understand ourselves, others, and the world around us. This mental map is once again an expression of our fundamental need for control and order. It takes our ongoing hodgepodge of experiences and from them first excludes those that seem irrelevant to our survival. Then those that we are unable to easily incorporate into familiar, tried-and-true categories we have created to give meaning to our experience are filtered out. In many respects this mental map is an indispensable tool that makes our lives smoother, safer, and simpler. However, when it is applied rigidly and inflexibly, it becomes a kind of mental straitjacket that soon proves to be dangerously confining. At some point, the burden of maintaining this worldview in the face of mounting contradictions and unfulfilled expectations proves to be too much and it collapses. That is the moment when the fear that urged us to maintain it at all costs becomes most acute—a time of both great peril and great promise. We have become disillusioned. But looking at ideology only from the perspective of the individual is just half the picture. Remaining within this narrow view will hamper any efforts at unveiling the many other situations when ideology is at work and undoing it when it exercises an adverse impact on our well-being.

The need for a broader perspective is advocated by Augoustinos (1999) who observes that historically there are two traditions of research on the concept of ideology. In the one based on an individual focus, attention is given to the role of ideology in the construction of individuals' reality and the way in which this influences their conduct in everyday life. In the other, a critique is made of the way in which prevailing social norms and values become expressed in an ideology that then shapes how individuals come to understand "the way things are." As Prilleltensky (1989) observes, one such group of individuals are psychologists whose theories, knowledge, and practices reflect the assumptions and values of the dominant ideology at that time. In this second tradition, the identification and critique of this underlying ideology play a vital role in revealing how context-bound biases and false statements contained within it become falsely presented by psychologists as not only objective but normative. Because the hypothetical and assumptive nature of such assertions is not recognized, there is a clear danger that they legitimize unjust and harmful social practices and arrangements and portray them as natural and therefore unchangeable.

Portraying ideology only as a product of a person's own predilections and prejudices implies that he or she is then to blame for such errors and distortions and for acting in accordance with them. Once again, the problem is situated *inside* of the person, and the role of larger systemic factors is rendered irrelevant or even invisible. Under such conditions, the role of oppression in causing individuals to suffer is similarly rendered irrelevant or even invisible, as it is utterly meaningless to talk about oppression as simply an intrapsychic phenomenon. If the current state of affairs in a society is natural, inevitable, or normative, then no matter what terrible consequences such a state of affairs may necessitate for certain individuals, nothing can be done about it. For just this reason, any valid understanding of ideology must be expanded to include social, historical, economic, and political factors. As Augoustinos (1999) observes:

> The individual is viewed as failing to perceive reality accurately and failing to recognize his or her true self and group interests. Such approaches fail to acknowledge that reality construction is not an isolated cognitive task involving the direct and unmediated perception of the world. People are constantly and actively engaged in a complex and socially situated process of constructing reality, but they do this by using the cultural and ideological resources that are available to them....These resources are shaped by existing material and power relations

and are embedded in the very nature of people's lived social relations and practices. (p. 302)

By far the greatest influence exerted on how we go about constructing our mental maps comes from the multiple contexts in which we are embedded. Ultimately, our worldview is substantially an expression of an ideology that is held in common by members of the community to which we belong. One vital function performed by that ideology is to justify and make normative the prevailing economic and sociopolitical interests of that community. It is a total, more-or-less coherent system of ideas, beliefs, attitudes, and values that is so thoroughly internalized by members of a society that its assumptive nature typically goes unrecognized. It seems as natural to us as the very air we breathe. Ideology functions to explain the world and our relationship to it and to guide actions in accordance with these explanations. However, there is also a political function performed by an ideology which is rooted in the power relations that exist within a society. It is used by the dominant class to legitimize those power relations, to justify existing economic and political interests, and to portray those interests as both desirable and inevitable.

The way in which I am using the term ideology follows closely the work of Karl Marx and Friedrich Engels (1845/1932) and Italian Marxist philosopher, Antonio Gramsci (1971). This is because their views best capture the importance of material and social conditions in shaping how individuals see the world and themselves and the role that ideology plays in oppression. Of particular value is Gramsci's concept of *hegemony*. It refers to the reigning paradigm in a society. Hegemony consists of core dogmas, accepted wisdom, stereotypes, and values that become diffused throughout a society and inculcated in all its members by means of various forms of propaganda and through cultural institutions such as family, religion, and school. Hegemony performs an important political function. It is used to support the status quo, such that the ruling class maintains its sway over the subaltern class, securing its loyalty by means of various forms of ideological control. Because it exerts influence over the consciousness of all members of society, hegemony informs all aspects of human life—ideas, tastes, customs, morality, religion, and economic and political systems.

Mystification—Ideological Deception

The process by which hegemony masks and distorts extant material and social conditions and subsequently creates a state of confusion and clouded consciousness in members of a society is described as *mystification*. This echoes the earlier discussion of the human capacity for self-deception. However, it provides a valuable added perspective by elucidating that the process of deception is not something that has its roots solely within the mind of the individual. In his early writing, Marx (Augoustinos, 1999) noted how human consciousness was socially conditioned by the material and social relations that existed during a period of history. His colleague, Engels, coined the term "false consciousness" to capture how prevailing power relationships in capitalist society are concealed or distorted to secure the cooperation and consensus of the working class. However, over time Marx realized that an exclusively psychological understanding of false consciousness was incomplete. Mystification expands this understanding by acknowledging the ways in which actual material and social conditions within a society play a significant role in creating and maintaining the distorted and confused worldviews of its members. As Augoustinos (1999) notes:

> Mystification, then, is embedded in the very nature of capitalist society, in reality itself, and not in the minds of people. Reality itself generates deceptive appearances, and these phenomenal forms are used by people to make sense of their everyday social interactions and lived relations within capitalist society. The everyday social practices of capitalism reproduce and strengthen the phenomenal forms of the market. (p. 305)

The effectiveness of mystification nonetheless rests firmly on everything that we have learned about the human capacity for self-deception. Without this propensity mystification would inevitably fail as it builds upon all those processes involved in self-deception. However, though self-deception makes mystification possible, the substantive impact of material and social conditions in the process of mystification would be neglected if we were to restrict our focus solely on the individual. Many of the self-defeating and destructive lies that people tell themselves are not ones they manufacture on their own. Mystification and self-deception are related to each other but not synonymous. Mystification is essentially a social process in which the prevailing ideology creates plausible misinterpretations of the reasons behind events in people's daily lives and why certain things happen to them. These misinterpretations are aimed at legitimizing and sustaining the status quo. Like self-deception, mystification is utilized to quell the fear and anxiety that are triggered by uncertainty and insecurity. The ready-made answers and solutions to the everyday problems provided allay people's fears and lull them into a false sense of security.

Yet just as self-deception poses dangers, so too does mystification. By presenting the status quo as natural and inevitable, hegemony promotes a sense of passivity and fatalism among those who suffer most from inequality and injustice. The power of mystification is another reason for why, contrary to what reason may tell us, people actually consent to their own oppression and the misery that comes with it. By using fear to maintain the consent of the oppressed, the oppressors enforce consensus, inhibit awareness and critical thought, and stifle rebellion. It is only by understanding the social, historical, economic, and political forces at work in mystification that we will be better able to come to a clearer understanding of the substantial degree of human suffering that has its roots in those forces. And we will avoid the tragic and troubling tendency to blame the victims who suffer at the hands of those forces.

Neoliberalism—The Reigning Hegemony

What then is the current reigning hegemonic ideology? Staying within the perspective of the school of Critical Psychology founded by Holzkamp, the dominant ideology at present is based in later stage capitalism. Like a number of other authors (Chomsky, 1999; Giroux, 2008; Harvey, 2005; Klein, 2008), I believe more specifically that the ideology in question is *neoliberalism*. And like these authors, I believe that a careful analysis of neoliberal ideology is essential to understanding the current forms that oppression takes and the many ways in which it inflicts harm in virtually every aspect of human life. The argument for this clearly needs to be laid out in considerable detail, and so I must defer this for a later chapter. However, several examples in support of this argument can be offered here. I have chosen them because they will both be persistent themes in my examination of oppression.

The first is the previously made observation of the dangers of psychology's overemphasis on the individual. As the earlier quote by

Prilleltensky noted, this overemphasis has its roots in an ideology—that being neoliberalism. Though individualism has had diverse meanings and has been extolled as a value at different points in history, it has been a cornerstone of capitalist ideology. This is especially the case in the United States, where it has exerted such substantial influence that it has played an important role in the rise of neoliberalism throughout the world. Manders (2006) observes that the ethic of individualism is a core tenet of the belief system held by Americans. This includes values such as rugged individualism, autonomy, independence, individual choice, and personal responsibility. Similarly, in his article, Greene (2008) describes three different ideologies of individualism that have been endorsed in the United States over the course of its history. These three are the ideology of self-willed wealth, of full self-reliance, and of high self-esteem. Greene charts how shifting social, political, and economic conditions have been responsible for the evolving understanding of the importance of individualism in the United States.

A strong case can be made for the significance and desirability of the development of the notion of "the individual" in the course of human thought. This is particularly the case when the idea of the "individual" is associated with the recognition of each human being's inherent worth and dignity. As Wilber (1998) argues, the emergence of the concept of the individual during the modern era of thought brought with it the ascendance of science, the affirmation of human rights and equality, and the development of liberal democracy. Similarly, the importance of freedom, choice, personal responsibility and autonomy (all connected to individualism) to a meaningful and ethical life has been persuasively argued by many. However, the unbridled and extreme expression of individualism extolled by neoliberalism has also legitimately come under increasing scrutiny and criticism. For example, in an article on the prevalence of narcissism in contemporary society, I (Gruba-McCallister, 2007) describe how an extremely individualist ideology gives rise to a range of negative consequences including over-consumption, selfishness, extreme competition, and a sense of emptiness.

Along similar lines, in his article on the different ideologies of individualism in the United States, Greene (2008) contrasts the touted benefits of this ideology with the accompanying dangers.

> While amplifying material demand, individualism also appears to make "individualistic attributions for social problems" more

likely among American citizens. This, in turn, allows for questionable business practices and environmental destruction (Cairns, 1998) to proceed relatively unchecked. The USA lacks universal health care, but at the same time is a world leader in incarceration per capita. Highly individualistic values may also encourage selfish behaviors beyond what is necessary for subjective well-being and participation in a differentiated society... (p. 119)

Wayment and Brauer (2008) present research that finds excessive self-interest is related to social discord, poor health outcomes, and lower levels of self-esteem. Along similar lines, Mark Rank (2004) critiques the individualistic bias within the predominant paradigm for understanding poverty. Rooted in capitalist ideology, this paradigm locates the causes of and solutions for poverty solely in the individual. However, when this view is submitted to scrutiny using data on who are the poor and longitudinal studies of poverty, its argument is seriously weakened. For example, 35% of the poor are under the age of 18. Children who are born into poverty (and who often remain there) cannot be held responsible. Based on this, Rank argues that poverty is actually a result of systemic failures connected to the inability of the U.S. labor market to provide sufficient decent paying jobs to lift people out of poverty, the lack of adequate protections by the social safety net, and the impact of deprivation, discrimination, and oppression.

The point here is not that an individualistic perspective is utterly false and without merit. This is fully appreciated, for example, by Critical Psychology inasmuch as it advocates for a psychology from the standpoint of the subject—that is, from the unique perspective of an individual. However, it also recognizes that if such a standpoint is taken to an extreme by abstracting individuals from their world, that subjectivity is rendered impotent and meaningless. In keeping with the philosophy of Martin Heidegger (1927/1978), human beings must be understood as inextricably interwoven with the world in which they live out their subjectivity. Humans are *Dasein* or being-in-the-world. Critical Psychology asserts a two-sided reality to human beings. First, humans are societal beings exquisitely attuned to their life conditions due their dependency and the requirement that they can only fulfill their needs and interests through communication and collaboration with others. In addition to this, as subjects, human beings are not merely passively shaped by their circumstances but can also consciously influence and create them. What we find here are the errors posed by a one-sided, extreme, and rigid approach to understanding polarities of interdependent and mutually defining opposites. The individual and his/her world must be seen as a *dialectic* relationship. The importance of the dialectic will be another persistent theme in this book. One-sided points of view when applied to polarities that stand in a dialectical relationship to each other invariably give way to spiraling patterns of self-defeat and self-destruction.

An Introductory Excursion into the Subject of Suffering

The second example illustrating the destructive impact of neoliberal ideology harks back to my assertion that oppression is the most significant factor contributing to human suffering. Given this relationship, any discussion of oppression must include a careful consideration of the subject of suffering. While this topic is introduced here, a more in-depth examination will be reserved for a later chapter. Nonetheless, I must make clear that my examination of suffering will require a certain degree of humility. Not only is literature on suffering vast and complex, but the nature and purpose of suffering stands as one of the most challenging questions in the history of human thought. Nonetheless, the elucidation of the inextricable relationship between oppression and suffering provides insights pivotal to understanding not only why people engage in oppression, but also what stands in the way of providing understanding and comfort to those harmed by oppression. For the moment, my more modest goal is to illustrate the danger of neoliberalism by virtue of the substantial suffering it causes. To do so, I will look to one of the most eloquent analyses of suffering ever offered.

Though suffering poses many vexing conundrums, I have found that some of the wisest insights on the question of suffering can be found in the great spiritual traditions. The following comes from Buddhism, but these insights have been echoed time and again in other traditions. Buddhism identifies three forms of suffering or what is called *dukkha*. The first is called *dukkha-dukkha* or obvious suffering such as things that naturally cause us pain (e.g., physical injury or rejection by a loved one). The second is *viparinama-dukkha*, which is suffering that is caused by constant change and the transient nature of human life (*anicca*). In the story of how the Buddha came to understand the nature of suffering, it was his witnessing old age, sickness, and death that led to his realization of how such transience causes us to suffer. For now, I will need to set these first two forms of suffering aside and focus on the third form. That form is called *samkhara-dukkha*, which is suffering due to the ways in which our experience is conditioned by the attitudes and motivations that we attach to it. Among the most destructive motivations are greed, fear, and selfishness. According to the Buddha, this third form makes up most of our suffering.

In the teachings of Buddhism, these unwholesome motives are rooted in a form of willed ignorance or stubbornly holding fast to illusory ideas and beliefs about the nature of ourselves and the world. This ignorance is maintained by rigidly imposing our idiosyncratic expectations upon reality. Because these expectations are shaped by mistaken habits of the mind that fail to see things as they are, they inevitably are disappointed. When this happens, we experience loss as our expectations are dashed and preconceptions put into question. With loss comes fear. This fear causes us to suffer because we are frustrated by reality's stubborn resistance to our fruitless efforts to control it and shape it to our desires.

This suffering then is often compounded further by a resistance to sitting with our pain. While this reactivity to suffering is in some sense natural, it presents one of the most destructive of all pitfalls for us. Instead of accepting and learning from our disappointment, we are offended by the discovery that we are not the very special and important person we presume ourselves to be. As our losses seem to accumulate, we may eventually be devastated. But even in our darkest hour we still refuse to accept what is painfully being made clear. Rather than relinquish our illusions and abandon our false expectations, we allow ourselves to be ruled by our fear and cling all the more tightly to the very expectations that have been exposed as false.

We have been swept up in a self-defeating cycle, which I will argue lies at root of most forms of physical and psychological maladies. This cycle of spiraling suffering is depicted in the image of the Wheel of Samsara (the round of life and death) often found in Buddhist art. It portrays the ultimate form in which this vicious cycle occurs—that is, in the process of death and rebirth in which our ceaseless craving brings us back again and again to the realm of suffering while denying us the attainment of a state of lasting bliss. However, liberation is still possible by undoing these harmful habits of mind and coming to a true understanding of the nature of ourselves and reality.

The pattern described here no doubt sounds familiar as it mirrors the earlier discussion of the human propensity for self-deception and the futility of seeking to avoid the anxiety that comes with living life as an ever-changing process. Though the Buddha attained these insights regarding self-deception over 2500 years ago, they have never lost their relevance. Indeed, they seem to be a particularly apt description and critique of the disastrous cycle of destruction presently being spawned by neoliberalism. It is an ideology in which greed and selfishness are extolled as the highest virtues. It is maintained by using fear and playing upon the insecurities and uncertainties of those who live under its sway. In accord with its dictates, we continue with reckless abandon to rapaciously plunder the resources of our planetary home to secure maximum immediate rewards for the few while senselessly triggering an ecological calamity that will mean misery for millions. We engage in endless warfare to wrest the resources we covet from others who possess them, to aggrandize the egos of the war-makers, to instigate fear in those we deem to be kept under thumb, and to line the pockets of corporate heads of the military–industrial complex.

Based on neoliberal principles, we cheapen human life and trivialize human dignity through the transformation of all forms of human relationships into financial transactions in which everyone and everything has a price. The singular and all-consuming pursuit of more wealth than any single human being could ever need in multiple lifetimes is elevated as the quintessential mark of success, even if such greed is at the expense of the welfare of thousands. As a consequence, staggering levels of inequality have become an obscene reality. The pursuit of truth, compassion, and justice is dismissed as a ridiculous and antiquated idea, overshadowed by the ever-present web of lies manufactured by slick marketing and political spin.

There are those no doubt who would take serious exception to the way in which I have portrayed the "evils" of neoliberalism. I may be accused of turning a blind eye to the benefits and achievements of capitalism. It is not my intention to adopt the kind of one-sided view that I previously described as erroneous and harmful. It is also not my goal here to indict capitalism in its entirety. There are ample advocates for the blessings of capitalism, and I defer to them to make their case. What I hope to do here is to make my case for how the core tenets of capitalism have been taken to an extreme in our contemporary society and therefore have generated levels of inequality and injustice that constitute the most egregious forms of oppression.

Not all is bleak, however. Though the power of hegemony is considerable, it is not unassailable. Contradictory tendencies and inconsistencies, as we have seen, exist in any ideology. These create tensions that make the ideology unstable and open to critique. Once revealed, the self-defeating nature of these contradictions can help to make the ambivalence of those subject to hegemonic domination more apparent to them. Thus, a counter-hegemony exists alongside a hegemonic ideology. This paves the way for dissent and resistance. While this conflict can be accompanied by pain and distress, it can ultimately impart a great blessing by serving as a means by which liberation can be achieved. And, though it may seem ironic, it is actually suffering caused by oppression that makes dissent, resistance, and liberation possible. Through suffering, transformation is possible. At first this may not be case. As Osterkamp (1999) observes:

> In the view of Critical Psychology, ideology is essentially seen as one-sidedness which allows the prevailing power relation to appear as "normal" and sees any resistance to them as "deviance" which needs to be silenced or explained away in one way or other. Silencing discontent with the given order and refractoriness to it, however, is only possible or tenable if the other side, that is, people's suffering from the given "normality," remains systematically overlooked and veiled. (p. 379)

While ideologies are often cleverly hidden, inevitably they are ultimately exposed through the various ways in which they prove to be harmful to the well-being of individuals impacted by them—the oppressed. "The essential criterion for the necessity of societal change, in this view, is its insufficiency to satisfy people's needs—that is, to recognize and alleviate people's suffering" (Osterkamp, 1999, p. 380).

A similar argument is made by Iris Marion Young (1990) in her discussion of the meaning of a critical approach in the study of justice. Such an approach must begin by examining the specific historical conditions that one immediately confronts and to evaluate these conditions in normative terms. Among the questions to be asked in such a critical approach is who benefits and who is harmed by these conditions because in the absence of such questions there is the risk of reaffirming and naturalizing those conditions. She goes on to elaborate:

> Normative reflection arises from hearing a cry of suffering or distress, or feeling distress oneself. The philosopher is always socially situated, and if the society is divided by oppressions, she either reinforces or struggles against them. With an emancipatory interest, the philosopher apprehends given social circumstances not merely in contemplation but with passion: the given is experienced in relation to desire. Desire, the desire

to be happy, creates the distance, the negation, that opens the space for criticism of what is. This critical distance does not occur on the basis of some previous discovered rational ideas of the good and the just. On the contrary, the ideas of the good and the just arise from the desiring negation that action brings to what is given. (pp. 5–6)

Once again it is the confrontation with suffering caused by oppressive conditions that makes possible the stirring of the desire to put an end to such oppression.

As my awareness of the substantial role played by oppression in causing a host of harms grew, this realization brought me back to an enduring interest that I had in the problem of human suffering. This preoccupation, of course, has been clearly shaped by certain facts of my life and the ways in which I have sought and continue to seek to contend with and understand those facts. Nonetheless, it was when I was working as a psychologist in a physical rehabilitation inpatient program that the relevance of suffering to my professional life became most salient. Dealing each day with the impact of unexpected and major loss in the lives of the patients to whom I provided therapy proved to be grueling work. Not only was there the emotional cost of seeking to remain open to the suffering of those with whom I worked, but also being reminded daily of my own vulnerability to a loss that could suddenly devastate my life.

As the toll of this work grew, I felt unprepared to offer the kind of service I felt that my patients deserved. I feared that I was becoming depleted by the anxieties that their loss and struggle awakened in me. In response to this, I launched into a serious exploration of whatever I could find on the subject of suffering and how to help those who suffer (as well as myself as one who suffered with them). A full discussion of what emerged from this exploration is part of what will be considered in a later chapter. However, among the most important lessons I learned is a point made in the work of Elaine Scarry (1985). Serious attention to the subject of suffering is a key to the advancement of knowledge and human development. Neglect of the relevance and reality of suffering results in a much-diminished appreciation for human life. This being so, to deny suffering—whether it be our own or that of someone else—brings with it the risk of also denying our humanity or that of another.

The Role of Oppression in Suffering

Here is where the subject of suffering becomes inextricably linked to oppression. As Friere (1970) astutely observes, a core element of oppression is the dehumanization of the oppressed. It is not merely that oppression strips its victims of humanity. The dehumanization of the victims of oppression is made possible in large part by denying the suffering being inflicted upon them. In Cudd's (2006) examination of the psychological harms of oppression, she includes objectification. While it might prove harder to behave terribly toward people we see as human beings like ourselves, it becomes much easier if we transform them into objects. Treating the oppressed as things deprives them of feelings, agency, and an entire range of human possibilities. At the same time, the experience of being objectified causes a whole host of other psychological and physical harms for the oppressed. These impacts will be discussed at greater length in a later chapter. For now, it suffices to establish that a critical element of oppression is not merely the inflicting of suffering on the oppressed, but the lack of recognition of the anguish caused by those harms. That lack of recognition is not restricted to the perpetrators. It is also found in the oppressed and leads them to doubt their own experience. The invalidation of the experiences of another human being constitutes a particularly egregious and all too frequent form of psychological violence. It is an essential element of the process of mystification. Consequently, this denial of suffering of the oppressed constitutes a significant obstacle to their liberation.

Friere (1970) adds another observation that expands our view of the suffering created by oppression. Though less obvious, oppressors are also dehumanized by their engaging in oppressive practices. Denial of the anguish of the oppressed and the multiple strategies employed by oppressors to justify their unjust treatment of others are not aimed merely at evading any recognition of the suffering of victims. They also evade confrontation with any discomfort, remorse, moral approbation, and guilt oppressors experience upon recognizing their role in oppressing others. Disowning this suffering is a potent way in which oppressors dehumanize themselves. Oppressors cannot escape the physical and psychological costs of oppression (Goodman, 2001). As in the case of the oppressed, their refusal to take ownership of the pain and discomfort that come with awareness of the wrongs they are committing stymies efforts to put an end to oppression.

The obstacle posed by oppressor's refusal to confront the pain they cause and their moral culpability in ending the exploitation and dehumanization of the oppressed were astutely observed early on by Friedrich Engels. He was the first person to write about the crushing burdens and cruel abuses of the working class at the dawn of the industrial age. In the Introduction to *The condition of the working class in England in 1844*, Engels (1892/1943) writes:

> In spite of all this, the English middle-class, especially the manufacturing class, which is enriched directly by means of the poverty of the workers, persists in ignoring this poverty. This class, feeling itself the mighty representative class of the nation, is ashamed to lay the sore spot of England bare before the eyes of the world; will not confess, even to itself, that the workers are in distress, because it, the property-holding, manufacturing class, must bear the moral responsibility for this distress. Hence the scornful smile which intelligent Englishmen (and they, the middle-class, alone are known on the Continent) assume when any one [*sic*] begins to speak of the condition of the working-class; hence the utter ignorance on the part of the whole middle-class of everything which concerns the workers; hence the ridiculous blunders which men of this class, in and out of Parliament, make when the position of the proletariat comes under discussion; hence the absurd freedom from anxiety, with which the middle-class dwells upon a soil that is honeycombed, and may any day collapse, the speedy collapse of which is as certain as a mathematical or mechanical demonstration... (p.18)

As Engels warns, persistently turning a blind eye to and a showing a lack of compassion for the plight of the oppressed may bring short-term benefits. However, such denial and deception cannot be successfully sustained and will one day lead to even greater calamity.

So, a series of paradoxes are once more unveiled in looking at the interdependent relationship that exists between oppression and suffering. One is the ways in which suffering often breeds oppression, such that those who have suffered channel their unhappiness by oppressing others and thus making them suffer just as they have. This suffering is extremely dangerous and destructive—so all-consuming that it eventually leads to the ruin of those who thought to escape their suffering by inflicting it on others. Another paradox is how the very same suffering caused by oppression can also lead to a heightened awareness of to it. The final paradox we discover is the realization that the end of oppression does not bring all suffering to an end. There is little doubt that the great majority of human misery would be eliminated. However, a certain suffering remains that is inherent to the human condition. Of all the paradoxes, this one invariably proves to be the most challenging. That is because it flies in the face of perhaps the most powerful of all illusions harbored by human beings—the desire and resolute belief that one can (and should) be free of all pain and suffering.

The Two Forms of Suffering and Their Interrelationship

The crucial insight of the Buddha and other thinkers that there are different forms of suffering helps us to elucidate these paradoxes. The first two rooted in natural causes of suffering (*dukkha-dukkha*) and the loss inextricably bound up with life as an unfolding process and suffering that comes with it (*viparinama-dukkha*) together can be seen as necessary and inevitable. This is suffering that comes with just being alive. For example, pain, whether in a physical or mental form, serves a vital function in alerting us to threats to our well-being toward which we must take some corrective action. Similarly, because life is a ceaseless process of change, we will inevitably suffer loss whether in the form of growing older, becoming ill, or eventually dying. This suffering that is built into the nature of existence itself will be called *inescapable suffering* (Gruba-McCallister, 1992; Gruba-McCallister & Levington, 1995). Removing this suffering totally from our experience is not only impossible but will actually prove detrimental as it deprives human existence of purpose and value.

   While this suffering exacts a terrible cost on human beings, it accounts for the smaller portion of human misery and distress. As argued by the Buddha and others, the third form of suffering described as *samkhara-dukkha* is by far the greatest source of misery. While our perspective, attitudes and motivations are to some degree influenced by factors beyond our choice and control, they nevertheless have been created by us and freely chosen as responses to our life experiences. Because they are habits of the mind that have been acquired through both experience and choice, they can be unlearned and different choices are possible. It is precisely for this reason that the Buddha prescribed the eightfold path to Nirvana, a set of disciplines that cultivate the attitudes and wisdom that lead to liberation. This second type will be called *self-created suffering* (Gruba-McCallister, 1992; Gruba-McCallister & Levington, 1995). As implied in the name, this form of suffering arises from the choices that human beings make and the destructive consequences of those choices. Possessing free will, human beings are moral agents and so are responsible and accountable for these consequences. Because this is suffering we create, it can be alleviated or removed by making different choices.

That is not to say that explaining how and why human beings make such destructive choices—what is called moral evil—is a simple and straightforward matter. One reason for this complexity is found in the earlier discussion of the current view of individualism. This perspective places an exaggerated emphasis on how the causes of evil reside within the person while obscuring or neglecting the role played by external influences. In fact, it was my encounter later in my professional career with Critical Psychology and theory and research on the social determinants of health that "awoke me from my dogmatic slumber" (to borrow a phrase from the philosopher Immanuel Kant). I became painfully aware of my uncritical acceptance of neoliberal ideology's bias toward locating problems within individuals. I am grateful for this awakening. It has enabled me to develop a more balanced and sophisticated understanding of how easy it is to confuse inescapable suffering with self-created suffering and the role that such confusion plays in forms of injustice and oppression. It exposed my own mistaken propensity to subscribe to mainstream psychology's neglect of the role of oppression and environmental deprivation in causing what it mistakenly calls "psychopathology" (Jacobs, 1994). Having come to a clearer recognition of the profound impact of these external factors, I am even more confirmed in my conviction that self-created suffering, unlike inescapable suffering, is neither inevitable nor irremediable.

This discussion brings to light just how important it is to accurately identify these two forms of suffering, and having done so, discern how best to respond to them. The hazards of confusing them are especially worthy of attention because both are at work in oppression. In the case of inescapable suffering, the recognition that some suffering is inescapable and necessary must be understood with some caution in the matter of oppression. This is because history has shown how this idea has been put to highly destructive use in the hands of those who, first, would use it to foist a fatalistic and nihilistic view onto those whose lives are devastated by suffering caused by oppression and, second, would then use it to disguise their own responsibility for causing that very suffering. Both these maneuvers are extensively used in mystification. This is achieved by means of confusing suffering that has its basis in harmful actions freely chosen by oppressors at the expense of the oppressed with suffering that is universal, natural, and thus incapable of being eliminated. Put another way, it is a form of deception that conflates self-created suffering with inescapable suffering.

Within the current neoliberal hegemony, for example, a vision of the world is created in which "the market" exists "out there" and operates autonomously in accordance with its own unchangeable laws (Esposito & Perez, 2014). Consequently, human beings must accept and accommodate themselves to these laws irrespective of their consequences. To not do so would be deemed irrational and deviant. If some people benefit more from the operation of these laws than others in the case of certain "market fluctuations," this is natural consequence about which nothing can be done. Likewise, if others are harmed by these same forces, that is a result of the working of the same immutable laws. What is obscured, of course, in this characterization is that there is nothing natural or inevitable about these "market fluctuations." They are actually consequences of manipulation by human beings in order to benefit themselves even if it is at the expense of others.

A recent disturbing example of this is the circumstances that led to the financial crisis of 2007. For example, unfair lending practices by larger financial institutions led to the exploitation of those who were given mortgages that they would eventually be unable to afford. Thousands of those individuals subsequently lost their homes while others prospered by their loss. Austerity measures were imposed on those most negatively impacted by the recession while the wealthy were left unaffected. Attributing the effects of the economy to the "market" is an example of what is called *reification*, in which an abstraction or mere concept takes on an illusory quality by being cast within an ideology as a concrete and objective entity. This is an example of *missing the metaphor*—another pattern that will be encountered again in my analysis of oppression. Such circumstances in which a metaphor is taken literally are unfortunately all too common and often give rise to suffering.

By attributing oppression to the operation of forces over which no one has any control, those responsible for such oppression obscure their responsibility and present their actions as actually benevolent and in the best interests of those who are oppressed. At the same time, those who are oppressed are rendered passive and helpless in the face of what they have mistakenly been led to believe are natural, inexorable forces. Moreover, by employing mystification, this type of oppression succeeds by avoiding overt use of coercion and force that would be more easily recognized and thus resisted. Instead, more subtle and indirect means of influence are employed that confuse the oppressed and induce them to feel at one with those who oppress them in the face of irresistible conditions. Fears and insecurity are manipulated in order to make the oppressed grateful for the treatment they receive (meager and harmful as it may be) and to convince them that any attempt at rebellion is evil and futile.

A comparable process of mystification occurs with regard to self-created suffering in which mystification is used to characterize an individual's suffering as his or her own doing when it is in fact not. In this case the most common manifestation of mystification is *blaming the victim*. In his classic work, Ryan (1971) ascribes the individualistic attributions for social problems to an ideological process aimed at maintaining the status quo. He provides the following description of blaming the victim:

> The stigma that marks the victim and accounts for his victimization is an acquired stigma, a stigma of social, rather than genetic, origin. But the stigma, the defect, the fatal difference—though derived in the past from environmental forces—is still located *within* the victim, inside his skin. With such an elegant formulation, the humanitarian can have it both ways. He can, all at the same time, concentrate his charitable interest on the defects of the victim, condemn the vague social and environmental stresses that produced the defect (some time ago), and ignore the continuing effect of victimizing social forces (right now). It is a brilliant ideology for justifying a perverse form of social action designed to change, not society, as one might expect, but rather society's victim. (pp. 7–8)

We have seen this pattern in how neoliberalism ascribes an exaggerated degree of responsibility for one's happiness or misery to the individual. This protects the status quo by attributing the full range of adverse consequences of social problems to those who suffer those consequences.

Neoliberalism's framing of poverty also illustrates this process. Greene (2008) cites research by Macionis (2002) that in a highly individualistic country like the United States, 60% of Americans believe that personal laziness is the primary cause of poverty. This contrasts sharply with more collective countries such as Mexico (25%) and Sweden (17%). A troubling facet of this research is that the poor themselves often attribute their poverty to laziness, reflecting the degree to which their experience of oppression has been internalized. Rank (2004) provides a sharp critique of this paradigm for understanding poverty solely in terms of individual inadequacies. He observes that there is a conservative and liberal version of this paradigm. In the conservative version, the focus is on undesirable personality characteristics like immorality, lack of discipline, and irresponsibility. In the liberal version, the focus is on inadequate human capital, such as a lack of education or marketable skills—what is sometimes called the deficit model. In either instance, the fault lies in the individual and it is the individual that must somehow be fixed, while the economic and social issues that cause poverty remain invisible and unaddressed.

From this examination of suffering, there emerges a core insight, which I acquired when I undertook my personal search of how to better cope with working with those experiencing profound and painful losses. This insight will prove valuable to my analysis of the problem of oppression. Suffering fundamentally takes two forms and these two forms are inextricably interwoven (Gruba-McCallister, 1992; Gruba-McCallister & Levington, 1995). One form cannot be understood or adequately dealt with without taking into consideration the other. The nature and causes of both forms must be understood to correctly distinguish between them. This then lays the foundation for how each requires a very different way of responding to and managing it. The failure to take these differences into account gives rise to ill-conceived and self-defeating efforts in which seeking to rid ourselves of suffering cause us to suffer all the more. This core insight can be stated as follows:

> *Self-created suffering is rooted in our futile attempts at evading and denying inescapable suffering. Our insistence that we should not have to suffer, our outrage at the suffering inherent in being alive, causes us paradoxically to suffer even more. And so we find that the greatest portion of suffering we experience is in the pursuit of not having to experience any suffering at all.*

To put this insight in more colloquial terms, people would rather be right than happy. This point has been made several times previously in discussing self-deception. The need for control and stability, accompanied by the anxiety associated with the unfamiliar, is often a source of considerable suffering. The inevitable losses we experience and the lack of control that we possess over a great deal of what happens are accompanied by inescapable suffering. That said, our refusal to accept this suffering as an inevitable part of life and our rigid resistance to relinquishing our need for control compound our unhappiness many times over. It is more important for us to cling to the familiar and to our dearest preferences even if they make us miserable. Whether our goal is to be right or to be happy, in the long term we are neither.

A similar observation that supports this assertion is that people who are unhappy and in distress often pursue a very self-defeating strategy to rectify this situation. Paradoxically, they try desperately to change the things in life that cannot be changed and then profess utter helplessness about changing the things in life that they can change. They are caught on the horns of a dilemma of their own making. Their failure to discern what can and cannot be controlled, to distinguish what is necessary versus what is possible, only serves to deepen their unhappiness. It's like beating your head against a wall and then castigating yourself for beating your head against a wall. This self-defeating pattern is tragically displayed in the many instances in which people rail and rage against the inescapable facts of their lives. "If only I had more loving and understanding parents. Why do I never seem to get a lucky break? If only I hadn't made that decision." Rather than finding ways of coming to peace with these things they cannot change and transforming their grief, disappointment and anger into healing, such individuals instead channel their frustration and disappointment into actions that are harmful, wicked, and at times insane.

Self-deception is also at work within this self-defeating pattern—a very powerful form of self-deception in which individuals maintain the illusion that the rules that govern all human beings somehow do not apply to them. Among these rules is what the creator of logotherapy, Viktor Frankl (1967) calls the tragic triad—to be human is to be fallible, finite, and mortal. What Frankl is asserting is another way of stating the first Noble Truth of the Buddha and the inevitability of the first two forms of suffering. The confusion of the two forms of suffering rests upon our stubborn refusal to embrace our humanity and the givens that come with it. In doing so, we refuse to accept our own inevitable suffering and the suffering of others. Our vain expectation to make our lives pain free, accompanied by our proclivity to always seek the easy way out, is based upon succumbing to lies (whether told by ourselves or others). The constriction of our experience and stifling of our feelings serve over time to shrivel our capacity for compassion and undermine our commitment to justice. As Erich Fromm (1964) describes so eloquently, our hearts become increasing hard, we drift farther and farther along a path that affirms death over life, and we make life more of a living hell for ourselves and others. Out of these harmful consequences comes our willingness to engage in oppression. Liberation, well-being, and happiness can only be attained if we are willing to suffer for our pleasures.

Returning to My Painful Awakening

So, I come full circle to the reflections on my experience of disillusionment at the start of this chapter. A number of confrontations with suffering and oppression led to my increasing disillusionment. First, there was the suffering I witnessed every day created by the many faces of oppression—exploitation, hatred, discrimination, and violence. There was also the suffering that I saw in those closest to me whose lives were either adversely impacted by oppression or who like me felt anger and distress at the injustices being perpetrated on the weak and vulnerable. There was my own suffering as I struggled to understand the lack of compassion shown by my fellow human beings and my own failures to show compassion and take action. But this distress was just the beginning. As it steadily became more intense, so too did the temptation to shut it out, to ignore what was going on all around me. I began to feel drawn to walk the path that would harden my own heart.

In other words, I was at the most critical of decision points regarding how to engage the suffering I naturally felt when faced with dire consequences of oppression. I saw, on one hand, the possibility that I might fall into a deep despair in which I would be overwhelmed by the immensity of the problem and rendered incapable of either caring or doing something about it. On the other, I saw how I might forsake and stifle the very human responses I was feeling and in doing so become the very type of person I held in contempt—cold and indifferent. There had to be some way to steer between these dangerous extremes and escape the vicious cycle that opened before me. That path required that I first embrace the pain I felt and accept it as the price for being caring and compassionate. I saw that without such suffering, compassion would never be awakened. However, it also meant that I would have to be willing to re-examine and, if necessary, abandon lingering mistaken beliefs and false expectations, particularly those that made me complicit with oppression. And that again meant a willingness to accept the fear and pain that this would bring.

I was not merely becoming disillusioned; I was actively identifying my illusions and shedding them. And through it all I was striving to be resolutely guided by the lesson I am making central to my examination of oppression. Awareness of oppression is only the beginning. As that awareness grows, so too does awareness of the immense suffering it causes to its victims, of the heartache we compassionately experience to their plight, and of the remorse we must accept for whatever part we play in causing such harm to others. Then that suffering must give way to resolve and action to do all we can to remove the causes of an unnecessary (and sometimes self-created) form of suffering. Only then will our firm commitment to compassion and justice take hold and pave the way to ending oppression and promoting liberation.

The centrality of these values of compassion and justice brings me to one other point I wish to make in my analysis of oppression. To ensure true liberation, we must recognize that oppression has a deleterious impact on all facets of human beings. I have previously critiqued individualism as an overly narrow perspective for understanding human beings. A complete understanding of human beings must be holistic. What that means is that in addition to looking at the biological, psychological, and social facets of the person, we must add the spiritual. During my personal and professional search for a meaningful understanding of and genuine response to the problem of suffering, I came to see how essential religion and spirituality were. It has been said by a number of thinkers that the very roots of religion are found in the human confrontation with pain, suffering, and evil. This was borne out for me when I found that the deepest and most helpful insights for how I could be of service to my patients came from diverse religious and spiritual traditions.

It is a specific function of religion within these traditions that is pertinent to the problem of oppression. Theologian John Hick (1989) describes this as the *soteriological character* of religion. This dimension of religion emerged in that exceptional period of human history in which the great wisdom traditions began—the Axial Age (800–250 BCE). At this period of human history, there was a notable growth in self-awareness accompanied by increased attunement to human moral weakness, insecurity, and propensity to suffer. New questions emerged for people living at that time including what happens when I die, in what ways do my actions today affect my fate after death, and why do bad things happen to me. Religious beliefs and values evolved to respond to these questions. While there was a deeper sense of the pervasiveness of evil and suffering in the world, Hick observes that the Axial religions espoused a cosmic optimism. This was the belief that human beings could move from this state of alienation to a radically better one in which salvation or liberation is attained. Great teachers professed that perfect bliss and fulfillment can be achieved when human beings move from their overly self-centered focus and excessive concerns for themselves and instead direct themselves toward a transcendent or ultimate concern that offers limitless better possibilities.

This soteriological character can be found in all the major faith traditions. It gives religion/spirituality a practical and ethical dimension. That is, what is a good life and how can we conduct ourselves in accordance with the moral precepts essential to a good life. One such moral imperative asserts that it is evil to cause others to suffer and that it is good to be compassionate toward others and seek to alleviate their suffering. In other words, the soteriological view elevated the values of compassion and justice. For example, we find the Hebrew prophets criticizing mere compliance with ritual and boldly proclaiming God's preference for the poor and the oppressed. Thus, they uncompromisingly condemned the host of injustices directed to the poor and oppressed and called for the perpetrators to repent, show compassion, and restore justice. Over time, with the rise of the social sciences in the mid-19th century, the impact of unjust political and economic systems became unveiled.

Once again religions responded to these revelations by expanding the vision of liberation beyond that of individuals to the liberation of entire groups. An excellent contemporary example is liberation theology (Ruether, 1972), which developed in the Catholic Church in Latin America. Like the Hebrew prophets of old, it proclaims the preferential option for the poor and engages in activism and political action to address poverty, human rights violations, and other social issues. Its exhortation to "Afflict the comfortable and comfort the afflicted," serves as a fitting summarization of this discussion of suffering and oppression. To achieve justice, oppressors must recognize and act upon the painful realization of their complicity in oppressive practices. This realization must then be followed by extending compassion to the oppressed to remove the causes of their suffering. Together justice and compassion will enable us to restore our humanity as well as the humanity of the afflicted.

Plan for the Remainder of the Book

Having laid out the general purpose and goals of this book, I will chart out how the following chapters will be structured to provide my examination of oppression, suffering, and mystification. The overarching goal pursued in opposing and ending oppression is the attainment of social justice. Thus, it is essential that there is clarity regarding what social justice is. This will be examined in Chapter 2. Chapter 3 will provide a careful examination of the subject of suffering in order to elucidate its core elements and the different forms it can take. A deeper appreciation of the various dimensions of the experience of suffering provides critical insights into the ways in which oppression is a substantial cause of suffering and the ways in which it affects human beings physically, psychologically, and spiritually.

Chapter 4 then turns to the other principal topic of this book, oppression. Oppression is examined as a social form of suffering. Prior to providing a comprehensive definition of oppression, some of the core principles of Critical Psychology are reviewed since they form an important framework for how oppression is examined in this book. Following the definition, this chapter elucidates the core aspects of the ways in which oppression is experienced, particularly as they overlap with elements of the experience of suffering provided in the previous chapter. Chapter 5 will then examine the processes involved in self-deception and their positive and negative consequences for human beings negotiating the range of challenges posed by life. This chapter begins with a brief overview of the structures and functions of consciousness. Following this, the chapter explores the relationship of self-deception to the basic physical and psychological defenses employed to deal with threat and elucidates lessons that can be learned from hypnosis applicable to self-deception. The chapter concludes by revisiting the problem of the ego as a paradigm for understanding self-deception.

Chapter 6 turns its attention to mystification. Since one of the primary functions of mystification is to render the dominant ideology invisible, the chapter begins by defining what is meant by ideology and describing its principal functions. The chapter next discusses the work of Gramsci on hegemony and how it takes the form of common sense or conventional wisdom. This is followed by an examination of how mystification can be viewed as the internalization of hegemony. Another perspective for understanding mystification is then offered, informed by the work of R. D. Laing on the destructive impact of the invalidation of experience. The chapter concludes with a discussion of the core elements of neoliberalism, the current hegemonic ideology. Chapter 7 builds on the previous chapter by reviewing the various means employed by neoliberal ideology to mystify suffering. A range of examples is examined, each connected to one of the central assumptions of neoliberalism—including the myth of the market, the primacy of the individual, the commodification of life, and happiness as the goal of life. The inconsistencies inherent in these assumptions are exposed, as are the ways in which these contradictions lead individuals to experience an even greater degree of suffering.

In the final chapter, Chapter 8, the theme of the potential of suffering to lead to positive change and transformation is revisited. The demystification of suffering and the disillusionment that follows it is disturbing and frightening, but a necessary step in the pursuit of justice. For that process to unfold, three critical steps must be taken: the naming, claiming, and reframing of suffering. The disowning and distortion of the experience of suffering by ideology must first be undone, enabling individuals to fully recognize what in fact they are experiencing. Next, resistance to the experience needs to be replaced by acceptance and the cultivation of a form of dispassionate attention or passive volition. Finally, working collaboratively and collectively with others leads to the development of critical consciousness. This allows for a reframing of suffering in which it is given a different meaning that is free of ideological distortions. The way is opened to imagine a more just world and to work with others to achieve it.

Chapter 2

Justice

Justice: The Means of Putting an End to Oppression

In the previous chapter, I make the case that all efforts seeking to put an end to oppression must be wedded with the pursuit of justice. This is because oppression is created by social and structural factors that constitute forms of injustice such as discrimination, exploitation, and violence. Morton Deutsch (2006) writes, "Oppression is the experience of repeated, widespread, systemic injustice" (p. 10). Similarly, in her detailed examination of oppression, Cudd (2006) states, "The main thesis of the book is that oppression is an institutionally structured harm perpetrated on groups by other groups using direct and indirect material and psychological forces that violate justice" (p. 26). However, while justice is essential, it alone cannot end oppression. The suffering caused by oppression can also evoke the powerful stirrings of compassion. Indeed, it has been argued by some (Hick, 1989; Nussbaum, 1992) that the experience of compassion would not be possible in the absence of suffering.

Compassion and justice are thus two values that are inextricably linked to each other and equally essential to respectfully, meaningfully, and effectively responding to suffering, whether it is our own or that of others. The close relationship between them is based on a critical insight into the nature of the human being and existence itself. Williams (2008) notes that compassion provides the moral foundation for justice based on the interconnected and mutually interdependent relationship that exists not only among all human beings but between human beings and all of life. By expanding the boundaries of the self, compassion enables us to feel one with the suffering of others and awakens the desire to remove that suffering. When that suffering is created by injustice, connecting with suffering can awaken anger and a sense of moral outrage that are equally vital to responding to that suffering.

Matthew Fox (1972) describes the interdependence of compassion and justice as two radical responses to life, based on the meaning of radical as "rooted." On the one hand, compassion expresses a contemplative tradition that reveals how one is "rooted" in a shared reality with others while, on the other hand, justice comes from a prophetic tradition of critiquing the status quo and working to "uproot" it in order to make it fairer and more compassionate. Fox describes this close relationship as follows: "I suggest that love today means before all else justice. Justice is the direction given to love. For the only way to love God is by loving one's neighbor; but the only way to love one's neighbor...is by justice. Very simply, he who says he loves his neighbor but ignores justice is a liar" (p. 105). This blending of awareness, understanding, reflection, critique, and action is also very characteristic of *praxis*, which has been observed by many such as Friere (1970) as essential to attaining liberation by working for justice.

Consideration must thus be given to both compassion and justice in order to oppose and eliminate oppression. However, for the moment I will focus on justice. This is first because, as noted earlier, oppression is a major form of injustice. In addition, when we witness the suffering inflicted on those who are oppressed, it may seem easier for many to feel sadness and concern at their plight while avoiding seeing beyond their pain to the systemic and structural factors at work. In other words, fixating on compassion—or what may seem like compassion as in the trite and meaningless offering of "thoughts and prayers" to those who have suffered a tragedy—is often a strategy for evading the call for justice. It is thus important to have clarity regarding what justice is and is not, what forms it takes, how it is integrally connected to oppression, and how it can inform efforts devoted to ending oppression.

The word "justice" evokes many different meanings. What may come to mind is the image of blindfolded justice holding a sword and scales that is intended to convey impartiality, equality, and a commitment to truth—all of which have been regarded as important elements of justice. Justice can evoke very conflicting notions as well. On one hand, it can convey kindness and clemency and, on the other, it can convey punishment and vengeance. This diversity of images of justice reflects the many meanings that have been attributed to it over time. In addition, the nature and meaning of justice has evolved, paralleling changing conceptions of the human person (Solomon & Murphy, 2000). Some ideas regarding justice, such as equity or fairness, have endured. Others have been revised and refined based on the increasing recognition of the value of the individual person and the centrality of rights to human dignity.

This chapter will provide an overview of key elements of the concept of justice. Following this overview, the principal forms of justice of justice will be described, with emphasis given to distributive and procedural justice as those most pertinent to the problem of oppression (Prilleltensky, 2012). Principal schools of thought regarding the meaning of distributive and procedural justice will be described. This will then provide the foundation for a more in-depth discussion of a contemporary view of justice that offers considerable insight into oppression and its impact on human well-being, the capabilities approach espoused by the Amatrya Sen (1999) and Martha Nussbaum (1992, 2003, 2004, 2006). The emphasis placed by the capabilities approach on promoting and enhancing human development offers a particularly powerful way of understanding the harms caused by oppression and how these can be corrected.

The chapter then concludes with a discussion of how key elements of social justice accord well with elements of human well-being (Prilleltensky, 2012). Concepts such as fairness, human dignity, liberty, freedom, human agency, and psychic and social harmony—all of which have been connected to justice—clearly can be related to those conditions that are necessary to end oppression and ensure well-being.

Justice and the Social Nature of the Human Being

The interconnectedness and interdependence that exists between human beings and between human beings and their world is not merely the foundation of compassion and justice. Our interconnectedness, particularly when placed within an ecological perspective, also exposes the fact that many of the causes of suffering cannot be viewed solely at the level of the individual. Rather, suffering often has its origins in the conditions in which human beings find themselves and over which they have little or no direct control. This idea that human beings are very attuned to and influenced by their physical and social environment has been described as "world openness," a concept with its roots in the work of philosopher Martin Heidegger (1927/1978). An important goal of Heidegger's work was to challenge the Cartesian dualism that characterized much of Western philosophy and that introduced a fundamental and irreconcilable split between mind and body. This split was then generalized to the nature of the relationship between persons and their environment. As a result, the essentially dialectical or interdependent relationship of human beings to the world goes unrecognized. Heidegger used the term *Dasein* to describe human beings, a term that literally means "being there" but is also translated as "being-in-the-world" to convey the inseparable relationship between human beings and their world.

In his article on the role of environmental failure/oppression in the development of psychopathology, Jacobs (1994) utilizes the concept of "world openness" to "...bring into focus the unprecedented degree of our species-specific dependence on the social environment" (p. 3). He goes on to add, "The term refers to the degree to which a species depends on learning, and thus exhibits a range of behavioral flexibility, as a routine part of the normal species way of life in its normal ecological niche" (p. 3). Jacobs' intent in emphasizing how the human species represents the pinnacle of world openness is, in part, to challenge the emphasis often placed on biological (or genetic) factors in causing psychopathology. While human biology is generally incapable of changing in response to the unique environmental circumstances, it is nevertheless the case that there exists a tremendous variation in human behavior in response to diverse environmental conditions, speaking to a high degree of human malleability.

This degree of world openness is linked by Jacobs with the fact that human beings' biological immaturity as a percentage of total lifespan is higher than that of any other species. As a result, the environmental and social conditions throughout the period of human infants' dependency exercise a profound impact on what they learn about themselves and the world and lay developmental foundations that continue to exercise a considerable influence on them for the remainder of their lives. In other words, as Jacobs (1994) explains, human beings possess "...an unprecedented vulnerability to inadequacies in the nurturant-developmental social environment" (p. 4). It is these inadequacies, particularly when they are of significant or traumatic proportion, that lead to psychopathology.

This observation by Jacobs regarding how various contexts in which human beings are embedded impact their development and well-being is clearly in line with Bronfenbrenner's (1979, 1989) ecological model and the substantial body of literature regarding social determinants of health (Marmot & Wilkinson, 2006). Likewise, Biglan (2015) makes a powerful case for the influence of the larger social context in either promoting well-being or causing a broad range of physical and mental health conditions. Adopting an evolutionary analysis, he provides evidence for the uniquely cooperative nature of the human species and for how many problems experienced by human beings stem from the environments in which they develop and live. He asserts, "Nearly all problems of human behavior stem from our failure to ensure that people live in environments that nurture their well-being" (p. 3).

Humans are essentially *social* beings. From the very beginning of life, they are made for and embedded in an intricate network of relationships, the quality of which substantially dictates the course of their development. Thus, while the concept of justice has been related to the dignity and sanctity of the individual, there is clearly and perhaps more importantly a social dimension to justice. Unless we situate our discussion of justice within the framework of how human beings relate to one another and to the various contexts in which they are embedded, not only will we fail to understand the core meaning of justice, but we will also be hampered in our ability to effectively promote it.

This essentially social dimension of justice is acknowledged by one of the most influential contemporary theorists on justice, John Rawls (1971). He states at the very outset of *A Theory of Justice*:

> Justice is the first virtue of *social institutions*, as truth is of systems of thought. A theory however elegant and economical must be rejected or revised if it is untrue; likewise laws and institutions must be reformed or abolished if they are unjust. Each person possesses an inviolability founded on justice that even welfare of society as a whole cannot override. For this reason justice denies that the loss of freedom for some is made right by a greater good shared by others. It does not allow that the sacrifices imposed on a few are outweighed by a larger sum of advantages enjoyed by the many. Therefore in a just society the liberties of equal citizenship are taken as settled; the rights secured by justice are not subject to political bargaining or to the calculus of social interests....Being first virtues of human activities, truth and justice are uncompromising (emphasis added). (pp. 3–4)

The social character of human beings that give rise to relations of interdependence is likewise highlighted by Miller (1999) in his examination of social justice. He notes that very early in the 20th century writers on social justice conceptualized society by adopting a viewpoint that emphasizes the interdependence of its various parts: "Society is viewed as an organism in which the flourishing of each element requires the cooperation of all the others, and the aim of social justice is to specify the institutional arrangements that will allow each person to contribute fully to social well-being" (p. 4).

Justice is a "social virtue," the measure by which we judge whether social arrangements and practices honor the inviolability of *all* society's members, particularly those who are excluded and marginalized. Justice pertains to fundamental principles regarding how human beings should establish and maintain relations with one another; how they should customarily treat one another; and how the benefits and burdens and the rights and obligations of societal membership should be apportioned or distributed (Frankena, 1962). Thus, key principles associated with the concept of justice are need, desert, and fairness (Miller, 1999). These principles govern the form and quality of human relationships and can be used to determine whether the way in which human beings organize themselves is conducive to each person being able to achieve the greatest extent of well-being possible while supporting the same goal for others.

However, as the quote by Rawls makes clear, recognition of this social dimension of justice in no way diminishes and demeans the sacredness of the human individual. The recognition of human dignity stands as a core commitment essential for achieving justice. As a result, Rawls strikes the necessary balance between the individual and collective facets of human life. As Rawls asserts, the principle of justice accords each individual human being an inviolability such that even the welfare of the remainder of society does not justify depriving a single person of his or her welfare or freedom. Such ideas are associated with principles such as equality and human rights in the literature on justice. Human beings are to be treated with respect and dignity not because of any superficial notions of equality such as in position, status, membership, or rank, but simply because they are human beings and as such have inherent worth. It is this recognition of the inherent worth of all persons that requires us to treat one another as equals.

The principle of the sacredness of each human being and the role it plays in establishing a moral code to which all are bound is often traced to the ethical philosophy of Immanuel Kant and what he called the categorical imperative. This imperative, which many see as a form of the Golden Rule, requires human beings not to treat their fellow human beings as means to an end or objects to be controlled or manipulated, but as ends in themselves. Vlastos (1962) writes:

...we acknowledge personal rights which are not proportioned to merit and could not be justified by merit. Their only justification would be the value which persons have simply because they are persons: their "intrinsic value" or the "sacredness of their individuality," as others have called it. I shall speak of it as "individual human worth"; or 'human worth' for short. What these expressions stand for is also expressed by saying that men are "ends in themselves." This latter concept is Kant's. (p. 48)

Thus, a concern of many theories of justice rooted in recognition of this inherent worth is some discussion of what constitutes the basic rights of members of a society. According and respecting certain fundamental rights that are due each person by birth is a way of recognizing their worth and dignity. For example, it acknowledges the basic needs that human beings possess to sustain and preserve their lives, make choices about their lives free of coercion, and pursue goals aimed at securing their well-being (i.e., life, liberty, and the pursuit of happiness).

The social nature of human existence must nonetheless be taken into account. When exercising rights, human beings must establish a sense of personal autonomy that is balanced by recognition of their interdependence with others and their duty to respect the rights of others. The conflict that sometimes exists between the individual and society and how best to harmonize or reconcile the relationship between them raise many challenging questions for theories of justice. How do we balance the needs of the individual with the needs of society? How do we reconcile the rights of one person with the rights of others, especially when they clearly conflict? When should the freedom of certain individuals be restricted or suspended in order to protect the common good?

To add to the complexity, such questions are not mere matters of definition and so cannot be settled based solely on rational deliberation. Because these questions deal with how human beings *ought* to behave, they are ethical or moral issues regarding good and evil, right and wrong. Frankena (1962) writes:

It may be said that a man's due or right is that which is his by virtue not merely of the law or of prevailing moral rules, but of valid moral principles, and that a society is just if it accords its members what is required to accord them by valid moral principles. According to this view, social justice consists in the apportionment of goods and evils, rewards and punishments, jobs and privileges, in accordance with moral standards which can be shown to be valid. In other words, social justice is any system of distribution and retribution which is governed by valid moral principles. (p. 3)

Establishing and defining these valid moral principles is essential to efforts aimed at eradicating oppression. We need to develop agreed-upon principles of social justice that can be used to evaluate whether societies, institutions, and the rules that govern them satisfy these principles. These principles will also provide important guidance regarding what means should be taken to rectify injustices and restore justice when these situations are encountered. Thus, established and agreed-upon moral principles must be applied not only to defining what constitutes the basic rights possessed by all individuals, but also how individuals are afforded the means and opportunities to realize those rights.

The Interdependence of Rights, Resources, and Opportunities

The significant influence exercised by the quality of the environment in which people are born and develop serves to highlight the relevance of the ways in which broader contexts impact the degree to which those rights are recognized and exercised. Without due consideration of resources and opportunities, merely according individuals' "rights" does not satisfy the claims of justice. To help understand why this is so, we can turn to the discussion of equal opportunity and social justice provided by Barry (2005). Barry makes clear that any account of social justice cannot be circumscribed solely by a consideration of the concept of human rights. It must also include the consideration of opportunities and resources. It is the dynamic interrelationship between opportunities, rights, and resources that dictates the course of human development and the degree to which individuals achieve well-being.

Resources are those things (both material and non-material) that can be employed by people to either achieve their goals or at least increase their ability to do so. There are resources of diverse types. For example, we might distinguish between external resources, such as material wealth or supportive community relationships, and internal resources, such as intelligence or athletic ability. *Opportunities* offer human beings the chance to take some action or achieve some goal when it is within their power to do so. We can think of opportunities as the range of options provided to individuals to realistically exercise choice or pursue a course of action. For example, individuals who are incarcerated have far fewer opportunities than those who are not. The concept of opportunities is often associated with a view of freedom sometimes described as "liberty." In this view, individuals should be *free from* obstacles, interference, constraints, prohibitions, etc. in order to be able to pursue the broadest range of opportunities possible for fulfilling their needs or achieving valued goals.

Barry asserts that social conditions play a significant role both in affording opportunities to individuals to fulfill their needs and achieve their goals and in making available to them the resources needed to do so. More important, these larger social forces often prove to be so pervasive and influential that they have the power to render ineffective whatever internal resources (abilities, talent, motivation) individuals may have to exercise their rights. From this perspective, when individuals by virtue of their membership in a particular social group disproportionately or excessively experience conditions that deprive them of the ability to exercise their rights, the conditions for social injustice or oppression have been met.

Challenging the pervasive individualistic view of social justice, Barry (2005) argues persuasively that mere personal effort, determination, will power, and persistence do not suffice in enabling individuals to secure the blessings of society while also avoiding the burdens. It is very difficult for individuals to pull themselves up by the bootstraps when they have neither the bootstraps to pull up nor the arms with which to pull. When we begin to consider the pervasive adverse impact that issues such as poverty, ethnicity, gender, or disability have on the ability of individuals to exercise their rights in the face of discrimination, exploitation, and oppression, we come to a stark realization of just how powerful social circumstances are in determining whether individuals are given a fair chance to fulfill their needs and achieve their goals.

To describe the necessary relation of rights to resources and opportunities, Barry (2005) uses the analogy of the starting gate of a race. He describes the ways that physical and social conditions into which individuals are born and grow exercise a profound impact on them due to the vulnerability associated with humans' dependence on others. Because of significant disparities in both resources and opportunities that exist for some individuals from the very start of life, they find themselves at an immediate disadvantage. It is as if they are people who do not begin the race in which they are competing at the same starting point. Depending on their starting position then, some have an improved chance of winning the race, while others are likely to get off to a poor start and then lag further and further behind as the race proceeds. Continuing with the analogy, all the persons participating in the race have the same goal of successfully completing the race—that is, the same essential rights and the desire to exercise those rights. They may also all be relatively equal in their native abilities at the start of the race and so possess the potential to successfully run it. However, because of the often stark differences that exist between the circumstances into which human beings are born, the reality is that they do not actually all start the race at the same point. Where each person starts life varies dramatically based on factors such as material resources, quality of the air and water, freedom from harmful environmental toxins, and level of stress. This starting point then dictates the rest of one's life course and the ability to realize one's inherent rights.

To make matters worse, often those same individuals who experience unfair disadvantages at the start of life then subsequently encounter even more obstacles or burdens that further hinder their attaining well-being. Thus, the problem of inequity is not merely evidenced in terms of where one begins life but persists as often such inequities mount throughout life. An ongoing lack of resources and opportunities for members of certain social groups serves to further hamper their ability to exercise their rights or to satisfy their most essential needs. Barry (2005) illustrates this form of cumulative inequity as each competitor beginning the race by carrying a twenty-pound weight. At the end of one lap, those who are in the lead have their packs lightened while those who lag behind them do not. This continues after each lap, making the gap between those in the lead and those behind greater and greater. As this analogy makes clear, those who are granted advantages in life often continue to accrue additional advantages and benefits that increase their ability to achieve success. Those who are disadvantaged find that their disadvantaged state steadily worsens, making it harder and harder for them to achieve success. The lives of those who are among the oppressed are dominated by a vicious and pernicious cycle of deprivation, discrimination and disadvantage. As this pattern unfolds over the course of their lives, its destructive impact becomes ever greater, digging them into a hole from which it becomes more and more difficult to escape.

A similar example to illustrate this destructive pattern of disadvantage is provided by Rank (2004) in his discussion of the problem of poverty. The term "capital" is often used to illustrate the types of resources that people have at their disposal to exercise their rights and avail themselves of life's opportunities. While the term capital has connotations to material resources, such as income, it has been extended to include human capital (e.g., knowledge and skills necessary for gainful employment) and social capital (the value and benefits provided to individuals by the social networks of which they are a part). Poverty is characterized by not only a lack of material capita, but also a corresponding lack of human and social capital. As in the case of material capital, such as cash, the more one has to invest, the more capital one accumulates over time, and those with little to nothing to invest are unable to acquire additional capital.

With this in mind, Rank (2004) describes inequities in opportunities and resources as a game of Monopoly in which different players begin the game with different amounts of money. As the game progresses, those players who begin with fewer resources (less money) have fewer opportunities to invest those resources in order to acquire additional wealth. Being unable to buy property and develop it, they are more easily victimized and impoverished by the wealthier Monopoly players who own a disproportionate amount of property. As in the example of the race, the disparity in resources among players affects the outcome of the game from the very start but becomes increasingly apparent as the game proceeds.

Looking at these analogies from a developmental perspective, what Barry (2005) and Rank (2004) are describing is the problem of *cumulative disadvantage* which represents a particularly egregious form of oppression that has devastating consequences for the members of certain social groups, particularly the poor. Barry states,

> Children start with, and grow up with, an enormous variety of different resources. On the basis of just a few facts about a child, such as its social class and its race or ethnicity, we can make a good prediction of where it will finish up in the distribution of earnings, the likelihood that it will spend time in jail, and many other outcomes, good and bad. (p. 41).

To illustrate this, Barry details research documenting how factors such as the unhealthy state of one's mother, poor nutrition, exposure to toxic metals and other environmental hazards, poor quality of prenatal and medical care, and a lack of parental time to devote to raising and caring for a growing child lead to progressively ever more damaging effects.

As a result, these children are severely disadvantaged even before they enter into the school system. These effects are then further compounded due to the inadequate and even inferior education provided to these children. These same points are made convincingly in a review of literature on childhood poverty by Evans (2004), which finds that poor children experience widespread and pervasive environmental inequities that have multiple adverse consequences for their future development. Put bluntly, the way in which society treats perhaps its most vulnerable and neediest citizens, infants and young children, is a shameful stain on its claim to being committed to justice. To so thoroughly disadvantage some children simply by virtue of the circumstances of their birth represents a form of oppression of the highest order.

Rawls (1971) also speaks to the injustice of cumulative disadvantage. He states that the basic structure of society consists of major social institutions whose function is to distribute rights and duties to its members. In doing so, social institutions also determine the distribution of advantages and disadvantages to its members. Examples are the political constitution upon which a government is based and the principal economic and social arrangements by which a society operates. By defining individuals' rights and duties, the basic structure of society also dictates each individual's life chances—life chances that for the most part are based on the circumstances that individuals are born into and do not choose. Because of the profound differences in life circumstances that such structures create, they must be of utmost concern in establishing a just society. Rawls writes:

> The basic structure is the primary subject of justice because its effects are so profound and present from the start. The intuitive notion here is that this structure contains various social positions and that men born into different positions have different expectations of life determined, in part, by the political system as well as by economic and social circumstances. In this way the institutions of society favor certain starting places over others. These are especially deep inequalities. Not only are they pervasive, but they affect men's initial chances in life; yet they cannot possibly be justified by an appeal to merit or desert. It is these inequalities, presumably inevitable in the basic structure of any society, to which principles of social justice must in the first instance apply. (p. 7)

Lack of control over how one begins life means that moral responsibility must be squarely placed on those responsible for creating circumstances of such glaring inequity and not upon those who suffer from it due to no fault of their own. People born into conditions of oppression do not wish these circumstances on themselves, but that doesn't spare them from suffering from their consequences. We clearly see once more the significance of the prolonged period of dependency of human infants on social justice. The health and happiness of children who are the future of any society rests squarely on members of that society establishing optimal, health-promoting conditions from the very start of life *for all children*. As Barry (2005) cogently observes, "...a new-born baby cannot possibly be responsible for the material and social conditions into which it is born, and...whatever 'decisions' a child may make for a number of years after that cannot be its responsibility" (p. 46). The processes of cumulative advantage and disadvantage, which are principally reflected in the unequal distribution of resources in a society, have a substantial impact on whether individuals are able to take advantage of opportunities, what choices they are capable of making, and what additional resources are available to achieve their goals. In other words, ascribing fundamental rights to individuals while depriving them of the essential means and resources needed to realize these rights essentially renders these rights meaningless.

The recognition of not only the injustice but also the implausibility of blaming those who are victimized by social inequities carries with it the demand that such inequities be removed in order to attain justice. It is an affirmation of the need to likewise remove the oppression responsible for those inequities. Barry (2005) underscores this point:

> The first demand of social justice is to change the environments in which children are born and grow up so as to make them as equal as possible, and this includes (though it is by no means confined to) approximate material equality among families. The second demand—which is more pressing the further a society fails to meet the first demand—is that the entire system of social intervention, starting as early as is feasible, should be devoted to compensating, as far as possible, for environmental disadvantages. (p. 58)

Looking at social justice utilizing the framework of human development and the conditions needed to promote human flourishing and well-being provides an excellent lens from which to understand oppression. It also provides a concrete means for illustrating how ideas of merit, need, fairness, impartiality, liberty, and non-injury relate to defining what justice is and how one determines whether the conditions of justice have been satisfied. In the next section then, I will consider concepts that have been associated with the meaning of justice and how the question of what justice is has given rise to a range of diverse perspectives.

The Many Forms and Facets of Justice

When one reviews the literature on justice, he or she will find that certain categories of justice have been identified. One way to come to a clearer understanding the meaning of justice is to consider these different views and the issues associated with each of them. The four principal types of justice identified are procedural, distributive, retributive, and restorative. I will be focusing principally on procedural and distributive justice. Thus, I will offer only a brief examination of the other two.

Retributive justice is concerned with the measures one takes to deal with those who violate the law or betray the public trust. Very early in the history of thought, the notion of punishment was connected to the meaning of justice. Considering the question of how to make punishment just, a determination must be made as to how to make a proportionate response to crimes and other infractions so that these measures are seen as justly administered and morally correct. The expression "Let the punishment fit the crime" describes this emphasis while also making the point that justice is not served when those who are guilty of certain offenses go unpunished. Thus, in addition to determining what type of punishment should be administered in response to offenses, retributive justice must also provide a rationale for what offenses merit any punishment at all. Further, the idea of retribution must be distinguished from revenge as the intent is to administer impersonally and impartially a proportionate punishment for a transgression (see Solomon & Murphy, 2000, pp. 205–277, for review of different perspectives on this view of justice). In other words, the punishment must be imposed after a person has been fairly and impartially tried for a justifiable offense and must be deserved based on the nature of his or her transgression.

Restorative justice is an alternative to retributive justice that has gained increasing attention as another way of dealing with crime and other forms of wrongdoing. The establishment of the Truth and

Reconciliation Commission in South Africa to address injustices and crimes committed during apartheid elevated international awareness of the practice of restorative justice (Rakoczy, 2006). Restorative practices turn attention away from punishment and offer a way of administering justice based on a peaceful and nonviolent approach. The intent of this approach is to create partnerships between offenders, victims, and the community at large based on mutual responsibility and dialogue. By this means, wrong-doers take responsibility for their actions, and the person who is harmed receives an apology in addition to some form of reparation from the wrong-doer with the goal of re-establishing some degree of wholeness or integrity to the victim. In the same vein, the goal of restorative justice is to reintegrate the offender into society. Thus, in restorative justice, crime and other forms of wrongdoing are seen as directed against the individual and the community rather than as an act against the state. The objective is to establish dialogue between the offender and the victim in order to restore the bonds of mutual responsibility, collaboration, and reconciliation that promote a strong sense of community. Restorative justice offers a promising alternative for the current emphasis on punishment and removal from society in treating criminals.

Procedural justice is concerned with ensuring the fairness of processes and practices involved in making and implementing decisions, with the goal of achieving fair outcomes. The idea is that if the rules are correct in determining the criteria for what constitutes a fair or just outcome, then the implementation of these rules will lead to just outcomes. For those who espouse a procedural view of justice, the means of attaining justice are given priority over the specific ends or the just outcomes themselves. Miller (1999) observes, "Social justice has to do with the means of obtaining welfare, not with welfare itself" (p. 7). Thus, a procedural approach does not look directly to outcomes to determine if they are morally sound and social justice has been met. Instead, great care is taken to construct what Rawls (1971, 2001) calls the conditions of justice, by which he means establishing and setting forth the presumptions needed to achieve just social arrangements and specifying the correct process for establishing how just outcomes are to be achieved.

This emphasis in procedural justice on rules and decision making goes back to Rawls' assertion that justice is established by means of the basic structure of society. This is because it is the political, economic, and social institutions of any society that establish the rules for how to allocate resources, resolve conflicts, punish transgressions, and settle other matters pertaining to justice. Thus, one form in which procedural justice is expressed is in how a society has decided to set up its legal system in order to enforce laws. Another significant form that procedural justice takes is the type of government that a society has established, such as a constitution or other bodies of law. In addition to a focus on legal proceedings, the administration of justice, and forms of government, procedural justice seeks to determine how best to develop principles for establishing whether the very processes used to make decisions about the allocation of rights, resources, burdens and punishment are fair.

Distributive justice is based on the recognition that "...social justice demands an equitable distribution of collective goods, institutional resources (such as social wealth), and life opportunities" (Hofrichter, 2003, p. 12). Theories of distributive justice consider how to derive just or morally correct principles for allocating the goods in a society (e.g., wealth, power, privileges) as well as ensure a fair distribution of burdens (e.g., taxes, military service, punishments). As a result, distributive justice focuses more on outcomes in order to determine if conditions of fairness have been satisfied. In those instances in which there is a disproportionate allocation of benefits or exposure to burdens, theories of distributive justice will often seek to reduce or eliminate such inequities by achieving a greater equality of outcomes. Thus, some of the challenges associated with distributive views of justice are what outcomes to focus on, how to measure such outcomes and the disparities that may exist between them, and how to achieve a fairer balance of outcomes across members of a society.

As such, distributive justice, in addition to its being connected with equity and fairness, is also generally linked to ideas such as the common good and respecting human rights. This connection is based on the understanding that the recognition of human dignity and fundamental rights that all human beings share requires that they are treated equitably. Principles of distributive justice prescribe that we not only treat one another equally, but that we have a duty to those who are in need to redress egregious and avoidable inequities.

Procedural Justice: Justice as the Basic Structure of Society

As noted above, taking the viewpoint of procedural justice requires us to consider how rules in a society have been established to achieve just outcomes. Various criteria have been identified for use in evaluating whether principles used to make decisions are fair. One is consistency, which means that like cases are treated similarly. For example, two individuals committing the same criminal offense in similar circumstances should typically receive the same punishment, or two individuals doing the same job should generally receive equivalent compensation. While rules must be flexible enough so that reasonable exceptions can be made when merited, for them to be fair they must be applied consistently or uniformly where they are applicable.

A second principle is that procedures should be fair and impartial. A good example is to establish procedures in the legal system to ensure that a case is tried fairly and minimizes the potential for bias or partiality regarding outcome. Various forms of favoritism in the application of rules have been targeted for criticism as have instances in which certain individuals are singled out for unfair treatment based on some form of bias or prejudice. In its most extreme form, the presence of bias in a decision-making process may lead to a predetermined outcome, such as when a person is granted some reward or privilege—a high-level job or admission to a prestigious university—not due to any merit but based on favoritism.

A third principle is that processes and procedures should be conducted in a transparent manner to avoid secrecy and deception. Transparency involves a critical element of a just society, trust. Indeed, trust has also been identified by psychologists as an essential element for mutually healthy relationships between human beings. One example comes from developmental psychologist Erik Erikson (1950), who saw the achievement of a sense of trust in the world as the first, and thus a pivotal, developmental task. The importance of trust is also encapsulated in transparency guarantees, one of the five instrumental freedoms identified by Sen (1999). Sen notes that in social interactions there must be some basic presumption of trust whereby individuals understand what they are being offered and what they can expect to get in their interactions with others. It also undergirds the understanding that agreements mutually made will be kept. He writes:

> *Transparency guarantees* deal with the need for openness that people can expect: the freedom to deal with one another under guarantees of disclosure and lucidity. When trust is seriously violated, the lives of many people...may be affected by the lack of openness...These guarantees have a clear instrumental role in preventing corruption, financial irresponsibility and underhand dealings. (pp. 39–40, italics in the original)

The importance of trust and transparency is also found in theories of justice that see social arrangements as based in contracts or mutual agreements among consenting members.

The final principle used to judge the fairness of a decision is that those who are impacted or influenced by decisions should be involved in this process to the greatest extent that is both possible and feasible. At minimum this means that those impacted by a decision should be given a hearing before a decision is made so that their input can be considered and weighed as part of the process. The philosopher Iris Marion Young (1990) was a passionate and eloquent voice in arguing for the importance of a diversity of voices in any decision-making process, particularly voices of members of those groups that are often silenced and marginalized. She asserted, "For a norm to be just, everyone who follows it must in principle have an effective voice in its consideration and be able to agree to it without coercion. For a social condition to be just, it must enable all to meet their needs and exercise their freedom; thus justice requires that all be able to express their needs" (p. 34).

However, depending on the circumstance and nature of the decision being made, individuals may be involved in the actual process to varying degrees. For example, the question of involvement in decision-making has much to do with the form of government that a social group adopts. Based on this, many thinkers have seen democracy as central to the establishment of social justice by virtue of its enabling individuals to be empowered to participate in the entire range of social institutions that impact their lives. To return to the work of Young (1990), she writes:

> Social justice entails democracy. Persons should be involved in collective discussion and decision making in settings that depend on their commitment, action, and obedience to rules....When such institutions privilege some groups over others, actual democracy requires group representation for the disadvantaged. Not only do just procedures require group representation in order to ensure that oppressed or disadvantaged groups have a voice, but such representation is also the best means to promote just outcomes of the deliberative process. (p. 191)

Similarly, Hofrichter (2003) makes the following assertions, "...social justice calls for democracy—empowerment of all social members, along with democratic and transparent structures to promote social goals" (p. 12). The principles of empowerment, collaboration, and participation that are so central to democracy are thus critical elements of social justice.

If we return to the previous discussion of early inequities and the analogies of running a race and playing Monopoly, we can see how issues pertinent to procedural justice can be used to determine whether these situations are just. One reaction individuals might have to the different advantages and disadvantages accorded children born into very disparate circumstances would be to declare that such situations are grossly unfair because the people responsible for creating such inequalities are "not playing by the rules." The assumption, in other words, is that in a society that overtly endorses values such as equality, fairness, and compassion, the rules used by that society to make decisions should mirror these commitments. When such rules are needed to protect the weak and vulnerable, such as children, then we can reasonably expect that those rules will most especially be adhered to. Those responsible for such inequitable treatment would thus be subject to our disapproval and moral indictment.

Staying with this example, another concern about inequity in the treatment of children is that it may be based on some form of bias, such as prejudice toward children from certain racial, class, or religious backgrounds. Such concerns naturally arise when we observe that it is indeed the case that a child's membership in a particular group does substantially influence his or her life circumstances. The suspicion of bias would clearly be justified. To be just, rules must be applied consistently and uniformly across those circumstances for which they are applicable without regard for the characteristics of individuals involved. Their purpose is to ensure a measure of impartiality and therefore fairness. So it is in games such as Monopoly or in forms of competition such as a race. Otherwise, the game or race is rigged from the very start since some players are granted an unfair advantage that makes the outcome slanted in a certain direction, if not altogether determined. Such impartiality is surely crucial with respect to factors that dictate human welfare, like those that have such influence on infants and young children.

Another facet of this inequitable treatment that raises issues about fairness is that while infants and children are substantially impacted by such decisions, they were not involved in them. This would seem to be self-evident, given that they are too immature to be able to provide meaningful input into these decisions. However, this fact also serves to highlight once again how their extreme vulnerability to the damaging effects of inequity makes it even more important that decision making adhere to the highest standards of fairness. As those who have been charged with their well-being, it is incumbent on the decision makers to represent their interests faithfully and in good faith. When they fail to do so, we can legitimately condemn their actions as not only unjust but immoral.

One can justifiably feel a sense of moral outrage when some people experience a greater degree of misfortune from adverse circumstances or suffer disproportionately at the hands of others due to no fault of their own. As Rank (2004) powerfully asserts, "I challenge anyone to make the argument that an eight-year-old child deserves to live in poverty as a result of his or her prior actions. That argument simply cannot be made" (p. 138). The challenge issued by Rank carries moral weight precisely because it is based on long-standing principles that have been used to define justice. However, while there is a moral dimension of justice, merely appealing to other people's conscience to do the right thing is generally not enough because they can either respond to or ignore the appeal depending on how they "feel" about the situation. This is why Frankena (1962) cautions that justice cannot be based on love for one's fellow human beings in the absence of a clear line of reasoning upon which to base this love because then justice would be subject to the vagaries of a mere emotional understanding of love for others. Justice must also be governed by rules that require equal treatment of all human beings irrespective of their background or station in life.

Reason and sound moral principles must thus be entwined with a capacity to experience a deep connection with our fellow human beings such that we understand that their desire for the good life and their capacity for happiness and fulfillment is no different than our own. This capacity for compassion for our fellow humans, along with a sense of moral outrage when any one of them is treated unfairly, gives expression to the call for fairness so central to procedural justice. Those who espouse fairness as a core principle of justice base this assertion on their belief in a fundamental equality that exists between all human beings. This equality likewise implies that rules or principles used to promote justice must be universally and absolutely applicable to all persons.

This idea of justice based on a belief in the fundamental dignity of every human person and essential human rights is rooted in a school of thought called *egalitarianism*. This idea generally has two meanings and gives rise to two different ways of achieving justice. The first is the belief that all human beings should be treated as equals with respect to having the same economic, social and political rights. The second is based on social philosophies that advocate for measures designed to remove economic inequalities that exist among individuals in a society. The first meaning is based on a procedural view in which the goal is to establish the means for creating a society that does not produce inequality, while the second is based on a distributive view of justice focused on identifying and then ameliorating circumstances of inequality that exist within a society. As such, the two meanings are not necessarily incompatible with each other as combining both approaches may result in a greater likelihood of achieving justice.

Turning to the first meaning, this form of egalitarianism connects human equality with the concept of rights. Frankena (1962) describes the basic theory of justice as the belief that all human beings ought to be treated with respect not in terms of their being equal in any particular respect(s), but solely based on their being human. He explains:

> A just society, then, is one which respects the good lives of its members and respects them equally. A just society must therefore promote equality; it may ignore certain differences and similarities but must consider others; and it must avoid unnecessary injury, interference, or impoverishment—all without reference to beneficence or general utility. (pp. 19–20)

This first meaning of equality has found support from different sources. It is common to find in religious and spiritual thought the belief that all people are equal in basic worth and moral status. For some religious traditions this is based on the belief that all human beings are created in the living image of God. Because all human beings are loved equally by God, we are required to extend the same love and respect toward one another. In other traditions such as Buddhism, Taoism, and Hinduism, the core of the human being is seen as a manifestation or expression of the same ultimate reality (Hick, 1989). Because all human beings share the same divine essence and the nature of this essence is love, then they are all equally deserving of love. This makes it one's duty to see the divine in others and to accord them the respect they are due.

Based on this spiritual realization of our essential oneness with all human beings, we can connect with them in a way that enables us to place ourselves in their situation. Thus, we may not only take offense at an unjust act directed against us, but also directed toward another. This realization, and the feelings it stirs within us, become the springboard to our desire to extend compassion to those who have been injured and take actions to redress the wrong that has been done. Some thinkers see this unavoidable reaction of distress evoked by the suffering of others as rooted in an innate sense of right and wrong that then forms the very basis for how we cultivate a sense of justice in human beings.

One example very early in the history of thought is the Chinese philosopher Mencius (around 372–298 BCE), who was a disciple of Confucius. He used the example of the horror that one feels when one sees a child about to fall into a well as evidence that all human beings share a sense of abhorrence for human suffering. This distress is experienced, according to Mencius, irrespective of what we believe might be the reactions of the infant's parents or others who may be present if we fail to respond to the imperiled infant. This is because it is our innate sense of right and wrong that gives rise to shame and disgrace when we fail to respond sympathetically to the distress of others. While these feelings naturally occur, they must be cultivated by proper environmental conditions that recognize and develop them further in order to achieve a just society. Those who share the view espoused by Mencius believe that it is by cultivating these natural moral sentiments of human beings that justice can best be achieved (see Solomon & Murphy, 2000, pp. 56–58).

Though religion and spirituality provide a very powerful basis for equality and thus for justice, one does not need to be committed to such a view to espouse this value. Sampson (1975) briefly discusses the history of the idea of equality in Western thought and cites the work of Brinton (1931) who described factors that contributed to the development of modern conceptions of human equality in the 18th century. The first of these factors was the creation of a unified physical science that sought to discover and describe the fundamental uniformity or lawfulness that lay beneath the diversity of physical phenomena. In like fashion, it was believed that despite the diversity of human beings, they needed to be understood as simple and same members of the human race, thus implying an essential identity of humankind. The second factor was the rise of the middle class. Prior to this development, the prevalence of the wealthy and powerful versus the poor and lowly led many to believe that this division was a natural one and so incapable of being changed. With increasing numbers of individuals achieving economic equality with the nobility, the doctrine of equality in other spheres such as the political and the social became more accepted. Finally, philosophers such as Rousseau began to argue persuasively for the natural goodness of all human beings and the significant role played by environment in influencing how human beings developed. Considering this, if people were treated alike or equally, then a state of equality would be achieved. Such philosophical ideas gave impetus to significant political ideas that inspired the American and French revolutions and the goal of establishing governments that promoted and protected human equality.

The assertion that the meaning of human equality must be grounded in the principle of fundamental human rights and equality in these rights across all individuals fits well with how most of us understand what equality means. However, despite this seeming plausibility, the question of rights has been the subject of disagreement and even controversy. While certain truths regarding rights and human equality have been declared "self-evident," as asserted by Thomas Jefferson in the Declaration of Independence, there has nevertheless been a good deal of disagreement about what fundamental rights human beings can lay claim to and whether there are any conditions under which these rights can be justly suspended or violated. For example, the Declaration of Independence declares these rights to be "life, liberty and the pursuit of happiness." In contrast, the leaders of the French Revolution proclaimed that these were "liberty, equality and fraternity." Likewise, many consider it just to violate a person's right to liberty if they are a violent criminal who needs to be kept imprisoned so as not to harm others. Similarly, we recognize limits on a person's right to the pursuit of happiness if it involves the abuse of illegal drugs or the harming of animals.

As a result, as Vlastos (1962) observes, while equality and rights have been linked together by many thinkers, the assertion that all human beings are equal in all rights would be very difficult to defend, even on the grounds of justice. There are some, for example, who hold a higher governmental office or who are in other positions of authority in society who clearly possess rights to which others in that society could not lay claim. Further, not everyone would have equal rights to such offices or positions—the claim that anyone can be president of the United States notwithstanding!

In response to this, Vlastos (1962) notes that there are some very fundamental questions that must be addressed to achieve a clear and definite idea of what is meant by rights as they relate to human equality. One is what the range of these rights is. This would involve specifying clearly what each of these rights are along with a rationale for how such rights are required in order to uphold equality. A second question is whether natural rights are absolute in the sense that no exceptions can be made to their claims. While it may be assumed that human rights must be absolute and therefore never violated, Vlastos notes that throughout the literature on the nature of human rights, that claim is never taken seriously. For example, a person's right to property may be justifiably be suspended under certain extreme circumstances as during a famine when food hoarded by some may be appropriated by the state to distribute to those without food.

The final question is how a doctrine of natural rights would address issues pertinent to a distributive view of justice. In particular, we would need to determine the place of natural rights with respect to what Vlastos calls the "five well-known maxims of distributive justice." These are as follows: (1) To each according to his/her needs; (2) To each according to his/her worth; (3) To each according to his/her merit; (4) To each according to his/her work; and (5) To each according to the agreements he/she has made. As implied by each of these maxims, the role of distributive justice is to determine how differences in individuals are justly recognized while also maintaining some commitment to human equality. Not all individuals have the same needs, and it is sometimes fair for those who need more to get more. It is for this reason that Vlastos (1962) concludes: "An equalitarian concept of justice may admit of just inequalities without inconsistency if, and only if, it provides grounds for equal human rights *which are also grounds for unequal rights of other sorts*" (p. 40, italics in the original). It is the task of distributive justice to determine such grounds, and so it is to this view of justice that we turn next.

Distributive Justice: Equal Concern for the Good Life of All

One way to think about distributive justice is its role in determining whether inequalities in certain outcomes in society are just or fair. In some instances, these inequalities may be admitted with no threat being posed to justice; while in others the inequalities may be so egregious that they violate the demands made by justice. Thus, theories of distributive justice concern themselves with three issues. The first is what goods (as well as what burdens) are to be distributed among members of a society. These goods can be seen in terms of wealth, power, status, resources, and other forms of reward. The second is who needs to be considered in making such distributions. This may include human beings, animals, individuals within a group or society, and different nations. The third is what rules or principles should be applied to achieve a just or fair distribution. As these questions reveal, distributive and procedural justice are closely interwoven. In this discussion, I will be focusing mainly on the first and third questions.

A good place to begin this examination is with Vlastos' (1962) discussion of where a doctrine of human rights fits with the five maxims of distributive justice. As we have seen, not all forms of equality are just. This makes it necessary to establish clear and soundly derived principles in order to determine which forms of equality are just and which are not. To illustrate we can return to the first maxim of distributive justice in which claims of a just distribution of goods must take into consideration that individuals can have very different needs. Vlastos notes that similar considerations may be involved based on differences between individuals regarding worth, merit, work, and agreements made. These types of differences are also described by Frankena (1962) as relevant to justice:

> One of the chief considerations which not only justifies but also establishes as *just* differences in the treatment of human beings is the fact that the good life (not in the sense of the morally good life but in the sense, roughly, of the happy life) and its conditions are not the same for all, due to differences in needs and potentialities. (p.15)

Thus, while we may accord equal respect for each human being's right to a good life, we can also accept that what may constitute the good life for one person will not be the same for another because of differences in their needs and potentialities. As a result, the way in which we would distribute goods or benefits to different individuals with different needs would not be equal.

Vlastos argues that while a person's intrinsic value or worth forms an important basis for why they should be treated equally, it also is the basis for why individuals must sometimes be treated differently in recognition of important facets of their individuality. The recognition of each person's intrinsic worth must be accompanied first by understanding that all human beings desire happiness and then respecting to whatever extent possible their being able to choose how to pursue happiness based on their unique needs and potentials. Vlastos derives this principle from the *eudaimonic* tradition, which has its origin in the philosophy of Aristotle (Nussbaum, 1992). This tradition emphasizes "doing and living well."

Eudaimonia is sometimes translated as "happiness." However, this does not capture all the nuances of how this term was used by Aristotle. For example, happiness often is associated with the pursuit of pleasure or the good things in life. However, a person may also choose to achieve eudaimonia through the rigorous and sometimes painful process of mastering a skill that brings with it an enhanced sense of well-being, such as in athletics. Thus, an alternative term used to describe eudaimonia is "flourishing." Another idea often associated with eudaimonia in early Greek philosophy is *arête*, which is translated as virtue. This concept is linked not to a moral sense of virtue, but rather to how doing anything well requires virtue or the cultivation of one's potential to achieve a certain degree of excellence. The goal of justice in this view would be to establish conditions that seek to cultivate well-being in all persons and enables them to enjoy the values life has to offer to the greatest extent possible. This tradition will be discussed later in relation to the capability approach to social justice.

Based on the individuality possessed by each person, the meaning of doing and being well is as diverse as there are different human beings. What constitutes well-being must, to some degree, depend on the individual. Frankena (1962) summarizes this point very well:

> The equal concern for the good lives of all members also requires society to treat them differently, for no matter how much one believes in a common human nature, individual needs and capabilities differ, and what constitutes the good life for one individual may not do so for another. It is the society's very concern for the good lives of its members that determines which differences and which similarities it must respect (and which are relevant to justice). (p. 20)

Promoting justice and well-being among disabled individuals would be an excellent way to illustrate this principle. Based on this view of justice, accommodations should be made for individuals with disabilities to promote their well-being, such as accessible public buildings or modifications that enable them to acquire gainful employment. This would require taking into account the different needs of persons with a disability to establish conditions in which they can maximize their ability to live and do well. Similarly, such differences will sometimes require unequal treatment for justice to be met. For example, the Individuals with Disabilities Education Act (IDEA) is a Federal law that ensures the essential legal rights of disabled children, and hence their families, by requiring schools to provide a free and appropriate education in the least restrictive environment. This goal is achieved by conducting a comprehensive evaluation of each child, whose results lead to the development of an Individualized Education Plan (IEP). The IEP determines the specific needs of each child and stipulates the methods and resources to be provided to meet those needs. Once the IEP is developed and approved, it is incumbent on the school district to provide services without consideration for whether the costs, time, and effort involved in doing so may be greater than for a student without a disability. Thus, the principle that some forms of unequal treatment are just informs certain laws such as IDEA.

Similar arguments about just differences in treatment or in outcomes can be made based on differential degrees of merit, work, achievement, etc. If certain individuals serve a society by performing work that requires extensive education and training, that brings a greater degree of benefit to others, or that involves a higher degree of danger or risk, we would typically see rewarding them for these things as fair or just. A similar example is if persons perform a job or task with a greater degree of skill or excellence. Making such determinations as to what does or does not constitute merit or benefit can be subject to debate, but the basic principles implied in differential treatment in such instances are generally accepted. For this reason, in the sphere of distributive justice the terms "equity" or "fairness" may be more frequently used to determine conditions of justice than "equality" because the goal is not to show preferential or biased treatment and, wherever possible, to treat similar cases similarly.

However, our sense of individuality is not merely based on different needs and potentials. It is also expressed in the way that human beings uniquely exercise their agency through the choices they make. Thus, Vlastos (1962) adds a second requirement of what constitutes the good life for human beings: they must be able to choose things of value from competing alternatives. To appreciate Vlastos' point, consider being told what to like or dislike or forced to choose something versus being able to freely decide such matters for yourself. We both express and experience our values through the choices that we make. In making this point, Vlastos is aligning the idea of human rights with another idea with which it is generally associated—human freedom. This recognition of each person's freedom to pursue happiness or well-being as he or she chooses becomes the other necessary component of human rights relevant to distributive issues. Belief in equal human worth and respect for human rights is based on the recognition that one person's well-being and freedom is as valuable as any other's and that "...a person's well-being and freedom are aspects of his individual existence as unique and unrepeatable as is that existence itself" (Vlastos, 1962, p. 49). We can conclude then that recognition of a person's inherent worth must include according respect to him or her both by virtue of what he or she shares in common with all others *as well as* what sets him or her apart as an utterly unique individual. Different views of distributive justice propose different ways of settling matters that arise in how best to demonstrate respect for others.

Two different, but related, forms of freedom must also be included when discussing matters of justice. *Freedom from*, also sometimes referred to as liberty, expresses that dimension of freedom that involves the removal of barriers, limits, and other forms of interference or harm that would infringe on persons' exercise of choice in pursuit of their well-being. Frankena (1962) articulates the role of freedom from in ensuring justice as follows:

> A just society must protect each member from being injured or interfered with by others, and it must not, by omission or commission, itself inflict evil upon any of them, deprive them of goods which they might otherwise gain by their own efforts, or restrict their liberty—except insofar as is necessary for their own protection or the achievement of equality. (p. 21)

Once more we see how the broad pursuit of equality may nonetheless result in specific forms of inequality. For example, there may be times when we must protect individuals from choices or actions that would be harmful to themselves or others. This view of freedom is clearly relevant to the issue of oppression as in situations when individuals from a certain group have their rights, opportunities, and resources limited or taken away in order to benefit members of another group.

The second form of freedom, *freedom to*, does not focus on the absence of restraint or limitations on one's choices, but instead on the ability to act or direct one's own life. This form of freedom refers to the earlier discussion of how the recognition of personal agency and right to self-determination is one way of respecting a person's inherent worth. By means of individuals exercising their freedom to make choices and take action, they are likewise empowered to shape their own lives and to realize their potential in whatever ways they choose. Prilleltensky (Prilleltensky & Nelson, 2002) observes that freedom to, or what he calls self-determination, is one of the central values that must be advocated by psychologists in order to promote personal well-being and oppose oppression.

Through this discussion of freedom and human rights, we can gain a better understanding of certain paradoxes that theories of justice must contend with. One is the relationship between the individual and the collective. "Freedom to" is situated squarely within the individual based upon its expressing the unique capacity of each human being to make choices and direct his or her life. Alternatively, "freedom from" is bound up with the social or collective sphere of human life as it involves the degree to which one is either able or unable to exercise choice based on limiting factors imposed by or involving others. Another way to understand the tension between the individual and the collective is when freedom as self-determination or self-expression must be balanced by the recognition of our duty or obligation to others. This point is made quite eloquently by Simone Weil (1952), French philosopher and social activist. Weil asserts that obligations have precedence over rights and give rights their power and meaning. She believes this is so because the authority of obligations comes from their being rooted in a transcendental or spiritual order. Weil writes, "Rights are always to be found to be related to certain conditions. Obligations alone remain independent of conditions. They belong to a realm above conditions, because it is situated above this world" (pp. 3–4). Because obligations are independent of conditions, the same fundamental obligations are binding on all human beings although they may be performed in different ways dependent on conditions. For Weil, our obligation toward our fellow human beings is a way of recognizing and respecting their fundamental worth and dignity.

Justice Equal and Unequal

As indicated by the previous discussion of distributive justice, the doctrine of egalitarianism and the meaning of equality with respect to justice can take different forms. The distributive view of justice naturally must consider the relevance of differences between human beings and how such differences should be judged in weighing the claims of justice. Two ways of addressing the question of whether and when differences are just are in terms of equality of outcome vs. equality of condition. One of these perspectives focuses on whether people "get" the same and the other focuses on whether people are "treated" the same.

The question of equality sometimes requires an examination of differences in outcomes that usually refer to the material conditions of certain individuals, although it may also consider differences in other valuable outcomes such as status, privilege, and power. A common position taken in this view of social justice is that a society should strive to achieve the goal of either reducing or eliminating inequalities in the material conditions between individuals, particularly when these inequalities are disproportionate and thus have a more adverse impact on the well-being of certain individuals. An example might be to establish a more uniform standard of living across individuals in a society.

This point of view raises certain challenges. One is how does one concretely quantify or measure the outcomes to determine whether efforts made to remove disparities have been successful. The literature on distributive justice is filled with a range of different opinions about how to measure material conditions and how to make meaningful and relevant comparisons between different individuals or groups in terms of the distribution of benefits and burdens within a society

One of the most influential schools of thought regarding this question is *utilitarianism.* Utilitarianism is a normative approach to ethics in which the morality or rightness of an action is determined by its utility or its contribution to happiness or pleasure as summed across all people in a given group. It is a form of a broader viewpoint called *consequentialism*, which bases the morality of an action on its outcome. It is unlike a *deontological* approach to ethics, which looks at the goodness of acts and nature of duty irrespective of the goodness of motive or consequences. This approach would be more focused on rules or obligations (and thus more likely found in a procedural view of justice). By basing the goodness of actions on pleasure or happiness, utilitarianism attempted to make outcomes quantifiable. The objective of this approach is often framed as the greatest happiness principle or "the greatest good for the greatest number." Because no one person's happiness counts more than any other person's, utilitarianism espouses an impartial view that its proponents see as conducive to promoting justice.

The establishment of utilitarianism is usually credited to British philosopher Jeremy Bentham (1988). For Bentham, pleasure and pain were the only intrinsic values and so these became the basis for making determinations about what was just and unjust. Following this line of thought, British philosopher John Stuart Mill (1961/1998]) refined the use of pleasure and pain as the means of measuring the morality of actions. He asserted that cultural, intellectual, and spiritual pleasures were of greater value than mere physical pleasure and thus should occupy a higher place in determining how to change the lives of human beings for the better. In addition, he moved away from making pleasure the goal of actions and substituted happiness. This was based on his observation that the pursuit of pleasure of itself did not always lead to happiness.

Since being advanced by Bentham and Mill, utilitarianism has evolved into many different forms and has been used as support for a diverse range of political views. It is still widely endorsed. A full examination of the different views of utilitarianism and debate as to its merits is beyond the scope of this review. Sen's (1999) discussion of utilitarianism offers a useful overview

In contrast to equality of outcome, one can focus on equality of condition. In this case the goal is to establish a desirable set of circumstances in a society that would subsequently promote the achievement of equality. Once more, there is a range of opinions about what those desirable circumstances are and how best to achieve them. Some advocate various political approaches such as democratic citizenship or civil liberties (Young, 1990). The goal here is to enable individuals to maximize their participation in a range of decision-making processes that subsequently influence outcomes pertinent to their well-being. However, a particularly important example of this view is equality of opportunity because of the prevalence of this idea in countries like the United States as the vehicle for achieving social justice.

Earlier, opportunity was noted as an important ingredient for achieving social justice as it connects the expression of persons' rights with making it possible for them to take actions to realize those rights. In light of this, equal opportunity would require the provision of a social environment in which people are not excluded from activities necessary to express their rights or to achieve well-being (such as education, employment, and health care) on the basis of characteristics that they are incapable of changing or circumstances over which they have no control. While many would regard this approach as sound in principle, in practical application it poses many challenges. This is observed by Barry (2005, pp. 37–45), who makes a compelling argument that the enduring and powerful impact of long-term cumulative advantage and disadvantage makes the achievement of truly equal conditions for success illusory.

Nonetheless, the rise of the ideologies of neoliberalism and individualism has made the concept of equal opportunity a widely endorsed approach to promoting social justice. This has come with certain dangers (see Young, 1990, Chapter 7). The first is that it increases the likelihood of situating the causes for success and failure in the competition for the good things in life within the person, while obscuring the impact of structural and systemic factors. Another is that it has legitimized certain inequalities, even very substantial ones as in the case of income or well-being. This commonly takes the form of individuals being given a fair chance to succeed but then blamed for not putting forth the hard work and commitment needed to do so. Finally, this point of view sees competition as a reflection of natural forces and processes, not a result of an ideological system created and maintained by human beings. In this view if competition gives rise to certain forms of inequality, these outcomes are natural, inevitable, and therefore incapable of modification by human intervention.

In contrast to this predominant viewpoint, there is growing dissent among those who see most forms of unjust inequalities as expressions not of individual failings but structural failings (Rank, 2004). Because of this debate, certain fundamental questions regarding the justness of inequalities must be carefully considered, as different solutions lead to very different outcomes. These questions are: (1) Can equality or fairness be achieved or is inequality inevitable? (2) Is the goal of equality desirable or morally right, or is inequality (or certain forms of inequality) desirable? (3) What factors give rise to forms of inequality? (4) If equality is achievable, what measures can and should be taken to achieve it?

Given the importance of these questions to understanding oppression, Sampson's (1975) description of the debate between two contrasting solutions to the distributive problem—equity and equality— is instructive. He argues that human beings initially devise economic solutions to the distributive problem and that these solutions then become extended into principles for how to conduct noneconomic social relations, such as love, concern, helping, or harming. This strong connection between economic structures and other forms of human relationships helps to highlight why it is important to attend to distributive issues in the study of oppression. Sampson describes the first of two approaches to the distributive problem as follows:

> The equity solution is based on a principle that divides resources (e.g., outcomes of wealth, income, status, game

points) according to defined inputs (e.g., ability, intelligence, hard work). Thus some persons are said to deserve more of the valuable resources because relative to others they have more invested. It is argued by some analysts of social stratification...that only by providing such heavily invested persons with proportional outcomes can we ensure that others will be willing to make similar investments later; and this is important to societal survival. (p. 48)

This position has been described by others as a *meritocratic theory*, which espouses that goods such as wealth, income and social status should be apportioned based on individual merit, which is typically defined in terms of a combination of an individual's talent and hard work. Beauchamp (2003) asserts that this is the dominant model of distributive justice in the United States and calls it *market- justice*. He elaborates, "Under the norms of market- justice people are entitled only to those valued ends such as status, income, happiness, etc., that they have acquired by fair rules of entitlement, e.g., by their own individual efforts, actions or abilities. Market-justice emphasizes individual responsibility, minimal collective action, and freedom from collective obligations except to respect other persons' fundamental rights" (p. 269).

The alternative solution to the distributive problem is described by Sampson (1975) as well:

The equality solution, by contrast, is based on a principle that divides resources equally, arguing that differential investments do not provide a legitimate basis for differential outcomes. Equality does not require a homogenization of persons who may indeed be differentiated in many ways (age, sex, authority, levels of skill, years of training, etc.), but rather argues that these differentiations do not require differential access to resources. All persons deserve much the same. (p. 49)

Unlike, the equity solution, the question of merit or desert is settled in such a way as to equalize outcomes across individuals as much as possible. Thus, when unfair differences in outcomes occur, those espousing the equality position will seek to rectify these disparities. While those espousing the equity position favor competition, those espousing the equality position favor cooperation.

Sampson (1975) agrees that the equity solution is the one most commonly endorsed by modern Western capitalist societies like the United States, but that the assumptions that underlie this view are often unexamined because it is assumed to be simply the way things naturally are. A particularly destructive example of how egregious inequalities are deemed "natural" that continues to exercise influence is Social Darwinism. Darwin's theory of evolution described the process of natural selection in which competition among individual organisms for limited resources lead to certain outcomes based on adaptation. As the theory of evolution gained credence, other thinkers began to apply this principle to social evolution. Principal among them were English philosopher Herbert Spencer and Francis Galton, who was an early psychologist and Darwin's cousin. The term "survival of the fittest," often ascribed to Darwin, was in actuality coined by Spencer. The implication of this term is that in the social sphere inequalities resulting from open competition were the natural outcomes of a process by which those who were stronger achieved better outcomes than those who were weaker. Based on this misrepresentation of Darwin's ideas, it was asserted that those who came out on the losing end of this process were unfit to compete and thus deserved less.

A later version of this idea intended to temper some of the harshness of the original view emphasizes the need to establish social arrangements whereby all individuals have equal opportunities to compete openly. Once established, the resulting unequal distribution of rewards is fair and just based on differential ability, talent, and effort. This is the argument often used by those who advocate equal opportunity as the means to achieve social justice. Here is how this viewpoint is described by Sampson (1975):

> This is the essence of our modern, Western, meritocratic principle that all persons are deserving of an equal opportunity to utilize their energies and talents to achieve whatever inequality of outcomes of wealth and social status is possible. In this view, inequality of outcomes within a society is justified on the basis of inequality of merit (i.e., inputs) among persons who, however, have had equality of opportunity to compete individually to achieve these outcomes. (p. 50)

Social Darwinism commits a grave error called the naturalistic fallacy. By proposing that what is presumed to be a natural law, survival of fittest, is also a moral law, this viewpoint confuses an "is" with an "ought." In other words, since it is natural for the weak to have less and not prosper, it is morally correct to do nothing to assist them. In addition, because such inequality is the result of a natural process of competition in which some are better able to compete than others, it is useless to do anything to interfere with this process.

An example of an important figure in psychology whose work supported oppression can be found in Francis Galton (1892), who put forth a meritocratic argument to justify grave injustices, including the wholesale killing of thousands. In his book, *Hereditary Genius*, he proposed that mental traits were inherited in the same way as physical traits. He went on to assert that certain races were inherently superior (in this case, the British race) and that measures should be taken to ensure that the "blood" (i.e., genetic pool) of those of the superior race not be contaminated by those who were inferior. Galton went as far as advocating for legal measures to prevent such contamination, such as the involuntary sterilization of those deemed genetically inferior, including those who occupied the bottom rungs of society and the disabled. In doing so, the well-being of the human species and the unfolding of evolution would be attained by furthering the interests of the strong and letting those who are weak and thus "not fit" to respond to the demands of life gradually become fewer in number. Galton coined the term "eugenics," and in subsequent years the Eugenics Society (of which, interestingly, Darwin's son, Leonard, was president from 1911 to 1928) engaged in propaganda that led to the passing of Sterilization Laws in a number of states that allowed individuals deemed genetically weak or sick to be involuntarily sterilized. The same perverse logic was used to implement a policy in Nazi Germany that led to the active extermination of thousands of children and adults afflicted with disabilities and mental disorders (Silberman, 2015).

Sampson (1975) details how the equity solution makes an error akin to the naturalistic fallacy by asserting that it is based on human nature and so is the expected and most desirable way to resolve the distributive problem. He states,

> In their zeal to develop basic principles of human behavior, social psychologists often have erroneously assumed that an equity principle is either the only solution to the distributive problem that has ever existed, or, as the most preferred solution in the contemporary Western world, must therefore characterize a fundamental quality of human psychological functioning." (p. 49)

The equity principle is seen as rooted in the "fact" that humans are naturally selfish and self-interested. As a result, the tendency of individuals to be competitive and to approach relationships to maximize personal gain is seen as natural and inevitable. Based on this, even when individuals seemingly behave in an altruistic and cooperative manner, they still do so out of self-interest. The morality of rational self-interest put forward by novelist and philosopher Ayn Rand (1964) is a well-known example of this viewpoint.

Seeing inequalities due to individual competition as part of a "natural" process also poses the danger of making any efforts aimed at ameliorating or eliminating such inequality futile. Thus, such theorizing serves to support the status quo, even if it is unjust. As Sampson (1975) clearly argues, the assertion that the equity view is merely objectively describing some natural process is a fallacy. Actually, these findings are rooted in historical, political, ideological, and cultural factors. For example, Sampson cites studies that find that male subjects more frequently employ an equity approach to distributive problems, while female subjects employ an equality approach. These differences are not based on natural differences between males and females but are best explained by socialization practices prevalent in Western society, particularly the United States. The non-critical endorsement of the equity approach is also deeply rooted in neoliberal ideology with its emphasis on competition, profit, and coming out on top.

Sampson concludes his article by speaking directly to the need to pursue social justice, questioning the equity solution as the preferred or even the natural solution to the distributive problem. He observes that the prevalence of the equity solution has contributed to various forms of oppression, including growing inequities among groups within society, disparities in power between men and women, and other threats to cooperation and equality. Sampson believes that psychology can provide valuable evidence that when solutions to the distribution problem are unjust, they lead to threats to cohesion and order in human relationships and impaired well-being. Useful alternatives must be advanced to these mistaken beliefs, which give rise to oppression. He writes:

> The humane tradition argues that egalitarianism is a solution to human injustice that should not be readily dismissed by the circular and culture-bound argument that it is unnatural or impractical. If the United States protests of the sixties have

taught us anything, it is the need for careful reevaluation of the unmitigated agency that characterizes too much of life, at the cost of the possibilities for communion. It is only through seeing and then reaching for the utopian vision that the present forms might be changed. (p. 59)

The Capabilities Approach: Social Justice and Human Development

An example of a theory of social justice that seeks to integrate a procedural and distributive understanding is the capabilities approach. The creation of the capabilities approach is credited to Nobel Laureate economist and philosopher Amatrya Sen. In *Development as Freedom,* Sen (1999) focused on issues of social justice particularly pertinent to human development and how best to address the disparities in wealth, income and other resources in international development. Sen offers a critique of other prevailing approaches to evaluating and promoting well-being among individuals and between countries. One example is his critique of an opulence view focused on wealth or other acquired commodities as excessively materialistic. Sen points out that wealth or commodities are not valued ends in themselves. Rather, he states that "The usefulness of wealth lies in the things that it allows us to do—the substantive freedoms it helps us to achieve" (p. 14). Sen also asserts the following:

> Development has to be more concerned with enhancing the lives we lead and the freedoms we enjoy. Expanding the freedoms that we have reason to value not only makes our lives richer and more unfettered, but also allows us to be fuller social persons, exercising our own volitions and interacting with—and influencing—the world in which we live. (pp. 14–15)

For Sen, freedom is central to development or well-being. Sen uses the term "substantial freedoms" to refer to the basic building blocks for enhancing and enriching people's lives. Substantial freedoms are things of value distributed among human beings that can range from very basic goods (such as food, longevity, or health) to what might be called higher level goods (such as education or the ability to engage freely in the political process). The *intrinsic* importance of freedom means that it is significant in itself as it promotes the sense of agency that human beings need to experience in making choices, bringing about changes and exercising other forms of initiative. The *instrumental* role of freedom consists of the ways in which different types of rights, opportunities, and entitlements contribute to expanding individuals' freedom and with it their well-being. Sen (1999) describes five forms of instrumental freedom for individuals:

- Political freedoms or opportunities to decide how they are to be governed, to engage in free speech, to vote, etc.
- Economic facilities or opportunities to utilize economic resources to consume products or for purposes of economic production or exchange
- Social opportunities that include education, health care, and effective involvement in economic and political activities
- Transparency guarantees, which were discussed earlier as the openness needed for establishment of trust
- Protective security, meaning policies that establish a social safety net that prevents individuals from falling into abject poverty, starvation, etc. in instances of tragedy, duress or crisis

The term "capabilities" refers to what human beings are able to be and to do. Because capabilities are practical opportunities, they are distinguished from the actual level of achievement attained by an individual (referred to as *functioning*) and includes activities as well as desirable states. This distinction is useful for several reasons. First, it makes clear that development requires both the enhancement of certain human forms of functioning and the broadening of the capabilities that enable individuals to do so. Second, it considers the role of individual choice and responsibility *as well as* economic, political, and social structures in development. While part of the intrinsic importance of freedom is recognition of the agency each person possesses to make choices from the capabilities afforded them and so attain certain functionings, a sense of personal responsibility must also accompany such choices. To some degree, the achievement of happiness or well-being is up to each person. However, many larger forces over which individuals exercise little or no control significantly impact the capabilities available to them. Sen (1999) summarizes this point:

> Responsible adults must be in charge of their own well-being; it is for them to decide how to use their capabilities. But the capabilities that a person does actually have (and not merely

theoretically enjoys) depend on the nature of social arrangements, which can be crucial for individual freedoms. And there the state and the society cannot escape responsibility. (p. 288)

Philosopher Martha Nussbaum (1992, 2003, 2004, 2006) has taken up Sen's idea of capabilities in her own work. Both Sen and Nussbaum situate the capabilities approach within an Aristotelian and Marxist tradition based on its focus on human well-being and flourishing. Nussbaum (1992) also speaks of an Aristotelian essentialism in both her and Sen's work that is opposed to the dangers of subjectivism and relativism in those schools of thought that regard all value statements as historically and culturally contingent and thus incapable of generalization. While recognizing the dangers of absolutism in the ethical realm, Nussbaum argues that unless an accurate account can be given of the most important functions of a human being, there is the risk of unjust circumstances that deprive individuals of their humanity going unchallenged. For Nussbaum, some form of essentialism is needed to ensure the recognition of two crucial human sentiments necessary for human beings to live together, compassion and respect.

Nussbaum (1992) thus seeks to integrate an absolute and relative understanding of how to promote human well-being. In discussing this, Crocker (1992) observes, "The important point is that the capabilities approach can retain the notion of a culturally invariant (absolute) core to both well-being and deprivations while at the same time construing any *specific* means of provisioning as relative to historical and cultural contexts" (p. 592). Human life has certain defining features that are enduring, irrespective of time and place. However, these universal facets of the human person must be defined generally and modestly enough to recognize the diversity of ways in which these needs are expressed and met. This becomes the basis for how Nussbaum develops a list of essential capabilities.

Nussbaum (2006) agrees with the assumption that human beings are free, equal, and in possession of a fundamental dignity that must be respected. The primary basis for the worth of persons is their power of moral choice, which they exercise by means of valuing certain goals and then pursuing them. By respecting and promoting the liberty of choice possessed by all persons, we are also respecting and promoting their equal worth. Nussbaum then adopts a more outcome-oriented approach characteristic of distributive justice. Thus, she must define what societies should be in terms of the kind of life that human beings can and would choose because such a life would be valued. For Nussbaum, these outcomes are based on fundamental capabilities.

Nussbaum advances a *thick vague theory of good* that looks beyond Rawls' focus on primary goods such as wealth and income. The thick vague theory of good focuses more on ends rather than means and, as a result, offers a much fuller description of what constitutes the good life and human well-being. These goods are described in vague terms to allow for many different versions based on social, cultural, and historical differences, while retaining an element of universalism. This then becomes the basis for what Nussbaum (1992, 2006) proposes as a list of capabilities. In compiling her list, she is guided by two ideas. One is that capabilities express something essential about what it means to be human because when they are lacking, life fails to be human at all. She writes, "The Aristotelian essentialist claims that a life that lacks any of these, no matter what else it has, will be lacking in humanness" (p. 222). This point aligns very clearly with the view of oppression as a form of dehumanization. The second is that the priority of justice is to establish conditions whereby every person is allowed a decent level of capabilities for each of the functions needed to have a generally good life.

What this means is that the capability approach first establishes a minimal or ground floor threshold below which life would be so impoverished that it would cease to be human and a second threshold somewhat higher than the first, below which areas of functioning would be available in such a reduced way that life would be possible but not one that anyone would consider as good. Thus, the goal is not to create a society that would provide its citizens opportunities to function at the bare minimum. However, having set such a threshold, there must then be allowances made for individuals to improve upon this level of functioning through personal choice and in ways that are up to them. As a result, for Nussbaum, capability to function rather than actual functioning should be the goal of legislation and public planning and policy. Oppression is not merely evidenced in reducing members of certain groups to an abject level of living, but also in depriving them of the resources and opportunities to exercise personal choice in the pursuit of fulfilling their capabilities.

The list of capabilities proposed by Nussbaum (1992, 2006) is as follows:

- Life: The ability to live a full human life or one not reduced to the degree that it is not worth living

- Bodily health: Good health, adequate food, adequate shelter
- Bodily integrity: Safety and security from harm; ability to move freely, to achieve sexual satisfaction, and exercise choice in matters of reproduction
- Senses, imagination, thought: Ability to use these functions in ways that make one feel truly human
- Emotions: Attachments to people and things, experience of the range of human emotions (love, grief, gratified, justified anger, etc.) that make life meaningful, safeguards against experiencing developmental arrest or setbacks due to excess fear and anxiety
- Practical reason: Ability to form one's own conception of the good and to engage in reflection about one's life goals
- Affiliation: Ability to live with and toward others, being treated with respect by others
- Other species: Ability to live with concern for and in relation to the rest of the natural world
- Play: Laughter, play, recreation
- Control over one's environment: In its political form, the ability to participate in political processes and choices about how one is governed; in its material form, the ability to hold property and property rights, seek employment on an equal basis with others, and be free from unwarranted search and seizure.

Based on this list, Nussbaum advocates for a view of justice that promotes a just distribution of a set of capabilities, each of which are distinct and diverse among members of any society. In doing so, individuals may experience a sense of dignity and worth due them by virtue of their humanity. To do otherwise is to deprive individuals of their humanity, as Nussbaum (1992) makes clear in this quote:

> Human beings are creatures such that, provided with the right educational and material support, they can become capable of the major human functions. When their basic capabilities are deprived of the nourishment that would transform them into the higher-level capabilities that figure on my list, they are fruitless, cut off, in some way but a shadow of themselves. (p. 228)

A Proposed Definition of Social Justice

I have concluded this examination with the capabilities approach because it provides an understanding of justice well suited to efforts aimed at ending oppression and promoting liberation. This is based, in part, upon its focus on human development. The concepts of cumulative deprivation and disadvantage discussed earlier in this chapter provide a powerful illustration of how oppression exerts an adverse impact on a human being's development. Similarly, development has been made a central framework for understanding well-being and optimal functioning (see Wilber, 2000). While the relationship between development and justice is framed differently across different perspectives, an area of agreement is that the objective of justice is to establish conditions that promote the greatest degree of development, and thus well-being, possible for all persons. Such views subscribe to a form of what is called a *teleological or perfectionist* theory aimed at maximizing the achievement of fundamental human potentials or capabilities or at making it possible for human beings to live the most perfect life they can. This is also known as the eudaimonic tradition in philosophy.

The study of human development has occupied a central place in psychology. It is often asserted that health is best achieved by promoting the optimal level of development of which individuals are capable. The converse is that dysfunction is based on some form of developmental arrest. In this view, promoting well-being involves assessing an individual's capabilities as well as resources and opportunities for realizing them. In addition, attention must be given to supporting factors that enable individuals to realize their potential and removing obstacles or impairments that have blocked their growth. Development is often conceptualized based on a stage-theory view in which certain developmental tasks characteristic of each stage must be successfully negotiated in order to achieve optimal growth. Successful negotiation of this process involves a dynamic interaction between the individual's unique potentials with a range of environmental factors that function to either foster and cultivate these potentials or frustrate and thwart them. Thus, while the environment clearly plays a vital role, individuals do as well by exercising their capacity for self-determination in the choices they make and the goals they set for themselves.

Integrating the list of capabilities developed by Nussbaum with essential human needs proposed by psychologists can yield a conceptualization of human development that more fully integrates both the innate and inner potentials of human beings with the environmental conditions that must be established for individuals to flourish. An example of this would be Maslow's (1971) proposed hierarchy of needs. The lowest needs on this hierarchy (basic physical needs and security needs) are included by Nussbaum (1992) as the capabilities of life, bodily health, and bodily integrity). The next levels of the hierarchy are the needs for self-esteem and affection, which again can be found in Nussbaum's list with respect to her categories of emotion, affiliation, and control over one's environment. Though Maslow's highest need of self-actualization is not found explicitly in Sen's and Nussbaum's work on capabilities, this meta-need should not be neglected as a valued goal in the promotion of justice. Though the term "self"-actualization has been justifiably critiqued as reflecting the over-emphasis of an individualistic perspective, enabling persons to maximally realize their capabilities and the freedom to pursue possibilities are essential features of a just society. This actualization will only be possible when we realize the inextricable relationship between the good person and the good society.

This perspective on development and justice also considers understanding human beings at both an individual and collective level. Nussbaum created her list of capabilities to be both general and vague enough to capture those capabilities that are general enough to be universally applicable to all human beings and flexible enough to allow for human diversity. Psychological theorists of human development have sought to do the same in describing concepts of human needs and developmental potentials. The example of the Individuals with Disabilities Education Act used earlier in this chapter illustrates how the distinctive needs of each person must be understood and appreciated to provide optimal environmental conditions for those needs to be met, while also allowing for individual initiative and choice. However, I would propose that in the interests of true social justice, the model provided by IDEA be adopted for any member of society. That is, due consideration should be given to carefully and completely assessing each person's specific needs and potentials followed by efforts made to provide the appropriate resources and opportunities to realize those potentials.

Further, responsibility to achieve the greatest degree of potential does not fall solely on the individual or on society in this framework for social justice. This again fits with Nussbaum's and Sen's work, in which the need for human beings to experience themselves as free agents capable of deciding for themselves the goods they will pursue and the goals they will set is central to the achievement of a just society. This view is in line with the interaction of rights, resources and opportunities in the pursuit of justice. Nussbaum (1992, 2003) drew a clear relationship between capabilities and human rights. In the psychological context, rights can be seen as fundamental human needs, akin to Maslow's (1971) ideas. Resources are typically things external to individuals that have the characteristic of better enabling them to achieve their goals. Opportunities refer to making it within an individual's power to pursue a course of action to achieve a desired goal. Thus, while we situate rights "within" individuals and in so doing, see them as personal characteristics or attributes, we must also recognize that the course of development is based upon the inextricable interaction between these personal characteristics and environmental circumstances. The optimal conditions for growth are features of the "external" environment that either enables individuals to realize their potential or thwarts their ability to do so.

I would like to propose a working definition of social justice to guide my analysis of oppression. In his article on compassion and social justice, Williams (2008) sets forth the basis for this definition:

> ...concerns of social justice seem each to emanate from one crucial and overriding humanistic concern: *development and sustenance of social conditions within which all persons have the greatest opportunity to realize their potentialities, both as unique individuals and as members of greater communities and societies.* In this light, issues of social justice might be most properly rooted in the *eudaimonic* tradition—that tradition which takes human well-being, fulfillment and flourishing as the highest good and, consequently, directly confronts the various personal and social impediments to the realization of this good (pp. 6–7, italics in the original)

Following from Williams, I propose that a just society is one whose systems, structures, and processes promote the optimal development of all its members with respect to fulfilling those potentials unique to each of them without regard for arbitrary or prejudicial differences in merit or worth, while also establishing conditions within which individuals are able to realize and express their capacity for freedom and self-determination. Commitment to the promotion of human well-being and social justice is embedded in this definition as both are best attained through efforts aimed at maximizing human development.

Chapter 3

Suffering

A Recap of Some Prior Points

In this chapter and the next I will be taking up the subject of suffering, which was first discussed in the introduction. This chapter will examine the causes and consequences of suffering from the perspective of the individual. The following chapter will examine the social and systemic causes and consequences of suffering. Based on my argument that oppression is the single greatest societal factor contributing to human suffering, it will form the central focus of analysis of social causes of suffering. In adopting this approach, I continue to seek to understand suffering holistically. Employing an individual lens in this chapter will highlight biological, psychological, and spiritual facets of the person. Exploring oppression will elucidate the essentially societal nature of human beings. Taken together this will give an account of the diverse range of factors contributing to suffering and the various dimensions of the experience of oppression.

Examining suffering from the perspective of individuals will also shed light on the importance of the value of compassion and its inextricable relation with suffering. In her important book on suffering, theologian and social activist Dorothy Soelle (1975) asserts that it is a categorical imperative that we strive to abolish conditions under which people "...are exposed to senseless, patently unnecessary suffering, such a hunger, oppression or torture" (p. 3). This categorical imperative is not merely based upon the immorality of such suffering, but the call to respond to the feelings stirred in us when we witness the suffering of another. A significant reason people suffer is because they are forced to by others. Poverty, violence, and oppression cause the victims to feel abased, enslaved, powerless, and transformed into objects of contempt. A lack of compassion, or ability to connect and identify with the suffering of others and to deem it unmerited, plays a significant role in inflicting suffering on others. By the same token it can be argued that all human beings possess an innate capacity for compassion. Fostering a fellow feeling that enables us to recognize a fundamental connection we share with others gives rise to the desire to remove their suffering. Thus, the cultivation of compassion is essential to putting an end to oppression.

Before beginning the analysis of the individual dimension of suffering, it would be useful to summarize key points made about suffering in the Introduction. These points will be revisited and expanded upon in the pages that follow.

1.   Suffering is a universal experience and so inherent to being human. This form of suffering can be called inescapable. From a Buddhist perspective, this suffering is caused by the transient nature of existence, which gives rise to unavoidable experiences of loss, such as illness, aging, and ultimately death. These losses cause us varying degrees of pain and distress (Rahula, 1974). A similar idea advanced by existential philosophy is existential anxiety. Each loss is a reminder of the ultimate loss, death. This anxiety is often experienced as uncertainty, insecurity, and apprehension. The roots of existential anxiety are pain, guilt and death.

2.   Human beings have a powerful need for control, order, and stability, which served some evolutionary purpose and continues to operate at a biological and psychological level. Situations that challenge our sense of order and predictability and threaten our ability to maintain control are stressful and trigger fear. As a result of the pervasiveness of the experience of loss, this need for control is constantly challenged, accompanied by fear. Similarly, having to negotiate life as a dynamic process of constant change means that existential anxiety is a fixed part of our experience.

3.   The way in which we respond to the fear triggered by loss or to existential anxiety can give rise to two different outcomes. One is that it can create even greater suffering. This has been called self-created suffering, which constitutes the greatest source of our pain and unhappiness. Self-created suffering is caused by human beings adopting mistaken beliefs about themselves and the world and then persistently applying these beliefs to dealing with experiences involving natural and inevitable suffering. Most fundamentally, this is the illusion that one ought to be exempt from any form of suffering and that life should

conform to all of one's expectations and desires. In denying our suffering, we end up denying our very humanity—often with disastrous consequences for ourselves and others. In the very effort of evading suffering we cause ourselves (and often others) to suffer even more. Thus, self-created suffering is based on a form of self-deception that gives rise to a self-defeating pattern that has unhealthy and destructive consequences.

4. The other way in which one may respond to inevitable encounters with suffering is to come to terms with loss, insecurity, and anxiety and find in these the opportunity to creatively and productively respond to the challenge posed. In other words, suffering can promote personal transformation and social liberation.

5. Though the resistance human beings experience to pain and suffering is built into their bodies and minds, social influences can play a significant role in reinforcing and fostering that resistance. Such social influences, in the form of a dominant ideology, play a powerful role in maintaining extant power relations, justifying oppression, and suppressing social liberation.

Suffering and Loss

Suffering defies any definition or convenient categorization. Indeed, any attempt to render it as some abstraction carries the risk of making it impersonal and depriving it of any meaning. Above all, suffering must be regarded as a lived reality that defies articulation for the one who is suffering. With that caution in mind, we must still attempt in our modest way to provide some way of approaching and elucidating this suffering. The following two quotes offer a helpful starting place that respects the lived experience of the suffering while also revealing core elements of that experience. First, Frank (2001) writes:

Suffering involves experiencing yourself on the other side of life as it should be, and no thing, no material resource, can bridge that separation. Suffering is what lies beyond such help. Suffering is the unspeakable, as opposed to what can be spoken; it is what remains in darkness, eluding illumination; and it is dread, beyond what is tangible even if hurtful. Suffering is loss, present or anticipated, and loss is another instance of nothing, an absence. We suffer the absence of what was missed and now is no longer recoverable and the absence of what we fear will never be. At the core of suffering is the sense that something is irreparably wrong with our lives, and wrong is the negation of what could have been right. Suffering resists definition because it is the reality of what is not. Anyone who suffers knows the reality of suffering, but this reality is what you cannot "come to grips with." To suffer is to lose your grip. Suffering is expressed in myth as the wound that does not kill but cannot be healed. (p. 355)

Next Morgan and Wilkinson (2001) write:

Suffering is always more than physical pain; more than violence; more than material deprivation; more than destruction; more than loss: suffering is a state of being which "unmakes our world" (Scarry, 1985). Suffering imposes an emotional and social distance between people which is beyond language (Weil, 1950: 77–8). In a profound sense, only those afflicted can bear authentic testimony to the intensity of their plight. In extreme forms, it so dominates consciousness that it is difficult to be aware of anything beside [*sic*] a sense of pain. Yet precisely what we are conscious of can scarcely be assumed in words. (p. 203)

Taken together, these eloquent passages capture several themes that will be elaborated in this chapter. The first, by now very familiar, is that suffering is a response to loss. The most typical emotions triggered by loss are sadness, grief and—most extreme—depression. However, there may be other reactions as well including anger, a sense of numbness, confusion, and apprehension. Any sort of loss can cause one to suffer, although the loss need not be something unwelcome or unpleasant. For example, while an unexpected situation involving good fortune may initially be experienced as positive, over time it may upset one's sense of the familiar and expected and cause unhappiness. Studies of individuals with even considerable amounts of wealth find that this often does not bring happiness (Csikszentmihalyi, 1999).

The ultimate loss toward which all other losses point is our death. One's total annihilation evokes the greatest sense of dread. Even in its more attenuated forms, such as a sense of emptiness, feeling suddenly thrust into an utterly foreign situation, or a nagging sense of foreboding, this most extreme of all losses can be terrifying. It can be experienced as an absence or void—a deep sense of emptiness. As David Bakan (1968) observes, the threat of the dissolution of everything embraces the dialectical relationship between the person (fear of dying) and the world (fear of loneliness and isolation). The quote by Morgan and Wilkinson (2001) cites the work of Elaine Scarry (1985), who ascribes suffering to more than mere loss but instead to the "'unmaking of one's world." This again harkens back to the interdependent relationship between human beings and their world. It is not the unmaking of "the world" but of "one's world."

This is because the unmaking of one's world is essentially equivalent to the obliteration of one's self. This is the primal anxiety described in existential literature. Existential anxiety is rooted in the person's awareness that his or her very being is always at issue. R. D. Laing (1960) calls this ontological insecurity. Though this apprehension about one's annihilation is only truly realized upon death, threats to our sense of being are experienced in varying degrees throughout our lifetime—accompanied by varying degrees of suffering. These threats are not merely based in events outside of us, but far more often arise due to our capacity to think hypothetically and to imagine threats to our sense of being.

As the quote by Frank (2001) describes, the loss involved in suffering may be real or imaginary, actual or anticipated. These distinctions will prove to be very important not only to understanding suffering but also—as we will see—to the ways in which we try to evade suffering. As noted, one need not experience a real loss in order to suffer. Human beings suffer far more from imagined losses than actual ones. This is asserted in Buddhism's third form of suffering. This suffering is rooted in ignorance and based in mistaken habits of thought and distorted perceptions. Driven by craving or desire, human beings form strong attachments to objects and persons they believe are essential to their well-being and happiness. These attachments are expressions of human beings' need for control. By imposing their wishes and desires on life, human beings seek to deny the inevitability of loss. All attachments eventually must come to naught because of the transient nature of life.

Despite this, human beings cling to their attachments even more tightly, hoping to avoid suffering. But the mere possibility of loss, the chance that some cherished expectation may not be realized, brings disappointment and exposes us to the uncertainties of life. When our desires are unchecked, it is not long before they go unfulfilled. Our initial frustration soon gives way to fear. It is this very same fear that leads us to evade suffering and prevents us from understanding the true reason for our disappointment and dread. Rather than accept the loss and surrender to the suffering it brings, we cling even more tightly to our expectations and suffer more.

We see then that our heightened capacity for consciousness opens us up to degrees and forms of suffering that other species are incapable of. Human beings can step back and reflect on themselves. We can imagine and create a mental picture that functions as a frame of reference from which to understand the world (a worldview). In many instances, these imagined losses cause us to suffer even more deeply. Because these products of our imagination loom ever present, they can torment us despite never being realized. It is like the proverbial Boogie Man who lives underneath our bed. Each night he may fill us with terror, and that fear will remain with us until we actually look under the bed and find nothing there. This same capacity to think hypothetically is responsible for the second distinction Frank notes—actual or anticipated loss. This highlights how the temporal dimension inherent in the experience of suffering relates to loss.

A number of individuals have commented on the importance of this temporal element. One is physician Eric Cassell (1999), who observes that the experience of suffering requires that something has happened which influences an individual's perception of future events. It may not be the loss we are experiencing now that causes us to suffer, but the one we anticipate that is yet to come. This orientation toward the future is reflected in concern that should suffering persist, we would be unable to bear or cope with it. In the direst situation, persons may fear that they have no future because their suffering portends death. Fears that one's anguish may continue unabated or that one may have no future are not uncommon among individuals with a chronic or progressive disease. On a very similar note, Radley (2004) distinguishes pain from suffering by observing that in suffering there is the fear that one will be overwhelmed by the pain and left helpless and beyond help. One is thus again deprived of any sense of having a future.

Even for those who are not suffering an illness, the relevance of the future in suffering is crystalized in the realization that our death awaits us. From the moment of our birth, our eventual death becomes a constant possibility. We often try to evade being reminded of our mortality by casting it off somewhere into the distant future. But our future is entwined with our lives in the here and now. In our hopes, plans, and projects, we structure our lives in a way that is oriented toward what is yet to come. At the same time, death looms always in our awareness. Though we think this ultimate loss will come at some distant time, the truth is that it can befall us at any moment. Expectations alone, however, are not the only way in which time enters the experience of suffering. Our past is also entwined with the present. Our memories are not static entities; nor are they factual renderings of things that have happened. We constantly reshape our past in the here and now, and it is this version of the past that colors how we live in the moment.

Alan Watts (1966) speaks to this point. He observes that sometimes we envy animals because they are immersed in the immediate present. This makes their lives seem simpler and uncomplicated. Living in the moment, they experience pleasure and pain as part of the constant flux of existence. However, our more evolved state of consciousness—our ability to question, reflect, and give different meanings to our experience—provides us with an enhanced sensitivity that both enriches our lives and increases our vulnerability to suffering. We have a different and more complex consciousness of time. The ways in which we imagine what our future might be and recall events from our past are essential aspects of how we experience suffering. Watts writes, "The power of memories and expectations is such that for most human beings the past and the future are not *as* real, but *more* real than the present. The present cannot be lived happily unless the past has been 'cleared up' and the future is bright with promise" (p. 34, italics in original).

This impact of temporality on human consciousness sheds light on Frank's (2001) description of suffering as "the wound that does not kill but cannot be healed." Self-created suffering is not confined to a single incident or a discrete cause. Unlike natural causes of suffering, in which a loss triggers pain and distress that comes and then passes, memories of past injuries and disappointments and our apprehension that we will be deprived of our imagined future lead to anguish that lingers interminably and offers no hope of relief. This brings a greater depth of suffering that was eloquently described by Kierkegaard (1941) as despair or "the sickness unto death"—an affliction that consumes the sufferer without killing him or her. Kierkegaard's analysis of despair in his work *The Sickness unto Death* offers a rich and powerful examination of the problem of suffering and the different ways in which suffering is experienced by human beings. His analysis provides a cogent exposition of the ways in which self-deception and the evasion of suffering give rise to a greater depth of suffering. For the purposes of this examination of the role loss plays in suffering, there is one key insight we need to take from his work. In the final analysis, the cause of suffering that endures and persists is not some specific loss that causes us to be wounded. In time and with patient care, wounds will typically heal. Rather, the true cause of this suffering is the troubling realization that we are vulnerable and so capable of sustaining such wounds.

The way in which Kierkegaard puts this is that human beings act as if they are in despair over something, but what they are actually in despair over is themselves. We erroneously attribute the reason for our suffering to some disappointment or setback in life, but what is painful and unacceptable to us is that we are not the persons we believe or wish ourselves to be. What we have lost is some illusion *regarding ourselves*. We are not as successful, as smart, as attractive, as physically resilient as we thought. It's not merely the case that the world is not the place we expected it to be. We are likewise not the persons we believed and expected ourselves to be. What certain losses require of us is the willingness and courage to abandon all pretenses about who and what we are. Rather than despise ourselves for our humanity and all the limitations that come with it, we need to humbly connect with our own suffering and show compassion for ourselves. In consenting to experience the suffering that is our due, we spare ourselves the greater portion of suffering that can be avoided.

Suffering and the Problem of the Ego

Kierkegaard's discussion of despair is one illustration of a very significant cause of suffering that has been described not only in philosophical literature but also religious/spiritual and psychological literature. It is often referred to as the "problem of the ego." When bad things happen to others or to us, one of the first ways in which we respond is to question what has happened and ask "Why?" At first this takes the form of "Why me?" The way in which we pose this question already reveals something about the problem of the ego. When we experience a disturbing loss, we often adopt a very narrow and egocentric perspective when trying to make sense of what has happened. Our attempts at understanding and responding to losses frequently are riveted around what impact these losses and disappointments have "on me." The overemphasis on the individual and the narcissistic focus that accompanies it (as discussed in the Introduction) make their appearance once more. For example, when things do not go our way, our feeling frustrated and offended soon gives way to the exclamation, "Life should be fair." However, most of the time when we make this claim, we are not actually expressing the wish that life should be fair *for everyone*. If we were to be honest with ourselves, we would admit that what we really matters to us is that "Life should be fair *to me*."

The problem of the ego would assert that this excessive preoccupation with ourselves—our own interests, needs, beliefs, etc.— is the default position that we occupy as we negotiate our day-to-day lives. Our central preoccupation is with ourselves. Social psychologist Anthony Greenwald (1980) provides experimental results that indicate the very powerful egocentric bias that lies at the heart of how we see ourselves. Information is better remembered to the degree to which it has to do with us. We are far more likely to take credit for our successes rather than our failures. As will be discussed in more detail later, whether information is processed and made part of our body of knowledge depends heavily on how well that information fits with our self-concept. However, our egocentricity and self-absorption are especially heightened in circumstances in which we have experienced a loss. This is because our deepest fear has been aroused—the loss of the most valued of all our possessions, our ego. Implicit in the question of "Why me?" is expression of our desire to deny or undo the loss or, failing that, to resist the pain caused by it. There is a sense of disbelief that this can possibly be happening to me, accompanied by a feeling of being deeply offended by what has occurred. Out of these reactions, efforts are directed toward making things okay again for me.

The amount of focus and energy invested in this common response to loss reveals just how powerful the ego is. But what precisely is the ego? The term "ego" has been used in various and even contradictory ways in psychological literature. To avoid this confusion, the way in which ego will be defined here is based upon spiritual literature, in which there tends to be a more shared understanding. Looking at the ego from this perspective is particularly relevant because it will mesh with key points about suffering that were summarized at the start of this chapter. The ego grows out of our need for order, control, and stability. It is something of our own making, composed of notions, beliefs, images, memories, and feelings that together form what we take to be our identity. Actually, much of what we believe to be real about ourselves (and about the world) is actually a set of fictions created by our minds and shaped by powerful social influences. As Erich Fromm (1960) observed, "The average person driven by insecurity, greed, fear, is constantly enmeshed in a world of phantasies (not necessarily being aware of it) in which he clothes the world in qualities which he projects into it, which are not there" (pp. 117–118). These fictions are nonetheless highly valued and strongly held as they are believed to be a bulwark against the trials and tribulations of life and the pain, fear, and insecurity that accompany them.

Ultimately, the problem of the ego is that it is both the dearest and most dangerous of our illusions. One of the most perceptive and penetrating analyses of this illusion and its dangers is provided by Alan Watts (1951, 1961, 1966, 1968), who calls it "the illusion of the skin-encapsulated ego." His use of this description is based on the common belief among people that the ego is something that essentially resides inside of "them," somewhere behind the eyes and between the ears. He goes on to describe this illusion as follows:

> The root of the matter is the way in which we feel and conceive ourselves as human beings, our sensation of being alive, of individual existence and identity. We suffer from a hallucination, from a false and distorted sensation of our own existence as living organisms. Most of us have the sensation that "I myself" is a separate center of feeling and action, living inside and bounded by the physical body—a center which "confronts" an "external" world of people and things, making contact through the senses with a universe both alien and strange. Everyday figures of speech reflect this illusion. "I came into this world." "You must face reality." "The conquest of nature." (pp. 5–6)

Bounded by the skin of our body, the ego is regarded as some living entity distinct and separate from the world and from all other human beings. The sense of the ego as a center of feeling and action also facilitates the belief that each person is unique and can autonomously exert control over his or her life.

However, as the above quote makes clear, Watts takes exception to this view of the ego. It fosters problematic feelings of alienation such that individual human beings experience themselves at odds with the world around them and other human beings. When particularly intensified, this may feel as if we are strangers who have been thrust out into a foreign and even hostile world. In time, this sense of alienation can even create splits within us between what seem to be opposing forces or clashing entities. We may feel torn between conflicting emotions or goals incapable of being resolved or reconciled.

In those moments when we act in ways contrary to what we intend or at odds with who we believe ourselves to be, the experience of alienation is particularly intense (Gruba-McCallister, 1993). Experiencing ourselves as a "skin-encapsulated ego" can eventually become a prison in which the person becomes trapped, isolated from others, and estranged from the world. This belief in the boundedness of the ego has also tended to foster a more competitive and even antagonistic relationship between the individual and others.

The full critique of the ego as a "hallucination" will need to be deferred to the discussion of the social roots of the ego in the next chapter. However, the ways in which it contributes to the experience of suffering at the level of the individual person will be considered here. Ever more importance assigned to the ego gives rise to a growing proclivity toward egocentrism or being overly focused on one's own narrow perspective. As we come to give preference to ourselves above all else, the various negative feelings and attitudes associated with the ego grow worse, including a sense of isolation, alienation, and conflict with others, the world, and ourselves. This narcissistic stance highlights the greatest danger posed by the problem of the ego. The ego moves from being more than just an illusion. It is an idol—something we prize and worship above all else.

At its most extreme, idolatry is nothing less than making a god of ourselves to which everything and everyone else must be sacrificed. Fromm (1976) describes this: "To be an egoist refers not only to my behavior but to my character. It means: that I want everything for myself; that possessing, not sharing, gives me pleasure; that I must become greedy because if my aim is having, I am more the more I have....I can never be satisfied because there is no end to my wishes ..." (p. 6). Our desperate craving not only to preserve the ego but to aggrandize it by possessing more and more becomes a frantic effort to hold loss at bay and to preserve ourselves at all costs. A threat to anyone or anything considered essential to propping up our ego evokes intense fear and is strenuously opposed. Such fear and resistance create suffering despite our hopes of avoiding the pain of loss. But, more important, because all these machinations are based on an illusion, they are destined to fail. In time, each and every idol is toppled.

The dynamics by which this illusion is created and maintained are based upon human beings' capacity for self-reflection and ability to categorize their experience into what are called *schemas*. Goleman (1985) writes, "...the mind packages information in 'schemas,' a sort of mental code for representing experience. Schemas operate in the unconscious out of awareness. They direct attention toward what is salient and ignore the rest of experience—an essential task" (p. 22). In other words, each schema represents a private theory that persons devise about all facets of their experience, including those bearing on who they believe themselves to be. These theories are not typically well thought out or elaborate and operate below our level of awareness. As a result, it would be difficult to articulate what these schemas are if asked. Nonetheless, they exercise a very powerful influence by shaping what we notice and what we don't notice as well as by coloring our experiences and giving them specific interpretations and meanings.

The very question of "who am I" would be impossible to consider without self-reflection because it requires us to be able to step outside of ourselves and examine ourselves as if we were another human being. As Watts (1966) describes this process by which the ego is created, he outlines how human beings employ various labels and categories to describe themselves, just as they would any other object. By and large, these notions about ourselves and the language we employ to describe ourselves are derived from a complex of social relations within which we are embedded. Over time, the ego as a concept or mental construction is fashioned using images, myths, models, and words. The collection of schemas regarding the self then shapes feelings and perceptions as we negotiate life. But in one important sense the ego is unlike any other concept. It occupies a unique and special place because it describes the one thing most precious to us—ourselves. The ego is fundamentally who we believe ourselves to be and by implication what we believe life is all about. Again Fromm (1976) highlights this point, "Our ego is the most important object of our property feeling, for it comprises many things: our body, our name, our social status, our possessions (including our knowledge), the image we have of ourselves and the image we want others to have of us" (p. 71). Hence, preserving things we consider essential to us—our social status, our security, our sense of well-being, and our very survival—hinges on preserving our ego.

The Buddhist analysis and critique of the concept of the ego helps to further clarify the nature of the ego as the most potent of our illusions (Rahula, 1974). If you were to pose the question "Who am I?", each entity in the entire laundry list of answers you were to give to the question can be thought of as an element making up your ego. Buddhism would consider each of these as an expression of your desire to fashion a sense of self that was permanent and impervious to loss. In other words, we often form a strong identification with or attachment to a whole host of objects, persons, roles, hopes, and dreams that we consider to be essential to our happiness and our sense of security. The process of identifying ourselves with these things also gives us the feeling that we can take possession of them and so control them. Some of these identifications can be so powerful that we have difficulty distinguishing who we are from these pivotal attachments that make up our ego. The very language we use to express these bonds simultaneously facilitates the process of identification. This is not surprising given the prominent role that language plays in the formation of concepts. Consider how one typically responds to the question "Who are you?": "I *am* (that is, equals) a father, a psychologist, intelligent, kind, an American, a Catholic, etc." There is an essential equation being made between "I" and these various identifications. This then becomes the basis for the illusory nature of the ego.

In making these equations, we are confusing who we are with each one of these very narrow identifications. We are trying to capture something as mysterious and complex as our identity by sorting specific facets of ourselves into fictitious categories, believing that somehow this makes our sense of self something tangible and substantial. By confining our sense of identity to these attachments, we are making a number of serious errors that are causes of substantial suffering. The first is pointed out by Italian psychiatrist Roberto Assagioli (1965) who observed, "*We are dominated by everything with which our self becomes identified*" (p. 22, italics in the original). Though we imagine that taking possession of what is critical to defining us provides us with control, quite the contrary is the case. Because so much importance is given to our attachments, we end up being slaves to them as we are willing to often make considerable sacrifices in order to maintain them. For example, if my career is the most important thing to me, all other aspects of my life will in time take a back seat to it. Rather than work for a living, one lives to work.

Preoccupation with our attachments, as well as attaining and retaining the objects of our desires, also fills us with anxiety and worry because we are aware that ultimately we have no control over them. The confusion of the ego with its attachments as a source of suffering has been asserted by Buddhism and other spiritual traditions. The reason for this, as articulated in the Four Noble Truths, is the transient and impermanent nature of our lives, the inevitable loss of every attachment and identification that make up our ego, and the suffering that accompanies it. Watts (1961) writes:

For the ego is the role, the "act," that one's inmost self is permanent, that it is in control of the organism, and that while it "has" experiences it is not involved in them. Pain and death expose this pretense, and this is why suffering is almost always attended by a feeling of guilt, a feeling that this is all the more difficult to explain when the pretense is unconscious. Hence the obscure but powerful feeling that one *ought* not to suffer or die (p. 69, italics in original)

What the quote by Watts captures is the distinction between the two forms of suffering. The ego rigidly maintains the powerful feeling that one ought not to suffer or die and so lives in the constant state of fear and guilt, although the actual reason for that fear and guilt may not be apparent. The futility of resistance to the inevitability of loss (and so suffering) is exposed by unavoidable encounters with pain and death. The illusory nature of the ego is punctured by these encounters.

There are times, however, when the magnitude of the loss is such that a person truly does confront the threat of his or her complete annihilation. Karl Jaspers (1984) describes these encounters as "limit situations" or "boundary experiences." These are true wake-up moments that occur in everyone's life at some point. In order to understand these experiences, we need to realize that people tend not only to equate who they are with specific attachments but also with the entirety of all their identifications, what might be called their worldview. Like the ego, this worldview is employed by persons to impose a sense of order and predictability on their experience. It also is the framework they use to interpret what happens to them and give meaning to their lives. Thus, it is not surprising that who we believe we are and how we look at the world (both of which are based on fictions and illusions) are seen as one and the same. What then gives rise to a boundary experience or wake-up call is a powerful experience that essentially shatters those illusions and completely turns the predictable routines we have created upside down. As a result, the safety and security that our familiar sense of the world once provided to us crumbles away.

As might be imagined, these experiences can be terrifying. However, behind that terror is a form of inevitable suffering that comes with any loss. It is the anxiety, dread, and guilt that accompany our encounters with Frankl's (1967) tragic triad of the givens of human existence—our fallibility, finitude, and mortality. The dissolution of the fictions that have distorted and constricted our outlook afford us the opportunity to confront genuine and critical issues that we have been trying hard to evade for so long. The way in which we respond to this crisis will dictate which of two options we pursue. In one we are presented with the prospect of reflecting upon the inadequacy of what we once believed and broadening our worldview. However, while there may be this potential benefit, all too often the distress we experience is so painful that it ends up thwarting any consideration of how to seize the moment to engage in open self-reflection and create a more encompassing and valid viewpoint.

Rather than squarely confront the upheavals that come with the inherently fluid nature of life, human beings return to seeking out ways to buffer themselves from the threat posed by the unknown and unpredictable. They erect a barrier around what they had mistakenly espoused as irrefutable and indubitable beliefs and then adamantly go back to defending them with a life-or-death attitude. This rigid and inflexible stance has its roots in the mistaken connection made between what has been lost and one's own impending annihilation. Human beings' propensity to closely identify themselves with their worldview so often proves to be the source of a great deal of their suffering. They make the mistake of assuming if their worldview becomes seriously questioned, their very sense of self is jeopardized. The destruction of one's worldview and one's annihilation, however, are not the same.

When torture and war are involved, we can clearly see how individuals might well fear that the unmaking of their world would be accompanied by their actual destruction. However, "limit situations" are not solely found in such dire circumstances. They can be experienced in less extreme situations such as serious illness, the death of a loved one, the loss of a cherished goal, or an experience of extreme humiliation or shame. What remains the same in each of these instances is that we suffer because the comfortable and predictable world we once knew is turned upside down. Our sense of control is stripped away. With the protective barrier that once provided us with a false sense of security gone, we suddenly find ourselves no longer able to deny fears, worries, and supposed threats that we had tried so hard to evade. The moment of greatest crisis comes when we realize that all certainties have been laid to waste, and we wonder whether we will ever be able to restore any degree of order and control. In the depth of that crisis, we may come to the realization that we are faced with a pivotal choice. In one direction lies even greater suffering should we choose to cling to what has been lost, and in the other lies the possibility of growth and renewal should we willingly sacrifice what has been lost.

The potential for wake-up experiences to lead to growth and renewal will be considered at the end of this chapter.

Suffering: Disintegration and Separation

The discussion of the role of loss and problem of the ego reveals another common theme pertinent to suffering. This is how suffering threatens to disrupt or destroy the sense of one's wholeness, integrity, or harmony. An example of this theme is given by Cassell (1991) who writes, "Suffering occurs when an impending destruction of the person is perceived; it continues until the threat of disintegration has passed or until the integrity of the person can be restored in some other manner...Most generally, suffering can be defined as a state of severe distress associated with events that threaten the intactness of person" (p. 33). This view of suffering highlights that an important way in which we understand what it means to be a person is based upon our ability to experience ourselves as whole and intact. As this relates to the previous discussion of the ego, the typical way we maintain our identity is by resisting anything that might deprive us of one or more essential elements composing it. Moreover, this emphasis on integrity reflects our understanding of the centrality of the diverse network of relationships within which we exist to our personhood. Undermining these relationships also poses a threat to us.

Implicit in this analysis is the belief that wholeness, unity, integrity, and harmony represent well-being and a good to be sought and maintained. This understanding is expressed in the etymological roots of words such as "health" and "heal," which come from Old English and Old Norse "to be whole, sound, or well." The word "holy" is also related to health. In contrast to this desirable state, to be broken or to be faced with the possibility of disintegration is something undesirable, harmful, and so to be avoided. This state of disunity, separation, and un-connectedness is the experience of alienation discussed earlier. As we saw, it can be experienced in our relationship to ourselves, to other human beings, to the physical world, or to a higher or transcendent order or being. This sense of separation, isolation, or estrangement is accompanied by feelings of emptiness, numbness, abandonment, rejection, shame, or guilt. Though the meanings given to alienation have been diverse and debated in philosophical, theological, psychological, and sociological literature (Schacht, 1970), it has often been employed in analyses of self-deception, oppression, and mystification. Thus, it will continue to be an important idea for my own analysis of suffering and oppression.

It is easy to see how a significant loss can pose a threat to our sense of wholeness and integrity, leading then to the experience of alienation and suffering. The reason for this can be described in terms of a dichotomy or conflict embedded in every experience of loss that gives rise to a sense of disharmony, disintegration, and estrangement. The relevance of this to the experience of suffering is highlighted in the analysis of suffering by Moulyn (1982), who writes:

> We have been thrown into a terrestrial existence which is rent by many blemishes, imperfections, contradictions, unresolved problems, dichotomies, and fractures. These blemishes and fractures are inherent in the human condition and they are the source of the many levels of suffering. Inasmuch as we have to accept our being thrown into the world, we also have to accept periods during which we suffer. But instead of devaluing suffering and rejecting it as something that should not befall us, we ought to make an effort to become aware of the meaning of suffering. Its value and its meaning are that it heals the blemishes and fractures in our problem-ridden existence. (p. 4)

Certain conflicts in life that pose contradictions and conundrums are inherent in the human condition. They give rise to a range of feelings including tension, anxiety, dread, and even terror. All these responses are forms of inescapable suffering. But as Moulyn observes, this is only half of the experience. We are also faced with a choice as to whether we will accept these periods of suffering rather than deny and devalue them. The way in which we respond to these experiences determines whether we deem that there is any value or meaning in the suffering they cause. If we allow them to, these experiences can awaken our resolve to synthesize the opposing elements of the conflict we face and restore a state of integration and harmony. That path leads to healing. But there is always the other path, the path rooted in our refusal to accept the necessary suffering that comes with life. That path widens the fissures and exacerbates the conflicts. It is the path that leads to self-created suffering. This tension between wholeness and brokenness, between unity and disintegration, is still another expression of the paradoxes posed by suffering. How we negotiate these paradoxes is pivotal to understanding the experience of suffering on both an individual and a collective (or social) level.

These paradoxes can be organized around particular polarities intrinsic to human experience, which Spinelli (2014) calls existential tensions. These represent inescapable sources of conflict and suffering that recur as we move through life. Spinelli states that we organize our worldview and our understanding of ourselves around these polarities as we seek to come to terms with the issues they pose. Moulyn (1982) and Bakan (1968), for instance, both assert that the two most serious threats to our wholeness and integrity are the fear of loneliness and the dread of death. Both these threats can be expressed using just such existential tensions. The first is, of course, the most fundamental of all polarities, Life vs. Death. Philosophical and psychological literature through time has been replete with references to this fundamental dimension of human experience.

The second polarity, equally fundamental to existence, has been described by Arthur Koestler (1967) as the Janus effect. By this he means that there are two opposing tendencies in all living organisms that express the polarity of whole vs. part, autonomy vs. dependence. This basic polarity means that wholes and parts in the absolute sense do not exist anywhere in nature. Rather, all persons or things making up a living system have characteristics of both whole and part and must ceaselessly engage in trying to balance or reconcile these tendencies. The expression of wholeness, called *the self-assertive tendency*, can manifest as assertion, competition, and aggression. The expression of partness, called the *integrative tendency*, can manifest as cooperation, dependence, and self-transcendence. With respect to negotiating our relations with other human beings, the Janus effect can be seen in the tension between the degree to which we strive to be self-sufficient, independent, distinct, and autonomous versus relying on others and being dependent, submissive, and identified with something bigger than we are. As Koestler (1967) makes clear, these polarities cannot be dealt with by adopting a one-sided, either-or attitude. Having both partness and wholeness in our very nature, we are always trying to find ways to balance these opposing tendencies.

As suggested by Moulyn (1982), Spinelli (2014), and many other thinkers, the course of each of our lives is inextricably involved in negotiating a host of situations in which we must deal with issues that express these very fundamental polarities. Examples include determining whether our actions are right or wrong, making a life or death decision, or establishing whether someone is a friend or foe. These polarities are an expression of the *dialectical nature* of human existence. The idea of the dialectic was touched on in the Introduction.

From a dialectical perspective, there is an interdependent relationship that exists between two opposites. This is because, contrary to being incommensurate with each other, they mutually define and depend upon each other. Moreover, the human mind is inherently capable of thinking dialectically such that in knowing one thing, we implicitly know its opposite. This is because any idea implies its opposite. The dialectical nature of many of the polarities that we experience in life makes resolving the apparent conflict they pose more complicated. Our generally preferred way of dealing with these sorts of conflicts is to adopt an either/or mentality that strives to separate the two sides of the polarity into distinct, iron-clad categories. Such black-or-white thinking may sometimes succeed in settling some issues, but far more frequently it fails to appreciate the complexities and nuances involved. Moreover, dichotomizing can exacerbate conflict and intensify opposition.

Nevertheless, the fact remains that when faced with these polarities, we must contend with them. The dynamic and ever-evolving nature of our lives requires this. As Erich Fromm (1947) observes, "It is one of the peculiar characteristics of the human mind that when confronted with a contradiction it cannot remain passive. It is set in motion with the aim of resolving the contradiction. All progress is due to this fact" (p. 52). Further, the way we deal with these confrontations determines the course that our lives take—that is, toward well-being, wholeness, and harmony or toward unease, fragmentation, and discord. As Moulyn (1982) asserts, conflicts, incongruities, and other threats to our integrity bring with them the potential both for suffering and for growth. The unsettling of our sense of wholeness and harmony may cause us distress, but the upheaval of established and rigid patterns of thought and action is almost invariably the prelude to what may be productive change.

It is thus not difficult to see how the process of managing these disruptions and upsets can be demanding and rigorous. Kierkegaard (1941) provides an eloquent description of this process in his discussion of despair as the arduous path of negotiating inescapable existential tensions. For Kierkegaard, the human being is constituted by the polar opposites of being finite and infinite, temporal and eternal. We feel torn between these polarities as they seem to be constantly pulling us in opposite directions. This tension gives rise to suffering as no permanent state of harmony between these opposing tendencies can be achieved. When that tension seems to be too much to bear, human beings are tempted to resolve the conflict by clinging to one side of the polarity to the exclusion of the other. Kierkegaard describes various forms of despair that result from these desperate and futile attempts to escape from the demands that both these facets of who we are exert on us. Despite the anguish that this rigorous process may require, we must show the resolve and courage necessary to ceaselessly strive to synthesize polarities that can never be permanently resolved. For Kierkegaard, this means living our lives authentically and embracing the anxiety that comes with it. Any effort on our part to evade this demand paradoxically causes us to suffer more.

However, are all of life's polarities incapable of being resolved? We have seen that there are two distinct forms of suffering and, correspondingly, two distinct forms of polarities that give way to them. This makes it critical that we understand the difference between these two forms of conflict and how best to approach addressing each of them (Gruba-McCallister & Levington, 1995). One way to understand the difference is the distinction made in theological writing between natural evil and moral evil. Natural evil is the cause of suffering that cannot be avoided because it is rooted in the very fabric of the universe in which we live. This harkens back to Frankl's (1967) tragic triad and what I call inescapable suffering. The polarity of life and death is one significant source of natural evil. This polarity can never be successfully resolved. It represents a source of tension and conflict throughout our lifetime.

Moral evil, on the other hand, is the suffering and harm caused by the choices that human beings make. For example, we are dealing with a moral choice each time we must decide whether to treat another human being justly and compassionately. This has also been described as self-created suffering. A similar and useful distinction is offered by Fromm (1947). Existential dichotomies, such as life and death, are inherent to the human condition and so must be confronted and accepted as they cannot be avoided or eradicated. Historical dichotomies, on the other hand, such as wealth vs. poverty, are created by human beings. Thus, they are subject to being altered or eliminated by taking different actions or making different choices.

One final issue that is implicit in this distinction is controllability. We have seen how this very powerful human need is so much a part of the problem of suffering. Natural evil and existential dichotomies are not subject to our direct control; whereas, moral evil and historical dichotomies are things over which we have control. Moral evil and historical dichotomies will prove to be important concepts when the subject of oppression is taken up later. Engaging in oppression is clearly a moral evil, and such evil actions create historical dichotomies that are the source of considerable suffering by virtue of depriving members of oppressed groups of a sense of wholeness, integrity, and well-being.

One final way in which to understand the two forms of polarities that have been outlined here is by describing the very different ways in which they are experienced. This also provides insights into how they cause suffering and offers ways of responding to that suffering. A distinction proposed by John Kafka (1971) in his discussion of the role of ambiguity in promoting healthy growth is extremely useful here. In certain instances, the fractures and dichotomies we experience can be understood as a contradiction. The opposing elements making up a contradiction can easily be distinguished and separated from each other. This is because no relationship of interdependence or reciprocity exists between them. An example would be coming to an intersection in which two signs are posted, "Stop" and "Don't Stop." In this situation, the alternatives we are faced with are straightforward as we must decide to do one or the other. Until our decision is made, we may experience ambivalence about what to do. But this promptly disappears once we act on one of the alternatives. The example of a contradiction can be used to elucidate what is involved in historical dichotomies that are a profound source of oppression. The egregious inequity created by the gap between the rich and poor is neither inevitable nor natural (despite declarations often made to the contrary). There are very clear-cut choices that decide whether we have a more equal society (Rank, 2004). Do we seek to establish a society in which the distribution of blessings and burdens is equitable? Do we act to eliminate avoidable causes of harm to those who are vulnerable? When choices are made that cause egregious harms that are avoidable, they are morally condemnable because individuals could have decided otherwise. The same can be said of other dichotomies responsible for oppression (e.g., inferior vs. superior, included vs. excluded). Apathy, indifference, and inaction in response to these avoidable forms of suffering causing oppression are morally condemnable.

The experience of suffering may also arise from polarities in which there is a dialectical and interdependent relationship between the opposing elements. In this instance, it is not opting for one of the two alternatives that directly causes the suffering. Rather it arises from the struggle one experiences from being caught on what feels like the horns of an irresolvable dilemma. Kafka (1971) calls this a paradox. The example of a paradox given by Kafka is a sign that reads "Don't read this sign." In order to obey the sign, one must read it, but in reading it, one disobeys it. Another example is when a friend tells you to try hard to have a good time at a party. Having a good time or not is something that happens spontaneously. You cannot force yourself to have a good time. In paradoxes such as this one, the choices cannot be easily distinguished or separated from each other. Instead they seem murky and easily blur into each other. Rather than ambivalence, one experiences ambiguity and confusion. There is a sense that one is caught in a quandary that offers no easy answer or means of escape.

According to Kafka (1971), paradoxes provoke the experience of uncanniness in which our familiar sense of the world is suddenly turned upside down (derealization) and our view of ourselves is in question (depersonalization). Another way in which this experience is described is as a state of acute alienation. In the most extreme case, a paradox can lead to the boundary experience described earlier. Persons lose all sense of their bearings due to the loss of their worldview. Unable to comprehend what is happening, lacking words to describe what they are thinking and feeling, the state of uncanniness is accompanied by a keen sense of anxiety that can be described as dread and even horror. It can thus give rise to extreme and desperate responses to restore some measure of safety, security, and stability (Goleman, 1985).

Existential dichotomies are examples of paradoxes. This is because they offer no straightforward or simple solution. We have seen, for example, how human beings must assert their individuality and autonomy while also recognizing their essential dependence on others. As Watts observed, the single-minded pursuit of absolute security only leads to a growing sense of insecurity. Avoidance of the prospect of death can lead one to retreat further and further from life. Kierkegaard's (1941) observation that the process of living requires each person to ceaseless engage in efforts to synthesize these opposing polarities shows a keen appreciation of the way in which these existential dichotomies outline the ongoing challenges of human growth and development. Though these paradoxes defy any attempts at our control or final resolution, this does not mean that we are left helpless and with no options. Fromm (1947) addresses this point:

> Man can react to historical contradictions by annulling them through his own action; but he cannot annul existential dichotomies, although he can react to them in different ways. He can appease his mind by soothing and harmonizing ideologies. He can try to escape from his inner restlessness by ceaseless activity in pleasure or business. He can try and

abrogate his freedom and turn himself into an instrument of powers outside himself, submerging himself in them. But he remains dissatisfied, anxious, and restless. There is only one solution to his problem: to face the truth, to acknowledge his fundamental aloneness and solitude in a universe indifferent to his fate and to recognize that there is no power transcending him which can solve his problem for him. Man must accept responsibility for himself and the fact that only by using his own powers can give meaning to his life. But meaning does not imply certainty; indeed, the quest for certainty blocks the search for meaning. Uncertainty is the very condition to impel man to unfold his powers. (pp. 53–54)

Fromm's analysis of the strategies used to evade existential dichotomies sheds valuable light on certain hazardous strategies that often can be found in oppression. Ideologies such as neoliberalism do offer seductive solutions that falsely promise to put all our fears to rest but ultimately end up tricking us into surrendering our freedom and submitting ourselves to the machinations of those in power. Neoliberalism is built upon instilling a constant craving in citizens that they mistakenly believe will only be satisfied by consumption. But even as we acquire more and more, our sense of anxiety and insecurity intensifies (Kasser & Kanner, 2004). We throw ourselves into our jobs assuming that hard work will one day lead to success, but that success constantly eludes us. Inevitably, we are betrayed by this ideology, and our dissatisfaction, unhappiness, and fear are still there. Yet Fromm offers hope in one solution he proposes by asserting the power that the suffering evoked by existential dichotomies has to tap into the capacity of human beings to transcend it and transform it into growth.

Understanding existential dichotomies provides additional insights into suffering based on how the hegemonic ideology frames these dichotomies as if they were problems that can be solved (that is, confusing existential dichotomies with historical ones). One of the most maddening is how oppressors seize upon the quotation by Jesus, "The poor will always be with us," as an excuse to do nothing to ameliorate poverty. Yes, it is true that even in a more just world some individuals will suffer from having less. There will be times when the needs of certain individuals will go unmet even if substantial effort is made to eliminate poverty. While we may be able to realistically alter or remove the conditions responsible for their suffering, we cannot conveniently "fix" the pain and harm that these conditions have caused them. The demands of justice only require that we do all in our power to resolve historical dichotomies and put an end to avoidable causes of suffering.

But even then, turning a blind eye to the suffering that remains is a form of oppression as it is a denial of the humanity of the victims. Their suffering demands our attention and validation, especially when our efforts have failed to ameliorate it. And when we extend this compassion toward them, we will find that we experience suffering as well—a suffering just as natural and as inevitable. This suffering too cannot be remediated. Both the oppressed and those who either witness or even participate in oppression will encounter a time when their world has been turned upside down. All illusions will be stripped away. Our greatest fears will stare us in the face. That is the moment when a consequential moral decision must be made. And so, it is this moral dimension of suffering to which we must now turn.

Suffering and Evil

The earlier quote by Frank (2001) states that suffering is experienced as something that should not be. Something has occurred that is irreparably wrong. Here Frank is invoking the ethical and moral meaning of suffering. The study of ethics historically has placed the problem of good and evil at the center of attention. Consideration of the causes of suffering and ways to better understand and manage it are inextricably bound up with questions regarding what the good life is, how ought human beings be treated, and what is just and unjust. The existential dichotomy of good versus evil lies at the heart of the problem of suffering because of the vast amount of suffering created by evil actions and because on some level suffering is often seen as a form of evil. In his critique of psychology's neglect of the issue of evil, Miller (2013) makes an impassioned case for this:

> To simply characterize human activities as wrong, stupid, destructive, or hurtful is insufficient in some circumstances. Though criminal is sometimes synonymous with evil, in contemporary society it is mostly used to refer to actions that are illegal and punishable by the law. However, some human actions are so vile and destructive that they undermine the very basis of human existence. These actions destroy the fabric of meaning and community that make it possible to lead productive and fulfilling lives and reduce humans to physical shells that are empty, cold, and dead inside. There is evil in the

world that psychology must address, and it consists simply of this: Any act that destroys our trust in the reciprocity of human relationships and creates the belief that individuals need only look out for themselves and not one another is human evil. The more subtle, convoluted, devious, dishonest, and deceptive an act of utter self-interest is, the more evil....Blatant self-interest is destructive, but by being transparent it helps to delineate those who [sic] we can trust from those we cannot. Duplicitous self-interest that masquerades as kindness and concern for others is what most thoroughly erodes trust and faith in humanity. It seems that the greatest evils are perpetrated with the most deception and generally result in the greatest immediate advantage to the perpetrator. (pp. 232–233)

Miller's quote is particularly useful because its description of evil echoes themes that have already been encountered in the discussion of suffering. Evil, like suffering, unmakes one's world. It destroys the very fabric of human existence by transforming its victims into mere lifeless objects, thus depriving them of their humanity. In the process, the evildoer also becomes dehumanized. Perpetrators of evil demonstrate an extreme degree of egotism and self-centeredness that lead them to place their interests above those of all others. This narcissistic orientation colors their relationships, rendering them incapable of establishing connections with others characterized by mutual respect and understanding. Instead they seek to manipulate and control others and see them as a means to attaining their own selfish ends. Evil proves destructive to relationships as it creates or accentuates ruptures, divisions, and fragmentation rather than harmony and integration. Evil is often cloaked in a façade of kindness, concern, and benevolence so as to mask the evildoers' actual intent. Thus, any understanding of evil must include an examination of deception, including self-deception. The self-deception behind evil actions often ends up being self-defeating. All these themes will be considered more closely in this section.

Miller (2013) asserts that psychology's neglect of the subject of evil can be rectified in part by a closer study of philosophy and theology. There is a long tradition in moral philosophy to pose questions about how to understand and relieve suffering and establish what is good and evil (Nussbaum, 1995). However, even greater importance has been given to the subject of evil in theological literature. Most religious traditions see the issues of suffering and evil as inextricably interwoven. The linking of suffering and evil is central to theodicies, a term coined by German mathematician and philosopher Gottfried Leibnitz in 1710 to designate a way of answering the question of how an all-good and all-powerful God permits evil and the suffering that comes with it. Further, even non-theistic religions often seek to grapple with questions such as why bad things happen, why good or innocent people suffer, and why human beings inflict harm on themselves or others. A brief review of some of the major ideas from these religious traditions will thus not only substantiate the necessity of recognizing the moral dimension of suffering, but also help to elucidate some of the key elements of evil noted earlier.

A natural place to begin this examination is to ask whether evil and suffering are one and the same and, if not, what relationship exists between them. Recognizing that there is a diversity of views on this, it is commonly asserted nonetheless that there is a distinction between them. The term "evil" is more often used to describe human wickedness as expressed in acts rooted in aggression, cruelty and selfishness (Hebblethwaite, 1976). This is again referred to as moral evil. In his examination of extreme forms of suffering, Staub (1989) elucidates the role that this form of evil plays in oppression, "The essence of evil is the destruction of human beings. This includes not only killing but the creation of conditions that materially and psychologically destroy or diminish people's dignity, happiness, and capacity to fulfill basic material needs" (p. 25).

Staub also offers several more observations that illustrate the role of deception and self-deception in evil. The first is that evil cannot be judged based upon the conscious intentions of the perpetrators. This is because the ability of individuals to distort or hide their motivations may make them unaware of their true intentions for doing harm. Contrary to thinking they are doing something evil, perpetrators may attribute harmful actions to serving a noble purpose, such as truth or justice. Additionally, they may regard the suffering of victims as merited due to some wrongdoing on their part. Such defenses are often employed because of the powerful need that individuals have to hide their evil motives and actions from others in order to preserve a positive self-image. We will see later how strategies like these are employed by a hegemonic ideology to justify oppression and gain the consent of the oppressed to the harms being inflicted on them.

In contrast, there is natural evil that cannot be attributed to human wickedness. Examples here are forms of physical and mental suffering caused by things like aging, illness, or natural disasters. Even suffering not caused by human wickedness is deemed evil in the sense of being undesirable and contrary to a "good life." Just because the suffering inflicted by natural evil is due to larger natural forces over which we have no control, this does not mean that it has no connection to oppression. One reason for this is because a common way of disguising or rationalizing oppression created by human beings is to falsely attribute "natural" causes to others' suffering or to erroneously claim that victims of oppression are responsible for suffering that is actually based in natural causes over which they have little or no control.

For example, while thousands of people die due to natural disasters every year, it is nevertheless the case that injustice and inequity place members of certain groups more in harm's way. The vulnerable, excluded, and discriminated members of society are typically more at risk of being the victims of these disasters (Cutter, 2006). In his study of the deaths caused by the heat wave in Chicago in 1995, Eric Klinenberg (2002) describes how ethnic and racial factors and elements of the social environment in which isolated and excluded individuals lived placed them at greater risk. However, the City of Chicago obfuscated the actual causal factors in its report on the disaster by essentially attributing the disaster to an extreme and deadly climate event—i.e., an act of God.

Conversely, the higher morbidity and mortality rates of those who are at the lowest rungs of society are frequently attributed to their choosing to engage in unhealthy and destructive behaviors and neglecting to take care of themselves. The argument is that it is bad health habits that lead to their sickness and early death. However, this deceptive characterization utterly ignores the now well-established literature on the adverse impact of inequality on the poor (Marmot & Wilkinson, 2006). The unfair circumstances into which individuals are born and which, over time, exert an increasingly damaging impact on their health are not ones that these individuals choose and are often beyond their control to alter. And yet it is precisely these factors that undermine their well-being.

This does not mean that human choice plays no role in creating evil. There is considerable self-created suffering based upon choices which human beings make. Hebblethwaite (1976) writes

> By far the most common explanation, within the theistic religions, of a great deal of evil and suffering is based on the fact of human freedom. If at least one of God's purposes in creation was to establish a world of personal beings over against himself

and able to enter into personal relations with each other and with him, then they must have been created free to choose either good or evil. The only alternative was a world of puppets programmed to act rightly, and that would not have been a world of persons. Indeed the notion of acting rightly would have no application, since moral goodness necessarily involves free choice. The possibility of a wrong choice had to be allowed. Moral evil and the suffering it causes are to be explained as resulting from this necessary condition of a world of persons. (pp. 51–52)

As Hebblethwaite observes, the question of morality would not enter into judging the choices human beings make in the absence of freedom. If people are compelled to act in a certain way (like puppets) by some external force, they are not the authors of their actions and so cannot be held accountable. While there are circumstances in which this may be the case, many choices people make are ones in which there are alternative possibilities from which to choose. One of the principal reasons for why there is always at least one alternative course of action when making a decision again resides in human beings' capacity for thinking dialectically. Because one thing always implies its opposite, human beings can confront any circumstance and imagine that it can be otherwise. The ability to question and imagine that comes with self-reflection ensures that any given possibility can always imply an alternative option, and thus ensures free will. This essential ingredient of freedom is recognized by May (1981), who describes it as "...being able *to harbor different possibilities in one's mind even though it is not clear at the moment which way one must act*" (pp. 12–13, italics in the original).

Erich Fromm (1964) adds one other element to this process. The process of weighing various options and deliberating prior to making a choice also cannot be removed from a moral framework because choices are informed by values. Rollo May (1981, p. 6) calls free will "the mother of all values" because it is basic to our capacity to value anything at all. The very act of freely choosing one possibility from others is to give preference to one of them, to value it above the others. Embedded in every choice is an awareness that every person has about the motives and intentions behind his or her actions. Fromm (1964) writes, "Awareness means that the person makes that which he learns his own, by experiencing it, experimenting with himself, observing others and, eventually, gaining a conviction rather than having an irresponsible 'opinion'" (p. 133). Individuals may (and often do) deny or disavow the values and motives that inform their actions. Nonetheless it is precisely our actions and the consequences they have that expose our values and intentions far more than anything we might say to the contrary. Again, Fromm writes, "Man's freedom lies in his possibility to choose between the existing real possibilities (alternatives). Freedom in this sense can be defined as acting on the basis of awareness of alternatives and their consequences" (p. 143).

Freedom is thus inseparable from responsibility. Choices have consequences. Sometimes these are not of great significance and other times they are. However, irrespective of the magnitude of impact of any particular choice, it is the pattern of choices human beings make that ultimately charts the course of their lives. The framework in which Fromm (1964) places this developmental process is viewing these choices as affirming either a biophilous (good, life-affirming) or necrophilous (evil, death-affirming) orientation. The biophilous orientation sees the good as that which reveres, advances, and enhances life, growth, and the flourishing of human possibilities. From this orientation, human beings are respected and accorded the compassion and dignity that they deserve. The social conditions promoted by the biophilous orientation are characterized by justice and abundance. Conversely, the necrophilous orientation advances evil by being opposed to life. It seeks to possess and control and thus transforms nature and even other human beings into objects. In its extreme form it adopts a sadistic attitude aimed at achieving complete control over other human beings and in the process humiliating, enslaving, and doing with them as one pleases. The social conditions promoted by the necrophilous orientation are characterized by injustice and oppression.

It is clear that the consequences of each choice one makes extend outward toward the world upon which he or she is acting and inward in the shaping of his or her character. Goldberg (1995), in reflecting on Fromm's work, observes that the character of individuals is forged and shaped over time by the choices they make. We essentially learn by doing. Each moment in our lives we are called upon to choose between good and evil. No matter how minor or major the decision may be, it leaves its mark upon us and shapes the moral choices we make in the future. For Fromm, each evil choice hardens our hearts and each good choice softens our hearts. The hardening of our hearts strips us of all that makes us human—reason, freedom, love. As we become inhuman, we treat others inhumanely as well and so inflict suffering on others and ourselves.

What is not elucidated in this explanation about free will is specifically why human beings choose to do bad things. Like the questions raised about why there is so much suffering in the world, many answers have been proposed and not surprisingly no consensus has been reached. However, despite this complexity and disagreement, this question cannot be completely neglected when examining the relevance of evil to the problem of oppression. Any such neglect would block meaningful efforts aimed at discovering reasons for why people engage in oppression and finding ways of ending its destructive impact. One of the answers most often proposed to this question is one we have already encountered. The experience of exercising our freedom and the necessity of accepting responsibility for the consequences of our choices bring with it considerable fear. The power to create ourselves through the choices we make and to constitute the world in which we live by endowing it with meaning is often experienced as frightening, an onerous burden from which we try to escape.

Fear of the burden of freedom has been a frequent topic in existential philosophy. Kierkegaard (1980) traces the entwining of free will and suffering to the story of Adam and Eve. In this story we witness the birth of free will with the attainment of the capacity for self-reflection, the ability to examine ourselves, and to think hypothetically. All this begins with Adam and Eve eating the fruit of the Tree of Knowledge of Good and Evil. The seeds for this first act of free will were actually planted by God explicitly prohibiting Adam and Eve from doing so. Kierkegaard observes that telling Adam and Eve that they "may not" do something actually awakens in them for the first time the realization that they "can." They have the choice to act contrary to this prohibition. As symbolized by the tree from which they ate the forbidden fruit, Adam and Eve acquired awareness that with knowledge of good there simultaneously comes knowledge of evil. They can think dialectically, and that leads to a very dramatic change in how they experience the world and themselves. The capacity for self-reflection makes Adam and Eve self-conscious. This is illustrated by the shame experienced by Adam and Eve upon discovering that they are naked. They are also now able to pretend and act as if something is the case even if it is not. And so, for the first time they are able to lie and be deceptive when they deny that they have done anything wrong when confronted by God. But most important, the ability to imagine and think hypothetically means they can distinguish between good and evil. They can question and challenge what seems to be given and imagine an alternative. Again, if a person is faced with a situation in which one and only one option is possible, free will is meaningless. However, for Adam and Eve a world of seemingly endless possibilities had been opened.

The story of Adam and Eve also makes it very clear that with free will comes suffering, as made evident in their banishment from paradise. But why is this so? Kierkegaard (1980) continues with his analysis by describing the suffering that accompanies freedom as dread (or anxiety). This dread is an expression of the "dizziness" of freedom— the realization that with freedom comes a vast number of possibilities from which one must eventually choose. One might think that this "dizziness" would be exhilarating and exciting—and in a certain respect they would be correct as free will had made both Adam and Eve god-like. The ability to imagine enables us to face any situation without succumbing to the hopeless notion that it is fixed and unchangeable. Nothing is given once and for all. There is always the possibility that it can be otherwise—the very basis for hope and optimism. However, that is not the complete story. As Kierkegaard observes, dread or anxiety is an experience characterized by a deep ambivalence in which we are simultaneously drawn to and repelled by our ability to imagine alternatives and choose from multiple options.

What this means is that in recognizing their freedom individuals can no longer take refuge in the comfort and certainty that can be provided by a world that is fixed, predictable, and orderly. Likewise, there no longer are incontrovertible rules readily available to us that prescribe precisely what to do when faced with any of life's diverse circumstances. The tried and true that we have habitually looked to when faced by uncertainty is shattered by the intrusion of the unknown and unexpected. Yalom (1980) describes this as *groundlessness*, which frightens us by the lack of any structure, ultimate authority, or magic answers to guide our decisions. As a result, this dizziness is also experienced as a deep sense of apprehension and even paralysis. Not knowing in which direction to throw our weight, fearing what will follow any choice we make, we feel suspended between two horns of what feels like an unresolvable dilemma.

In order to understand the anguish and fear that attend exercising our freedom, we must return to a core element of suffering discussed previously—a sense of loss embedded in experiences of emptiness, uncertainty, and feeling uprooted. May (1981) utilizes what he calls the "pause" to describe the experience of exercising free will. This is meant to describe that moment when we are facing the array of options open to us and become aware of the various forces that seem to be exerting influence on what choice we will make. It is at this moment before any decision or commitment is made that May believes a person is most vulnerable to anxiety. Embedded in the experience of the pause is an encounter with a void or sense of groundlessness as the individual, prior to making any commitment, is rooted in nothing and no one. In other words, for the moment everything is open, nothing is settled, and only the person can make a choice. The experience of the pause can thus bring with it a profound sense of doubt and uncertainty that can be extremely unsettling.

The exercise of free will is inextricably interwoven with the necessity of confronting loss. This occurs in various ways. To begin with, whenever we make a choice from a range of options, we are not only realizing one possibility, but at the same time we are negating countless other possibilities that for the moment are lost to us. For example, in the act of committing myself to one person in marriage or pursuing a particular career path, I must accept that all the other choices I could have made are "dead to me." Further, when I recognize that some choice is open to me to pursue, I must also recognize that for all intents and purposes it represents something that is currently not the case. If I set a goal for myself to someday become an accountant or nurse, I am admitting that at present I am neither of these things. This is still another way in which freedom requires me to confront a sense of lack or emptiness that can give rise to suffering. This can particularly be the case at those times when individuals look back over their life and feel a deep sense of grief and disappointment at all the opportunities that have passed them by or all the hopes and dreams that they never dared to pursue. And finally, in exercising my freedom there is no guarantee that I will realize my possibilities or attain my goals. My future is not completely under my control, and there are no guarantees that come with any choice I make. Dashed hopes and dreams unfulfilled are a common cause of suffering. The experience of loss that accompanies the exercise of freedom can thus take many different forms.

The suffering that accompanies freedom can, in fact, become so intolerable that an individual engages in strategies designed to recoil from making any choice at all or to seek some means of surrendering his/her freedom to someone or something else. A detailed examination of these strategies will be conducted at a later point. However, there is one form of evasion that merits examination here as it provides some further valuable insights on the nature of suffering. This comes from the work of M. Scott Peck (1983) whose thinking was influenced by the work of Erich Fromm. Like Fromm, Peck sees evil as contrary to life and as rooted in an exaggerated need to control others in a way that stifles their humanity. However, there is another element of Fromm's (1964) work on suffering that has not been examined. This element— the role of malignant narcissism—occupies a central place in Peck's analysis. This will touch on points made previously in the section on the problem of the ego.

For Peck, it is not the committing of wrongdoings that characterize evil people because we all are imperfect and make bad decisions. Rather, evil people have an extreme need to maintain an image of their being perfect, righteous, and above reproach. Thus, they cannot tolerate becoming aware of or being confronted by their failure and inability to attain the perfection they crave. As Peck (1983) observes, "It is not their sins per se that characterize evil people, rather it is the subtlety and persistence and consistency of their sins. This is because the central defect of the evil is not the sin but the refusal to acknowledge it" (p. 69). They cannot tolerate it because when confronted with their misdeeds and evil actions, it pains them. The call of conscience and its demands for righteousness and justice are a source of suffering for them rather than an invitation to examine their actions, feel remorse, and choose differently. To evade this pain, evil individuals engage in self-deceptive measures. One of the most common is projecting their evil on others and scapegoating them. They also lash out against anyone who presumes to question their righteous self-image or expose their misdeeds. Evil individuals also often possess an exaggerated sense of morality and thus are not truly unaware of their transgressions. This presents a paradox in which they are painfully aware of the wrong they do and harm they cause, but at the same time desperately try to evade their awareness through rationalization and other defensive measures in order to reassure themselves of their righteousness and to appear good to others whose opinions matter to them.

This inability to admit to flaws, weaknesses, or failures, paired with a tendency to project what they disown about themselves unto others, is rooted in malignant narcissism. Fromm (1964) contrasts this with a more benign form of narcissism that promotes self-preservation and bases one's sense of esteem on what one has attained and achieved through his or her own efforts. In contrast, malignant narcissism is an irrational and excessive form of self-love in which persons transform themselves into their own absolute, an idol to be worshipped and before which all else must be sacrificed. Motivated by selfishness and greed, they desire to possess more and more even if it is at the expense of others. Their egocentric focus means that they are incapable of empathy with others and so their relations tend to be exploitative even to the point of not valuing the lives of others at all. Their insatiable need for control is manifested in an unrestrained willfulness that refuses to submit to anyone or anything. Though such individuals convey a sense of superiority and invulnerability, they actually feel a gnawing sense of insecurity and are constantly frightened of being confronted with their own evil and sense of imperfection. This fear of exposure terrifies them. Once again, they employ a range of defenses in order to avoid such confrontation.

Individuals who can be characterized by this form of malignant narcissism are unfortunately not uncommon. However, malignant narcissism must be understood as existing on a continuum, a matter of degree. As Fromm (1964) asserts, the development of an evil character is a gradual process that unfolds over time. Further, while it may become more and more difficult to stop one's movement toward a necrophilous orientation, by virtue of our possessing free will it is always possible for us to choose differently and change direction. He sagely observed, "Man's heart can harden; it can become inhuman, yet never unhuman. It always remains man's heart" (p. 150). That said, it must also be understood that human history is replete with countless examples of individuals who demonstrated a degree of malignant narcissism of demonic proportions responsible for horrific acts of destruction and terrible tragedies. It is certain that malignant narcissism is a powerful force at work in all forms of oppression.

The Muteness of Suffering: Promise and Peril

There is one final element of suffering to be discussed that is highlighted in the quotes by Frank (2001) and Morgan and Wilkinson (2001). Suffering is "the unspeakable" and so beyond words. It is an experience of such intensity and power that it cannot be articulated. Anything we might say pales in comparison to what we are feeling. Because it defies expression, there is the risk that an individual's experience may remain invisible and sets what seems an unbridgeable distance between him or her and others. Despite this, it must always be remembered that the sufferer retains absolute authority regarding the experience, and he or she alone can bear testimony to it.

The muteness of suffering has often been observed by a range of writers. One such person was mystic and social activist Simone Weil

(1997) who made significant contributions to our understanding of suffering with her idea of *affliction*. Both the promise and peril posed by the muteness of suffering can be found in her writing. Weil suffered from a number of physical maladies, including years of frailty and chronic pain. Toward the end of her life, she was diagnosed with tuberculosis. Despite this, she continued to engage in ascetic practices (food restriction), which some feel may have then contributed to her death at the age of 34. Weil's many years of social activism on behalf of the poor, dispossessed, and exploited working class enabled her to gain valuable insights into the horrific impact of oppression and the means by which we can oppose it. Included in this is the tension that occurs amid affliction between a sense of isolation and estrangement and the experience of communion and sharing.

In an article, Helsel (2009) explains how Weil's experience with chronic pain shaped her understanding of the nature of suffering and her theology. Affliction is one of the most profound and powerful descriptions of suffering that one can find. It is caused by an event of such magnitude that it exerts complete control over a person's life. Thus, it impacts every facet of a person. It is more than something physical and mental; it also has social and spiritual impacts. The social impacts afford important insights into the role of oppression in affliction. Those who are the afflicted are not merely ignored but are the object of degradation, repulsion, and hatred by others. These feelings of contempt and loathing are then directed by the afflicted against themselves. From a spiritual perspective, the suffering of the afflicted is so intense that they feel abandoned and estranged from God. This makes their suffering even more unbearable as there is nowhere they can turn for comfort or help. They feel robbed of any sense of the future and any possibility of hope; they instead are faced with total annihilation.

For Weil, such a powerful experience of suffering robs individuals of the ability to communicate the depth of their despair. The muteness of suffering and the degree to which it is an utterly personal experience lead to additional pain in the form of loneliness, a sense of isolation from others, and fear of abandonment. Inability to share their experience intensifies the sense of disconnection and estrangement they feel toward themselves, other human beings, and even God. This echoes the previous discussion of the theme of separation and alienation in the experience of suffering. Despite the private and lonely nature of pain, Weil saw that it also paradoxically demands that it be shared with others in order to overcome the alienation that it has created. Because of the inadequacy of words and the essential incommunicability of the experience, any hope of help is possible only through the anguished outcry of the sufferer. In the sharing, there can still be risks of alienation as one may still be rejected, ignored. or misunderstood. However, there is also the promise that one's anguish can be alleviated through the restoration of communion not only with others, but with oneself and ultimately with God. In coming to a deeper understanding of our experience of affliction, we may also be better able to understand, and connect with, the affliction experienced by others. And so, for Weil, the muteness of suffering offers the potential for healing and transcendence, even though the potential remains that the sufferers may become trapped within their subjective experience of suffering. Inability to give full and genuine expression to their pain makes it much more likely that those who suffer experience invalidation, insensitivity, and stigmatization.

This same dilemma surrounding the private nature of suffering is noted by Scarry (1985). The deeply personal and subjective nature of the experience of suffering leaves little doubt of its validity in the mind of the sufferer. Nonetheless, as Scarry sagely observes, this same subjectivity can make this suffering invisible and intangible to others. The invisibility and incommunicability of suffering make it much easier for observers to question or even doubt the reality of the pain of another. They can doubt the sincerity of the sufferer and presume that his or her pain is feigned or even self-induced and thus deserved. This sort of judgmental and callous response is especially pernicious when suffering is inflicted on individuals and then dismissed as contrived or merited by the very same people who inflicted it. This is akin to the pattern of blaming the victim, with the added indignity of those doing the blaming being the ones responsible for the harm done to the victims.

The muteness of suffering thus contributes to its denial and mystification. We have already seen that humans innately experience anxiety and dread in the face of the prospect of loss and suffering, accompanied by resistance and denial. This response occurs whether we are confronted by our own loss or loss experienced by another. Anything that might buffer us from our fear and discomfort will readily be seized upon. Suffering that cannot be expressed provides us with an excuse to turn a deaf ear and blind eye. The next step is to stigmatize victims and, in doing so, achieve a sense of emotional and social distance from them. This distance makes it less likely that we will enter into the experience of the victim and make a compassionate response.

This denial and mystification of another's suffering justifies many forms of oppression in the eyes of the oppressors. Being deprived of a voice is itself a commonly practiced form of oppression. Unable to bear witness to their experience, the oppressed are more easily marginalized and disenfranchised. To put words to one's experience, no matter how inadequate and imperfect they may be, is essential to being recognized and accepted as a human being in one's own right.

The tension between the muteness of suffering and its social dimension is examined by Radley (2004) within a medical setting. Acknowledging this tension, he then describes the quandary it poses to both the sufferer who seeks solace and to those witnessing the suffering and questioning what their response should be:

> When undergoing suffering, people may find it impossible to convey that which engulfs them. What is communicable to other people is the apprehension of, or the memory of, changes to self and world that suffering induces. It is quite possible, then, that others identify these expressions of pain and loss as being suffering itself. Out of this it is possible to consider the person "as sufferer" in the light of having coped with the events that attach to his or her illness situation. Social judgments can then be made concerning the degree to which the person coped well with difficulties, so that suffering itself becomes a means by which the person can lay claim to a higher moral status. Once communicated in this way, suffering gains a social form, or rather the person's experience is made available as a concrete instance to which ideologies of coping can be applied. (p. 34)

In trying to describe their pain, those who suffer employ language in order to somehow concretize or categorize it. This may render their suffering easier to communicate to another and correspondingly easier for others to also categorize the experience and devise some means to respond to it.

However, as theologian and social activist Dorothy Soelle (2001) observes, in the process something essential and meaningful about the experience is lost. Suffering is a type of extreme and extraordinary human experience in which we discover the helplessness and even the perils of language. There is an entire dimension of human experience in which we know more than we can say. Scientist and philosopher Michael Polanyi (1967) called this *tacit knowledge*. Suffering is one such experience. On the opposite side of the spectrum, one of the defining characteristics of elevated states of awareness (mystical or peak experiences) is their ineffability or inability to be put into words (James, 1958). It is interesting that in her study of mystical or elevated states, Laski (1968) found that states of intense suffering can also be a trigger for such experiences. The problem is not merely that words are insufficient to capture what we wish to express. Under such circumstances we would do well to remember what the philosopher Ludwig Wittgenstein observed, "Whereof one cannot speak, thereof one must be silent." There are times when language can prove harmful either because we mistakenly try to distill something essential to our experience within the narrow confines of words or because language is employed as a means of distorting or denying our experience. Another way in which these dangers can occur is when language is utilized as an instrument of power for purposes of control or domination. This will be discussed at greater length in the later chapter on mystification

As the quote above by Radley (2004) makes clear, the situation involving communication between those who suffer and professionals who seek to provide care is rife with hazards. We may clearly invite those who suffer to tell their story. Such narratives play a critical role in helping them make sense of their suffering and providing it with some meaning (Kleinman, 1988). But we must take care not to convey the requirement that they communicate their suffering in order for their suffering to be acknowledged and to receive care. This places an unfair and unreasonable expectation due to the muteness of suffering. Additionally, this expectation is often based more upon the discomfort, fear, and guilt aroused in those who witness suffering than in the desire to be of help. Language offers a means of "explaining" or "categorizing" suffering from a safe and comfortable distance (Dass & Gorman, 1985). Radley points out that the inherently moral nature of suffering requires that we make a moral response to it. Compassion can be extended to those who suffer through the acknowledgment of its presence and simply by its being recognized for what it is—including its muteness.

The Transformative Power of Suffering: Compassion

Given what has been written thus far, it is abundantly clear that one cannot overestimate the horrors and destructiveness of suffering. Thus, it may be surprising to find that throughout the extensive literature on suffering there have been writers and thinkers who have attested to another side to it. This other side of suffering is its potential to be a stimulus for growth, an opportunity for loss to provide a means of promoting transcendence, and an essential ingredient for the cultivation of compassion. Make no mistake; this is typically not the way in which suffering is portrayed in the predominant ideology that shapes our fundamental beliefs and values. Nor is it the view that informs the models of care for those who work with those who suffer. In the commonly accepted view of things, suffering is seen as having absolutely no value. It is regarded as antithetic to the pursuit of happiness so highly valued in American culture. It is an evil that, if possible, should be completely eradicated. This perspective is captured well by Moulyn (1982):

> The question why we suffer has generated many answers of a cosmological, ethical, religious, logical, and philosophical nature...Whatever the answers, the question why we suffer always starts from the premise that it is against the natural state of affairs, which is happiness. This premise is grounded on the belief that suffering is a sign of evil, that our wrongdoings and our sins are the causes of our sufferings. One concludes that suffering is valueless because it destroys happiness. (pp. 5–6)

This one-sidedly negative view of suffering is just as dangerous and problematic as the viewpoint that seeks to dismiss or underestimate how harmful it is. In both cases, there is a lack of appreciation for the fundamental existential paradoxes that are embedded in the experience of suffering. Those paradoxes may sometimes confound our attempt to grasp what we are undergoing, but without them there is no real opportunity of giving meaning to the experience of suffering. It is in the struggle or coming to terms with loss that a way forward is discerned, and not in fixing our attention on the past and what has been lost or on some imagined future that can only be our way out. As the poet Rainer Maria Rilke wrote:

> Be patient toward all that is unsolved in your heart and try to love the questions themselves, like locked rooms and like books that are now written in a very foreign tongue. Do not now seek the answers, which cannot be given you because you would not be able to live them. And the point is, to live everything. Live the questions now. Perhaps you will then gradually, without noticing it, live along some distant day into the answer.

No matter what form avoidance of suffering takes, it blocks our efforts to meet suffering with the open and compassionate response required to promote healing.

As I noted in the Introduction, it was a rude awakening for me to find how little serious attention was devoted to the problem of suffering by those in professions charged with providing help and comfort to the afflicted, including medicine and my own profession of psychology. physician Eric Cassell (1991) observes:

> When I discussed the problem of suffering with laypersons, I learned that they were shocked to discover that it was not directly addressed in medical education. My colleagues of a contemplative nature were surprised at how little they knew about the problem and how little thought they had given it, whereas medical students were not sure of the relevance of the issue of suffering to their work. (p. 31)

While physicians have responsibility to offer more than just relief to those who are suffering, Cassell found that medical literature and education had little to say about this. Rather, a great deal of focus was given to pain. Though there is clearly some connection between pain and suffering, as Cassell notes, they are not synonymous. Cassell concludes that the focus on pain to the neglect of suffering is based on the narrowness and inadequacy of medicine's traditional concern primarily for physical disease and the persistence of their holding to a mind–body dualism. As a consequence, medicine not only fails to fully attend to the suffering of those with physical afflictions but also to the psychological distress inextricably related to illness and to the suffering sometimes caused by medical treatment itself. Cassell's analysis is also valuable because it illustrates the role played by the politically and economically dominant biomedical model in the neglect of suffering— a critique that we will see raised again when investigating more closely the role of neoliberal ideology in perpetuating both suffering and oppression.

More recently, psychologist Ronald B. Miller (2005) offered a cogent and passionate critique of psychology's neglect of suffering. Like Goldberg and Crespo (2003) and others (Kleinman, 1988), he asserts that suffering must be situated within the moral realm and the practice of ethics. He also argues that psychology must eschew its evasion of the inherently moral nature of its study and practice and give open and careful consideration to the insights regarding suffering that have been offered by philosophy and theology. It was these insights that enabled me to gain a very different perspective on suffering and find in it a way of honoring both its destructive and painful nature as well as its potential to promote healing and growth (Gruba-McCallister, 1992; Gruba-McCallister & Levington, 1995). The very same suffering that arises from our encounters with conflicts, ruptures, and contradictions has a constructive element. It stimulates efforts to translate these conflicts into positive change by discovering answers and solutions that ultimately either eliminate avoidable suffering or provide meaning to inescapable suffering (Moulyn, 1982).

There have been eloquent and influential voices who have spoken to this constructive side to suffering. One is theologian and social activist Dorothy Soelle (1975). As an ardent advocate for social justice, Soelle condemns the considerable suffering inflicted through poverty, torture, war, and other abuses of power. For that reason, it is essential that we establish the causes of suffering and under what conditions it can be eliminated *as well as* the meaning of suffering and under what conditions it can make us more human. These two areas of inquiry echo the distinction between inescapable suffering and self-created suffering. Discerning between these two forms of suffering is essential to avoiding misunderstandings that then lead to ways of dealing with suffering that exact even greater costs from the afflicted. While we may acknowledge the universality of suffering, we must take great care not to use this as an excuse to deflect from the role that historical, economic, and political factors play in doing significant harm—harm that is avoidable. This way of thinking leads individuals to experience what Soelle calls *apathy*, the inability to acknowledge and participate in the suffering of the oppressed.

According to Soelle, it is apathy, not pleasure, that is the opposite of suffering. She writes, "Apathy is a form of the inability to suffer. It is understood as a social condition in which people are so dominated by the goal of avoiding suffering that it becomes a goal to avoid human relationships and contacts altogether" (p. 36). For those who are not suffering or who are inflicting suffering on others, this apathy causes them to essentially feel nothing. Soelle compares this to Fromm's necrophilous orientation. This is because such lack of feeling expresses a form of sadism or an insensitivity that gives rise to contempt for humanity itself and the devaluing of the human person. This insensitivity is cultivated by a society based on an ideology that teaches individuals to deal with their own suffering and suffering due to injustice using illusion, minimization, and suppression. Victims of societal suffering are exhorted to passively submit and patiently endure it based on the false promise that someday (usually after death) they will know happiness and attain their just rewards. This inculcates and reinforces a sense of powerlessness in the victims that undermines their self-esteem, exploits their dependency, and deprives their life of meaning.

A second eloquent voice speaking to the transformative power of suffering is Elaine Scarry (1985). While suffering is a power that unmakes one's world, it has another side to it. She notes that the word "labor" is associated both with the experience of pain and with the idea of work. These two meanings are interwoven in the expression, "a labor of love" as it conveys the understanding that a certain degree of pain and suffering is an essential part of the creative process. This can be explained on a very basic level. The collapse, destruction, or disintegration of some idea, commonly accepted point of view, or long-held belief is a necessary first step for something new to emerge. Polish psychiatrist Kazimierz Dabrowski (1964) proposes a theory based on this process, which he calls *positive disintegration*. Development can be conceptualized as a series of stages or levels through which human beings move in order to achieve progressively higher levels of functioning and well-being. However, in order to move from one stage to the next, there needs to be a disintegration or breakdown of the habitual forms of thinking, feeling, and coping at our current level of development. These are moments of loss that bring with them a certain degree of anxiety, uncertainty, and suffering. But what can emerge from this suffering is the motivation to grow and mature. There are several bodies of research that support this view of development, including Antonovsky's (1987) salutogenic model that explores factors that facilitate health-promoting responses to stress, and the clinical research on post-traumatic growth (Calhoun & Tedeschi, 1999).

Another way in which suffering and creativity are entwined is witnessed in the arts. The word "passion" is illustrative of this connection as its etymological root is in Sanskrit "pati," which means to suffer. To suffer for one's art is for many to transform their personal experiences of pain, loss, disappointment, and oppression into works of great power and beauty. The channeling of one's passion is often a pivotal element in significant achievements across various areas of human endeavor. Ludwig van Beethoven, considered by many to be one of the most eminent of all composers, produced his greatest work while grappling with the progressive loss of his hearing (Sullivan, 1960). As

Scarry asserts, notable examples of creative work are the product of voluntary and controlled suffering.

One final influential spokesperson for the transformative potential of suffering was Viennese psychiatrist Viktor Frankl. Frankl was a Holocaust survivor, imprisoned in concentration camps from 1944 to 1945. His wife, mother, and brother all died in the Holocaust. These experiences, which he chronicles in his book *Man's Search for Meaning* (1959), were seminal in shaping Frankl's work and philosophy. He founded a school of psychological treatment called logotherapy. Frankl examined how human beings dealt with a very dramatic and dire confrontation in a set of circumstances giving rise to suffering over which he, like other concentration camp prisoners, exercised no control. Despite the horrors of such a situation, Frankl believed that even under such conditions individuals could still discover the ultimate purpose and meaning of their lives. When all other choices are taken away, the one freedom that remains to persons under these conditions is the attitude or stance they assume toward these unchangeable facts. It is by means of assigning attitudinal value that persons can find meaning in their suffering—a meaning that allows them to transmute their anguish into something that enables them to surmount it.

In adopting this stance, Frankl (1967) was a sharp critic of a prevalent view at that time that saw the pursuit of pleasure as the principal motivation for human behavior (hedonism). He also criticized the belief that homeostasis, or a state of static balance, was necessary for well-being. The homeostatic view sees the tension and conflict created by disruptions to one's sense of stability, order, and balance as both distressing and destructive. In order to remove this tension and discomfort, efforts are directed at restoring the previous state of balance. This is an inherently conservative point of view that regards change as undesirable and something to be resisted to maintain the status quo and keep things as stable as possible. Eliminating tension and restoring equilibrium brings with it pleasure, linking homeostasis with a hedonistic viewpoint. Making pleasure and the maintenance of balance the ultimate goals one should pursue in life, leaves little if any room for suffering.

However, as Frankl makes clear, the pursuit of both these goals is self-defeating. The limitations and problems of making pleasure the central goal of life were critiqued in the chapter on justice. For example, Amartya Sen (1999) argued that the utilitarian view fails to appreciate that wealth and the acquisition of resources are not valued as desirable goals in themselves, but due to the ways in which these things enable us to do the things we want to do and exercise our freedoms. Likewise, Frankl argues that happiness or pleasure cannot be the goal in life. First, because the harder we strive for pleasure, the less likely it is that we will attain it. Second, pleasure is not an end in itself but the byproduct of our pursuit of goals that have value, importance, and meaning to us.

Likewise, making homeostasis our primary goal is also misguided. Such a goal is rooted in an extreme need for control, a desire to render life into something that is utterly predictable. Such stability and order are an illusion. We have seen that the dynamic character of life is based on the inevitability of change and loss. The more we resist change (and the tension or distress that comes with it), the more we find our efforts futile, leading to the frustration and disappointment we were hoping to escape. Avoiding change is thus avoiding life and instead inviting death. Without change, our existence would sink into a stifling, boring, humdrum state. Rather than run from upheavals, we need to see them as opportunities to change in a positive and productive way.

For Frankl, the experience of suffering exposes a tension or conflict of great import. He (1967) writes, "Man does not need homeostasis at any cost, but rather a sound amount of tension such as that which is aroused by the demand quality...inherent in the meaning of human existence" (p. 21). What he means by this is that suffering opens a rift between what is and what ought to be. It shakes us out of automatic and habitual patterns that we are reluctant to examine or to alter. And because people would rather be right than happy, it is these very patterns that so often are a source of suffering for us and for others. Our proclivity to inertia, to pursuing the path of least resistance, is often so powerful that it is not until these patterns have been dashed to pieces that we awaken to the realization that they are neither inevitable nor desirable. The demand exerted on us by the "ought," by some higher value, obligation, or duty that we have to ourselves and others opens the window to new insights. These insights then can become the ferment for a commitment to strive to realize the higher values of justice and compassion—the keystones to unveiling and ending oppression.

Before this chapter is concluded, there is one other "fruit" of suffering that needs to be acknowledged—and that is compassion. The inextricable relation between compassion and justice has been a persistent theme. In the chapter on justice, the article by Williams (2008) is cited in which he asserts that compassion is the moral foundation of social justice. His extended treatment also discusses the role that suffering plays in making compassion possible. In this respect,

Williams' view accords with a long-standing perspective on suffering found in religious literature. In Christianity this is referred to as the Irenaean theodicy (Gruba-McCallister, 1992; Hick, 2007).

Recall that a theodicy is a system of religious thought used to explain the presence of evil and suffering in the world. Irenaeus was one of the early Christian fathers who lived in the second century. He proposed a teleological theodicy, which means that the suffering and unhappiness we experience in the present must be understood in conjunction with the ultimate goal toward which our lives are directed. Human beings are engaged in the process of self-perfection or what Hick (2007) calls "soul-making," For the process of seeking to improve and grow to unfold, human beings need to possess the ability to exercise choice as moral agents. That is, they must be able to make choices between good and evil. This, of course, means at times they will make choices that lead to suffering for themselves and others. It is not the suffering caused by these choices that offers the opportunity for growing more perfect, but the way we respond to this suffering. There are two fundamental responses open to us. The first, as discussed earlier, is to meet it with resistance and avoidance and so harden our hearts (Fromm, 1964).

The other is to let suffering awaken our natural capacity for compassion. There is an ever-growing body of research that supports how the societal nature of human beings provides us with the means to establish deep relationships with others, to connect with their feelings, to experience distress when we witness it in others, and to experience the desire to help them (Gibson, 2015; Jensen, Vaish, & Schmidt, 2014; O'Brien, 2014). This is not a new idea. The Chinese philosopher Mencius, who lived from 372 to 289 B.C.E., believed focus should be placed on the cultivation of *hsin*, which was both the chief organ of the circulatory system and the chief organ of thought. This is sometimes translated as "heart–mind." Every human being's heart–mind feels for others. Thus, there is an automatic response of shock and distress that human beings experience when witnessing the suffering of another. This offers a very contrary view to the one espoused by the current predominant ideology in which human beings are characterized as narcissistic, selfish, and competitive by nature. Little wonder that in such a climate compassion is not only devalued but stifled.

Williams (2008) observes that compassion expands rather than contracts the boundaries of the self because it is other-regarding. It is a reminder of our shared humanity and so opens the way for a deeper empathy between individuals. It is based upon our interconnectedness.

In seeing another's anguish, we are reminded of our own vulnerability and fallibility and recall moments of our own encounters with suffering. Even if the other's circumstances are different than any we have known, we can nevertheless acknowledge that "There but for the will of God go I." Some seek to set conditions on whether compassion is extended to another. For example, one might weigh whether the person's suffering is merited or deserved. Another might consider the degree of severity of the other's suffering. However, such judgments threaten to undermine a moral imperative to identify with the pain of another and seek to relieve it. This is particularly the case because of the degree to which social conditions and values influence how we render these judgments. If in some way a person may have brought on his or her own suffering, that does not mitigate the impact which it has on him or her and others. As Williams (2008) asserts, as a virtue compassion cannot be selective. The suffering of another must never be a matter of indifference to us no matter what the circumstances.

This brings us back to how essential recognition of the spiritual nature of human beings is. The fundamental interconnectedness of human beings is not some notion or belief that one may or may not choose to believe. It is a given, and because that is so our capacity for compassion is not something we may or may not choose to believe exists. It is a moral imperative that we suspend all judgment when faced with suffering. It does not matter who, what, why, or how. We need to heed that stirring deep within us that is awakened and the connection we feel to the sufferer. Returning to the soteriological function of religion first described in the Introduction, the transcendence of the narrow boundaries of the ego and commitment to the values of compassion and justice have been the ethical insights of the great teachers. It is in our nature to sympathize with others in their sorrows (as well as their joys), and without this capacity for fellow-feeling not only would morality not exist but neither would human society itself. As Hick (1989) concludes, "Love, compassion, self-sacrificing concern for the good of others, generous kindness and forgiveness...is not an alien ideal imposed by supernatural authority but one arising out of our human nature (though always in tension with other aspects of that nature), reinforced, refined and elevated to new levels within the religious traditions" (p. 325). And so, with that imperative now firmly fixed in our minds, let us proceed to examine the sundry forms that social suffering takes—the problem of oppression.

Chapter 4

Oppression

Oppression—the Social Sources of Suffering

In this chapter I will continue my examination of suffering but do so by shifting the focus away from the lens of the individual. This does not mean that we should not take the experience of any individual's suffering as inconsequential and unimportant. This tendency to dismiss or trivialize the experience of one who is suffering has already been identified as a regrettable but not uncommon response of perpetrator and victim alike. Suffering frequently stands as irrefutable testimony to the workings of oppression on the many millions who have been targeted by injustice. Meeting suffering with resistance inflicts additional harm in the form of self-created suffering and undermines any resolve to remove avoidable causes of suffering. The invalidation of a person's experience of suffering is a particularly pernicious form of violence perpetrated on those who are oppressed. This invalidation will be discussed at greater length in a later chapter. It is a key element in the process of mystification frequently practiced by oppressors to, first, disguise their role in inflicting harm on the oppressed and, second, foster a sense of alienation within their victims that causes them to doubt their own experience.

In the case of oppression, it is a person's membership in a group that exposes him or her to a greater likelihood of suffering. The suffering caused by oppression afflicts multiple individuals by virtue of their group membership. On one hand, while it may be shared by many people, the experience of anguish cannot be fully grasped by considering it some undifferentiated, collective phenomena. To do so would be transforming something concrete, definite, and uniquely nuanced into something abstract, general, and impersonal. But to confine our attention to the subjective and unique ways in which each member of a group experiences oppression would likewise not suit our purpose as it would obscure the many social causes of suffering. As Osterkamp (1999) asserts, "People's suffering as the essential criterion of society's insufficiency and the need for change, for instance, is not plainly visible but it can only fully be comprehended once there is a language to talk about it as well as some idea of human nature which can be violated and, thus, cause suffering" (p. 380).

The "idea of human nature" that Osterkamp refers to here is a key principle of Critical Psychology, introduced earlier, that recognizes the dialectical relationship of the subjective/individual and societal/ collective nature of human beings. This perspective enables us to strike the proper balance between two key dimensions of suffering critical to understanding oppression. Returning to a central argument of this book, oppression is the single greatest factor contributing to human suffering. The ways in which oppression gives rise to suffering cannot be fully grasped by adopting a narrow lens that omits the prominent role played by insufficiencies in a society rooted in injustice. As Osterkamp observes, without a language for describing these processes, the social causes of suffering are invisible. The ways in which existing power relations and prevailing ideological beliefs and values inflict suffering on the oppressed are often obscured by portraying the status quo as not only normal but inevitable.

Not only does this render victims of oppression impotent to do anything to alter their circumstances; it also imposes a silence upon them. This silence must be broken through to render the ideology transparent, to expose its taken-for-granted assumptions, and to cultivate conditions that allow individuals to question the status quo and their role in maintaining it. Critical Psychology challenges the assertion that human beings are shaped and controlled solely by the hegemonic ideology and prevailing social structures and practices. It acknowledges their two-sided nature and the ways in which suffering follows from violating both their societality and agency.

The first form of suffering is created by the insufficiency of that society to satisfy people's needs. According to the work of psychologist Abraham Maslow (1971), these needs range from the most basic physical ones to the need for affection and self-esteem to higher spiritual needs. Irrespective of what needs go unmet, such privation thwarts the ability of persons to realize the fullest extent of their development. We can think of this dimension of suffering as related to a distributive view of justice—that is, privation and impoverishment caused by the unfair and inequitable distribution of the resources and opportunities available to members of a society to fulfill their needs.

What is at issue here is not a form of deprivation that is shared across a society, but rather inequities in which there are abuses of power and members of the dominant group exploit members of subordinate ones. Additionally, this form of suffering arises from the interdependent relationship that exists between human beings who must rely upon each other and mutually cooperate in order to fulfill certain needs. While this is true for all human beings, it is particularly true for those more reliant on others due to factors such as age, vulnerability, and ability.

But that only captures half of the equation. Human beings are not completely helpless and passive in this process. As Schraube and Osterkamp (2013) point out, while human beings may not exert influence over or create conditions at the overall societal level, they do actively participate in producing, influencing, affirming, and transforming the specific life circumstances under which they live. Critical Psychology affirms the capacity of human beings for self-determination that affords them the opportunity to act and achieve control over resources for the satisfaction of needs. Thus, it is not merely deprivation that causes suffering but experiencing oneself as being deprived of control and at the mercy of others in order to meet those needs. Schraube and Osterkamp summarize these two sides to suffering as follows:

> Human suffering or, generally, any injury, including anxiety, has the quality of being exposed to and dependent upon other-directed circumstances, dissociated from possibilities of controlling essential, long-term conditions, i.e., constraints on possibilities to act. Correspondingly, overcoming suffering and anxiety, and the human quality of satisfaction is [sic] not obtainable merely by actual satisfaction and protection, but only by achieving control over the resources of satisfaction— that is, the conditions upon which one's possibilities of living and developing depend. (pp. 20–21)

Mere recognition of one's dependency is not a cause for anguish since such dependency to a degree is an inescapable part of our being social. However, when that dependency exposes us to being taken advantage of unfairly, we may be subjected to harm due to exploitation. We may then consider our dependency as some flaw or personal failing. This will only be amplified when we are exposed to an ideology that espouses the ideal of the person as being self-contained, independent, competitive, and self-reliant (Sampson, 1985). Such is the ideal espoused by neoliberalism. Knowing that I have little when others have so much is more than just an experience of deprivation. As will be seen when theory and literature on the impact of inequality are discussed later in this chapter, the experience of unfairness causes individuals to doubt whether they have what it takes to succeed. Their sense of agency and self-determination is weakened, and they experience a deep sense of shame first in the eyes of those who society tells them are the successful ones and then in their own eyes. Only by adopting a balanced and holistic understanding of all these diverse facets of being human can we comprehend the many ways in which oppression adversely impacts us.

Critical Theory and Psychology:
A Theoretical Framework for Understanding Oppression

The previous discussion of Critical Psychology's view of the human person underlines the importance of having some overarching theoretical framework from which to understand what oppression is and how it affects us. Because of the useful insights it affords us, I will continue to use this framework to analyze topics and issues in the remainder of this chapter and future chapters. This requires that I lay out some of the fundamental principles of Critical Psychology (and other forms of critical theory) prior to launching into a discussion of oppression.

Critical Psychology has its roots in Critical Theory, or what is sometimes called the Frankfurt School of thought. Its beginning can be traced to the founding of the Institute for Social Research in 1923, after which there has been a wave of thinkers associated with it up to contemporary times (Held, 1980). It included a range of neo-Marxist theorists from different disciplines who produced work in the areas of philosophy, psychology, sociology, and the arts. Many of these theorists sought to integrate Marxist philosophy, psychoanalysis, existential thought, and sociology. Common elements of this work were a critique of modernism and capitalist society, a commitment to social emancipation, and an interest in unveiling social forms of pathology.

The naming of the theory as "critical" highlights one key focus of its work. To be critical is to adopt a skeptical stance by questioning and rigorously examining all assumptions and statements of authority and truth pertaining to how we understand ourselves, others, and the world around us. It means not taking anything at face value and instead challenging accepted authority and wisdom. One of the early founders of Critical Theory, Horkheimer saw critique as both an intellectual and practical effort following Marx's criticism of traditional philosophy as seeking merely to understand reality but not change it.

Such a critical stance is essential to detecting and exposing mystification. One must never be satisfied with accepting any and all prevailing ideas, beliefs, practices, and social conditions uncritically and based on mere habit. Rather, truth claims and what is often posed as "common sense" must be submitted to rigorous analysis. In this way, what is falsely presented as fact is dismantled by exposing the ways in which these notions are conditioned by the specific historical, economic, and political conditions out of which they arise. For example, a critique from a Marxian stance would skeptically expose the contradictions in the prevailing ideology in a capitalist society that extols individual freedom and the free market but instead produces the social reality in which inequality and exploitation abound.

As this example illustrates, the critique conducted by Critical Theory employs a dialectical method that uncovers contradictions which are inherent properties of reality. In the case of any ideology, its guiding principles and modes of action often proceed from an extreme position that eventually gives rise to outcomes contrary to the very claims and values it espouses. This self-defeating pattern provides the seeds of the undoing of that ideology and so makes possible resistance and change. By examining the normative thinking in an ideology (that is, what it prescribes as desirable and ideal) and contrasting this with the actual practical outcomes it produces, the veil of illusion created by that ideology can be pierced and clear criteria for criticizing it can be established. Moreover, actors can be identified to change it and an alternative view of society can be conceived and set forth as a goal.

Critical Theory saw capitalism as inextricably interwoven with the intellectual tradition of modernism. Thus, any critique of capitalism includes a critique of modernism. This period of intellectual thought, with its roots in the Enlightenment, is marked by the rise of science. Scientific advancement proceeded more rapidly due to the growing ability to measure sensory-motor data and to then apply the scientific method to the data in order to derive an understanding of ourselves and the world (Wilber, 1998). This reliance on sensory-motor data was accompanied by a materialist philosophy which asserted that all phenomena studied needed to be reduced to the essential "stuff" or material that it was composed of. This then allowed subjects of study to be rendered into things that were tangible, objective, and thus measurable. Topics that could not be reduced into such material terms were dismissed as not worthy of study or even as having any valid existence. This approach to study lent itself readily to the natural sciences, whose subjects were easily categorized as material entities. What this eventually meant was that natural science was set up as the model for all other forms of scientific inquiry, including those that studied human beings. The ascent of science also meant that there was a belief that the application of reason would provide the necessary solution to all problems. In other words, problems required essentially technical solutions.

Modernism brought with it certain blessings (Wilber, 1998). One was the "differentiation of the cultural value spheres" of the arts, morals, and science. What this meant was that each of these areas was accorded its own dignity and respect and so could pursue its work using its own tools, rules, and methods for exploration without interference from the others. Other benefits included the increasing recognition and respect accorded the individual, which contributed to the rise of liberal democracies; efforts that led to the end of slavery; and movement to accord rights to previously marginalized and disenfranchised groups. However, over time modernism began to veer into extreme directions that proved to be detrimental. The differentiation of the spheres of cultural values eroded as science grew in power, influence, and prestige. This extreme view was crystallized in positivist philosophy, which asserted the following principles:

- all knowledge is based in sensory experience
- the meaning of any phenomenon is grounded in observation
- concepts are representations of these data-based observations and are mere names or labels for these observations, having no existence in themselves
- truth claims can only be established using the scientific method
- facts that are objective are superior to values representing mere subjective judgments, often only reflecting personal preferences.

This imperial view of science as the sole means of attaining truth became an ideology or an official worldview called "scientism."

Scientism began to permeate every sphere of human thought and activity. As a result, it became interwoven with capitalist ideology. This was observed by sociologist Max Weber (1930) who sought to refine Marx's theories and make them more complete. His concept of *rationalization* or *instrumental reason* illustrates the weaving of scientism and capitalism. The predominant metaphor used by modernism described the universe is a machine. This metaphor was extended to represent many other things, such as the mechanization of labor (as in assembly lines), the establishment of bureaucratic systems with rigidly defined divisions of labor, impersonal authority and political neutrality, and even the transformation of human beings into automatons. Instrumental reason is a form of means–end thinking that is expressed in certain forms of domination such as adopting and following orders, completing repetitive and mindless routines, and operating within strict hierarchies defined by varying degrees of power and authority.

All these elements can be seen as contributing to a greater likelihood of abuse of power and oppressive practices. For that reason, Critical Theory engaged in a rigorous critique of positivism and scientism as part of its more general critique of capitalism. The methods of natural sciences were shunned as inappropriate for study in the areas of the human and social sciences. Conflating social and natural processes fails to appreciate the role that historical, economic, and political contexts play in social phenomena. Even in the natural sciences, the belief that one's stance is objective and value-free is a fallacy as our understanding of all phenomena is based on interpretation that is inextricably bound up in multiple contexts. Moreover, treating the social world as natural reifies it (in other words, transforms it into something static and unchangeable by seeing it as governed by fixed and universal natural laws). Such reification, according to Critical Theory, creates a socially manufactured illusion that the status quo is natural and inevitable and so incapable of change. The transformation of nature and human beings into simply a means to an end leads to subjugation of nature and treatment of men and women as mere objects to be used and exploited.

Many of these themes and critiques are taken up by Critical Psychology (CP). The term "critical psychology" first came into use in Germany in the 1970s. Klaus Holzkamp is considered the founder of the German CP movement and in recent years more of his and his followers' work has become available in English (Schraube & Osterkamp, 2013). I have already touched on some ideas from this school of thought. The next instrumental figure is community psychologist Isaac Prilleltensky and his colleagues, whose ideas again have been discussed in previous chapters. British psychologist and psychoanalyst Ian Parker (2007) has written a number of influential works on CP that integrate elements of discursive analysis (derived from postmodernism, which has also been an influence on CP), Marxist psychology, and psychoanalysis. Other influences on CP have come from liberation theology, the work of Paolo Friere (1970) in critical pedagogy, the work of Franz Fanon (1963, 1967) who wrote extensively on the adverse impact of colonialism, and radical psychology.

The first core principle of CP has already been described in the previous discussion of the societal embeddedness of human subjectivity and agency. A corollary of this first principle is that the principal root of the problems afflicting human beings is due to injustice and oppression in the status quo. Our interdependence not only with our fellow human beings but with the natural world (what was discussed as "world openness" in Chapter Two) makes it inevitable that we are exquisitely attuned to a vast range of environmental influences. The goodness of society cannot be separated from the goodness of the individuals that make it up. Teo (2015) writes, "Critical psychologists intend to challenge societal structures of injustice, ideologies, psychological control, and the adjustment of the individual. Instead of making individuals and groups into problems, CP attempts to work on problems that individuals and groups encounter in a given society" (p. 246).

To understand the ways in which problems in society impact individuals, we must understand the workings of power. Prilleltensky (2008) emphasizes the dangers of neglecting the pervasive role of power in shaping human well-being, liberation, and oppression. He adopts the position of Foucault (1995/1975) that power is suffused and dispersed through all aspects of human life. Power is exercised through discourse. Discourse refers to a set of ideas that have culturally important meaning. It plays a central role in how we interpret events and shapes how we subsequently behave. Foucault give particular importance to the disciplinary effects of discourse, or the way in which it leads to the internalization of societal norms that define what it means to be human and to which our behavior conforms. Thus, power often operates in ways that are not readily visible or under the mantle of neutrality.

This inescapable political dimension of human life is thus the second core principle of CP. Power is seen not merely as a personal attribute, which tends to be the commonsense view. This view is overly narrow because there is also relational power, or the ways in which social structures exert power over individuals that determine, limit, and channel their agency (or the degree to which they exercise freedom not only over the circumstances of their lives but the meaning and significance they attribute to these circumstances). This interaction between persons and their external circumstances is captured in Prilleltensky's (2008) definition of power as a combination of ability (rights and access to necessary resources) and opportunities, which together enable them to exert influence on events. This view of power returns to the need to take into account rights, resources, and opportunities whenever considering human agency. Various personal factors—including cognitive, physical, emotional, and behavioral—influence an individual's capacity to exercise power. These factors then interact with diverse environmental factors, particularly material ones, that can shape just how much power persons possess and the channels available to them to exercise it. This means that power is not a fixed attribute of a person. Rather, for most people a lack of power is not due to any personal failing on their part but to the material circumstances in which they find themselves (Small, 2005).

Likewise, power can be exerted in ways that promote oppression or that promote liberation and wellness. The predominant ideology exercises a substantial role in determining this as it dictates the degree and kind of power possessed by individuals in a society. This is due, first, to the ways in which ideology specifies and defines the means by which relations of power, control, and domination are established and maintained. Next, ideology determines the ways in which privilege is distributed in accord with material and cultural factors. Simultaneously, the ideology employs mystification to subtly and covertly shape the worldview of societal members including, as noted earlier, the internalization of cultural rules and norms. For members of dominated groups, this involves the induction of a sense of futility and passivity with respect to accepting their lot while justifying the status quo as natural and inevitable.

Given that CP upholds the importance of submitting all things to critical examination, it is not surprising that it directs its gaze on psychology itself and its role in oppression. This is sometimes called *psychologization,* or the increasing influence that psychology has exercised in society and on other disciplines for understanding human beings and the problems they experience. In fact, it has been argued that what is and is not deemed to be a problem and the methods by which such problems should be dealt with has increasingly come under the authority of the psy disciplines (Rose, 1998). These include any concerned with the study of the mind, behavior, and individual's mental life. Influenced by the work of philosopher and social theorist Michel

Foucault (1995/1975), Rose (1998) describes how this growing influence has meant a greater tendency for psychology to be wielded as an instrument of power by those seeking to ensure the maintenance of the status quo.

There are several advantages that these disciplines bring to *governmentality*, or the process through which governments produce citizens that are optimally suited to their policies and purposes. Rather than engage in overt, coercive, and even violent measures to ensure compliance and obedience, psychology and other psy disciplines offer the technologies and expertise to have citizens internalize societal rules and expectations and thus engage in supervision of their own conduct. This is particularly important in governments portraying themselves as liberal democracies that respect personal freedoms and individual autonomy. Individuals internalize rationalized schemes for understanding themselves and others and for acting in pursuit of their goals (what is called "regimes of the person"). Likewise, they internalize technologies utilized as means for governing themselves and shaping their conduct in ways that comply with the dictates of the dominant ideology. Rose (1998) writes, "Governing in a liberal democratic way depends upon the availability of such techniques that will shape, channel, organize, and direct the personal capacities and selves of individuals under the aegis of a claim to objectivity, neutrality, and technical efficacy rather than one of political partiality" (p. 155). Assuming the mantle of science, psychology employs what appear to be rational and objective explanations about so-called laws that govern human behavior to legitimize existing power relations.

This description of psychologization makes clear that it contains the same kinds of errors and dangers as scientism. The knowledge used to expand power and control over the conduct of human beings is portrayed as objective, rational, and value free because it has been derived from the application of the scientific method. Under the aegis of the positivist philosophy, scientists are portrayed as being disinterested in their pursuit of knowledge and not motivated by any political or economic interests. Further, the claims made by scientists are legitimated as serving only beneficial purposes based on the expertise and specialized knowledge and technology that they possess. All the critiques leveled against scientism are valid here as well. What is called descriptive is in truth prescriptive as both the findings and applications derived from psychology or other psy disciplines are value-laden and contaminated by economic and political interests. As noted previously, the values undergirding the neoliberal ideology of individualism, self-enhancement, meritocracy, and autonomy are widely endorsed in psychological theories and research. By claiming to be value free, these biases are effectively obscured and denied. Prilleltensky (1989) provides a fitting summary:

> Psychology is instrumental in maintaining the societal status quo by (a) endorsing and reflecting dominant social values, (b) disseminating those values in the persuasive form of so-called value-free scientific statements, and (c) providing an asocial image of the human being, which in turn portrays the individual as essentially independent from sociohistorical circumstances. (p. 800)

The role that psychology plays in facilitating, legitimizing, and even engaging in oppression will be explored in further detail in the later chapters on self-deception and mystification.

To combat the threats and correct the errors posed by mainstream psychology, CP is firmly aimed at offering an alternative and more accurate understanding of human beings. This is achieved in part by its commitment to taking history seriously and appreciating the inextricable relationship that exists between any understanding of human beings and the multiple contextual factors in which that understanding is located. Teo (2015) describes CP's adopting what are called social epistemologies, that see the ways in which the problems, methods, interpretations and applications involved in psychological study are all dependent upon the sociohistorical context in which they exist. As a result, psychology is a social enterprise influenced by power and financial interests. The dominant ideology permeates psychology just as it does every other facet of society. The values and beliefs upheld in that ideology control what psychology studies and what it does not study as well as how knowledge derived from these studies is used.

We have already seen how the individualist view of neoliberal ideology defines essential elements of what it means to be a person. People do things due to forces and causes within them, thus making them responsible for their actions. The expectation is not to set in place more just and fair conditions in order to improve the chances that people live a happy and productive life. Rather, individuals are expected to adapt themselves to conditions in which they find themselves—no matter what those conditions may be. If they fail to adapt, then society is not at fault. The individuals are deviant and at fault. If psychology or any other science hopes not to contribute to these questionable beliefs and practices, it must question its assertion of political neutrality and rigorously examine the ways in which it is used in the service of the ruling ideology.

In contrast to this mainstream view, CP fully accepts its ethical responsibility to not accept the status quo as fixed and unchangeable. It directs a critical eye toward the often-disguised precepts of neoliberalism and exposes the various ways in which they adversely impact well-being due to abuses of power. This requires CP to give particular attention to those most impacted by these abuses. It must look at the world through the eyes of the oppressed as its departure point. This provides much needed validation to the experience of those whose experience is all too often being neglected, silenced, marginalized, and pathologized. As Friere (1970) asserts, it is the oppressed who are the experts on the nature of oppression and who must lead the way to liberation. It is not enough merely to expose the reality of oppression. Understanding without action is impotent and useless. CP is devoted to working on problems that individuals and groups encounter in their daily lives that stand in the way of their liberation. As Teo (1998) makes clear, such a commitment to liberation is required to take the role of power in creating and sustaining injustice seriously. It is only through the analysis of power that liberation is possible. In the CP discourse, the suffering of individuals is inextricably connected to their position within the hierarchy established by societal status quo. Indifference and lack of compassion to the oppressed are unacceptable forms of apathy. Rather, psychologists must join with the oppressed and work together with them to change social structures and practices that are the causes of exploitation, derogation, domination, and injustice.

Oppression: An Overview

Power, privilege, and ideology will all continue to occupy a central place in the discussion of oppression. A number of issues will be examined in order to achieve a sound and complete understanding of oppression and its various dimensions. These include specifying its core elements; explanations that have been offered for why it occurs and what sustains it; how it impacts the oppressed and the oppressor; and at what levels it operates. A very comprehensive treatment of oppression is provided by Ann Cudd (2006), and so I will turn to her to provide the foundation for my examination. Cudd observes that there are four types of theories of oppression, a number of which will be familiar based on material that has already been covered. The first is psychological in focus and views oppression mainly as an internal state of mind or a feeling. While there is no question that this represents a significant area of concern, it suffers from the individualist bias we have encountered and fails to include the systemic and structural factors responsible for oppression. Its importance is that it captures the lived experience of the oppressed person. The second type of theory highlights the role that inequality plays in oppression. The topic of inequality was discussed in the earlier chapter on social justice. A certain degree of inequality in life is inevitable. The inequality referred to here is based on exploitation in which the material welfare of one group is attained through the deprivation of another group, the process of excluding access to resources is through coercion, and the degree and magnitude of exclusion is morally indictable (Wright, 1994). The adverse impact is due to members of the exploited group being deprived of access to resources necessary to their well-being, such as employment, adequate income, a quality education, or health care. Inequality can also be present when certain individuals are denied fundamental rights and entitlements afforded to others and as a result are not treated with the dignity and respect due them. Such inequality employs difference or the transforming of members of certain social groups as deviant, inferior, or evil (the process of "Othering") as a means by which to justify oppression.

Related to the second type of theory, the third sees oppression as the imposition of unfair limitations on certain individuals. This also adopts a more distributive view of justice. These limitations can be seen as infringements on the types and range of choices that individuals have in certain situations pertinent to fulfilling their needs. Essentially, they are deprived of the same types of opportunities and access to resources as more privileged members of society, and as a result their sense of freedom and agency is constricted and their development is stunted. The place in which persons begin life in the social hierarchy often dictates the kinds of options and opportunities they will be afforded, and over time the limitations they experience result in cumulative deprivation. The fourth type of theory sees the essential element of oppression as the systematic dehumanization of members of certain groups. This is a central theme in the work of Friere (1970). He analyzes oppression as a form of violence in which the victims are not recognized as persons. In the eyes of oppressors, they are objects to be dominated and controlled. Their inferior status means that they do not possess the same needs, wishes, and capacities as the privileged and so do not deserve the same blessings and benefits. Friere is careful to point out that oppression has a deleterious impact on oppressors, who also become dehumanized.

Embedded in these four types of theories is a debate between two views found in the literature on oppression. Nancy Fraser (1997) classifies these views of oppression espoused over time as those that call for redistribution and those that call for recognition. Each view roots oppression in one of the two principal categories for defining social justice. The redistribution view adopts the distributive justice view and so places its emphasis on the role played by the economic structure of society and the need to achieve a more equitable distribution of material resources as well as legal rights. It highlights the importance of the material forces at work in oppression. In contrast, the recognition view adopts a more procedural view of justice, which is concerned with the role of institutionalized domination and control based upon assigning certain members of society an inferior social status and denying them equality. The rights of individuals to engage in participatory decision making and to exercise the fundamental freedoms that enable them to express their agency and realize their capabilities go unrecognized.

A very extended and scholarly treatment of the limitations of distributive views of justice and the need to elevate the importance of democracy and participatory decision making to address these limitations is provided by feminist philosopher Iris Marion Young (1990). To achieve social justice requires having in place structures and processes that enable all members of a society to exercise their rights, participate in public discussion, and collectively deliberate on shared problems and issues and how they should be dealt with cooperatively. Involvement in institutions that make decisions bearing on their lives is essential to ensuring that the voices of all members of society are heard, their rights honored, and their needs, values, and beliefs taken into consideration. Young categorizes this exclusion as one of the principal forms of oppression called marginalization. Members of a group are not considered part of mainstream society and confined to its margins. Their exclusion is not merely political but also economic and social. As a consequence, they are not allowed to be full citizens in a society. Young summarizes her argument as follows:

> A goal of social justice...is social equality. Equality refers not primarily to the distribution of social goods, though distributions are certainly entailed by social equality. It refers

primarily to the full participation and inclusion of everyone in society's major institutions, and the socially supported substantive opportunity for all to develop and exercise their capacities and realize their choices. (p. 173)

While the different views of social justice shed light on distinct aspects of oppression and propose pertinent solutions, seeing the redistribution and recognition views as separate and distinct is ultimately unhelpful and misconceived. Even in her critique of the distributive view, Young recognizes the interdependence of fairness of distribution and fairness of procedure. Particularly at a time when morally indefensible levels of material inequality exist and grow ever more severe, neglect of the devastating impact this has on the health particularly of those at the lower rungs of society would jeopardize any chance at achieving justice. Further, as Swanson (2008) points out in her examination of the debate, the various causal factors at work interact in highly complex ways and so cannot realistically be disentangled from one another.

Seeking to provide a comprehensive definition of oppression that integrates diverse perspectives, Cudd (2006) asserts that defining oppression requires that four conditions must be met. The first is the *harm condition*, which states that the harm is due to an institutional practice. The second is the *social group condition*, such that oppression is directed toward individuals based upon their group membership by individuals who are members of a different social group. The third is the *privilege condition*, which states that members of the oppressing social group benefit from the institutional practices. The fourth is the *coercion condition*, which states that the harm caused is due to the exercise of coercion. Looking at these four conditions in detail provides a thorough understanding of oppression.

Cudd (1990) proposes that there are two ways in which the harms caused by oppression can be categorized. The first is material oppression, and the second is psychological oppression. Material oppression encompasses any harm to one's physical being due to various forms of violence and deprivation or denial of material resources necessary to a decent life—including income, wealth, the quality of one's living conditions, health care, and adequate nutrition. It is logical that these more basic needs be granted primacy because they are the earliest and most basic needs that must be met given the dependence of the infant on caregivers. It is essential that we recognize the pivotal role that the prolonged dependence of the human infant plays in the course of his or her development. This makes plain the significant impact of the adequacy of environmental conditions to meet those needs. Moreover, dependence is not restricted to the earliest years of life. Throughout the course of human development, fulfillment of basic and essential physical needs is pivotal to health and a decent life. Deprivation of these needs is the most destructive form of oppression as it leads to a higher likelihood of illness and death. Moreover, these needs are the foundation on which ongoing human development depends. Following once more from Maslow's (1971) hierarchy of needs, if basic needs go unmet, then higher psychological and spiritual needs are less likely to be met.

Cudd begins her examination of the material forces of oppression with the most obvious—violence. The starkest form this takes is physically harming individuals through the application of physical force, whether it is on a small or large scale. Violence may be either random or systematic. In either case, violence is harmful not only to the target of the violence, but also to those who witness the violence due either to the importance of those individuals to the witness or to vicarious trauma. Violence must also be understood within a timeframe. Acts of violence in the past and continuing into the present pose the threat of occurring in the future. This means that victims are also harmed by persistent fears of future attacks, making them anxious and constantly vigilant to any sign of impending violence. Thus, over time violence gives rise to terror and, for many, trauma. When violence is structural, it is accepted or tolerated by the power structure within a society so that little or no consequences accrue to the perpetrator and victims have little recourse to justice. Cudd (2006) writes, "Fundamentally, systematic violence is oppressive because it alters the sense of the possible of its victims, victims who are not only the direct objects of violence but also those who share group membership with them. Systematic violence circumscribes their choices to their own detriment and for the benefit of others" (p. 116). Though this is the most serious form of violence, less severe forms such as harassing, intimidating, or deriding individuals in a manner that stigmatizes them and marks them as different and inferior are also detrimental.

The next major types of material forces that inflict oppression are economic in nature. Economic institutions and practices systematically disadvantage and harm members of certain social groups first through deprivation. In other words, forces that cause people to be poor and to not have what is necessary to secure an adequate, much less valued, existence through the ability to produce and consume goods and services. Poverty as a glaring and morally unacceptable consequence of oppression will be discussed in greater detail later in this chapter. Less severe is economic inequality, which entails having fewer economic opportunities due to membership in a social group as compared to more privileged groups. This inequality again is avoidable, unfair and undeserved. It typically has its roots in a pervasive form of oppression: exploitation. The most extreme form of exploitation is enslavement, which also often involves some form of violence. More generally, exploitation is a social process in which members of a privileged or dominant group can accumulate resources, wealth, status, and power from energy, efforts, and labor by the subordinate group. This form of oppression was a cornerstone of the work of Karl Marx (1978).

Such exploitation operates fundamentally through the extant class system within a society based on the dominant economic system. It establishes membership in groups that can be designated as the haves and the have-nots. Economic institutions and practices in a society define key elements of what work is, who does what kind of work, who works for whom, how one is compensated for the work one does, and how the value of what one produces is distributed. Implicit in the rationale given for the economic system are beliefs and values that justify who is awarded high status, high-paying jobs and who is not, as well as who can improve one's social position and who cannot. Along with this rationale, the very way society is structured and in which institutions function assures that the existing hierarchy and distribution of economic power in that society remains unchanged. The haves acquire more and more and the have nots experience ever more deprivation.

The second form of harm incurred by oppression is psychological in nature (Cudd, 2006). She writes, "Psychological oppression occurs when one is oppressed through one's mental states, emotionally or by manipulation of one's belief states, so that one is psychologically stressed, reduced in one's self-image, or otherwise psychologically harmed" (p. 24). Prilleltensky and Gonick (1996) agree with Cudd that psychological oppression has a material basis. This relationship can be explained by understanding how oppression functions as both a state and a process. The process involves the abuse of power through the systematic domination, manipulation, and control of the oppressed group by the privileged group. The oppressed are objectified and treated as a means by which the privileged achieve their own ends through various forms of social control. This domination is justified by means of a hegemonic ideology that actively shapes the consciousness of the privileged and oppressed alike. The adoption of this worldview facilitates the maintenance of unequal power as it is regarded as natural, inevitable, and even beneficial and therefore incapable of being changed. The same ideology becomes the basis for the interpersonal, cultural, economic, and political forces exerted by societal institutions to maintain the status quo. The state of oppression "...*entails a state of asymmetric power relations characterized by domination, subordination, and resistance, where the dominating persons or groups exercise their power by restricting access to material resources and by implanting in the subordinated persons or groups fear or self-deprecating views about themselves*" (Prilleltensky & Gonick, 1996, pp. 129–160, italics in original).

It is these alterations in how human beings see themselves, or what can be called impacts on their identity, that constitute the psychological consequences of oppression. Considering this, some clarification of what is meant by identity is needed. Each human being seeks to establish him- or herself as an individual in his or her own right and identity plays an important role in this process. On a personal level, identity is a set of schemas or internal templates constructed by individuals to establish some degree of order and stability to their experiences, to make sense of and give meaning to life, and to plot a course for their ongoing personal development. On a social level, identity includes characteristics, labels, or features that distinguish us as individuals while also establishing a connection to social groups who share these things with us to some degree. These characteristics can be physical (relating to our body), psychological (beliefs, values, feelings) and social (roles, group membership). One purpose of identity is to maintain stability and provide the person with a sense of coherence or intactness. However, it is also essential to individuals' well-being that their identity is flexible enough to change over time and adapt to ever-evolving demands and circumstances. One final critical aspect of identity is the degree to which individuals can hold themselves in esteem.

Various negative effects of oppression on an individual's identity have been found. These include the following:

- A sense of worthlessness, inferiority, and low self-esteem due to the internalization of degrading images and attributes
- Feelings of surplus powerlessness, which refer to feelings of personal impotence beyond what would be expected with

respect to actual limitations placed by the social context (Lerner, 1986)
- Learned helplessness (Seligman, 1975), passivity, apathy, and over-dependency
- A sense of pessimism and fatalism that often leads to depression
- Humiliation, degradation, and feelings of shame related to defamation, harassment, social distancing, marginalization, and violence
- Feelings of guilt and blame for the oppressive conditions that impact them
- Anger, which is often suppressed, directed at oneself or at other members of one's social group
- Experiences of alienation in which one feels estranged from or in conflict with oneself and disconnected from others or socially isolated
- Experiences of objectification in which individuals feel stripped of their humanity, such as their ability to exercise freedom or influence their lives
- Development of disorders related to trauma

Reviewing this list of negative impacts, one can clearly see the profound impact that one's environmental and social circumstances and, most particularly, the dominant social ideology exerts on an individual's identity. However, it would be a significant error to interpret this to mean that persons are passively shaped by external forces. If that were the case, any chance of opposing and eliminating oppression would be bleak indeed. I must return to a point made early on in this book. There is a dialectical and interdependent relationship that exists between individuals and society. While our societal nature makes us vulnerable to environmental influences, the nature and extent of those influences are tempered and shaped by individuals exercising their agency and their innate capacity to actively create meaning and purpose in their lives.

Oppression, Alienation, and Feeling Divided Within

One of the most dramatic examples of the impacts of degradation, social exclusion, exploitation, and other forms of social control can be seen in accounts written about the harms caused by colonization and cultural imperialism. Colonization generally refers to domination of another territory or country by a central system of power that has forcibly invaded and inhabited it. Colonization includes establishing control over the indigenous peoples and the colonizers appropriating the resources of the colonized land for their own use. Cultural imperialism is a term used by Young (1990) to describe one the five forms of oppression. It occurs when the dominant group universalizes its experience and culture, thus establishing them as the norm. Asserting the dominant culture as the standard and as essentially representing all humanity, all other cultures are deemed deviant and inferior. Those who hold to these devalued cultural beliefs and norms become stereotyped and marked as other and less than. With their inferior status in place, efforts are made to abolish their culture and, when possible or deemed desirable, indoctrinate them into the dominant culture.

One of the most influential writers on this form of oppression was the psychiatrist, political philosopher, and revolutionary Frantz Fanon (1967). Fanon was born on the island of Martinique, which was then a French colony, descended from African slaves and indentured Indians. Thus, his work draws from his own experience as well as his analysis of the experience of others who underwent oppression as a result of colonization. He was influenced by the philosophy of Marx as well as by existential philosophy. In the 1950s, he collaborated with eminent existential philosopher Jean Paul Sartre in producing critiques of capitalism, Western hegemony, anti-African racism, and France's involvement in the French–Algerian war. An important idea that Fanon drew from both Marx and existential philosophy is *alienation.* The role of the experience of alienation in suffering was discussed in the previous chapter. We will be revisiting it here as it relates more specifically to oppression.

Marx's use of alienation was influenced by its treatment in the philosophy of Hegel (1807/1966), although Marx was a sharp critic of Hegel's work. In Hegel's philosophy, alienation referred to being estranged from one's essential nature or what one truly is. The state of alienation gives rise to negative effects, including a decline in one's self-worth, a sense of having lost control to some external force, feeling at odds with oneself and others, and a feeling of being disconnected and isolated. Marx made alienation central to his critique of capitalism and sees it rooted in the struggle between the two social classes of the bourgeoisie (capitalists) and the proletariat (working class).

The process of alienation initially is the cause of material harms, which then give way to psychological harms. This alienation operates at multiple levels. It begins with the working class being alienated from what they produce. Because the working class works for a wage and does not own the means of production, they can claim no ownership of what they produce. Rather, they experience themselves as under the control of what they make as it is the capitalist who is enriched by it and who coerces them to work for wages. This sense of being disconnected from the work produced colors the relation of the working class to the entire world of objects, including nature itself. Not benefiting from what they produce and ending up spending their wages on the very commodities produced by either themselves or others constitute a material harm. At the next level, members of the working class become alienated from the labor process. They function merely as the means for capitalists to achieve their goal of profit. The labor process is experienced as regimented and controlled by others and offers workers no sense of ownership or personal involvement. Work becomes a means of earning wages so that no intrinsic satisfaction is gained from one's labor.

Marx encapsulates his astute analysis of alienation of the workers in his idea of *commodity fetishism* (Rehmann, 2013). Adopting a religious concept, Marx describes how the social relations involved in producing, selling, and consuming goods are transformed from interpersonal processes into mere economic relationships between things. Once again, we see the process of dehumanization at work coupled with the elevation of riches and money to an idol to be worshipped above all others. Rehmann (2013) summarizes:

> The decisive argument of Marx's critique of fetishism is this: since the producers have no democratic control over what is being produced, how it is being produced, or how the surplus is being distributed, the products of their labour pile up on the other side of the divide—they become the wealth of the capitalist owners. Commodities turn into an alien power that is used against the workers by replacing them with new technologies, by firing them, by impoverishing them, by making them "superfluous." (p. 40)

The third level of being alienated from the labor process touches very directly on the psychological harm caused by alienation. As a result of being estranged from what they create and from the time and energy they devote to creating it, workers no longer feel connected to something inherent to their very nature as human beings. Marx calls this "species being," by which he means that an essential element of human nature is to be socially cooperative and to be creative. Human beings need to be able to channel their powers through engaging in purposeful activity and the act of producing. Capitalism deprives human beings of engaging in such creative, free, and conscious activity and, as a consequence, dehumanizes them. The fourth and final level of alienation follows from the previous feelings of alienation. If persons are alienated from themselves, they will also be alienated from other human beings. The competitive and exploitative nature of capitalism first gives rise to conflict between classes. However, alienation is not restricted to class conflict as it can include being alienated from members of one's own class. This conflict makes it more difficult for workers to achieve class consciousness, in which they realize that they have shared interests that they can fight for as one. The impairing of class consciousness benefits the privileged class as it stifles resistance and challenges to the status quo.

Fanon (1967) adopts Marx's work on alienation, as well as existential perspectives on this concept, to analyze the impact of oppression both on those who have been subjected to colonialism as well as the colonizers. He blends with these Marxist elements, material from psychoanalysis, and Hegel's analysis of the development of self-awareness based on the need for recognition. Adopting a perspective like Critical Psychology, Fanon then places his analysis within a sociopolitical, historical, and cultural context. Fanon sees the struggle for recognition among human beings through the lens of a description in Hegel's (1907/1966) work, *Phenomenology of Mind*. Hegel describes the dynamic between master and slave, which is rather apt when considering colonialism. Using this example, Hegel makes the case that human beings only become conscious of themselves through the recognition provided by another person. This is another way of seeing how we are essentially social beings. The formation of our identity can only unfold through our interpersonal relationships. We have a basic need to be recognized because at a very basic level such recognition ensures that we are attended to and cared for. However, over the course of our development that need for recognition becomes the very basis for how we come to know and understand who we are. In forging an identity, we must rely on feedback we get from other people. This is the means by which we learn what impressions we make upon them and how they in turn view us. Through these interpersonal interactions we derive critical information that shapes what we think, feel, believe, etc. about who we are.

As the terms master and slave imply, there is often a significant power differential involved in this type of relationship. This insertion of power into the process of negotiating our need for recognition helps to explain oppression. The greater power possessed by the colonizer is exercised in such a way as to essentially negate the identity of the colonized through withholding of recognition. This is part of the broader process in which the native culture, language, and history is targeted for complete eradication by the superior culture because of its inherent inferiority. The colonized must be convinced of their inferiority to quash any resistance and thus ensure their complete domination. Demeaning stereotypes are often employed in this process aimed at convincing the target group of the necessity of refuting their native culture and adopting the culture of the colonizers. They are expected to assimilate the culture of the oppressor.

This dynamic sets up a conflict within the victims of colonization (and thus victims of oppression more generally). This is sometimes called "double consciousness" or "dual consciousness" based on the earlier work of W. E. B. Du Bois (1969), an African American sociologist and civil rights activist. Du Bois described how African Americans find themselves in a society in which they must look at themselves through the eyes of dominant others (that is, racist white society). Viewed from this perspective, they are regarded as inferior and objects of amused contempt and pity. This derogatory viewpoint becomes internalized and stands in opposition to their sense of identity as informed by their experiences and native culture. This then sets up a conflict around the toxic internalized influences rooted in oppression and resistance to those influences within the person.

In like manner, Fanon (1967) saw how the consciousness of members of a native culture is "colonized" or occupied by virtue of the internalization of the colonizers. This alien element within the identity of the oppressed is imposed through domination and coercion. It consists of disparaging and destructive images, attributions, and dictates that deform native identity and foster self-hatred. The power dynamics occurring outside of the oppressed are thus simultaneously enacted within them. When they seek to acquire the recognition from the privileged, they are only able to do so by complying with their authority and by allowing themselves to be defined by them. Their experiences and perspectives are invalidated and forced to go underground. Though repressed, however, these genuine elements of their identity remain and sometimes emerge in their efforts to reclaim their identity and attain liberation. Yet even at these times they come to realize the great risks and dangers they face, including not merely loss of identity but loss of their very lives. In the face of the harms and hazards of oppression, the oppressed must adopt different strategies in order to satisfy their need for safety and security. Sometimes they imitate the attitudes and behaviors of their oppressors. At other times they try to escape from their identity and assume another one that would seem to promise them safety and security. And as Fanon and Du Bois observe, another struggle is trying to negotiate dual identities.

Fanon (1967) eloquently and passionately describes this struggle by contrasting the dichotomy of black skin and white mask. On the one hand, the stereotypes imposed on the colonized by the oppressors mark them visibly as different and thus inferior and deviant (color of their skin), but at the same time their experiences, beliefs, values, and history are denied by the oppressors and so rendered invisible. Negotiating the demands of day-to-day life requires wearing many masks. They wear a white mask in order to get by in the white world and each time they wear the mask they negate their actual black, native identity. Fanon describes the process of "negrification," which is aimed at turning black persons into a "negro" and thus constructing their identity not only as Other but as marked by a difference that damns them. So thorough is the process that this becomes the sole means afforded to black persons for defining themselves, an imposed category that entraps them and does not allow them to escape. Even language reinforces this irreconcilable dichotomy in which white represents what is good and pure and black represents what is evil and corrupt.

This chasm within them inevitably leads to black persons feeling estranged and alienated from themselves on multiple levels—body, mind, sense of self. This alienation then spreads to significant others such as family or members of immediate social groups. The negative view held toward themselves generalizes to other black individuals and anything associated with being black. This has a range of detrimental effects. It undermines efforts at joining with others who share the experience of oppression to fight against it. It also can lead to acts of prejudice, discrimination, and even violence being directed at members of one' own group. At the next level, black persons may become alienated from elements of their own native culture, including language, history, and practices. Turning one's back on one's own culture because it is inferior solidifies the dominance of the oppressor's culture. Finally, on the deepest level, similar to what was observed by

Marx, alienation cuts black persons off from their most basic potentials to exercise their freedom, realize their possibilities, and create a productive and meaningful life.

Internalized Oppression

Throughout the discussion of the ways in which oppression creates a state of alienation that gives rise to multiple levels of conflict for the oppressed, a key element has been the internalization of the oppressor. This has been described as "internalized oppression" and can be considered a form of what Cudd (2006) calls indirect psychological forces involved in oppression. These are harms caused by members of oppressed groups to themselves because of their internalization of social beliefs and desires that then impact the choices and coping strategies they employ in order to deal with oppression. Though such harms do occur at the individual level, they can and do spread throughout all members of an oppressed group, as we saw from the previous discussion of Fanon's work. An examination of internalized oppression is particularly essential to achieving a better understanding of how and why oppressed individuals consent to and participate in their own oppression. In this sense, this form of oppression can be considered the most insidious and dangerous of all.

On the face of it, it would appear to be counter-intuitive that people would engage in behaviors or make choices that would expose them to the harms inflicted by oppression and undermine their efforts at opposing oppression and working for liberation. However, in my previous discussion of the two forms of suffering, I have provided some answers to this conundrum. These initial explanations will require additional elaboration to fill out the picture. However, that will be deferred to the later chapters on self-deception and mystification. For now, we need to gain a clearer picture of what internalized oppression is, how it develops, and how it impacts individuals. A very detailed treatment of the subject is provided in the book *Internalized Oppression: The Psychology of Marginalized Groups*, edited by E. J. R. David (2014).

Internalized oppression is the outcome of all the various processes involved in oppression discussed previously. It hinges upon the acceptance of inferior status by targets of oppression, accompanied by feelings of self-hatred, self-doubt, helplessness, and passivity. The most potent of the detrimental forces are those that tear away at the very essence of what is necessary for any human being to establish a sense of identity and a sound ability to negotiate life. That is the power that human beings can exercise over whether they can trust their own experience. David and Derthick (2014) write, "...the more oppressed an individual is, the more denial the individual has about his or her own reality as an oppressed person, effectively fragmenting the individual's experience of him- or herself and the world" (p. 9). The more that individuals mistrust their experience, the more this jeopardizes their inner sense of coherence and worth. Further, if they cannot trust their own perceptions, thoughts, and feelings, then they cannot trust others like them who have similar perceptions, thoughts, and feelings. Finally, without any ability to believe that their experience is valid, such individuals will be greatly challenged in their ability to determine what is real and not real. Under the most extreme forms, this can lead to madness. As will be seen, it is this insidious process of invalidation of experience that is behind the process of mystification.

Given the vulnerability and dependence of human beings from birth through their early years, it should not be surprising that the process of internalizing a sense of inferiority and a contemptuous view of oneself and one's group begins early in life. This learning is so powerful and goes so deep that essentially these negative stereotypes and toxic messages become unconscious and often operate in an automatic manner. They are not recognized as the products of social learning but are mistakenly assumed to be indisputable facts. As individuals' sense of identity becomes organized around these stereotypes and messages, they begin to function like self-fulfilling prophecies. Because they believe they are inferior, helpless, untrustworthy, lazy, etc. oppressed individuals begin to act in ways consistent with these beliefs. These behaviors, which are self-defeating and self-injurious, are the indirect psychological forces Cudd (2006) describes. Not only do they contribute to the person's oppression, they also have many long-term harmful consequences including depression, addictions and substance abuse, domestic violence, high-risk behaviors, and suicide. The processes by which internalized oppression impart beliefs, values, and behavior that lead individuals to consent to their oppression and undermine efforts at liberation are well described by Friere.

Like Fanon, Friere (1970) also concludes that oppressed persons experience an inner duality due to their internalizing the oppressor. Looking at the different dimensions of the internalized oppressor reveals major impacts. The first is that by adopting the oppressor the oppressed also adopt their standards, prescriptions, and guidelines. This is achieved by means of the internalization of the dominant ideology, which is so powerful and pervasive that both oppressor and oppressed fall under its sway. Because the oppressor is upheld as the true model of humanity, oppressed persons always see themselves as falling short and adopt a negative self-image. They uncritically accept the propaganda that society is good and just. If that is so, then their failures and deprivation are deserved because they are lazy, irresponsible, and ungrateful. This leads the oppressed to assume a fatalistic attitude toward their circumstances either because there is nothing they can do to change them or because they are resigned to the belief that their lot is God's will. This becomes a self-fulfilling vicious cycle as their passivity is seen as even further evidence that they are lazy and incompetent and get what they deserve. The internalized oppressor functions like an ever-present critical voice within them, against which they must constantly struggle.

The second dimension of internalized oppression described by Friere is that it leads the oppressed to fear their freedom. If they are as weak and inferior as they believe, then how can they trust themselves to make decisions that could have a major bearing on their lives? The fear is that they will only make things worse. This can also be seen in fear of challenging authority because of the retaliation that would be provoked. So, they choose not to join others like them to work collaboratively to achieve justice. Rather than make up their own minds, they submit to the prescriptions imposed on them by authority figures and let them make decisions for them.

As discussed in the previous chapter on suffering, the experience of exercising freedom and taking responsibility for one's choices is inherently anxiety provoking and sometimes painful. However, this anxiety is amplified for the oppressed due to their experience of coercion and domination. And so they approach their freedom ambivalently. While, on the one hand, they want to reclaim their agency and exercise their freedom, they fear ridding themselves of the image of the oppressor and the illusion of safety and stability it provides to them. And so, they adopt a spectator stance in which they withdraw from involvement in making choices and submit themselves to choices made by powerful others, even if those choices may prove disadvantageous and even destructive to them. This again has a self-defeating and self-destructive impact as it undermines their engaging in resistance and confirms the negative stereotype placed on them of being docile.

The third dimension described by Friere is rooted in the paternalistic attitude that oppressors adopt toward the oppressed. This is part of the strategy used to convince people who are oppressed to consent to their domination and to place their trust in those who exercise control over them. The domination and control are presented as being for the oppressed individuals' own good. The oppressors adopt the façade of beneficence and explain they are assuming authority based on the oppressed being incapable of managing their lives and doing what is in their best interest. The oppressed may find themselves feeling an irresistible attraction to the oppressor as their powerful protector and benefactor. When that identification becomes particularly powerful, oppressed individuals begin to relate it to people who share their oppression. Not only do they mistrust them and devalue them. They can act out violently against them. This is called horizontal violence by Friere (1970). One variation of this is when individuals in one oppressed group begin to compare themselves to members of another oppressed group, again using the standards imposed by authorities. In this case, such individuals may engage in harmful actions toward members of another marginalized group or consider the harmful actions done by the privileged toward those other groups deserved.

Oppression and the Privileged

Because oppression is enacted through relationships between human beings, it is not possible to fully understand it without also examining those who engage and benefit from it—the oppressors, or the privileged. As a number of writers on oppression have observed, there are adverse impacts on those who engage in oppression. Friere (1970) notes:

> Although the situation of oppression is a dehumanized and dehumanizing totality affecting both the oppressors and those whom they oppress, it is the latter who must, from their stifled humanity, wage for both the struggle for a fuller humanity; the oppressor, who is himself dehumanized because he dehumanizes others, is unable to lead this struggle. (p. 47)

In this quote, Friere not only acknowledges the all-embracing impact exercised by oppression but the role that the oppressed must play in leading the way to liberation. Because they are oppressed, they are the experts on the experience of oppression. Though the oppressors wrongly presume that they can escape from toxic consequences of a system based in oppression, they, too, would benefit from abolishing this system and establishing one that is more just. However, there are factors that stand in the way of this.

In her book *Promoting Diversity and Social Justice: Educating People from Privileged Groups,* Goodman (2001) provides a detailed account of the various ways in which oppression influences the experience and behavior of members of privileged groups. She lists three common traits of privileged groups that mitigate against their grasping both their involvement in oppression and the way in which they inflict harm as oppressors. The first is a lack of consciousness. As discussed previously, human beings have a powerful need for control. This applies especially to their worldview and their self-identity. Most privileged individuals have formed a view of themselves and the world that has not only internalized the dominant ideology but also the societal prohibitions regarding becoming aware of the beliefs, values, and preconceptions that make up that ideology. They do not consciously see themselves inflicting harm on oppressed groups or as being recipients of benefits by virtue of their privileged status. So much so, that to be confronted with these facts would be highly disturbing and threatening to them and give way to efforts to push these things out of their awareness. Thus, most people who engage in oppression do not do so consciously. This does not mean that oppressors are not morally accountable for their involvement, but they cannot consent to such accountability until their consciousness has been raised.

The role that ideology and unconscious underlying societal beliefs and values play in the everyday practices of oppression is again described astutely by Friere (1970):

The oppressors do not perceive their monopoly on *having more* as a privilege which dehumanizes others and themselves. They cannot see that, in the egoistic pursuit of *having* as a possessing class, they suffocate in their own possessions and no longer *are;* they merely *have.* For them, *having more* is an inalienable right, a right they acquired through their own "effort," with their "courage to take risks." If others do not have more, it is because they are incompetent and lazy, and worst of all is their unjustifiable ingratitude towards the "generous gestures" of the dominant class. (p. 59, italics in original)

In Friere's observation, the assumptions of a neoliberal ideology are glaringly apparent. First is the emphasis on acquisition and "having," so characteristic of our consumer-oriented society (deGraff, Wann, & Naylor, 2001; Wachtel, 1989). These dangers were sagely observed early on by Erich Fromm (1986), who spoke of how capitalist society transformed human beings into consumers with insatiable desires and all-absorbing greed. This obsession with consuming is wedded to the myth of scarcity, in which competition is necessary to get what one needs even if it is at the expense of another.

Additionally, lack of concern for others so long as one gets what one wants stems from the individualistic and narcissistic (sometimes also called Machiavellian) orientation embedded in neoliberalism (Gruba-McCallister, 2007). When the measure of one's worth is inextricably tied to how much one has, those who have an exaggerated sense of worth conclude that their excessive share of the goods life offers is theirs by right. They are the true winners in that myth we call the American Dream—the illusion that success comes to anyone who works hard and avails themselves of all the wonderful opportunities that life affords. Springing from narcissism is an all-consuming greed that does not have any sense of what is enough and that will transform everything into an object for one's possession, including other human beings.

These elements of the neoliberal ideology are for most people simply taken for granted. They adopt an uncritical stance and take what they experience at face value. Having been thoroughly indoctrinated in the dominant ideology, many of them may be well-meaning people who haven't the slightest inkling that they are nonetheless agents of oppression. It is for this reason, as well as the power that internalized oppression exerts over the oppressed, that most acts of oppression are not obviously coercive or imposed violently. The structural and systemic nature of oppression makes it hidden and typically unintentional. Philosopher Jean Harvey (2000, 2010) calls this *civilized oppression*. Harvey situates the workings of oppression in what she describes as distorted and inappropriate moral relationships. The more subtle ways in which power is negotiated in relationships between individuals occupying a superior and subordinate position can take many forms—for example, who can take initiative in a relationship, who is more exposed to expressions of disrespect, and who has easier access to the acquisition of social goods. The literature on *microaggressions* offers numerous other examples of how denigrating and damaging messages are conveyed to members of marginalized groups on a daily basis in what seem like casual encounters. If these matters critical to justice go unrecognized and unarticulated, the consciousness of the privileged about the role they play in all different forms and levels of oppression remains constricted.

The second trait that prevents the privileged from taking ownership of their participation in oppression, according to Goodman (2001), is denial and avoidance. Denial is one of the most primitive and basic strategies used by human beings to engage in self-deception. Despite this, it fails at completely silencing whatever uncomfortable truth may be distressing us. And so, the privileged have some sense that they are engaging in morally inappropriate behavior. This could blossom into a deeper or fuller realization that promotes liberation. However, before this can happen, the natural defenses that the privileged possess to manage unpleasant experiences and disturbing realizations must be dealt with. The use of these defenses is often rewarded by broader society because such awakening will eventually translate into a challenge to the broader status quo. To assist in allaying fears, the dominant ideology provides ready-made strategies and deceptive devices to evade discomfort. The negative impact of oppressive practices is reframed to remove responsibility from the privileged and place it elsewhere. This can be larger natural forces (as in cases of environmental calamities or disasters), long-standing stereotypes, the will of God (the role that religion can play in justifying oppression), and the "failings" of the oppressed.

The third and final trait of privileged groups that stands in the way of their joining forces with the oppressed is their internalized sense of superiority. Quite simply it feels good to be considered one of society's winners, a success, and a member of the "chosen" class. Daily life provides countless opportunities to reinforce this view and attitude among the privileged, while also more subtly terrorizing them with the threat of their possibly falling into the ranks of the despised and unwashed. Mullaly (2010) describes this contrasting phenomenon among the privileged as *"internalized domination."* Like the oppressed, the privileged are exposed from early life to learning that socializes them with beliefs and values that are then reflected in their demonstrating a hostile, demeaning, dismissive, and exploitative stance toward members of subordinate groups. With the hegemonic ideology firmly entrenched within their consciousness, the privileged see any threat to the status quo as a threat to them. If the threat is of sufficient magnitude, the resulting sense of terror can be called upon to justify even the most desperate and, for the targets, despicable countermeasures (Staub, 1989).

Goodman (2001) mentions several other impediments that can stand in the way of persons acknowledging that they have privilege. Despite our society valorizing competition, success, and power, there are still negative connotations associated with acknowledging, much less basking in, one's privileged status. Ironically, while the prevalence and degree of narcissism continues to rise in our society, the long-standing prohibition against pride continues to have weight. Next, the privileged status that they occupy is not always acknowledged by individuals. DiMaggio (2015), for example, reports findings that Americans are typically unreliable in assessing their social class status based on the actual factors that determine class. Many assume they are middle class when in fact they are not; and even for those who are not, many overestimate the likelihood that they will experience class mobility and ascend to middle class. Given this sort of confusion, the question of whether one is privileged or not may raise doubts. To add to that confusion, within our competitive society and based on the media playing on people's anxieties about whether they are living up to society's standards of success, people are highly inclined to engage in social comparison in order to figure out where they stand. Often, much of this is comparing ourselves to people who have more than we do. The result is that people tend to feel insecure about their standing and are less prone to count themselves among the privileged.

Notwithstanding the clear benefits enjoyed by the privileged and the power they possess that make them instruments of oppression, Goodman (2001) does outline the costs of oppression to the privileged. It is useful to be aware of these costs because they do provide a more balanced picture of the consequences of oppression. However, the more important reason for being aware of these costs is the potential they offer for mobilizing people of privilege to become more aware of the ways in which they are participating in the material and psychological harms inflicted by oppression. Seeing that they also are negatively impacted by the prevailing ideology has the potential of awakening them to the need for change.

This sort of disillusionment, as I have maintained, will inevitably be painful. Having dearly held beliefs shattered and one's eyes opened to the moral implications of one's actions will not initially be greeted with open arms. As we will see in later chapters, different forms of resistance will be used to shut out any realization and return to our illusions. However, if these resistances can be overcome, this paves the way for the privileged to move beyond their suffering and come to a deeper appreciation of the suffering of the victims of oppression. If this then opens channels for dialogue between them in how they can work together, then the possibility for achieving justice is far greater.

Goodman (2001) divides the costs to the privileged into five categories. The first are psychological costs that arise from the constriction of consciousness noted previously. The privileged, in order to maintain their illusions, must close themselves off from their experiences as well and so experience the alienation that comes with this. Though they may feel empathy for the poor and disadvantaged or feel a twinge a shame at abusing their power, they do not avail themselves of these opportunities to expand their self-knowledge. They may also feel pressure to remain within their socially prescribed roles, which may bring entitlements and advantages but also restrict them from considering alternative ways of being. These injuries can lead to psychological problems. The social costs are essentially found in the alienation that is created between privileged individuals and those of subordinated groups. Lack of trust and understanding fuels tension between them and increases the potential for violence. One's social network shrinks because of avoidance of establishing relationships with those outside one's social circle.

Moral costs are based upon an awareness that by either engaging in oppression, being complicit with it, or turning a blind eye to it, one is acting contrary to moral dictates that elevate compassion and justice as core values. This can evoke shame and guilt. The intellectual cost for the privileged is ignorance of the history, culture, and traditions of other groups. An ethnocentric attitude is not uncommonly found in people who engage in oppression in which they assume that their culture is superior. Because of this, other cultures have no value and so are not worthy of study or interest. An interesting element of this is that many privileged people are completely blind to culture, seeing it as something irrelevant to defining human beings. For that reason, they often have little interest in or awareness of their own cultural history, values, and traditions.

Finally, there are material and physical costs of oppression to the privileged. Oppression tears away at the fabric of society at every level. Higher levels of oppression are associated with higher levels of unrest, instability, insecurity, crime, and violence. These are threats that the privileged cannot shield themselves from. Moreover, privileged people often fail to appreciate the many ways in which failures to decrease oppressive policies and institutional practices end up being more economically costly. Adequately funding schools to provide a quality education decreases incarceration later in life, which is far more costly. Compelling individuals without access to health care to turn to more expensive options such as emergency room visits for non-critical issues is another example.

The Levels of Oppression—Cultural

Thus far, I have principally examined oppression at the personal level. However, this perspective is too narrow to capture all the dimensions of oppression as both a process and a state. Thompson (1997) proposes what he calls the PCS model for analyzing oppression, which includes the personal, cultural, and structural. These dimensions may each be described individually, but in practice they are interdependent and interact in sometimes complex ways. In moving on to the next two levels of oppression, I will be drawing attention to what I believe to be the irrefutable major causes of oppression—poverty, inequality, and the social determinants of health. While none of these causes is unique to our times, there is sound evidence that the magnitude of inequality and its impact on impoverishing even more people and consigning them to social and environmental circumstances that lead to a host of adverse physical and psychological consequences is greater at this time than at any other, particularly in the United States. To understand how this is so, we must first understand the degree to which neoliberal ideology has permeated virtually every facet of human life, particularly in the form of a consumer culture. And we also need to deconstruct the dominant narrative that poverty and inequality are due to individual characteristics of the poor and marginalized and instead are firmly rooted in the political, economic, and social structures and policies established by neoliberalism.

The importance of understanding and respecting culture in order to achieve a more just society has attracted increasing interest in recent years. For example, in psychology and other service professions there has been far more attention given to the diversity that makes up societies and that characterizes the individuals who seek out those services (Goodman et al., 2004). This area of multicultural theory and practice is one way to understand what is meant by culture. It includes important ways in which individuals define themselves and associate themselves with certain groups. For example, ethnicity, age, gender, class, religion, and disability are all areas considered relevant to better appreciating the experience of diverse individuals in the literature on multiculturalism. While there is no question that these ways of defining culture are important and provide a lens through which to understand oppression, a more encompassing view of culture also needs to be employed.

Culture forms an important bridge between larger structures that consist of institutions and systems (e.g., political, economic, and educational) whose policies, rules, and practices organize life within a society and the individuals that make up that society. Culture performs an essential function by providing individuals with an overall worldview from which to understand life. This consists of beliefs, values, myths, guiding ideals, and norms that are embedded in prevalent symbols, metaphors, stories, discourses, texts, and language. The very way in which human beings at different times and in different places have defined what it means to be a person has been rooted in culture (Kirkmayer, 2007). The purpose of culture on the broadest level is to provide us with a sense that we live in an orderly, predictable, and meaningful universe. In other words, it is another way to understand how the human need for control is attended to and facilitated. It has been proposed by some that the most important function of culture is to buffer human beings from the awareness of their mortality. A notable example of this view is *terror management theory* (Solomon, Greenberg, & Pyszczynski, 1991). Influenced by the work of Ernest Becker (1973), this theory sees culture as a set of shared fictions sustained by social consensus that provides meaning and value to life by conferring self-esteem through the provision of social roles and associated standards of conduct. This sense of life having meaning and the belief in their possessing value enables human beings to face the inevitability of death with a greater degree of equanimity.

Culture thus profoundly shapes our understanding of what it means to be human. However, in doing so it does not provide a completely open and embracing framework for processing and giving meaning to our experience. Rather one of the functions of culture is to filter experiences in order to make them fit within certain organizing schemas. This ensures that only certain experiences are allowed, and a limited range of meanings can be given to those experiences. In this regard, one can see that culture performs a very important political function. While there may be multiple competing cultures available to individuals in a society, only one culture is dominant. And that dominant culture expresses the hegemonic ideology, the same ideology that is reflected in the worldview of the powerful and privileged.

Ultimately, only this worldview is validated and valorized, while all opposing ones are dismissed, degraded, and forbidden. The power to define reality once again is a potent tool wielded by the privileged to maintain the status quo and to dominate subaltern groups. It is the function of principal institutions and major cultural agents to ensure that the core beliefs, values, and norms of the dominant culture are inculcated, disseminated, and maintained. Nonetheless, while the power of the cultural agents is considerable, it is neither irresistible nor insurmountable. The availability of alternative or countercultures always offers dissenting views. Further, due to the capacity to think dialectically, human beings can question and examine their basic assumptions and decide whether or not to ratify them.

The role that ideology, language, and discourse play in the process of enculturation will be examined in more detail in the later chapter on mystification. For the moment, I will offer some focus on a very central aspect of contemporary dominant culture: the role that it plays in oppression. This is the transformation of our society into a *consumer culture*. A major instrument used to achieve this transformation has been mass media. This realization of the power of the media to serve as a tool for the imposition of the dominant culture can be traced to the work done by two theorists of the Frankfurt School, Horkheimer and Adorno (1944/1995), on the culture industry. It was their observation that in the later stages of capitalism the growth of mass media and the entertainment industry provided a new means of social control and ideological indoctrination.

The culture industry fulfills several purposes that facilitate oppression. One is to promote the continued commodification of life central to the capitalist economic system. The expansion of advertising and its infiltration into virtually every aspect of life is a clear example of this. The use of advertising to manipulate individuals to buy products and boost corporate profits while often plunging them into deepening debt is just one facet of how it carries out the priorities of neoliberalism. As Chomsky (1999) so lucidly critiques, the rise of neoliberalism, accompanied by a decline in a vital and functioning democracy, has been attained in large part by changing citizens into consumers. He writes, "The corporate news media, the PR industry, the academic ideologues, and the intellectual culture writ large play the central role of providing the 'necessary illusions' to make this unpalatable situation appear rational, benevolent, and necessary if not necessarily desirable" (p.14).

The methods of advertising were expanded into what Chomsky observes was a booming public relations industry. One of its early pioneers, Edward Bernays, believed that principles of psychology should be used to consciously and intentionally manipulate the opinions and perceptions of the public in order to control them, get them to consent to the existing power structure, and adopt the picture of reality aligned with the dominant ideology. A more detailed examination of propaganda will be conducted in the chapter on mystification.

A final function of mass media and entertainment is to divert the attention of individuals away from the problems created by the status quo and instead induce them into a make-believe reality designed to soothe their fears and distract them from their cares and worries. Rather than provide citizens with information that is pertinent to their lives and well-being and would enable them to engage in democratic participation, mass media employs sensationalism and superficial fluff to excite or sedate them (Bourdieu, 1998).

The expanded infiltration of what Horkheimer and Adorno called the culture industry into ideological control and the establishment of a consumer culture go hand and hand. In their extensive treatment of consumer culture and its various impacts, Kasser and Kanner (2004) provide valuable insights into how it has become a powerful force contributing to oppression. It is difficult not to conclude that the United States, under the poisonous influence of neoliberal ideology, has become an increasingly death-affirming culture (borrowing again from the work of Erich Fromm). In 2018 the U.S. Congress passed and the President approved a federal budget that allotted $700 billion for the military while making cold-hearted cuts to services for the poor, elderly, children, and disabled. Rather than use this money to address poverty, provide universal health care, make higher education affordable, or remove lead from drinking water, politicians boosted the profits of industries devoted to instruments of mass destruction. This military budget represented a 40% increase from the $500 billion approved in the years 2003 to 2005 when the United States was still immersed in the quagmires in Iraq and Afghanistan. At the time I was writing this chapter in March 2018, 7,182 students had been killed in gun violence (since 2012), compared to 6,915 combat death (since 2001). This figure does not include the many others who die of gun violence each year. Despite this, limits on access to firearms are shunned by those accepting millions of dollars from gun manufacturers. Politicians turn a blind eye to the collapsing social safety net and the crumbling infrastructure. They seek to pass legislation to deprive individuals of health care. The list of their offenses against life could go on for quite a length, but the point is made. However, the death-affirming attitude that lies at the very core of our culture is found not only in these more blatant examples.

Unless the roots from which these poisoned fruits grow are exposed and removed, no real progress can be made. The elevation of wealth and profit, the reduction of the value of human beings to dollars and cents, the obsession with having more and more no matter what the consequences, the plundering of every resource the earth has to offer—all these integral elements of consumer culture are the moving forces behind the lack of regard we have for life. This is why we cannot neglect the devastating role of consumer culture and the mindless pursuit of having more and more while being less and less (Fromm, 1976). This quote by Kasser, Ryan, Couchman, and Sheldon (2004) provides a fitting summary of what is meant by consumer culture:

> If we look at contemporary culture, we see that the media propagate messages to purchase items and experiences, that myths are passed on that say that America is the land of opportunity, that governments work to support capitalism, that business people make decisions based on how to maximize profit, and that consumers amass debt to buy products such as sport utility vehicles and large-screen television sets. These actions can be viewed from many angles, but they must also be understood as reflecting the combined beliefs of a large number of individuals who have internalized the capitalistic, consumeristic worldview. Thus, the culture of consumption is, in part, a shared worldview lodged within the psyches of the members of culture. However, we must also recognize that living in a culture of consumption means that individuals are exposed to pressures to conform to the beliefs and values of this culture. Accordingly, the worldview in a society shapes the identities and lives of members, leading them to hold the goals and engage in the practices...that support the culture. (pp. 12–13)

To substantiate the adverse impacts of consumer culture, Kasser et al. (2004) cite a number of empirical studies. They describe what they call the creation of the *materialistic value orientation* (MVO), which includes the belief in the importance of pursuing the goal of affluence and financial success, having the right kinds of possessions and images, and defining oneself and one's status in terms of the wealth and possessions one has acquired. One of the primary ways by which an MVO is cultivated in individuals is by inducing experiences of insecurity. Advertising and other forms of propaganda employ fear and cultivate worries and doubts about one's self-worth and safety because these feelings have been demonstrated to increase materialistic values and attitudes in order to compensate for these feelings. This has been found both with individuals as well as on a national level as individuals in poorer countries have been found to be more materialistic than those in richer countries.

The second means by which individuals develop an MVO is through social learning, by exposure to materialistic models and values. This begins at the very start of life as many companies now openly admit their intention to "brand" children through investing millions of dollars in advertising to them (Schor, 2004). The intention of much advertising is to engender what are called upward social comparisons in which individuals look to more powerful and successful models to evaluate themselves. This only serves to intensify insecurity while at the same time promoting the false promise that purchase of the product advertised will restore positive feelings for oneself. Research again confirms that people with a high MVO are more likely to engage in social comparison, believe more strongly that making money is the key to proving their worth, and are more likely to purchase goods in order to secure the approval of others.

The clearest evidence of the deceptive claims made by advertising to those with an MVO is research showing that higher levels of MVO are associated with lower ratings of life satisfaction. Higher MVO levels have also been found to be correlated with narcissism, likelihood of reporting physical symptoms of distress, greater drug use, lower self-esteem, and poorer quality of interpersonal relations. People with a stronger MVO report feeling less competent, having less empathy for others, and being more manipulative in their relationships with others in order to get ahead. Finally, examining the impact of MVO on a broader scale, it has adverse social and ecological consequences. Individuals with a higher MVO tend to demonstrate less civil behavior toward others and less social interest.

The role that the rise of narcissism and consumerism has played in the corresponding declining sense of community has been described by Harvard sociologist Robert Putnam (2000). In this aptly titled book *Bowling Alone*, Putnam proposed the concept of *social capital* to refer to the value and benefits derived from being a part of social networks based upon trust, reciprocity, and information. The extreme emphasis on individualism associated with the consumer culture has been accompanied by a decline in persons' access to social capital and thus the benefits that come from a strong sense of community. From an environmental standpoint, the unchecked rate of consumption is a pivotal element in the ecological crisis facing the world, as seen in climate change, deforestation, less access to clean water, and loss of land for agriculture.

In his article about the "empty self," Cushman (1990) outlines a very similar argument about how neoliberalism socially constructs an understanding of who we are that is in the service of its political and economic priorities. He traces the origins of the empty self to the end of World War II. At that time, the United States had become the greatest economic superpower in the world. The mass production of material needed to conduct the war had finally lifted the country out of the Great Depression. However, that meant the end of the war posed a dilemma. How would that industrial boom continue if companies were not making planes, tanks, etc.? Where would the many thousands of GIs returning from war find employment? How could the expansion of the economy continue? With the specter of the Depression still looming, it was clear that U.S. industrial might had to be channeled into producing consumer goods and that there had to be people ready and eager to buy them. While part of the emptiness of the self was due to the continued decline of family, community, and tradition fostered by an individualistic ideology, that emptiness needed to be deepened in order to provide the motivation to

> ...seek the experience of being continually filled up by consuming goods, calories, experiences, politicians, romantic partners, and empathic therapists in an attempt to combat the growing alienation and fragmentation of its era. This response has been implicitly prescribed by a post-World War II economy that is dependent on continual consumption of non-essential and quickly obsolete items and experiences. (Cushman, 1990, pp. 600–601)

Neoliberalism does not create our sense of inner emptiness so much as it seeks to amplify it. As I argued in an examination of the rise of narcissism associated with consumer culture, there is a certain sense of incompleteness that is naturally experienced by all human beings

(Gruba-McCallister, 2007). The deepest longings of individuals stirred by our confrontations with an ever-present inner emptiness can be channeled in positive as well as negative ways. For some, that sense of emptiness can lead to a search for a deeper and more fulfilling meaning, to commit to a worthy cause that requires their serious commitment, or to form a powerful emotional bond of devotion to another. However, that same sense of emptiness is recognized by those who would capitalize on it by stirring feelings of discontent and doubt. These uncomfortable feelings and the manipulation of human vulnerability then are employed in ways to benefit the wealthy and powerful—generally at the expense of those being targeted. One way is to seduce them into engaging in a futile search for fulfillment. As Lasch (1979) describes this, "In a simpler time, advertising merely called attention to the product and extolled its advantages. Now it manufactures a product of its own: the consumer, perpetually unsatisfied, restless, anxious and bored. Advertising serves not so much to advertise products as to promote consumption as a way of life" (p. 137). Another influence it exerts is to undermine individuals' confidence in their ability to direct their own lives and exercise their freedom in deciding what is best for them. And so instead they are lured into looking to those held up by society as attractive, powerful, and successful exemplars to make decisions for them and to allay their fears.

Thus, we are faced with a disturbing paradox. To make the economy thrive and to keep the power structure intact, advertising and other forms of social indoctrination must intensify the degree of self-absorption and self-importance people feel while at the same time undermining their self-esteem and feeling of security. The result is the veneer of narcissism adopted by individuals, behind which hides a perpetually fragile sense of self. While extolling the importance of being autonomous individuals who must stand on their own two feet and pull themselves up by their bootstraps, they are simultaneously made to feel incompetent and incapable. Because of their untrustworthiness, it becomes the "onerous" task of the rich and successful to rescue and direct them. Though their "social network" is constantly expanding through Facebook and Twitter, their sense of isolation, disconnection, and alienation continues to gnaw at them. How could individuals not feel tied into knots from which they are unable to extricate themselves or ensnared by the nagging calls of insatiable desires that confirm rather than still their emptiness? No living person is untouched by the woes being inflicted by our consumer culture. However, the burden of consumerism and the commodification of life fall more heavily upon the poor, the exploited, and the marginalized.

The Levels of Oppression—Structural

The final level at which to examine and understand oppression is structural. This means the role played by social, economic, and political systems and the ways in which these systems determine social practices and political policies to advantage privileged groups at the expense of oppressed groups. These abuses of power will be examined by focusing on the central division along which oppression occurs within a neoliberal ideology—class. This does not in any way imply the irrelevance of other social divisions and distinctions. In fact, analyzing oppression in a unidimensional way will inevitably provide an extremely skewed picture. It is increasingly accepted that human beings have multiple identities and belong to different social groups. As these different identities combine and interact, some become more or less salient in circumstances involving oppression. A person may occupy an oppressed status based on one identity and an oppressor status on another. The concept of *intersectionality* has been adopted to describe the ways in which many different dimensions of identity come together and interact in complex ways for each person (Wineman, 1984).

At a time of growing inequality in income and wealth and the power and privileges that accompany these, special attention to class as a significant way in which contemporary society is structured is crucial to any analysis of oppression (hooks, 2000). To begin then, we must define class. This is not as straightforward as it seems. For example, class is not synonymous with socioeconomic status or the amount of income one makes or wealth one possesses, though these things do have some relevance. Individuals may have similar incomes, but nevertheless have completed different degrees of education or are employed in very different types of occupations. For that reason, they may not have shared values or common ideas and may pursue very different lifestyles. Other political and social factors influence what class individuals occupy. Day, Rickett, and Woolhouse (2014) explain that social class is a complex interaction of family background, individual experiences, membership and social networks, language and speech style, and lifestyle in addition to the more traditionally used indicators. One other factor that adds complexity is that individuals subjectively experience what class they occupy in ways that are inconsistent with typically used external measures.

Irrespective of what definition of class we employ, there is no question that it has a significant impact on virtually every aspect of a person's life, particularly in the case of poverty. Continuing to center this analysis of oppression from a Critical Psychology perspective, poverty and inequality must be placed at the very center of any serious analysis of oppression. We can begin to see this negative impact by examining *classism*, which is a collection of attitudes, beliefs, and behaviors expressed in everyday practices and institutional structures, and policies that oppress the poor. These attributes are then used to justify the contempt and disgust directed toward the poor and to legitimize their exploitation in order to serve the needs and purposes of the privileged. For example, traditional psychology has been complicit in these negative portrayals of the poor by describing them as low in intelligence, lacking in motivation to improve themselves, and engaging in criminal, immoral, and irresponsible behavior (Day et al., 2014; Smith, 2010).

The depth and degree at which the aversion and dehumanization of the poor is experienced is vividly illustrated in research conducted using brain imaging or MRI scans to examine the automatic and thus unconscious responses people make when looking at pictures of those who occupy the lowest rungs of society such as the homeless (Harris & Fiske, 2006). What this research found is that the patterns of brain activation when people were shown such photographs mirrored the disgust triggered by exposure to pictures of garbage, mutilation, and human waste. Moreover, the activation of those parts of the brain ordinarily connected to perceiving another human being did not occur when viewing pictures of a homeless person. As Harris and Fiske conclude, the findings indicate that our prejudice toward the lowest of the low goes very deep indeed. Not only are they regarded as no better than trash or waste; they are not even considered human.

This notion of the poor as "waste" and "trash" was present at the very beginning of the United States, as documented by Nancy Isenberg (2016) in her book *White Trash*. Isenberg discredits convincingly the fictitious narrative that early settlers of the New World sought to establish a country unlike the class-bound society of England and instead establish one in which all would be regarded as equal. Instead, the reality is that men of privilege in joint-stock companies driven by profit seized the opportunity of ridding England of undesirables and criminals by sending them off to settle the colonies. Their agenda was to reduce the population of the poor and destitute in England and, at the same time, send free or even slave labor to work in the colonies. And so individuals who were essentially regarded as waste and trash were callously cast away with little regard for their lives. The majority of people who landed on the shores of the New World were considered completely expendable and meant to be placed at the service of the privileged few. These expendables included vagrants, petty criminals, prostitutes, debtors, and even children who were swept up from the streets of London to make up for labor shortages in a practice called "spiriting." Despite the expectation that this "refuse" would end up dying off, as Isenberg points out, these individuals would make up a permanent underclass in the United States that continued to be considered of inferior breed and incapable of improvement.

Isenberg's book dispels still another illusion long held in the United States that it is a classless society. It is the meritocratic myth of the American Dream that the opportunities and resources to become successful are available to any and all who are willing to work hard. Extensive research has since shown that this class mobility scarcely occurs and, if anything, Americans are far more in jeopardy of seeing their economic status decline (Rank, 2004). In an article in *Science* Chetty, Grusky, Hell, Hedren, Manduka, and Narang (2017) did a comprehensive study of data using sophisticated statistical analysis and found that the rates of absolute mobility have fallen from 90% for children born in 1940 to 50% for children born in the 1980s. They conclude that the probability of children earning more than their parents has declined over the past century in the United States. Moreover, most of the decline in absolute mobility can be attributed to the increased inequality of distribution of economic growth in recent decades rather than any slowdown in the growth of the gross domestic product.

The sheer magnitude and pervasiveness of poverty and inequality is undeniable. For the moment, I will restrict myself to inequality in the United States. In the report *Income and Poverty in the United States: 2016* (Semega, Fontenot, & Kollar, 2017), it was reported that the overall poverty rate was 12.7% or 40.6 million. Children under 18 represented 18% or 13.3 million of those in poverty. Although children make up 23% of the population, they account for 32.6 % of those in poverty. Between 2009 and 2012, U.S. households experienced less income mobility than in previous years. Also, between 2009 and 2012, 34.5% of U.S. households had at least one spell of poverty lasting two or more months. Common causes for falling below the poverty level are unemployment and catastrophic illness.

Turning to statistics on inequality, a study published in *Nature* in 2017 was the product of collaboration between social scientists from fourteen different institutions (Kohler et al., 2017). It was the largest study of its kind, examining factors throughout human history that contributed to economic inequality as well as looking at current trends in inequality. It employed a well-established and accepted measure of inequality called the Gini coefficient, ranging from 0 (least inequality) to 1 (most inequality). Using this measure, the Gini index for the United States was .81, which represents an extreme degree of inequality. For comparison purposes, the Gini index for the ancient world (as in Patrician Rome) was estimated to be .59. Inequality existed at earlier points in history as well, but these levels were still exceeded by the U.S. rates. The authors were aware of the alarming implications of such levels of inequality, noting that a society can sustain only so much inequality before giving way to significant social unrest. As will be seen shortly, irrespective of whether such a significant crisis emerges, the degree of inequality has devastating consequences for well-being.

By itself, there is no greater risk for virtually every type of physical, psychological, and social malady than poverty, and this has long been recognized. The wide range of impacts of poverty is summarized in the following quote by Hofrichter (2003):

> Individuals at a socioeconomic disadvantage are more susceptible to death and disease, regardless of specific diseases, due to their greater exposure to conditions that produce disease. A strong relationship exists between degree of economic inequality and child poverty....These cumulative disadvantages occur within a historical legacy of socioeconomic and racial inequality. Poverty and correlated living conditions impose constraints on many aspects of everyday life that affect access to requisites for good health such as good nutrition, adequate housing, education, transportation, recreational activities, and environmental conditions....Social and psychological effects of absolute poverty are also harmful. Uncertainty, lack of control over one's life, helplessness, chronic stress, anxiety, and depression all contribute to ill health and even death. (pp. 16–17)

This quote makes it amply clear that there is not a single aspect of life that is not potentially adversely impacted by poverty. This exemplifies the oppression of the poor due to exploitation, marginalization, discrimination, and violence. Laura Smith (2010), who has written extensively on psychology's mischaracterization and neglect of the poor, documents how the negative stereotypes of the poor are used to justify the abuses of power that are creating an economic apartheid in our country as the poor get poorer and the rich get richer. The oppression of the poor occurs at both the highest levels in the form of inequities in political, educational, healthcare, judicial, and environmental policies and in the everyday social practices and attitudes that demean and dismiss them.

While facts and figures provide cogent evidence of the material and psychological harms inflicted on the poor, they themselves are ultimately the final and definitive experts on their experience of these harms. It is only through the narratives of the poor that flesh and blood is given to those grim figures. This added dimension is provided by both Smith (2010) and Rank (2004), who give words to the anguish and struggles of the poor. Within those narratives, one finds expected themes. These include having to live always on the edge of crisis or disaster as they struggle with deprivation in all areas daily. Due to the lack of essential resources, the poor must often make difficult and unjustifiable decisions about what necessary needs they must neglect in order to meet other ones. The tenuousness of their situation means that the possibility of plummeting into chaos is ever present. Such a precarious existence forces them to live life one day at a time and precludes any chance of presuming to have hopes or dreams for the future. The contempt and lack of regard shown to them mean that they live with stigma and are treated with disrespect. Painfully aware of their excluded status, they frequently experience shame and a sense of being left on the outside.

Given these bleak conditions, it is little wonder that the poor frequently experience despair, depression, helplessness, and hopelessness. They may turn to destructive solutions to manage these feelings, such as violence, drug and alcohol addiction, and suicide. They are also more likely to suffer from severe mental disorders (Rogers & Pilgrim, 2003). And as already noted, they have an increased risk of developing a wide range of physical disorders and die prematurely not only due to these illnesses but also due to lack of access to health care.

Though the existing dominant ideology portrays the poor as responsible for these abysmal conditions, the evidence that the causes are structural is far more valid and persuasive. Thus, it is critical that these structural causes be elucidated if we intend to strike at the core issue behind the suffering created by poverty and inequality. Rank (2004) devotes a substantial part of his book disputing what he calls the current paradigm that attributes poverty to individual characteristics of the poor and instead provides several lines of argument that poverty is due to structural failings. This makes clear that poverty constitutes deprivation and so is an injustice. The first of the structural failings is that the capitalist system is so structured that there will always be a lack of adequately well-paying jobs to support all individuals and their families who are looking for work. This is referred to by economists as a natural unemployment rate. For a free market economy to function effectively, a certain percentage of workers must be out of work since full employment would interfere with the ability of employers to attract and hire workers at what they deem to be a competitive wage. Furthermore, given the dramatic changes that have occurred in recent times in American industry, the number of low-paying jobs not requiring advanced education or specialized skills has grown much faster. Thus, a far larger portion of the U.S. workforce falls into the low-wage sector than do workers in other developed countries. The declining power of unions to effectively negotiate with management has also contributed to this situation,

The second major structural factor has been the progressive weakening of the social safety net to prevent poverty. As noted previously, the way funding is distributed in the federal budget provides ample evidence that the priorities of the federal government increasingly do not include providing public assistance to those in need. This disparity is again notable when compared with many other industrialized nations that invest far more of their budgets in providing the kinds of services and assistance that prevent poverty, including unemployment compensation, universal health care, childcare assistance, and aid to the disabled and destitute.

The third structural factor cited by Rank (2004) is revealed when one reviews data that provides a life-course analysis of poverty. This looks at patterns of the likelihood of people in the United States experiencing poverty over the course of their lifetime. What these data reveal is that over time a steadily increasing number of Americans will experience at least one year below the poverty line. In fact, a clear majority of them will experience poverty at some point during their adult years. This life-course analysis of poverty is important because it undermines the argument that poverty can be attributed merely to characteristics of the individual. While these risk factors may indeed be found in individuals, this vulnerability is only realized when some detrimental external event occurs that precipitates a crisis that jeopardizes their social standing. Rank observes that while there may be individual characteristics that help in part to explain why some people lose out in the economic game, it is larger structural forces such as layoffs, lack of health insurance, economic downturns, or social unrest that ensure there will be losers. He describes this situation using the metaphor of musical chairs in which there will never be enough chairs for those playing the game. Someone will always come out a loser.

An additional powerful line of evidence that illustrates the degree to which poverty and inequality is dictated by political policy comes from the economist, Paul Krugman (2007). He provides convincing data and analysis that the increasing level of inequality between the wealthy versus the poor and middle class is due to the rolling back of New Deal legislation placing social and political checks on business executives and increasing income tax on high incomes since the 1970s. He describes the Great Compression, so named by economic historians Claudia Goldin and Robert Margo, between the 1920s and 1950 in which there was a sharp decline in the gap between the rich and working class. This was achieved by New Deal policies, including a strengthening of the social safety net, wage controls, and, most important, a more equitable tax policy.

As Krugman observes, the sudden decline in the wealth of those at the top of the economic hierarchy was largely due to taxes. In the 1920s the top income tax rate was only 24%, and the estate tax on the largest inheritances was 20%. During Franklin Roosevelt's presidency, the top income tax rate rose to 63% during his first administration and to 79% during his second. It continued to increase and rose to 91% during Eisenhower's administration. There were corresponding increases during this time in the corporate tax rate and the estate tax. These policies gave rise to a higher level of affluence across the income levels while not sacrificing productivity and growth of the American economy. Sadly, however, it has been the conscious and deliberate disassembling of these progressive policies that not only has sacrificed these gains but has sent inequality soaring.

The final body of research that speaks powerfully to the structural determinants behind poverty and inequality and that offers penetrating insights into oppression has been mentioned earlier. It is the work that has been done on the social determinants of health. The earlier quote by Hofrichter (2003) touched on what these factors are and why they matter. The pioneering work was done by Marmot and Wilkinson (2006), who examined the various ways in which the social environment exerts a powerful influence on health. The World Health Organization has defined the social determinants of health as the conditions in which individuals are born, grow, live, work, and age. This definition makes clear that these determinants must be understood from a developmental perspective as the impacts they exert on health often are cumulative over time. Among the factors included as social determinants are neighborhood and physical environment (safety, housing, and transportation), food (access to healthy food and sufficiency of food), employment, education, community, and health care. Each of these factors has been investigated in terms of the respective protections and risks they provide that either contribute to health or increase the risk of morbidity (the likelihood of becoming ill) and mortality.

Work in the area of social determinants of health has led to more attention to a life-course perspective on rates of morbidity and mortality. This is because where people begin life and where they are in the social hierarchy exercises such a powerful impact on their health. For example, there is substantial evidence that individuals who experience severe material disadvantage and unhealthy psychosocial environments early in life will suffer cumulative adverse health consequences that continue well into adulthood (Evans & Cassells, 2014). The risk posed by social determinants is not equitably distributed throughout society but vary significantly across different populations. These disparities are aligned with disparities in political, economic and social power. Rose and Hatzenbuehler (2009), citing extensively from the work of Nancy Krieger (2005), explain the link between inequality and health using the concept of *embodiment*. Embodiment is a concept that refers to the ways in which we literally incorporate on a biological level the material and social world within which are embedded and live. It is in the very same sense that we embody oppression or, referring to the work of Cudd (2006), the way material harms give way to psychological harms.

This notion of embodiment was also put forward by Marmot and Wilkinson, who saw stress as playing an integral role in how inequality gets under our skin. Wilkinson and Pickett (2009) present an impressive array of findings based on the degree of inequality found in rich countries. Their decision to restrict their focus to developing countries was because the magnitude of poverty and deprivation found in poorer nations overrides any impact that inequality might have. The abject conditions under which most of the population live in poor countries exert a far greater impact on their health. The health indicators examined by Wilkinson and Pickett included community life and social relations, mental health and drug use, physical health and life expectancy, educational performance, obesity, teenage pregnancies, violence, rates of imprisonment, and social mobility. Their overall finding was that as the degree of inequality grew, there was a corresponding decline in all indicators with respect to the health and well-being of individuals and their communities.

The manner in which stress helped to account for these findings was based on how central our societal nature is to understanding the way we look at and evaluate ourselves. Our self-esteem is derived in part from our perception of where we stand vis-à-vis others and to what degree we live up to the standards and norms that society holds up as indicators of success and achievement. We can see how the previous discussion of consumer culture fits into this analysis as the markers of achievement are heavily based in material success. Likewise, the literature on consumer culture revealed the considerable effort put into increasing individuals' level of personal insecurity and encouraging them to make upward social comparisons. It is little surprise, therefore, that in societies marked by high levels of inequality, those at the bottom of the ladder will experience a larger number of threats to their social self, which then increases their level of anxiety and stress. Their heightened level of shame also poses the threat of confirming the attributions of being inferior imposed on them by society, thus deepening their distress even more. This may then stimulate efforts on their part to improve their image by increasing their competitive strivings and working harder to get the positive feedback they crave. However, their occupying a lower social status impairs these efforts by depriving them of the control as well as the resources and opportunities necessary to succeed.

The pattern described above is essentially a vicious cycle in which the poor and those suffering from extreme inequality are condemned no matter what they do. While images of success, fame, and fortune are dangled before them and they are bombarded with messages that these things are not only what they should desire but within their reach, their hopes of "making it" are constantly thwarted. And each failure casts a shadow not on the deceptive culture that has peddled these illusions, but instead on them. These experiences fulfill the very negative stereotypes that the more powerful and privileged hold of them. In fact, with each new frustration, the poor and oppressed become more and more fearful, but also convinced, that these stereotypes are true.

While the demands placed on the poor are greater than those on the privileged, the degree of control they have over their lives is far less. The outcome is a level of stress that not only increases but becomes unrelenting. And according to Wilkinson and Pickett (2009) and the research on embodiment, it is precisely this stress that tears away at their health on a physical and psychological level, leading to a higher risk for illness and an earlier death. As Rose and Hatzenbuehler (2009) conclude, "In this framework, people's bodies (including their brains, minds and emotions) contain the cumulative impact of their material existence and its meaning, primarily as an outcome of unequal levels of stress and its biological impact" (p. 463).

Chapter 5

Self-Deception

Providing a Critical Foundation—A Basic Description of Consciousness

An investigation of self-deception is necessary to understanding the ways in which ideological forces shape, distort, and obscure consciousness via mystification. The subject of consciousness is inescapably bound up with how oppression inflicts suffering. The topic of consciousness has been encountered in previous chapters but no formal definition or description of what is meant by consciousness has been offered. Until now a commonsense way of understanding consciousness has been assumed. This framework is no longer enough as it will not permit a clear description of the processes of both self-deception and mystification. Thus, a more detailed and formal framework for describing consciousness is provided here. However, the overview provided will still in some ways be cursory because of the complexities that are inevitably encountered when trying to fully grasp just what consciousness is. With that understood, some guiding definitions and principles are offered regarding what consciousness is in terms of the essential functions it performs and the structures around which it is organized.

For purposes of this discussion, the following definition will be employed: *Consciousness is the medium by and through which we know, evaluate, and act upon our experience of ourselves and the world.* The way in which I have framed this description is to avoid characterizing consciousness as a thing. In this regard, I agree with Combs (2002, 2009), who sees consciousness as the essence of experience, as a kind of subjective presence that exists in constant relationship to the world and so is always oriented toward some specific object. Similarly, Garcia-Tomeu and Tart (2013) proposed the following definition of consciousness: "...consciousness refers to the subjective awareness and experience of both internal and external phenomena. These phenomena may include but are not limited to internal sensations, perceptions, thoughts, emotions, and the sense of self, as well as perception of all classes of external objects, events, and other stimuli" (p. 123). This observation that consciousness is always conscious of something is called *intentionality* in phenomenological philosophy (Husserl, 1962). This again makes clear the essentially relational nature of existence.

This core assumption of phenomenological philosophy—that all things exist in relationship with each other (Spinelli, 2014) has also been a persistent assertion of mystical schools of thought within world religions (Watts, 1951; Wilber, 1980). Consciousness expresses this inescapable fact of inter-relatedness as it is the medium by which human beings actively participate in the ever-unfolding process of engaging in and with the world. On one hand, one can think of consciousness as a beam of light that is constantly and intentionally directed by the human subject toward an object that then becomes disclosed as the point of focus for the moment. This introduces a certain element of stability and permanence as individuals reify or categorize that moment of consciousness in order to impose order or structure upon it. However, given the dynamic nature of the process, these moment-by-moment characterizations prove to be partial, incomplete and ultimately an artifice. Psychologist William James (1890/1981) thus adopted the metaphor of a stream to capture how consciousness is continuous while also being ever-changing. Using this description also helps to make clear why it is better to understand consciousness as a verb (process) rather than as a noun (thing).

There are three dimensions or lines of relationship along which consciousness engages or processes experience. This serves to help explain the core functions performed by consciousness and the structures along which those functions are organized. The first is the *cognitive* dimension or how we seek to know something. In this sense consciousness is the means by which we acquire information in order to expand our grasp of what exists and what it means. Implicit here is that there is a world that in some ways exists independently of us, although there remains a vital and inescapable relationship that we have with it. This world can be accessed by means of faculties such as attention, sensation and perception. The data acquired is used to organize, categorize and construct representations of our experience. The term *schema* was used previously to refer to these basic units of experience (Goleman, 1985). Schemas are made up of hypotheses or assumptions that condense data into categories that capture similarities underlying diverse experiences. These categories then are employed to label and interpret these types of experiences going forward. Schemas are expressions of our basic need to impose order and stability on what would otherwise be an overwhelming onslaught of information.

This collection of schemas then become integrated into a more inclusive structural framework that establishes a sense of continuity to our lives and experience and holds at bay chaos and the threat it imposes to our sense of security. This broader structure can be called a *worldview* (Spinelli, 2014). Because it is something constructed by human beings, it contains biases. These are selective and narrowed understandings that reflect the overall approach that persons have adopted for coming to terms with life and for realizing their overall life project. Core elements of the worldview, according to Spinelli, include fundamental beliefs, values, and attitudes regarding oneself, others, the world, and the relations that exist between all of these. Because these schemas and structures are invented by persons, the degree of fit between them and the data provided by their actual experience varies. Some exclusion, editing and distortion inevitably occur in the process, often in accord with the need to maintain the core beliefs, assumption and values of the person.

Based on this cognitive dimension of consciousness, experience can be described based on the polarity of Subject and Object or Knower and Known. This again establishes that consciousness must be understood in relational terms as the principle of intentionality requires that for every subject there must be an object. It is meaningless to talk about either independently of the other. Each makes essential contributions to our knowledge and understanding. Phenomenological philosophy describes the contributions of the object as the noematic element. This consists of what the object discloses to the subject, what it reveals to the knower in the relationship. The contributions made by the subject are called the noetic element. It refers to the ways in which the central elements of a person's worldview actively shape the experience and endow meaning on it.

The subject–object polarity on which consciousness is based provides one further set of insights pertinent to the upcoming discussion of self-deception. Expressed again in metaphoric terms, consciousness unfolds moment by moment based upon whether it is directed *outward* away from the self or reflected *inward* back upon the self. These two modes form a dialectical relationship as both are inextricably interwoven. However, they are also mutually exclusive in the sense that consciousness cannot perform both operations at the same time. In other words, when consciousness is directed outward, its awareness of itself is inhibited and temporarily suspended. Likewise, when consciousness is directed inward, its awareness of the outside object is inhibited and temporarily suspended. Under ordinary circumstances, consciousness unfolds as a ceaseless fluctuation between these two poles of experience. However, as will be seen, this process can also become one-sided, rigid, and inflexible, which then increases the likelihood of self-deception.

Each of the two modes of consciousness has distinct characteristics that can be described and that result in very different ways of experiencing ourselves and the other (or object of our awareness). These distinctions play an important role in the existential philosopher, Jean Paul Sartre's (1953) perceptive analysis of self-deception in his major work, *Being and Nothingness*. Beginning first with the mode in which consciousness is directed outward, Sartre describes this as *prereflective or nonthetic* consciousness. In this state, persons become deeply absorbed in the object of their awareness as it occupies the focus and center of their awareness. The state of absorption is so powerful that for the moment all awareness of ourselves is absent because we are plunged into the world of objects outside of us. Aligned with this absorption, persons as knowers may feel a close identification with the object of awareness, even to the extent of, at least for the moment, blurring the distinction between knower and the known. This can lead to a sense of extreme identification of persons with another person or an object. The previous discussion of the problem of the ego made clear the hazards associated with such intense identification.

On the other hand, the state in which we turn consciousness back on ourselves and make ourselves the object of our awareness is described by Sartre as reflective or thetic consciousness. At moments like these, we become more self-aware and engage in an examination of and deliberation on our actions and inner experiences. We compare our experience in the moment with other experiences drawn from our memory and interpret and evaluate that experience accordingly. As in the case of prereflective consciousness, reflective consciousness can also take a more extreme form in which we become excessively absorbed in ourselves or painfully self-aware, such as the experience of shame. Heightened states of self-consciousness may also be found in an exaggerated sense of self-importance, a kind of idolizing of oneself.

To illustrate what this polarity might feel like, Sartre gives the example of a bit of peeping tom who out of curiosity begins to snoop into what is happening in the apartment of a neighbor. And so, one day he decides to look through the keyhole of the neighbor's apartment door and soon becomes entranced with what he sees. As Sartre observes, while engaged in this snooping the person involved loses all awareness of himself. Instead he becomes completely drawn into the scene he observes from the keyhole. It is as if he has physically transported himself into the apartment of his neighbor. And that is where he remains until he suddenly hears someone from behind him saying, "Ahem." He has been caught engaging in what would be deemed an unacceptable intrusion into affairs that do not concern him. At that very moment, his consciousness is drawn out of the apartment and flips dramatically to being directed back on himself. He becomes painfully self-aware as he has fallen under the critical glance (and seemingly control) of the person who has caught him. Sartre employs the powerful metaphor that it is like a pin being stuck into a butterfly. The person is immobilized by the critical look of another.

This discussion of the peeping tom lends itself to consideration of the second dimension that can be used to describe a core function of conscious. That is the role played by consciousness in evaluating experience, or what I will call the *affective* dimension. Affective typically refers to our emotions. Embedded within our emotions in addition to feeling is also some value assigned to experiences that give rise to those emotions. On the most basic level, these affective assessments given to our experience can be understood in hedonistic terms as those things that give us pleasure and those that give us pain. Experiences associated with pleasure are assigned a positive value that can be described as like, love, or good. Those associated with pain are assigned a negative value that can be described as dislike, hate, or evil. As Freud (1961) observed at some point in his theorizing, the polarity of pleasure versus pain can ultimately be understood as an expression of the polarity of life versus death. That which is positive is that which affirms and advances life; that which is negative is that which affirms and advances death.

The feeling and accompanying assignment of value dictates the ways in which persons act upon the experience. In a later discussion, the affective dimension will be described as inextricably interwoven with the cognitive one. This is because human beings seek to identify themselves with experiences associated with pleasure or positive feelings and seek to deny or disown experiences associated with pain or other negative feelings. One way in which this disowning unfolds is that the negative experience is regarded as alien to the person—or as "other," not-me. These dynamics of alienation are an integral element of self-deception. Likewise, many times the appraisal of or judgment made about experience occurs automatically and without our being aware of it. This type of appraisal that occurs in a prereflective state of consciousness will also play an important role in the beginnings of self-deception. Such appraisals need to be distinguished from those in which the evaluation of an experience is made when persons assume a reflective stance allowing for examination and analysis prior to rendering a judgment.

The third dimension pertinent to a function performed by consciousness has to do with how persons act upon those experiences and, in doing so, act upon themselves, others, and the world. This is called the *conative* dimension, and it pertains to how persons act on thoughts and feelings. This reminds us that consciousness is not a completely passive process of simply taking in information, but that much of how we understand life is the product of a structure we create for giving it sense, purpose, and meaning. There are two basic ways in which we act upon our thoughts and feelings that closely parallel the previously described polarity of prereflective consciousness and reflective consciousness. Deikman (1976) described this as bimodal consciousness, which performs two functions. The first is the receptive function, which is oriented toward taking in information from the environment. In this mode attention is more diffuse, and the subject and object are less differentiated from each other (i.e., prereflective). The second is the active function, which is oriented toward manipulating or exerting control over the environment, attaining and achieving goals, and avoiding pain. This mode is associated with reflective consciousness.

I (Gruba-McCallister, 1993, 2002) have distinguished these two modes as active and passive volition. The inclusion of "volition" in these descriptions is intended to stay faithful to the conative dimension as it recognizes human will as involved in consciousness and the ways in which humans act upon experience. Looking at these two forms of volition also illustrates how the three dimensions interact with one another to create characteristic ways in which we know, evaluate, and act on ourselves and the world. In exercising active volition, we are aware that we are exerting effort and applying ourselves to the accomplishment of some task. The objectives are control, manipulation, and mastery. A stance is assumed based on being evaluative and analytical in considering how to make use of objects to meet needs and achieve goals. Finally, in exercising active volition we are performing functions that are under our voluntary control (that is, actions that are under our conscious attention and control).

At first glance, the term passive volition may sound like a contradiction. However, this is not to be confused with complete lack of control or submissively allowing things to be done to oneself. Passive volition is a form of control in which we willingly abandon ourselves to a process and permit it to happen. It is a "letting be" attitude in which we have granted consent to whatever may unfold. This means that passive volition is open, receptive, and non-evaluative. Persons do not interfere in a process and allow it to proceed while fully participating in it. In a state of passive volition, individuals experience themselves as completely absorbed in someone or something else and so experience a temporary loss of self. Examples of such experiences are being deeply moved by some work of art, becoming absorbed in some pleasurable activity, performing some physical feat smoothly and effortlessly, or falling in love. Passive volition is an essential ingredient in learning relaxation techniques or practicing meditation or some other spiritual exercise. As can be seen from the description, passive volition is associated with a prereflective state of consciousness. It is involved in performing functions that are not under our voluntary control (i.e., that occur without consciousness or attention, such as vital body functions like breathing, heartbeat, digestion).

Several more points can be drawn from this discussion of consciousness. The first is that consciousness does not refer to a single, unitary process. Rather consciousness forms a continuum that is made up of different types or states of consciousness. This was famously observed by William James (1958), who asserted that our waking state (which many of us mistake as consciousness) is just one state of consciousness separated by very filmy and almost imperceptible barriers from a number of other states of consciousness (such as deep sleep, dreaming, trance). Every day all of us move from one state of consciousness to another, often without even realizing that we have made the transition. Charles Tart (Garcia-Romeu & Tart, 2013), a prominent researcher in this area, has found that these different states of consciousness are distinguishable. Each can be described as a unique dynamic configuration of psychological structures that are experienced by individuals as distinct from each other. Each state is qualitatively different from others, such that they can be identified and studied. Another way to state this point is that there are different ways in which we can know ourselves and the world. The discussion of self-deception and mystification will identify and describe some of these different ways of knowing.

A related and similar point is that consciousness can be divided (Hilgard, 1986) or, put simply, human beings can do more than one thing at a time. This point again will be pivotal to understanding self-deception. Hilgard, a prominent researcher in the area of hypnosis, finds in hypnotic phenomena some valuable insights regarding consciousness. Those same insights will shed considerable light on self-deception and mystification. This ability to do more than one thing at a time relies on certain functions being performed without persons being aware. These functions occur in parallel smaller streams that operate simultaneously within a larger stream of consciousness. Sometimes they can operate in a harmonious and integrative fashion, and other times they can conflict and be at odds with each other. The capacity for human beings' thoughts, emotions, and behavior to be motivated by factors of which they are unaware brings the concept of the unconscious into discussion—again, an area of substantial theory and research. I will be arguing that the term "unconscious" is both confusing and inaccurate in that it implies something occurring essentially in the absence of consciousness. In that the absence of consciousness signals the end of life, this is clearly nonsensical. Instead, what we call "unconscious" is better understood as an altered state of consciousness distinct from ordinary consciousness (Gruba-McCallister, 1993).

A Matter of Life or Death

The roots of self-deception lie in an innate response found in many species, including human beings, that has been shaped by evolution and so has existed for perhaps millions of years. It is called the fight-or-flight response. It is triggered by circumstances that pose a danger to the homeostatic or balanced state the body seeks to maintain. This happens when something unpredictable and unexpected happens that so challenges our ability to adapt to the change that our very survival is threatened. This response occurs automatically—that is, without our consciously thinking about it. This automaticity is clearly an evolutionary advantage in that the time it would take to realize that a danger is being posed may delay the actions necessary to cope with the threat. This threat triggers a state of hyperarousal that mobilizes different parts of the body to respond by either attacking the threat or fleeing from it. This includes increasing heart rate and lung function, constricting the blood vessels, providing more energy to the muscles to act, slowing down or stopping digestion, and dilating the pupils to improve sight.

The fight-or-flight response originates from the autonomic nervous systems (ANS), which is responsible for a range of automatic functions of the body (i.e., functions that occur without our conscious awareness). The ANS is divided into two parts. The sympathetic division's main function is to activate the physiological changes involved in the fight-or-flight response while the parasympathetic division is involved in de-escalating the state of arousal and returning the body to homeostasis. The ANS developed much earlier in human evolution and so is involved in very basic physical functions (hunger, thirst, sex, emotions).

The importance of the fight-or-flight response to illness and health was expanded upon through the work done by Hans Selye (1974, 1976) on stress. While Selye was in medical school, he observed that people who were ill had very similar reactions even though they had very different diseases. These included things like loss of appetite, weight loss, and decreased energy. He wondered if these things might be part of a syndrome of "just being sick." He later returned to this observation when he was doing research with rats to discover a new hormone. This research required him to regularly give the rats injections (an unpleasant and life-threatening experience for them). When he later conducted autopsies on these rats, he again observed a common pattern of changes in their bodies. Their adrenal cortex became enlarged; the thymus, spleen, lymph nodes and other parts of the lymphatic system shrank in size; and the rats developed bleeding ulcers in the stomach and upper gut.

Selye concluded that the experience of repeated injections had triggered a state of extreme arousal in the rats, a fight-or-flight response. What made the situation worse was that it was one that the rats could neither escape nor resist. Selye reframed the fight-or-flight response as the *stress reaction.* From this discovery, Selye launched some of the most important work about how humans and animals alike become sick and die due to stress. Selye defined stress as the nonspecific response of the body to any demand made upon it. The demands that triggered stress were called stressors, and they could range in severity depending on the degree of demand imposed. The response made is nonspecific because it is identical irrespective of the stressor.

The fight-or-flight response was part of the first stage in this stereotyped stress reaction called by Selye the General Adaptation

Syndrome (GAS). That first stage is the *alarm reaction*, in which a threat to the balance or homeostasis of the body is perceived and recognized and the body is mobilized to resist the threat. This state is very brief and so intended to deal with the threat quickly and efficiently if possible. The second stage is called *adaptation* or *stage of resistance*, in which the body works to cope with the stressor and restore homeostasis. However, if the threat persists, these efforts fail to deal with the danger and restore balance. The body cannot sustain this heightened state of arousal without inflicting damage to itself. It no longer has the energy or resources to manage the situation and enters the stage of *exhaustion*. At that point illness and even death occur. This pattern, described by Selye as unfolding in the GAS, will prove to be extremely important to understanding self-deception and the ways in which it gives rise to a self-defeating pattern that has harmful effects.

Subsequent research has been done to clarify what makes certain events stressors that then give rise to the stress reaction. Selye (1974) himself observed that events occur all the time that pose some challenge to our homeostasis, and we are constantly called upon to adapt to changing conditions. In this he echoes the Buddha's insight that the transient nature of life is the basis for suffering. Given the constancy of change, Selye sagely observed that the answer to dealing with stress is not to strive to remove it from our lives because that is impossible. It is likewise true that not every unpredictable or unexpected situation causes us distress. The key to whether a stressor will trigger a stress reaction is how we interpret the situation. This insight was substantially elaborated on by psychologist Richard Lazarus and his colleagues (Lazarus & Folkman, 1984). Lazarus found that two cognitive appraisals were made of a stressor prior to eliciting of the stress reaction. In other words, it is indeed the way in which persons think about or interpret the situation that is critical. The primary appraisal is whether the situation poses an immediate threat or the expectation of some future discomfort or danger. The second appraisal is whether persons feel they have the necessary resources to deal with the threat. Both appraisals occur without our conscious awareness—again, because that is more of an evolutionary advantage.

These two appraisals echo familiar themes. In the case of the first one, the issue is a matter of life or death. The powerful response that human beings have to anything that raises the question of whether their being is at issue is a core element of the experience of suffering and oppression. Terror management theory (Solomon, Greenberg, & Pyszczynski, 1991) is one useful framework for understanding the significant role that fear (in particular, fear of our eventual death) plays in how human beings behave. Likewise, the second appraisal speaks to another persistent theme regarding the importance placed by human beings on feeling in control and maintaining order and stability. Just as a certain degree of anxiety regarding death is natural and inevitable, a desire to maintain control serves some useful and important functions.

These points are echoed by Goleman's (1985) extended treatment of self-deception. He explains that the mind innately possesses the capacity to protect itself by narrowing attention and inhibiting awareness. Some of the filtering function of the mind is a legacy of evolution, as it is found not only in humans but in other species. Our senses and perception have already been shaped to process only certain forms of information and to attend to some data and not to others. However, in addition to this first type of screening that filters out certain types of sensory input, Goleman observes that lacunae or blind spots are created in our attention under conditions in which we experience anxiety caused by a threat to our survival. A critical function of attention is to gather information vital to our survival. This capacity to block attention, however, also becomes the basis for self-deception. This is because a compromise is struck in which we restore a sense of security by narrowing attention; however, in exchange, our grasp and understanding of a situation is distorted and skewed in line with our need for control and maintaining pre-existing expectations and assumptions.

Goleman connects this process to endorphins which are neurotransmitters that function like opiates in the brain, a kind of painkiller. He also relates the process to the stress reaction described by Hans Selye. This fits within an evolutionary framework in that there is an advantage to the way in which dimmed attention soothes pain. The tuning out of pain under conditions of threat enables humans and animals to more effectively attend to the immediate dangers present. Goleman (1985) writes:

> Fitness for survival falls to members of a species who, when events warrant, are best able to ignore their pain while dealing with the threat at hand. The high survival value of pain-numbing would explain why it is found in primitive brain areas, which humans share with more ancient species. Indeed, opiate receptors have been found in every species examined, including those with nervous systems as primitive as leeches. (p. 38)

In the ideas of both Lazarus and Folkman and Goleman, there is a pivotal assumption made regarding this process. The appraisals made of the situation and the alterations of attention and awareness to screen out or reinterpret the threat are operations that occur without our conscious awareness. Due to the process of evolution, there are certain situations universally found among human beings that will elicit a fight-or-flight response. These can be encapsulated by common forms of phobias or irrational fears found among human beings (fear of strangers, water, heights, animals, enclosed spaces, etc.). However, over time, what is designated as a threat becomes increasingly more subjective and so is shaped through the process of social learning. It is these acquired fears and anxieties that are of far greater importance to self-deception as well as to oppression and the process of mystification. What remains the same is the automaticity with which these operations occur, and that automaticity now needs to be examined more closely.

In the earlier discussion of consciousness, it was pointed out that consciousness can sometimes process information, evaluate situations, and carry out actions outside of our awareness. Of course, the pioneer of this idea was Sigmund Freud, who did ground-breaking work on the role of unconscious motives in much of human behavior. Since that time there has been extensive research that has substantiated that the human nervous system is structured to carry out a wide range of activities that occur outside of consciousness. In fact, the argument can be made that the processing of any information would not be possible without this capacity. Consciousness can be understood as a serial information processing system in which we can access data and act upon it, employing parallel streams of consciousness (Hilgard, 1986). Hilgard speaks of two types of functions that can occur without conscious awareness. The first type encompasses executive functions that include planning goals, initiating actions in accordance with those goals, and sustaining such action in the face of obstacles and distractions. The second type includes monitoring functions such as maintaining alertness, scanning input, being vigilant to threats to safety, using selective attention to edit disturbing information, and exercising critical judgment (appraising). This automatization of functions as a result of evolution, or the formation of habits through learning, has the advantage of setting the mind free to devote time and energy to other matters. It is often advantageous to be able to do more than one thing at a time, but, as we will shortly see, this automaticity also poses some clear dangers.

Since Freud's theory was advanced, the questions of whether the unconscious exists and, if so, how best it can be explained have been subjects of heated debate. The debate will not be settled here. Still, some framework for understanding how the nervous system can carry on activities outside of awareness is essential for any explanation of self-deception. I stated earlier my position that what we call the unconscious is actually an altered state of consciousness distinct from our ordinary conscious awareness. To provide a rationale for this position, I will turn first to what we can learn from hypnosis, which I also believe to be an altered state of consciousness. Hypnosis is a particularly apt topic of interest, based on the observation made by individuals such as R. D. Laing (1967), Alan Watts (1951, 1961, and 1966), and Erich Fromm (1960) that the means by which society inculcates individuals with illusions that lull them into a state of self-deception and contribute to their oppression is akin to being inducted into a hypnotic trance, The second line of argument that I will be using in analyzing the role of the unconscious in self-deception comes from phenomenological and existential philosophy.

What We Can Learn from Hypnosis

Different ways of describing the organization of the mind have been proposed to accommodate operations that occur without conscious awareness. Among the earliest such thinkers were individuals who were involved with the study and use of hypnosis (Crabtree, 1993). One of these was French physician Pierre Janet, who proposed the *dissociative model* (Ellenberger, 1970). For a time, this was the dominant model and even Freud, who studied in Paris with Janet, subscribed to this view. However, he subsequently rejected it and adopted what is called the *depth model*, which then secured wide acceptance (Ellenberger, 1970). However, as interest in sexual abuse and other forms of trauma increased, attention returned to the dissociative model. This return was also supported by research in hypnosis. As previously mentioned, Hilgard (1986) was one of those proponents.

Hilgard asserted that the unity of consciousness is illusory. One way to think of dissociation is that there exists within each person a series of parallel strands or streams of consciousness that are vertically separated from one another. In this view, consciousness is divided such that several streams can co-occur in a seemingly independent fashion. This opposes the horizontal organization of consciousness advanced by

Freud. Each of these strands can be identified as being relatively coherent patterns of behavior with a sufficient degree of complexity to represent what might be thought of as a "part" of a person possessing a certain degree of internal organization. In some instances, these distinctive strands are rather basic in nature, such as an automatized routine performed in a required situation or to meet a certain need. Certain well-learned and habitual skills might fall into this category, such as driving or performing some athletic skill at which one is very proficient.

There is another way in which to think about these "parts" of ourselves. Some theorists employing an integral psychology framework (Foreman, 2010; Ingersoll & Zeitler, 2010) conceive of our sense of identity as a self-system composed of several elements or parts. These include the antecedent self, which can be thought of as the source from which consciousness emanates—the witness present at all levels of awareness. The proximate self is the unique subjective sense we have of ourselves, the way in which we see and understand ourselves. It can also be equated with the ego as it consists of the sum of our identifications, all those things with which we have formed powerful attachments. The shadow, on the other hand, is made up of experiences that we disown and push out of our awareness because we find them aversive, painful, or threatening. By disowning these experiences, we make them "other" and either pretend as though these experiences never occurred or that they are in no way connected with us. In other words, the disowning of these experiences involves self-deception, telling lies to ourselves that enable us to reject integrating these experiences into our sense of identity.

Finally, different strands of consciousness can be viewed as subpersonalities (Assagioli, 1965) capable of acting like a person for a short period of time. These subpersonalities are semi-permanent and can act with a certain degree of autonomy from the rest of the elements of the self-system. At times, these subpersonalities, like the shadow, are aspects of the self that have been dissociated or split off and pushed out of awareness. From this description, we can see that individuals can have a sense of identity characterized by different degrees of integration and harmony. The degree to which persons experience themselves as having a cohesive sense of self is dependent upon the degree to which dissociation or splitting off of experiences has been engaged in. This will be taken up further in the discussion of alienation that follows.

These strands are separated by what is called an amnesia barrier that prevents their integration or contact with each other during those times when dissociation between them persists. In other words, to varying degrees these "parts" may or may not be aware of one another. These "parts" or "divisions" are also sometimes called forms of *co-consciousness* which typically include memories organized around an emotion associated with events bearing some similarity to one another. The degree and severity of dissociation that occurs between these co-consciousness streams can vary and have different degrees of negative impact on the well-being of individuals. A certain amount of dissociation of minor variety occurs in everyday life with no adverse effects. Examples might be daydreaming, becoming so absorbed in a book or a movie that one loses track of oneself and of the passage of time, or engaging in some athletic activity such as running. Hypnosis is also an altered state of consciousness that is cultivated by inducing experiences of dissociation. Further, many of the phenomena that are associated with being in a hypnotic trance—such as hypnotic amnesia, age regression, pain control, and positive and negative hallucinations—are examples of dissociative states.

Finally, dissociation can function as a defense mechanism or coping strategy. When functioning as a defense, dissociation implies the presence of two or more incompatible or conflicting strands of consciousness that are structured in such a way as to exclude all but one from conscious awareness. Dissociation is automatically employed by individuals to deal with extreme circumstances such as trauma. This is achieved using two specific strategies, both of which are essential elements of dissociation. The first is *derealization.* When something overwhelmingly frightening and painful happens to persons, they can deny that it is actually happening. They enter a state of consciousness in which the world seems to take on an unreal quality as if they were looking at it from a distance or projected on a television screen. As a result, individuals feel detached and disconnected from the immediate circumstances they are in in order to provide themselves with some sense of safety. What was once familiar now feels strange, almost as if it were a dream.

The second is *depersonalization.* This can be described as feeling as though something is not actually happening to you but to someone else. This also can help persons deal with extreme anxiety or the sense that their existence is at risk. As in the case of derealization, persons feel a sense of detachment from themselves. It is as if they are observing themselves from a distance. This then enables them to attenuate or block out their physical sensations, perception, emotions, and thoughts. If taken to an extreme, depersonalization may lead to the creation of the kind of alter-ego that may take on a life of its own. While extreme examples of derealization and depersonalization are described here, they can be experienced in less extreme forms in daily life.

With the dissociative model described, we can return to the subject of hypnosis, beginning with an essential feature of how persons are inducted to enter a hypnotic trance. The process is facilitated by having individuals turn their attention away from themselves and instead toward another fixed point of focus. That point of focus can be just about anything, but the intent—returning to the earlier discussion of the structure and function of consciousness—is to cultivate a prereflective state of consciousness in which individuals' attention becomes deeply absorbed in something other than themselves. As this attention grows stronger, they first increasingly lose a sense of themselves. Simultaneously, the object of their awareness assumes greater prominence and power. What occurs was previously described in Assagioli's (1965) principle of identification, which stated that anything with which we become closely identified eventually dominates us by virtue of our investing it with so much of our attention. In the process, we can lose ourselves and become enslaved to our identifications because we mistakenly assume that such identifications can in some way encapsulate and constitute our entire sense of identity and worth.

One consequence of this outward focus is that individuals in a trance become much more suggestible. They are far more receptive to accepting suggestions, instructions, or assertions made by the hypnotist, in part because the words or directives of the hypnotist assume a greater degree of authority and power. This suggestibility is also due to another and more important feature of the trance state, and that is called *the suspension of the critical function*. Instead of pausing to consider and evaluate the information being received, people who are hypnotized accept it at face value, unquestioningly. This loss of the critical function is due to the predominance of a prereflective state of consciousness while in a trance. As suggested by the term "prereflective," our ability to detach ourselves from the immediate situation and reflect on it critically has been temporarily suspended. Our ability to maintain any skepticism or caution about what we are experiencing has been rendered inoperative. Things are just as they appear to be. We stop at the obvious, and we confuse the way things appear with the truth. This suspension of the critical function is an especially dangerous feature of this state of consciousness as it makes us much more vulnerable to the influence of others, particularly powerful others. It paralyzes our ability to question what is being posed as irrefutable. As a result, the capacity of a person in a trance to accurately engage in reality testing (i.e., distinguish what is real and what is not) is compromised. One can clearly see how individuals in such a state would be far more susceptible to propaganda and other forms of mind control that are associated with oppression.

It should be remembered, however, that the suspension of critical judgment is temporary. Even in a hypnotic trance, individuals are not rendered completely passive and subject to the control of the hypnotist (although this is a misconception fostered in fictional and dramatic accounts). One way to understand why this is so is something called the "hidden observer" that was discovered by Hilgard (1986). What Hilgard found was that while subjects were in a hypnotic trance there was a part of them, or a form of consciousness, that was capable of being aware of things that hypnotic subjects seemed not to be aware of. For example, in an experiment in which individuals were hypnotized to feel less pain, when told to submerge their arms in ice water, they would report little or no pain while at the same time the "hidden observer" would report the level of pain that was actually being experienced. In a sense, there is a part of the person that remains aware of what is happening, monitors the information being processed, and so can provide accurate observations. This part can also exercise a protective function by alerting hypnotized subjects when some suggestion is contrary to their values or when some danger is posed to them requiring immediate action—which would lead to the person emerging from the trance.

Before discussing several other important and relevant features of trance, there is one other very powerful force that paralyzes our critical faculties, and that is fear or anxiety. To illustrate this, I will use an experiment conducted by psychologist O. Hobart Mowrer (1948) delineating what he called the "neurotic paradox." In this experiment, Mowrer used rats that he placed in a cage that had three compartments (A, B and C). Compartments A and B had floors that were grids that could be electrified, while C did not. In compartment A there was a light that would be used as a signal. The experiment began by turning on the light and then electrifying compartments A and B. Upon receiving the shock, rats eventually fled to compartment C to escape the shock. Based on classical conditioning, the rats learned that the light was a signal that the shock was going to be administered. This then triggered their escaping the shock by fleeing to compartment C when the light went on. One could say that at this point the rat had formed a phobia to the light.

In the next phase of the experiment, the light again was turned on; this time compartment A was not electrified, but compartment B was. Based on what they had learned, as soon as the rats saw the light, they automatically ran to compartment C. But this time the conditions were different because the rats were shocking themselves unnecessarily since remaining in compartment A would have spared them being shocked. However, their heightened state of arousal did not permit them to think before acting. The mere threat of re-experiencing pain was enough to trigger the desire to escape. This is what Mowrer referred to as the "neurotic paradox." In other words, the rats had developed an irrational, habitual pattern of behavior that inflicted pain on them that could have been avoided. This avoidant pattern had become so rigid and inflexible that the mere hint of danger caused them to panic and engage in a self-defeating strategy of coping because they inflicted on themselves the very pain they hoped to avoid.

The next question was how to "cure" the rats of their neurosis? This was the final phase of the experiment. A barrier was placed between compartments A and B so that when the light was turned on, the rats were prevented from escaping to C. As might be expected, initially this caused the rats a great deal of panic and agitation as they tried everything they could to escape without success. Eventually their efforts at resistance and agitation were exhausted, and they were forced to realize that the light no longer signaled danger. Turning on the light no longer triggered a panicked reaction. At that point the barrier between A and B was removed and when the light turned on, the rats remained in compartment A where they were safe and no longer unnecessarily shocked themselves. They had been cured.

The lessons learned by the rats in this experiment have relevance to human beings, who also learn dysfunctional ways of managing anxiety in certain situations that lead them to engage in similar self-defeating patterns. Mowrer believed that this experiment illustrated what he called the *two-factor theory of learning.* As noted previously, what was responsible for the rats learning to avoid a situation posing a danger to them was the fight-or-flight response. This hyper-aroused response is mediated by the autonomic nervous system (ANS), as evidenced in the immediate and automatic reaction of escaping from the pain signaled by the light. This first form of learning is involuntary and occurs automatically as soon as a sign of danger is presented. This is a more visceral type of learning rooted in emotions, basic needs, and physiological functions. Also, it is a more primitive way of experiencing and dealing with the world, as the ANS developed earlier in evolution to perform very basic physiological functions including attention, emotion, memory, hunger, thirst, and sex,

However, and more important, when the ANS is activated, it inhibits the use of the other principal nervous system—the central nervous (CNS), which includes the brain and spinal cord. These portions of the nervous system developed later and make it possible to engage in higher level functions. Of particular importance, the CNS enables human beings to use reason and logic, to create abstractions such as categories or schemas to organize and label our experience, to delay and consider courses of action prior to taking action, to critically evaluate a situate, and to set long-range goals.

The important lesson here is that states of extreme arousal—such as fear, anxiety, or rage—based in the ANS inhibit the ability to make use of the higher order functions of the CNS. To put it in informal terms, when we are fearful, anxious, or overcome by anger, we are far more likely to act stupidly. Research has found that it is not only the risk of harms created by fear that increase when higher order thought and planning are inhibited; impaired executive functioning has also been found more likely to lead to aggressive and violent behavior, particularly of the more impulsive type (Paschall & Fishbein, 2002). This is because these extreme states of arousal paralyze our critical faculties, impair our ability to rationally think things through and examine conditions from a more detached standpoint, and weaken our problem-solving skills.

The unreflective immediate response made to a perceived threat that arouses anxiety or extreme anger may provide quick relief, but such relief is only temporary and ultimately does not resolve the matter at hand. It is not long before the shortcomings of the immediate solution and the accompanying long-term adverse consequences become apparent. We may deceive ourselves into thinking that the temporary relief offered by the short-term solution has provided us with the safety and security we hoped for. But behind that deception is a lingering anxiety and fear that only intensifies because the source of our distress remains unresolved. That lingering anxiety then prompts an even more desperate effort to persist with the ineffective solution, which then, of course, intensifies the anxiety even more. Our stubborn refusal to squarely confront the issue facing us and truly come to terms with it has spiraled into a destructive, self-defeating cycle.

In all of this, the limitations and potential dangers of a prereflective stance in how we understand and deal with our experience are amply illustrated. These limitations are evidenced in persons in a hypnotic trance in their heightened suggestibility, loss of initiative, declining ability to plan, and reduction in reality testing. One other potentially hazardous characteristic of this state not yet discussed is called *trance logic*. Statements that would be seen as contradictory and logically inconsistent under ordinary circumstances are not contested but accepted while in a trance. For example, a person may be told that their arm will start to rise in the air all by itself whether or not he or she wishes it to. Or that their eyelids are growing heavy and beginning to shut despite any effort on their part to keep them open. Another feature of trance logic is that verbal statements and metaphors presented to the hypnotized person are taken literally. If told that an iron bar has been placed in their right arm that makes it impossible for them to bend it, hypnotized persons will be able to keep the arm elevated for a much lengthier period of time. In a sense, this happens because the person literally believes that an iron bar makes it impossible to bend the arm.

These features of the trance state have positive potentials that are utilized to achieve a broad range of therapeutic benefits provided by hypnosis. But these same features pose perils as well. Among those perils are self-deception and the potential these features have for making people vulnerable to ideological control and manipulation that have oppressive consequences. Seeing these characteristics in their most extreme form helps to underline the harms they can cause. These very dangers were observed and described by neurologist and psychiatrist Kurt Goldstein (1963), who studied soldiers who had suffered damage to their prefrontal cortex, the part of the brain that can abstract, critically analyze, imagine alternatives, and plan. Goldstein contrasted these abilities, which he called the abstract attitude, with the loss of these abilities, which he called the concrete attitude. The loss of the abstract attitude had devastating consequences affecting every area of an individual's life.

First, these individuals were no longer able to organize or manage their own lives because they had lost the capacity for self-direction and for developing and carrying out a planned sequence of actions. Because they were no longer able to inhibit their own impulses and emotions, they required a highly structured and supportive environment to manage and protect them. Like hypnotized individuals, those with a concrete attitude due to brain damage were unable to think hypothetically or to assume an "as if" attitude. They interpreted whatever they were told literally. For example, if asked what it means that a drink is on the house, they would respond that it meant that a drink was literally sitting atop the house. They were stimulus-bound and tied to the immediate situation they found themselves in. If asked to look outside the window on a sunny day and say that it was raining, they rigidly refused to do so because it was not raining. This was because they were no longer able to question the raw facts facing them or conceive of an alternative to those circumstances.

Because their ability to maintain a sense of control and stability in their lives was so compromised and fragile, they adopted rigid and inflexible patterns of behavior to negotiate life from which they felt completely unable to deviate. If something disrupted any of these patterns or routines, they experienced what Goldstein (1963) termed a *catastrophic reaction.* This was a state of extreme anxiety in which individuals felt as though their very existence was under threat because the world as they knew it had suddenly collapsed. Such extreme forms of rigidity, concreteness, and propensity to see the world in literal terms was also observed by Goldstein in individuals with the diagnosis of schizophrenia.

To summarize, these are insights we can acquire from research on hypnosis and other states of dissociation as they pertain to self-deception and its relationship to mystification and oppression:

- A prereflective state of consciousness is more conducive to self-deception due, first, to the accompanying loss of the critical function. The ability of individuals to inhibit reactive responses to what is perceived as a threat is compromised. Reactions tend to be more extreme and rigid. Because the capacity to critically examine, evaluate, and analyze information is suspended, such information is more likely to be accepted and taken at face value. This makes individuals far more suggestible, particularly with individuals perceived as authorities.
- The narrow focus on something other than oneself that accompanies a trance state and prereflective consciousness is more likely to create narrow attention to data congruent with pre-existing attitudes and expectations and to screen out information that would allow for a fuller and more complete understanding of a situation.
- The object of awareness is invested with a greater degree of attention which then endows it with an exaggerated importance and weight. Consequently, it exerts an excessive

influence over persons. They may become overly identified with the object and experience themselves as falling under its control. Anything that jeopardizes this sense of close connection will be experienced as catastrophic and trigger an extremely adverse reaction.

- Prereflective states of consciousness increase the likelihood of experiencing extreme dissociative experiences accompanied by powerful feelings of alienation in the form of derealization and depersonalization. Such states of heightened alienation are the next to be examined in this analysis of self-deception.

The Dialectics of Alienation

The experience of alienation has already been described as an essential element of both suffering and oppression. It is thus little surprise that alienation reappears again as an equally essential component of self-deception. Previously, derealization and depersonalization were identified as inherent aspects of the process of dissociation. These are also critical to describing the experience of alienation. The archetypal experience of alienation is one in which we feel as if we are not ourselves or that our accustomed understanding of the world has been disrupted. In the chapter on suffering, an extreme case of this was called a boundary experience (Jaspers, 1984), one of life's wake up calls. All sense of familiarity, stability, and order is suddenly stripped away and replaced with a sense of estrangement from ourselves, others, and the world. However, less extreme cases of this happen in everyday experience. It may be a time when we act out of character or do something completely at odds with what we intended to do. We may have gotten extremely angry at a friend over something insignificant. Or we may have resolved to avoid engaging in some bad habit only to find ourselves engaging in it in the next moment.

Using a phenomenological approach, it is important to describe such experiences as clearly and completely as possible as this will provide considerable insight into their core elements. It is not uncommon at such times to say things such as the following: "I was not myself. Something came over me. I couldn't help myself. It was just such an irresistible urge. That couldn't have been me." Embedded in this language is something that lies at the heart of the experience of alienation. It is the disowning of a painful experience that challenges our core beliefs, assumptions, and values. This is then followed by attributing our thoughts, feelings, and behavior to someone or something else. We invent a distinct entity that seems to have a life and power of its own and is able to take possession of us. All of these bear the marks of dissociation, the splitting of consciousness into distinct parts in order to preserve the sense of identity we have created for ourselves and the worldview we have established to maintain a sense of control. It is precisely these kinds of defensive maneuvers that lead to the creation of the shadow, the sum of all those experiences that we have disowned and disavowed.

Staying with how the experience is described, we can identify with the speaker because the descriptions capture what alienation feels like. This is because these descriptions accurately depict the automaticity that accompanies the process of dissociation. Bakan (1968) helps to explicate this point and how self-deception unfolds into a self-defeating strategy that exacerbates one's sense of brokenness and fragmentation and so intensifies one's suffering. Bakan sees important parallels in the work of Freud and Selye in that both demonstrated that the core of what constitutes disease is not the initial injury or conflict that causes alarm and distress, but rather the way in which the body and the person respond to or defend against the threat. He writes, "Paradoxical as it may appear, I suggest that *'defense' is a key notion for unlocking at least some of the mystery of the disease process"* (p. 22, italics in the original). In other words, the very measures we take to make things better, actually make things worse.

For both Freud and Selye, the event that triggers these defenses is the threat of a disruption of balance or homeostasis, followed by efforts aimed at restoring it. Pain (or suffering) is the companion of this threat, which signals more than a disruption of homeostasis—rather, the actual annihilation of the person. However, in this regard pain assumes a paradoxical character as it has both a positive and negative value. On the positive side, it provides an essential signal that a threat or danger is posed that requires attention and action. In the absence of pain, we would engage in any number of behaviors that would risk further damage to ourselves. On the negative side, it is experienced as aversive and frightening and so triggers reactions intended to decrease or eliminate it. This same paradox is mirrored in the strategies often used to deal with pain because these responses are extreme, rigid, and out of proportion to the threat posed. In other words, when we try too hard to resist or avoid pain, we only make pain worse.

In the case of Freud, the deployment of defenses in response to a psychic conflict functions as a compromise formation. It may temporarily forestall danger or threat, but not eliminate it. What may seem like protection from injury ends up in some way exacerbating the situation. Thus, for Freud what constitutes the core of neurosis is not conflict but the constellation of defenses employed by persons to protect themselves. In the case of Selye, the problem of prolonged stress leading to illness or death was noted in the earlier description of the General Adaptation Syndrome. Selye called these diseases of adaptation because it is the very automatic processes employed by the body to resist threat and try to adapt to the harmful circumstances that end up turning against the body. The reason is, first, because the threat being posed is prolonged and, second, because the efforts launched to remedy the situation achieve the exact opposite effect. Additionally, when the defenses employed become rigid and extreme, adaptation will inevitably fail because people fail to account for what is a constantly changing set of circumstances. Thus, we do not get ill because of the original injury. Rather, it is the stress reaction engendered by the injury that steadily weakens the body because it is unable to manage or eliminate the threat. In both instances, the dynamics of self-defeat are clearly illustrated.

These self-injurious responses are also embedded in a form of self-deception because in both instances the assumption is that the defenses being used are not only necessary to one's survival but will also be efficacious in dealing with the threat. When experience tells us that both assumptions are erroneous, this caveat is unheeded and no corrective actions are taken. Instead, the self-defeating methods are even more rigidly adhered to and applied. A large reason for this is the belief that these reactions are happening outside of our control and of their own accord because of their automaticity. This point is described astutely in the following extended quote by Bakan (1968):

> Neurosis may be defined as a condition in which some regular response occurs in the individual in spite of his conscious wish that he not make that response. In obsessions, phobias, and compulsions, the classical forms of neurosis, the individual has thoughts or fears, or engages in acts in opposition to his conscious intentions, and even to his disadvantage. The responses indeed appear to occur as though there were "some extraneous force at work." It is precisely this *automatic* occurrence, occurrence independent of the conscious ego, that marks the response as neurotic. The way in which events take place *automatically* in the organism is what Freud identified as reflecting the work of the death instinct. Now, when we read

Selye describing how physiological reactions are triggered quite automatically, resulting in the injury of the organism, we are led to the opinion that automatic defense processes constitute the major factor in disease and death. Both Freud's death instinct and Selye's diseases of adaptation may be identified with those automatic mechanisms in the organism, the primitive, elementary, and instinctual mechanisms, which are phenomenologically extraneous to the conscious ego. (p. 29, italics in original)

We experience mechanisms of defense as phenomenologically alien to the ego or self. Because that is what the experience feels like, persons adopt a language that fits with their experience. Similarly, according to Bakan, because the experience of pain is aversive and frightening, it appears not to be part of the ego or the person but rather as something alien that happens to him or her. However, no matter how natural it may feel to consider pain and our defenses as ego-alien, we must realize that in neither instance is this true. As long as it remains ego-alien, this form of self-deception will bring with it mounting negative consequences. The only means of avoiding this self-defeating spiral is to reject the invented distinction or split in consciousness that has been made by means of dissociation and to recognize that we have been deceived by appearances. Bakan (1968) writes:

How could the injuriousness associated with the mechanisms be mitigated? Clearly, the way to overcome the injuriousness of a mechanism is to change that which is ego-alien to something which is not ego-alien, to recognize that which may have the sense of being "other" (as the word "id" so strongly suggests) is really the person himself, to overcome the automaticity of the functioning of such mechanisms that have on the *appearance of defense* so that indeed the person may be really defended instead of injured by them. (p. 30, italics in original)

Ironically, despite Freud's (1959) later rejection of dissociation in favor of the concept of repression, in an early paper on the psychogenesis of hysteria he employs it astutely to describe the very patterns noted. He elucidates how there is no "it" or alien force responsible for our defenses. As Bakan states, Freud observes how the "other" is actually the persons themselves. In this paper, he describes the successful treatment of a woman unable to feed her newborn children. In his work with her, Freud discovered that because of the lack of any physical basis for this problem, she was experiencing a form of hysteria, which he then proceeded to successfully treat with hypnosis. Following his description of the case, Freud offers his ideas about the psychical mechanisms behind this disorder. In doing so, Freud attributes hysteria to a *perversion of will*. In other words, the experience of persons with hysteria is that they have been seized by a power over which they seem to have no control. However, a closer examination reveals that this is not the case.

Freud explains that human beings have certain ideas that have affect attached to them. This take two forms. The first is the idea of persons doing some particular thing, taking some action—or *intentions*. The other is the idea of some particular thing happening to them—or *expectations*. The affect attached to intentions and expectations is dependent on two factors—how important the outcome is for the person and the degree of uncertainty the person feels about achieving the desired outcome. The more important the outcome is, the more troublesome the doubts about carrying out the intention. This uncertainty takes the form of a collection of distressing antithetic (opposing) ideas. This could be expressed as "I will be unable to carry out my intention because it is too difficult" or "I am inadequate to the task, and there are many other things that might happen other than what I desire." What this means for Freud is that whenever we form an intention that carries with it an expectation, uncertainty regarding our ability to successfully carry it out gives birth to a counter-intention.

This is a restatement of the idea that human beings have the capacity to think dialectically. Every thought, feeling, or intention implies its opposite. Such contrariness in our approach to ourselves and life is the breeding ground for alienation. Nonetheless, we generate our own counter-intentions and alter-egos. What we thus imagine to be some alien entity or force at work is something that we ourselves have created. It is only in realizing this that we will successfully resolve the experience of alienation without resorting to solutions that only intensify conflict and widen the chasm that we erect within ourselves.

What remains unanswered is why we are so easily seduced into this mistaken way of thinking. Understanding where this vulnerability comes from will also prove important to undoing the damage caused by self-deception. The answer lies in the previous discussion of the state of consciousness found in a hypnotic trance—that is, a prereflective state of consciousness. In such a state, the object of awareness assumes great significance and weight. It seems to absorb the knower and to exercise a kind of control over person that renders them helpless. For the moment, awareness of ourselves is attenuated, almost as if we have disappeared and only the object of our focus remains. Also, in the prereflective state there is a suspension of the critical function. Experience is not submitted to any form of critical analysis or judgment but instead is taken at face value. Thinking becomes concrete, and information is understood in literal terms.

The trance state is a form of dissociation, and the same type of dissociation occurs, as we have seen, under conditions of extreme arousal such as intense fear, anxiety, or anger. At times like these, defenses are mobilized without our conscious awareness to meet the threat. We are in an automatic mode in which something like a robot takes over control. This automaticity serves some adaptive function but also has elements that are not adaptive. Phenomenologically, persons experience these automatic functions as forces that operate outside of their conscious and volitional control. *But here now is the important point. It is precisely because we are experiencing these processes while in a prereflective state that we interpret them in this way.* The experience is understood in a literal and concrete manner. In fact, the language we use to describe what we are experiencing is metaphoric, a kind of poetry that seems to fit what is occurring. We are employing our imagination to make sense of experience. It is *as if* something came over me, *as if* I was caught in the grips of some irresistible force, *as if* I had suddenly been seized by some alien power.

But in a state of prereflective awareness, all sense of appreciation of the "as if" is temporarily lost. We are so thoroughly absorbed in the account we give of events that we lose all sense of detachment from what we are saying and see it as fact rather than fiction. *We are missing the metaphor*, and very often when we take metaphors literally bad consequences follow. The experience of alienation is one of those times. The literal interpretation of our experience facilitates self-deception and leads us to surrender our sense of agency and autonomy to a figment of our imagination. There is no "other" or alien force at work. As Sartre (1953) observes, self-deception contains a troubling contradiction. How can the person lying (and thus knowing what is in fact true) and being lied to be one and the same person? Another danger is that the same process of alienation may lead us to assume a passive and helpless stance and mistakenly give power and control over not merely to external circumstances but to powerful others. We may literally feel that we have fallen under their spell and submit uncritically to their wishes and commands.

While we may believe that we are not exercising a choice because events seem to unfold of their own accord or we experience ourselves as compelled by some urge or force, this is not true. In the experience of alienation, we are in fact employing passive volition, which is a form of control available to us. Whether we recognize it or not, we have given our consent to let something happen, or permit a process to unfold, seemingly of its own accord. This becomes particularly clear in those instances in which we actively oppose urges, desires, and other forms of experience that are involuntary and find that not only do they resist our control but instead become more powerful. By surrendering our agency, what begins as a metaphor (something fashioned and created by our own imagination) takes on a life of its own, defies efforts on our part to reassert control, and threatens to destroy its creator as in the classic tale of Frankenstein. And these types of situations are not inconsequential, particularly when those metaphors fashion a false and harmful understanding of ourselves, others, and the world.

Such illusions of our own making, if accepted uncritically and at face value, have disastrous consequences. Grossman (1995) in his book, *On Killing,* provides dramatic evidence for this in his description of how metaphors such as "Gook," "Kraut," or "Nip" were used to characterize enemy combatants and makes them into less than animals. This sense of emotional, cultural, social, and moral distance dehumanized the enemy and so made it much easier to convince soldiers to kill them. We have similarly seen how the dehumanization of human beings and transformation of them into things are inherent to oppression.

The power of passive volition to achieve a vitally important form of control has been empirically established in research on how individuals can learn to control what were once thought to be involuntary responses. Such responses, which have been found to be capable of individuals' control, include blood pressure, heart rate, brain waves, respiration, and hand temperature, among others. Further, various methods for cultivating passive volition and utilizing it to achieve such control have been studied. These include biofeedback (Green & Green, 1978), meditation (McDonald, Walsh & Shapiro, 2013), and hypnosis (Wickramasekera, 2013).

The issue is not that we have either lost control or never had it to begin with. Nor is it that the true reasons behind our thoughts, feelings, and actions are buried forever in our unconscious. What has happened is that we have created a rift within ourselves between conscious and unconscious, subject and object, deceiver and deceived; and because it is a rift of our own creation, it is a rift that we can heal. These supposed contradictions and unresolved conflicts are, in truth, the interaction of two sides of a polarity that are interdependent and inseparable. They represent what Fromm (1947) called existential dichotomies built into human existence that cannot be eliminated or avoided but must be confronted and dealt with. Trying to tease apart these opposites and keep them separate will only lead to self-deception and self-defeat. As Sartre (1953) points out in his discussion of the role of prereflective consciousness in self-deception, "Thus the subject deceives himself about the meaning of his conduct, he comprehends it in its concrete existence, but not in its truth" (p. 91). Freud (1920) makes a similar point, "...the dreamer really does know the meaning of his dream; only he does not know that he knows, and therefore thinks that he does not" (p. 106). The truth is there to see; it is our resistance to confronting it because it is too painful or too frightening that obscures it. That is why there is such a significant and consequential difference between knowing and knowing that we know. When our experience goes unexamined, when we are content to restrict ourselves to mere appearances, when we refuse to question what is presented to us as fact—it is at these times that we are liable to lapse so easily into self-deception and succumb to all the dangers that come with it.

To avoid self-deception, we must live out our existence as an ever-changing process, no matter how demanding, how rigorous, how scary, or how painful that may be. That process is enacted within the structures formed by the polarities of *knower–known, good–evil*, and *active–passive*. As existential dichotomies, these polarities can neither be eliminated nor resolved by clinging desperately to one side of the polarity to the exclusion of the other. However, this does not seem to deter us from efforts to do so. This is made particularly clear in Sartre's (1959) discussion of self-deception, or bad faith. He asserts that human beings cannot rest in negotiating the fluctuation between prereflective to reflective consciousness. He contrasts these two modes of consciousness as *being-in-itself* (prereflective), which represents objects without possibilities, freedom, and consciousness, and *being-for-itself* (reflective), which represents subjects that have possibilities, freedom, and consciousness. Using this framework, the experience of alienation is one in which human beings wish to evade the anxiety involved in exercising their freedom. The different sides of polarity represent choices we must make moment by moment, stances we are free to assume toward our experience. The requirement to make these choices, and in doing so fashion ourselves and the world, is experienced as a burden that we want to escape. And one way in which we frequently do this is to assert one side of the polarity to the exclusion of the other. These one-sided, extreme stances invariably result in denying or distorting our experience and introducing what we believe to be irreconcilable splits in our relationship to ourselves, others, and the world. It attempts to create a false sense of permanence where process and change are inevitable.

Several examples remind us of how this one-sidedness fails by helping to illustrate these points. Freud (1959) observed in his paper on the development of hysteria that a counter-intention is unavoidably formed each time persons assert an intention. This counter-intention may introduce an element of doubt that is troubling as it threatens to undermine the original intention. However, by the very act of resisting that counter-intention, persons fail to eliminate or avoid it. Instead, such resistance invests the counter-intention with energy that only makes it stronger and more irresistible. What we resist persists. Over time the counter-intention becomes so powerful that it takes on a life of its own and seems to actively thwart our original intention or pervert our will.

A similar dynamic can be found in Jung's (1933) concept of the shadow as that element of the personality that represents everything we have rejected and disowned. Jung subscribed to the principle of opposites, akin to the earlier discussion of counter-intentions, in which every tendency in the psyche has a corresponding opposing tendency that performs a compensatory function to maintain a certain degree of balance or integration in the psyche. Thus, if persons were to try too hard to resist or deny their shadow, this compensatory process would lead not to the weakening of the shadow, but rather to it becoming more powerful and, at some point, erupting into awareness and taking control of the person.

Finally, Frankl's (1953) discussion of the therapeutic technique of paradoxical intention provides another perspective on the dynamics of self-deception. Frankl observes that in the case of certain conditions such as phobias, anticipatory anxiety plays a significant role in the distress experienced by individuals. Essentially, anticipatory anxiety is being anxious about becoming anxious or being apprehensive about finding oneself in a situation that one fears. For example, if a person has developed an irrational fear of drowning, he or she will become anxious if faced with the prospect of being near the water. What is at work in this dynamic is described by Frankl as excessive attention and wrong passivity. Individuals with irrational fears become too focused on or preoccupied with anything connected with what they fear, and in the process, they actually bring on the very thing they hope to avoid. In hypnosis this is called the law of reverse effect, in which the harder you try not to do something, the more likely it becomes that you will. A popular expression of this is being told not to think of a pink elephant. By wrong passivity, Frankl means that when individuals strive so hard to withdraw from situations because of anticipatory anxiety, not only do they narrow their lives but often they find themselves ultimately in the very situations they hoped to escape.

Another self-defeating pattern is one that Frankl sees in persons with more obsessive or compulsive types of disorders. These individuals experience thoughts (often abhorrent and frightening) that come to them unbidden or find themselves irresistibly engaging in some repetitive pattern of behavior. In this instance, what Frankl finds at work is excessive intention and wrong activity. These individuals tend to be overly preoccupied with their symptoms and believe that the only way to overcome them is to fight hard against them. Like the example of counter-intentions and the shadow, resistance of obsessions and compulsions is doomed to fail. The misplaced amount of attention and intention occurs due to adopting a one-sided, rigid, and extreme stance toward one of the three polarities that define consciousness. Frankl describes this as seeking to achieve a balance between closeness and detachment within the relationship between subject and object. The remedy for excessive attention is to cease being so fixated or close to one's symptoms and to achieve a distance from them that enables individuals to see them more realistically. In some instances, such distance helps us to see how ridiculous our fears and our symptoms are. This illustrates the healing power of humor. We can only laugh at something once we have achieved a certain degree of detachment from it. The remedy for excessive intention, which again is rooted in being too close to what distresses us, is described by Frankl as de-reflection—that is, learning to ignore what ordinarily disturbs us and instead focus our attention on something other than ourselves. Self-absorption is just another form of becoming stuck in an overly reflective stance and forgetting that there is a big world out there besides us and all our cares and concerns.

The Problem of the Ego Re-Visited

Before concluding this examination of self-deception, it would be useful to return to the problem of the ego described in the chapter on suffering and situate the role of alienation and one-sided extremism into this framework. What the problem of the ego makes clear is that the greatest deception of all is the false, constricted, and manufactured view we have created of ourselves—the ego as defined by our attachments, desires, and identifications. It is little wonder in light of this that the most powerful feelings of alienation we experience are directed toward ourselves. In so many ways, we are strangers to ourselves and relate to ourselves through the distorted lenses of the biases, myths, and fantasies we have created of ourselves and that we have been induced to believe about ourselves. However, the degree to which we feel this self-estrangement can vary, and these variations carry consequences of varying degrees of severity. It is this alienation that then proceeds to infect our relationships with other human beings, the physical world and—for those religiously and spiritually inclined—with the Absolute.

This process of alienation begins from the very start of life in the formation of our identity, or what psychiatrist Harry Stack Sullivan (1953) called the self-system. According to Sullivan, in the course of their development infants form different "parts" of themselves based on the way they are responded to by their caretakers. Infants seek to secure feelings of approval and tenderness because these experiences are positive and pleasant, while avoiding disapproval and punishment because they arouse anxiety, shame, and guilt. Experiences of approval become integrated into the good-me, or the person we would like to think we are. Experiences of disapproval create an interpersonal form of anxiety as infants believe that the love they seek is being withdrawn from them. These experiences are integrated into the bad-me. The bad-me relates to experiences in which we have done things for which we feel regret or remorse. The good-me and bad-me eventually combine into a single self-image.

It is the third part of the self-system that connects most directly to alienation. That is the not-me. It is an experience of a very different order because it has its roots in intense situations associated with a high degree of anxiety, terror, and dread. At such times, individuals are unable to comprehend what is happening to them. The emotions evoked are called "uncanny," and the expression used by Heidegger for these emotions (*Unheimlikchkeit*) gets to the heart of what is meant. One no longer feels "at home" because the world is no longer the familiar, stable place it had been. It is an experience of utter confusion and horror.

The purpose of the self-system is principally to control awareness by employing a range of different defenses to suppress or repress threatening events, maintain a sense of security and harmony in one's relationships, and direct the development of the personality. This makes it is easy to see how Goleman (1985) connects the self-system with ways in which attention and awareness are modified and lead to self-deception. What this description by Sullivan also makes apparent is how powerfully social forces, in the form of a network of interpersonal relations in which individuals are embedded, shape the ways in which we understand ourselves. Those same social forces subsequently give rise to varying degrees of alienation. And those social forces can be manipulated in order to cultivate states of alienation with the objective of controlling individuals. One way in which that control might be exercised is to oppress individuals from certain social groups. Another way is to facilitate the oppression of those individuals using ideological manipulation conducted by the oppressors.

The ego as a social creation is a theme also taken up by Alan Watts (1966), who regards our normal sense of self as a "hoax" perpetrated on us, a role that we have been tricked into playing by our own consent. He sees this process as similar to hypnotic subjects submitting themselves to suggestions given to them while in a trance. Watts further elaborates on the creation of the ego, stating, "This whole *illusion* has its history in ways of thinking—in the images, models, myths, and *language systems* which we have used for thousands of years to make sense of the world. These have had an effect on our perceptions which seems to be strictly *hypnotic*" (p. 51, italics in the original). Once again, it is the dominant ideology in any society that is the principal influence on these images, models, myths, and language.

What Watts (1966) is reiterating is the way in which the societal nature of human beings makes them inescapably vulnerable to the "immense power of the social environment" This power shapes how our attention, what we choose to notice or not to notice, is first motivated by fear. However, we not only selectively focus on what is advantageous to our survival but also on ways to preserve our status and security—feelings manufactured in the creation of the ego by extant social structures and forces. That power is then further consolidated by language, myths, models—everything we use to make sense of and classify our experience—that have likewise been provided by society. Thus, illusions, the partial truths, and seductive inventions that keep us trapped in this socially induced trance do not exist outside in the physical world (although that is often where we presume them to be). They are based in the schemas and worldview we have consented to by submitting ourselves to the power of social institutions.

Like hypnotic suggestions, we have uncritically internalized the tools and rules they have supplied to us for making sense of our experience.

In the descriptions by Sullivan (1953) and Watts (1966), we find the most powerful tool wielded by social institutions and the ideology that they rest upon is anxiety, dread, terror—a fear of our very annihilation. It is through fear that social forces exercise the power to define us and the world. This is most dramatically illustrated in how the powerful and privileged frequently employ intense experiences that uproot people from all that is familiar and safe. These heightened states of alienation are used to create a sense of profound confusion and convince individuals of the necessity of disowning what may be vital and valid aspects of themselves. Instead, they are convinced to adopt illusions that do not serve their interests but the interests of powerful others, who convince them that these illusions must be defended with a life-or-death attitude.

For Watts (1972), the three essential causes of evil that arise from the ego are insecurity, pride, and inertia. These, too, are the tools of the powerful and the privileged. Insecurity is the persistent fear of the annihilation of the ego that may follow from any experience of loss. It is found in our morbid fear that our hopes and expectations will not be met and that we will be plagued by frustration and disappointment. We have already seen how insecurity is used to foster the materialistic value orientation that fuels our obsession with consumption (Kasser and Kanner, 2004). Pride has its basis in our capacity for reflective thought. However, it is more than merely our ability to take ourselves as an object of our awareness. It is unbridled and extreme as we idolize ourselves. In pride, the ego elevates itself to a god-like status and regards itself as a law unto itself. It exults in its achievements and everything that it has acquired and attained, seeing these things as solely attributable to its own power. We have already encountered the problem of pride in the extreme narcissism and individualism fostered by our neoliberal ideology (Gruba-McCallister, 2007). Such exaggerated self-importance, of course, hides an underlying vulnerability that responds in extreme and destructive ways to the slightest injury. Inertia is resistance to change, the preference to always take the path of least resistance. It is the expression of an unchecked need for control that insists on maintaining order and stability. And we have seen throughout this discussion of self-deception the dangers and harms created by our insatiable need for control.

Once more, we see that the problem of self-deception and the many ways in which it inflicts harm cannot be understood in isolation. It is not merely a set of intrapsychic processes enacted to cope with internal conflicts and private fears. It most certainly relies on processes that reside within human beings. However, knowledge about these processes and ways in which they can be manipulated has been appropriated by those who commit countless acts of social injustice. The vulnerabilities of human beings exposed in this discussion of self-deception are cravenly employed by perpetrators of countless forms of oppression. And so, we must next turn to a discussion of mystification as the means by which these injustices are not only inflicted but justified.

Chapter 6

Mystification

Ideology and Its Seeming Invisibility

The role of ideology—and most particularly the current dominant ideology of neoliberalism—in oppression and the suffering it inflicts on its victims were asserted in the Introduction. The various ways in which neoliberal ideology perpetrates material and psychological harms on the oppressed have subsequently been only broadly sketched out. These have ranged from persistent but minor detrimental impacts that steadily gnaw away at individuals' sense of safety, security, and self-worth to chronic and cumulative forms of oppression that lead to more extreme consequences as found in deprivation, discrimination, and dehumanization. Some pathways by which ideology leads to such detrimental consequences have been explored but need now to be more fully examined. This examination will draw upon ideas that have been outlined in the previous chapters. It will also extend the relevance of the material presented on self-deception, by illustrating how "intrapsychic" defense mechanisms alone are inadequate in explaining the creation and persistence of pernicious illusions that perpetuate oppression and obscure the suffering inflicted on the oppressed.

These defenses are utilized and expanded upon by the dominant ideology in order to further disguise and distort facts and lead individuals to question and doubt their experiences. Thus, any discussion of ideology must be accompanied by a discussion of the process of mystification, or the ways in which ideology distorts perceptions of reality and provide plausible misinterpretations of experiences in order to defeat and deflect any attempts at examining and opposing the status quo. The most important function of mystification is to essentially render the dominant ideology invisible and in doing so portray the social order based upon that ideology as natural, normal, and thus inevitable.

From what has been discussed thus far, the most obvious form of suffering caused by oppressive ideologies is what has been called self-created (that is, suffering resulting from the adverse consequences of choices made by human beings). This includes the host of material and psychological harms described in the chapter on oppression—all of which to some degree are avoidable and capable of amelioration. That being the case, a closer scrutiny of the role that ideology plays in how human beings make choices helps to disclose the role it plays in oppression. The power of ideology resides in the ways in which it shapes individuals' most fundamental values and beliefs because these values and beliefs inform many of the choices individuals make. Research has demonstrated that ideology is a very potent force behind human motivation, a force that can be channeled into everything from war and atrocities to acts of great compassion and sacrifice (Jost, 2006; Jost & Amodio, 2012). The exercise of agency occurs through channels provided by each person's worldview. This worldview is deeply inculcated into individuals and contains social, economic, and political understandings, sympathies and antipathies, and predilections that then become motivating forces behind patterns of behavior expressed in choices—both major and minor. This does not negate that human beings exercise some degree of agency independent of environmental influences. Neither does it completely exempt them from the consequences of the choices they make.

However, human agency cannot be understood solely from an individual perspective, as if persons were self-contained, autonomous entities that can function independently from the contexts in which they live (although this is a common error perpetuated by neoliberal ideology). An appreciation of the power of ideology helps us to see that human beings' awareness and understanding of agency must always be situated within a structural and systemic perspective. This is because ideology exercises such a profound and lasting effect on how human beings understand themselves and make sense of their capacity for choice. Even looking at agency from an individual perspective, no serious proponent of free will has proposed that human freedom is without limits.

For example, Heidegger (1927/1978) observed that individuals must commit themselves to their thrownness, the givens or facts of their lives, before taking up the task of living authentically by exercising choices that are possible to them. Likewise, Sartre (1953) saw human beings exercising choice within the polarity of transcendence and possibility (being-for-itself) and facticity and necessity (being-in-itself).

The facts of our lives are not things we have chosen; they are givens that set limits on us. The one choice we have regarding these givens is what stance we will assume toward them. However, while this distinction may seem straightforward on the face of it, as will be seen when a harder look is taken at neoliberal ideology, a great deal of confusion can be sown in the minds of individuals regarding what actually is and is not subject to their control and choice. Ideology achieves this not merely by causing individuals to doubt their agency but by misleading them about what choices are and are not available to them.

The circumstances into which individuals are born and live always exert an influence on human agency by setting limits on whether and how it can be exercised. However, the impact of circumstances can extend beyond that. Even if it is granted that human beings have agency, that alone does not guarantee that they will acquire the experiences necessary to help make them aware of their agency or to encourage them in ways that they are willing to exercise it. At the start of life some degree of agency is present, but its scope and range exist as a potential. It is a sort of tool that human beings have at their disposal. To use any tool, you must first become aware that you possess it and it is available to you. Next you must learn what it is, how it works, and what it can be used for. You need to become competent in the use of the tool. So it is with our capacity to exercise choice. As social beings, we require sufficient conditions that enable this capacity to unfold and develop over time. These conditions must allow us to develop awareness of our ability to exercise choice and then provide opportunities to practice making choices and experiencing the consequences that follow from them.

In other words, certain social circumstances enable human beings to learn how to be free; while others can lead people to learn to be unfree. Bandura's (1997) concept of self-efficacy is useful in this context as it refers to the degree to which human beings develop the belief that their actions can exert an impact on their circumstances. As his research illustrated, through learning human beings can develop varying degrees of self-efficacy. One of the consequences of ideology and mystification is that those who experience oppression have a lower sense of self-efficacy (Prilleltensky, 2008). Thus, the impact that ideology has not only on the choices we make that contribute to oppression, but also on whether we are willing to accept responsibility for those choices is complex because the process can be shrouded in distortions manufactured by mystification.

Our concern must not be restricted to the suffering created by choices we make that lead to avoidable distress and disappointment. Mystification is also at work in our experiences with inescapable suffering rooted in loss and disappointment. As observed by Osterkamp (1999), one of the most common and central functions of ideology is to provide seemingly plausible explanations for why things happen as they do. In just this way, ideology frequently explains away both the inevitable harmful consequences of oppression and the unavoidable participation of individuals in oppression. This is particularly common under a neoliberal ideology that advocates unbridled self-interest and competition in which benefiting at the expense of others is not merely condoned but idealized.

No matter what ideology may be dominant, human beings will at times behave in ways contrary to the requirements of social justice and the moral imperative to show compassion to others. What follows from this is inescapable suffering for those adversely impacted by injustice and lack of compassion. Any open confrontation with one's complicity in causing such suffering will likewise be an occasion that brings with it discomfort, shame, guilt, and regret—again, forms of unavoidable suffering. Osterkamp observed that when ideology provides a means of evading recognition of the suffering we have caused others and of disguising the suffering we feel should we acknowledge this, it is employing mystification to essentially sweep suffering under the rug. It normalizes and justifies the existing social order and power relations ultimately responsible for the harms that have been inflicted and, by doing so, removes wrong-doers from any form of condemnation. Put simply, the message we are left with is "Shit happens." There is no deeper rhyme or reason that we need to look for. So we are let off the hook and unable to benefit from learning from our acts of injustice. Likewise, the unjust status quo is held blameless and so not in need of change. The chief means by which this feat of mystification is achieved is by inhibiting critical reflection on how and why choices were made and by disguising the social, economic, and political forces that inflict harm.

This illustrates how the first phase in the process of mystification reframes self-created suffering as inescapable suffering. The pain that "appears" to be caused to the oppressed through the actions of the oppressors whose motives are based on an unjust ideology is portrayed as something quite different. Their suffering might be regrettable, but it is, after all, just a "sad fact of life." It is simply the unavoidable consequence of the operation of impersonal forces that are inevitable and thus beyond our control. As will be seen, in neoliberal ideology this is attributed to the natural and normal workings of the "market," to which all human beings must submit.

The next phase of the process is to portray the material and psychological costs of oppression as less consequential than they truly are. This makes them not subject to moral condemnation and so nothing that individuals should trouble themselves about. This transformation is facilitated, in part, by again seeing them as inevitable. When suffering is made to appear the outcome of blind and impersonal forces, what we are dealing with are facts and not ethical matters. After all what can anyone do about poverty, war, sickness, or violence? By convincing oppressors and the oppressed to resign themselves to the inevitable and inescapable facts of life, all notions of unfairness are made irrelevant. In the process, we are doing more than cultivating in them a passive and helpless attitude. We are simultaneously encouraging them to close their hearts to the pain of loss and disappointment—whether theirs or others'.

This is the apathy, the loss of the ability to acknowledge and participate in the suffering of the oppressed or one's own suffering that Soelle (1975) warned against because it eventually leads to the inability to suffer at all. In a single stroke, the suffering of not only the victims but also of the perpetrators and witnesses of oppression has been silenced by means of an ideologically effected invalidation of their concretely lived experiences. It is then just a matter of time before all manner of suffering is made invisible and inaccessible. But the weaving of illusions in the service of the powerful by mystification is still not complete. The denial and dismissal of the suffering caused by oppression in order to remove responsibility from the perpetrators are then strangely reversed by that very same ideology by blaming the targets of oppressors for their misery. It is they who have created suffering for themselves because of the irresponsible, immoral choices they have made. Once again, the difference between inescapable and self-created suffering is blurred by means of mystification in the service of upholding the prevailing ideology.

Yet there is one final phase of the process of mystification at work to well and truly ensure that any potential for liberation offered by the experience of suffering is thwarted. Shutting down the capacity to feel suffering in all those involved in the process of oppression has one ultimate objective: to narrow, dull, and if possible, shut down awareness altogether. By so constricting consciousness, people sink even more deeply into apathy and an incapacity to feel any genuine emotion except those prescribed by the ruling ideology. They go about their lives as if on automatic pilot, mindlessly performing routines intended to keep things going just as they are. So even when the injurious effects of the ideology seem to be plainly evident, such awareness may be no more than a flicker that quickly recedes and fades away.

Because the potential for consciousness to return remains, carefully constructed illusions ensure that the circumstances giving rise to suffering remain unexamined, unchallenged, and thus unaltered. Ultimately even the process of mystification itself must be mystified, and the banishing of awareness is designed to do just that. Such are the labyrinthine twists and turns of mystification and self-deception at work. This "dithering" back and forth from one end of polarity to the other is central to Sartre's (1953) discussion of self-deception and attributed to the evanescent or metastable nature of consciousness. Akin to the "knots" woven by deception and confused communication described by Laing (1972), the workings of mystification utilize paradox, the uncanny and the disturbing feelings accompanying it that leave its victims perplexed and immobilized.

Though the power of ideology and mystification may appear daunting, thankfully it is not insurmountable. In the investigation of mystification that follows, the one-sided and extreme elements typically found in ideologies eventually give rise to contradictions and incongruities that allow us to glimpse past the seemingly impenetrable façade they try to maintain (Osterkamp, 1999). In many ways, the dominant ideology that is the source of so many of our afflictions is hiding in plain sight. Its very obviousness is what makes it so easy for us to fail to recognize it even when it stares us in the face. We have come to take it for granted. It so is familiar and comforting that we cannot remember a time when it was not there.

Nonetheless, the proclivity of ideology to portray itself as truth and the utilization of mystification to evade the concrete lived realities of daily life will inevitably lead to breaches in the illusions that bind us. The erroneous assumptions and implausible interpretations that may initially appear to be seductive eventually are unable to hold up under the insistent anguish of the oppressed and the nagging guilt of those who hold some accountability for oppression. These experiences can assuredly be stifled but not extinguished. And so, Osterkamp (1999) is correct in asserting that when an ideology fails to satisfy human needs and stifles the ongoing development of their potential, these failures must in time become apparent and crystallized in the suffering they cause. However, the mere presence of that suffering is not enough to prompt a challenge to the ideology. A language appropriate to describing what has happened and a clear understanding of the ways in which human nature has been violated by this ideology are necessary to provide the means to recognize and meaningfully address this suffering. Most of all, the social causes of suffering—causes inextricably linked to the dominant ideology—must be exposed by undoing the process of mystification. It is the responsibility of anyone committed to social justice to take up these critical tasks and, in doing so, make it possible to awaken people to the suffering caused by oppression, to submit the taken-for-granted to critical reflection, and to pave the way for mutual and collaborative efforts to work for a more just society. With this is mind, we can turn to a closer examination of ideology and mystification.

Ideology and Its Essential Elements and Functions

As observed previously, there are diverse and conflicting opinions about what ideology means and about its utility as an explanatory construct. Jost (2006) writes that the prevailing opinion at the end of World War II was that ideology was no longer a valid subject of study. It was critiqued as lacking in consistency, stability, and constraint; failing to demonstrate any potency in motivating human behavior or any distinctive differences across types of ideology; and inadequately correlating any differences in psychological processes or styles across different ideologies. However, the pronouncement of the death of ideology proved to be premature. Jost defends this contention by summarizing research supporting not only the relevance and utility of ideology but also its ability to predict attitudes and behavior. He adopts a definition of ideology as an interrelated set of moral and political attitudes that have cognitive, affective, and motivational components. These attitudes provide explanations for why people behave as they do, and they exert influence on individuals' political behavior.

Research supporting the validity of ideology has principally examined the difference between the conservative and liberal forms. Two core dimensions help to distinguish these forms: attitudes toward inequality and attitudes toward social change. Individuals endorsing a conservative ideology believe that people are inherently unequal and thus deserve unequal rewards. They also value order, stability, authority, and tradition. Individuals holding a liberal ideology, on the other hand, are egalitarian, tolerate dissent, and are open to social reform. It is not surprising that these differences have been found to reliably motivate political behavior. Research has also established that most Americans can accurately identify their ideological allegiance. Findings reveal that because these attitudes are organized around abstract and core issues, they are very stable and predict behavior across a variety of situations. Differences between individuals holding these ideologies have confirmed earlier observations about personal characteristics associated with them. Those associated with conservatives include the following: a tendency to see the world as a dangerous place with a corresponding fear of death, crime, and terrorism; rigid, dogmatic, and prejudicial attitudes toward groups perceived as deviant and posing a threat; and an increased likelihood to attribute behavior of others to internal causes, accompanied by moral condemnation. Liberals demonstrate greater tolerance for ambiguity and openness and are more motivated by excitement, seeking out novelty, and engaging in creative pursuits.

The review of the findings summarized by Jost (2006) provides ample evidence of the relevance of ideology to the subject of oppression, particularly in the case of those endorsing a conservative ideology. But the importance of ideology goes much deeper than this. While the form that ideologies take must clearly be understood within broader historical, social, economic, and political circumstances (Rehmann, 2013), their existence expresses something inherent in and enduring about human beings. As Jost and Amodio (2012) observe, human beings are ideological animals. The reason cited for this should by now be very familiar. Human beings have a basic need to reduce uncertainty, maintain order, and experience a degree of control in negotiating life. Jost and Amodio turn once more to the work of Becker (1973) and terror management theory (Solomon et al., 1991) to illustrate that the primary function of ideology is to defend against the ultimate of all losses—our imminent mortality.

The worldview conferred by ideology serves to alleviate anxiety triggered by uncertainty, loss, and threats to a sense of predictability. Ideology provides human beings with a source of motivations that enable them to meet epistemological, existential, and relational needs. In other words, ideology provides people with a way of understanding the world, protects them against anxieties associated with a sense of insecurity, and helps them to feel connected with others who share their worldview. Jost and Amodio summarize this as providing certainty, security and solidarity.

While it is important to recognize what it is about individuals that lead to ideologies, we need to heed the caution of Augoustinos (1999) that this represents only a partial tradition of research on ideology. It preserves the individualist bias of psychology and other social sciences and so fails to consider the ways in which material and social circumstances also influence consciousness. While it is true that individuals actively shape and interpret their experiences to construct a version of reality, the material, resources and tools they have available to accomplish this task are afforded to them by society. The resulting worldview reflects the power relations and governing beliefs and presuppositions within that society. This dialectic of individual and collective must thus be retained in describing the functions of ideology.

Beginning with the *epistemological function* of ideology, it is a source of beliefs, understandings, and core assumptions intended to provide answers to substantive questions asked by human beings. Who am I? What is my place in the world? How should I relate to other human beings and the world around me? What is the purpose and meaning of life? How should I live? While these questions are all of major import, more often it is the more modest ways in which these questions insert themselves into the everyday lives of individuals that necessitate the ready-made, "common sense" solutions provided by ideology. In negotiating the social realities encountered in the circumstances that they face every day, individuals constantly look to the worldview provided by ideology to figure out what is going on and what to do. As Manders (2006) observes, the opinions, rationales, and coping strategies employed using the ideology are generally so mundane that they do not seem to merit any attention. They escape any examination and scrutiny because they are just part of a constantly present background from which we draw information as needed. However, because the beliefs in question are intended to address fundamental and substantive questions, their significance should not be underestimated. Often it is not until human beings are faced with a boundary experience (Jaspers, 1984), a major wake-up call, that these core assumptions are exposed because these larger issues have erupted into their awareness.

Looking next to the *existential function* of ideology, the beliefs and attitudes employed by individuals are not mere intellectual matters. They are associated with passionately held commitments and enforced by powerful emotions, even though these emotions are often not consciously apparent to individuals. They remain below the level of awareness because if they were to become conscious, there is the risk that what is triggering them will become conscious as well. This affective dimension of ideology is found in highly emotionally charged situations such as encounters with anxiety triggered by loss and uncertainty. This function is called existential because it is the deepest of all fears—the concern that one's very being is in question—that prompts individuals to utilize their ideology to cope with this threat.

Jost and Amodio (2012) provide evidence for this affective underpinning of ideology by utilizing what they call a political neuroscience approach. By this they mean connecting ideological processes to physiological substrates that help to elucidate how ideology is a form of motivated social cognition. The types of responses investigated are automatic ones elicited by what is perceived as situations that are dangerous and outside of one's control. These are responses mediated by the autonomic nervous system. This refers to the discussion of the fight-or-flight response, or stress reaction. Parts of the brain involved in conflict monitoring and threat processing have been found to play a role in the cognitive styles of conservatives and liberals and differences in information processing. This includes a higher degree of sensitivity to conflict and threat found in conservatives, corresponding to a greater likelihood of their experiencing heightened states of arousal. Thus, some of the most dramatic and extreme ways in which ideology motivates human beings are more than just an intellectual matter but are driven by powerful emotions. These same emotions do not merely motivate actions in accordance with strongly held beliefs but also serve to inhibit any critical reflection on those beliefs.

As was the case with the epistemological function, the affective dimension of ideology is not manifested solely in extreme circumstances but assists individuals in negotiating stressors and conflicts encountered in day-to-day life. To understand this, we must look at another feature of ideology, particularly the current ideology of neoliberalism. Manders (2006) helps to explain. Though ideologies are often presented as if they were coherent, rational, and beyond question, they are in fact riddled by inconsistencies and contradictions. Because the intent is to characterize ideology as absolute and universal fact, such contradictions are regarded as problematic because they provide opportunities to contest it. These contradictions expose chinks in the ideology's armor.

In the previous discussion of suffering, a significant source was encounters with life's dichotomies, contradictions, and fractures (Moulyn, 1982). These are moments when the fabric of life has been disrupted or even shattered by unavoidable loss. Similarly, these confrontations with life's dichotomies precipitate a sense of being unsettled, accompanied by the desire to find some resolution (Fromm, 1947), and in the process of doing so integrate the loss into some new understanding. For ideologies to remain unquestioned and unaltered, that suffering must be either silenced or attention diverted away from it. The tried and true beliefs and the ready-made solutions it provides must be applied to the problem irrespective of whether they are satisfactory or not. Often this rigid and unreflective application of a failing solution to a problem spirals into self-defeat and even greater suffering.

Manders (2006) calls these solutions *rationalities*, practical solutions for dealing with the concrete realities of daily life. He writes:

> The historical dominance of an ideology is not merely an intellectual affair. Its mass adhesion, its *popular* "rationality" as constituted in daily life and history, is also a matter of its emotional appeal. For in contemporary Western history, it is not an objective process of formal means–end rationality (alone) that secures the dominance of reigning ideology, although this is always a component of "popular-historical rationality." More significantly, the "real critical test" of hegemony of a particular mode of ideological thinking is its *experienced rationality*—its meaningfulness, its "sensibleness"—on the subjective, emotional and interpreted level of its everyday praxis. (p. 85, italics in original)

The form of reason being employed is not a critical one that seeks to analyze an issue and consider alternatives before engaging in action. Rather it is an instrumental, means-to-end form of reason in which individuals seek a quick, pragmatic solution that brings immediate benefits. Only over time does it become apparent that these short-term solutions ultimately prove to exacerbate problems in the long run and so make matters worse.

The third function of ideology is *relational*, a means of connecting with others who share it with us. Human beings have a powerful need for belonging. Because so much of one's identity is bound up with the ideology that one subscribes to, it is deeply affirming to be surrounded by others who also hold to that ideology. As Jost and Amodio (2012) observe, it creates a sense of solidarity that also performs a soothing and stress-reducing function. The work of social psychologist Erwin

Staub (1989) helps to illustrate this. He has done extensive work on factors contributing to mass killing and genocide. A common precursor of these events is what he calls "difficult life conditions," or times when a significant threat to individuals' beliefs, values, and expectations provokes fear of possible annihilation. When people's sense of efficacy and control are repeatedly frustrated, they feel increasingly vulnerable and frightened. They also feel a need to regain their sense of control and resurrect a sense of purpose and meaning. One way in which they may seek to do so is by submitting to a movement, ideology, or powerful leader that promises to give them the direction and guidance they feel they are missing. This is particularly the case in more authoritarian or hierarchical cultures. A shared ideology provides not only a bond to others but a sense of safety and security.

However, the same frustration that undermines their sense of control also is accompanied by increased anger and aggression. Individuals seek to mask or eliminate their suffering by distinguishing themselves from those who do not share their ideology and so pose a threat. This involves scapegoating others and proceeding to take harmful actions toward them. In other words, if the suffering that inevitably follows adverse life circumstances cannot be accurately identified and accepted as such, it becomes incorrectly crystallized into a specific fear directed toward others. When the ideology or authority attributes problems to members of another group, this aggression is directed toward them as a means of reclaiming power by taking it from them. This exercise of control over others extends as far as killing them if need be.

Erich Fromm (1941), in his book *Escape from Freedom*, describes a similar pattern. Difficult life circumstances can lead individuals to become so frightened and hopeless that they are willing to relinquish their freedom and their very sense of individuality to a higher authority, which often takes the form of an ideology. Under conditions of extreme threat and uncertainty, people become increasingly isolated from others and disconnected from themselves. These painful states of alienation are accompanied by an anxiety that one is progressively losing a grip on what once seemed certain and true. With the threatened collapse of their ideology, individuals may feel that they have lost their ability to exercise control over their own lives. Another possible reaction is feeling so overwhelmed by anxiety when faced with making choices that they fear making any choice at all. In either case such individuals will experience a diminished sense of agency and instead assume a helpless and passive stance in the face of forces they believe to be overwhelming. The burden of freedom becomes so painful and frightening that whatever fear individuals may have once had about relinquishing control to an authority is overshadowed by a fear of what they may lose in the face of a frightening and uncertain future.

For Fromm, the radically social nature of human beings distinguishes them from all other animals. Humans are innately motivated to be connected to others for their very survival and experience isolation as profoundly disturbing and painful. This need for connection under the circumstances described can become expressed in a willingness to abandon their individuality, relinquish their capacity for autonomy and self-determination, and submerge themselves in a form of mass identity. This harmful way of coping with the anxiety created by uncertainty, emptiness, and loss is also observed by Heidegger (1927/1978). Humans may attempt to flee from this anxiety by lapsing into an inauthentic mode of living in which they give up their individuality and conform to the collective, public identity of "the They" (das Man). One form of this is taking refuge in some form of absolute authority, whether it is a group, an ideology, or leader. By offering certainty and security, conformity to such authority promises to assuage anxiety and silence uncertainty. Fromm describes this as *automaton conformity*, whereby individuals blindly adopt the values and opinions endorsed by an ideology and essentially become mindless cogs in a machine.

Hegemony as Common Sense

With an overview of ideology provided, the importance of the work of Antonio Gramsci (1971) on *hegemony* is next considered. This will pave the way for an examination of the process of *mystification,* or the ways in which a dominant ideology operates on individuals' experience in order to make that ideology seem objective and true and garner popular consensus for the worldview it espouses. According to Gramsci, at any certain point in history one concept of reality is dominant and diffused throughout all of society. It informs society at all levels, including political, economic, social, religious, cultural, and moral. Gramsci describes hegemony as "common sense," or a conception of the world that is uncritically absorbed and utilized by average persons as they go about their daily lives. Manders (2006) goes on to elaborate what is meant by common sense. First, it is common because hegemony consists of beliefs, attitudes, and values that make up popular wisdom that is widely subscribe to. This is because ideology so thoroughly pervades and saturates society. Second, this system is not rigid; it must be flexible enough to adapt to the ever-changing circumstances that people face and to accommodate the contradictions embedded within them. Third, common sense is sensible, a resource utilized to answer practical problems that arise in day-to-day life.

But hegemony is not merely folk wisdom. It performs an essential political function that is often the basis for abuses of power and forms of oppression. Hegemony represents the worldview held by the ruling class and enforced within subordinate classes. It is the reigning paradigm, the "official version" of reality. The principal means by which hegemony exerts its power is by presenting the current state of affairs as objective, veridical, universal, and incapable of change. This is often what is communicated when people use the term "common sense." What they are saying is, "That's just the way things are." This so-called folk wisdom involves something that everyone already knows and takes for granted. Based on the inevitability and irreversibility of the world portrayed by hegemony, people are led to forsake their hopes and resign themselves to the conclusion that things in their present state are as good as they can get. As a result, any effort put into trying to change things is just a waste of time and bound to fail.

Hegemony asserts that the current power arrangements are the norm and justifies the prevailing hierarchy that assigns individuals to their place in the scheme of things. In doing so, it sanctions the social arrangements and practices that perpetuate the inequities, injustices, and material and psychological harms that result from oppression. The beliefs, values, and attitudes of the powerful and privileged are ruling forces in all spheres of life. A way of looking at the world endorsed by the powerful is first disseminated and then enforced by cultural institutions charged with ideological control. As such, hegemony becomes internalized by all members of society. Citing Gramsci's assertion that "every relationship of hegemony is necessarily an educational relationship," Giroux (2008) argues that hegemony functions as a form of public pedagogy.

In other words, the diffusion and internalization of hegemony is in a sense something taught to everyone using the language, discourse, metaphors, narratives, and moral precepts it provides. Once internalized, these "teachings" are then translated into how people think about themselves, others, and the world. This indoctrination is not restricted to educational institutions; nor is it something that only happens early in individuals' lives. Rather, all socializing institutions engage in the pedagogical process, and it continues throughout the lifetime of individuals. As Manders (2006) observes, this is essential because hegemony is not fixed or static but must be constantly produced in order to be sustained.

Manders elaborates on key elements of hegemony that help to fill out the description provided thus far. Hegemony involves a dynamic equilibrium that must be constantly negotiated between the privileged and powerful group and the groups over which they exercise control. While hegemonies are powerful, that power is not complete. Even the most basic assumptions contained in hegemony are contested, and dissent is always present. As a result, Manders points out that hegemony is a compromise. While efforts are exerted to hide them from view, ambivalence and conflict are always present. The alienation and ambivalence experienced by those dominated always offer the possibility of resistance and emancipation.

Hegemony is the basis for both economic/political domination and cultural domination. Locating the driving forces responsible for the worldview advanced by hegemony solely in the economic system is too narrow—as even Marx (1978) observed. Instead, what is revealed by a critical examination of hegemony is a certain degree of consistency in how its core assumptions and values are applied to all areas of human life. Certain key principles, guiding metaphors, and paradigmatic patterns of discourse seek to unify diverse aspects of human life under the umbrella of the dominant ideology. An example that will be discussed later in the examination of neoliberal ideology is the centrality of the "market" as metaphor, principle and moral ideal.

The next characteristic of hegemony is that its actual assumptive nature is not presented as such by the ruling group; rather, it is held up as an accurate depiction of reality. The manufactured nature of hegemony, its social and historical construction as an instrument of social control, is necessarily the facet most thoroughly disguised. Presenting hegemony as given, natural, universal, and fixed is aimed at fostering a sense of passivity and fatalism in the dominated. If things are the way the way they are, then resistance is futile. As a result, submitting to the facts—no matter how unpleasant or unjust—means that people will consent to their own exploitation and the accompanying suffering. This process resembles the previous discussion of internalized oppression, in which the sense of identity of individuals who have been oppressed becomes shaped by beliefs, values, and attitudes espoused by the dominant ideology. They then assess themselves using its standards and expectations.

The fourth characteristic of hegemony asserted by Gramsci (1971) is that it reflects national traits and characteristics. This underlines the role that historical factors play in the creation of different forms of hegemony at different times and in different places. In order to secure the consent of those who fall under the sway of hegemony, it must in some fundamental ways be in accord with already existing understandings they have about themselves and life. Those understandings are rooted in long-standing traditions, national myths, historical events of significance, and the stature assigned to esteemed individuals. In outlining the ideological hegemony of capitalism in the United States, Manders (2006) provides a clear illustration of its alignment with national traits and characteristics. The U.S. ideological hegemony includes the following elements: the ideals of freedom, democracy, and equality; the ethic of individualism; the ethic of competition; attitudes of authoritarianism and anti-authoritarianism; the ethic of nationalism; the American Dream; and the cult of efficiency. Each of these elements would easily resonate with U.S. citizens. These aspects of neoliberal ideology will be discussed and critiqued later in this chapter.

The final characteristic of hegemony is that it is historically necessary. For good or bad, what this means is that hegemony is essential to the organization and maintenance of every aspect of civil society—economic, political, religious, ethical, and cultural. Though an expression of a time and place, its power and authority are nonetheless presented as complete and universal. This distinguishes it from an ideology that might be arbitrary, rationally derived, or consciously constructed and adopted by individuals. Given the pervasiveness and weight assigned to hegemony, individuals experience it as psychologically valid. It is the principal means by which individuals develop consciousness of themselves and the world. The beliefs, attitudes, and values of hegemony are intended to render human experience intelligible, coherent, and to some degree manageable. However, the success with which hegemony is able to achieve this goal varies, and failures often call upon the use of mystification to obscure them or explain them away.

Social Character: Internalized Hegemony

Mystification plays a central role in why so many people actively and seemingly freely consent to their alienation and oppression. While the threat of direct force is never absent, in many societies conformity is achieved through the more indirect means provided by mystification. The success of this process depends upon the internalization of hegemony. The concept of social character developed by Erich Fromm (1941) provides a means for understanding just how hegemony is so successful in shaping individuals' identity and way of looking at the world. Social character is more than just how individuals consciously see and define themselves. As a product of life-long socialization and as an expression of how completely individuals are embedded in hegemony, social character also includes deep and often unconscious beliefs and motivations that reflect the internalization of the prevailing social structure and norms. As Manders (2006) observes, hegemony is not so much a matter of ideas as it is a way of being, what he calls an "operational praxis" that informs the way in which individuals live out implicit meanings and order their experience of social reality on a daily basis.

All forms of social character are historically constituted to align with the dominant ideology at that time. It includes notions of personal identity sanctioned and enforced by the status quo and desires instilled to serve the interests of the ruling order. Who we believe ourselves to be and our desires and aspirations may to a degree be a product of our own self-invention. Indeed, we may receive messages from society-at-large that we are largely responsible for our choices and the persons we have become. However, behind that culturally generated narrative, hegemony has been thoroughly inculcated into a character that suits its purposes and prerogatives. As Langman and Ryan (2009) observe, "Otherwise said, 'social character' can be seen as a form of internalized hegemony that impels socially required action through internal compulsion rather than external forces or rewards. Thus society harnessed the individual to work toward its ends and willingly accede to its patterns of authority" (p. 475). What we may experience as a personal desire or as a goal we have set for ourselves in fact expresses a social directive that benefits the powerful. A great deal of advertising consists of precisely this sort of mystification.

The processes by which larger social forces infiltrate consciousness and identity are laid out in considerable detail by Fromm (1960) in a book that, not coincidentally, examines possible parallels between Zen Buddhism and psychoanalysis. The most substantial source of suffering from a Buddhist perspective was described previously as samkhara-dukkha, or suffering having its origins in ignorance, illusions, and mistaken habits of thought. Out of ignorance arise cravings and desires that feel urgent and essential to our happiness but are bound to be frustrated. The emotions principally responsible for these destructive attachments are greed, fear, and selfishness. All three play a significant role in the current neoliberal hegemony that thrives on fear and extols greed and selfishness—the very same hegemony that shapes contemporary social character. Fromm's concerns about the catastrophic impact of capitalism, which transforms human beings into essentially mindless consumers whose obsession with having ensnare them in poisonous illusions, enabled him to appreciate the insights that Buddhism had to offer. His training as a sociologist and a psychoanalyst allowed him to integrate these insights into a formulation of social character as internalized hegemony.

Fromm begins by asserting that in order to survive any society must mold the character of its members so that they want to do what they have to do. They believe themselves to be free even as they fall under the power of implanted compulsions. These social functions are so thoroughly internalized that they are performed without thought and accompanied by the fear that something bad will happen should they fail to comply. To achieve this degree of compliance, the economic and political order of that society, along with the ideology upon which it is based, must be adopted unthinkingly. This makes the content of consciousness mostly half-truths, soothing deceptions, and plausible interpretations that do not represent reality but serve the needs of powerful. Fromm (1960) provides a detailed description of what occurs:

> ...most of what people have in their conscious minds is fiction and delusion; this is the case not so much because people would be *incapable* of seeing the truth as because of the function of society. Most of human history...is characterized by the fact that a small majority has ruled over and exploited the majority of its fellows. In order to do so, the minority has usually used force; but force is not enough. In the long run, the majority has had to accept its exploitation voluntarily—and this is only possible if its mind has been filled with all sorts of lies and fiction, justifying and explaining its acceptance of the minority's rule. However, this is not the only reason for the fact that most of what people have in their awareness about themselves, others, society, etc., is fiction. In its historical development each society becomes caught in its own need to survive in the particular form in which it has developed, and it usually accomplishes this survival by ignoring the wider human aims which are common

to all men. This contradiction between the social and the universal aim leads also to the fabrication (on a social scale) of all sorts of fictions and illusions which have the function to deny and to rationalize the dichotomy between the goals of humanity and those of a given society. (pp. 97–98, italics in original)

Fear, anxiety, and preying upon human vulnerability associated with their dependence on others are means by which these lies and fictions are instilled. However, as Fromm (as did Gramsci and others) observes, the successful internalization of hegemony depends upon the process unfolding in an indirect and seemingly beneficent manner. As DiMaggio (2015) points out, even as the upper class wages ideological warfare on the subordinate classes by promoting a business agenda that benefits itself at the expense of the disadvantaged, the powerful rely upon corporate public relations firms, product advertising, and slick-talking business executives to present things as in the best interests of all. As a result, the disadvantaged accept without question the motivations and behavior of the powerful as benevolent. The American (or whatever) way of life is clearly superior to all others and one should feel fortunate to be a part of it. Whatever problems it may have are correctable and so one must remain loyal and defend it. The internalization of a whole host of illusions generated by hegemony cements the success of this process.

The internalization of hegemony is ultimately achieved by means of society placing powerful controls within individuals that govern what and how they experience, how they come to understand or interpret experience, and how they then act on that experience. Experiences are only able to enter into awareness under the conditions that allow them first to be perceived and processed and ordered using categories within a conceptual system that has social origins. Fromm calls this a socially conditioned filter that screens out any experiences for which there is no category. One of the principal means by which this filtering process functions is by means of language. Fromm writes, "Language, by its words, its grammar, its syntax, by the whole spirit which is frozen in it, determines how we experience, and which experiences penetrate to our awareness" (p. 101). The pivotal role played by language in the inculcation of ideology has since been further endorsed and elaborated in postmodern thought (Burr & Dick, 2017). The profound impact that language exercises in the process of mystification is also acknowledged by Watts (1961), who explains that illusions are not to be found in the outside world but in the language-based concepts inculcated in us by social institutions.

The second aspect of the filter is the socially sanctioned form of logic that influences the thinking process of individuals. Fromm points out that the predominant form of logic incorporated into our social character is Aristotelean, which tends to frame issues in linear, either/or terms and so is unreceptive to recognizing the more dialectical facets of human thought. This type of black or white thinking is conducive to the formation of in-groups and out-groups that can lead to scapegoating. It is also commonly found in more authoritarian and dogmatic approaches to experience. And it is utterly unsuited to coping with the inevitable encounters with paradox that occur in life and give rise to heightened states of alienation. The final aspect of the filter is the actual content of experiences that each society permits individuals to be exposed to. In many ways the material that hegemony permits to become internalized functions as a set of expectations that are essentially self-fulfilling. We experience only what we are allowed to experience, and each time this happens these parameters become ever more thoroughly embedded and reinforced. Those experiences that are considered taboo are enshrouded in fear and condemnation, and risk social ostracization.

Calling upon his training in psychoanalysis, Fromm (1960) sees the social character developed by individuals as embedded in the unconscious, a form of automatic thought and behavior sustained by inhibition of the critical and self-reflective function. Social conditioning succeeds in large part because, as social beings, humans do not wish to become isolated or alienated from their social group. They risk painful consequences if they depart from the approved social understandings, norms, and rules. When experiences arise in conflict with what is permitted, they must be either forbidden awareness or distorted in such a manner as to conform to socially sanctioned categories. Adopting a Buddhist perspective, Fromm (1960) describes this as persons believing they are awake when they are actually half-asleep, bound as they are by a host of socially generated illusions. He writes:

> By "half asleep" I mean that this contact with reality is a very partial one; most of what he believes to be reality (outside or inside of himself) is a set of fictions which his mind constructs. He is aware of reality only to the degree to which his social functioning makes it necessary. He is aware of his fellowmen inasmuch as he needs to cooperate with them; he is aware of

material and social reality inasmuch as he needs to be aware of it in order to manipulate it. *He is aware of reality to the extent to which the goal of survival makes awareness necessary.* (p. 108, italics in original)

This creates a series of damaging rifts both within persons and between them. These feelings of alienation, while painful, offer the chance of awakening to a deeper and truer understanding of self and life. However, in order to awaken, the illusions must be identified and rejected.

More recently, Langman (Langman & Ryan, 2009; and Langman, 2015) has expanded on the work of Fromm and situated it within contemporary trends and the current dominance of a neoliberal ideology. In accord with the need for hegemony to be reflective of national traits and characteristics, Langman (2015) sees the current social character in U.S. society (and other comparable neoliberal societies) as intertwined with religiosity, anti-intellectualism, and admiration for those who are economically successful. Likewise, this character must be placed within the context of the characteristics of contemporary work as rule-bound, fragmented, repetitive, and not conducive to independent or critical thought. Finally, trends in popular culture to satisfy the desire for escapism and inhibit critical thought and reflection must be taken into account. Despite these factors, Langman also asserts the presence of contradictions, inconsistencies, and incongruities that, if seized upon, can become the foundation for dissent and counter-hegemony.

In keeping with the observation that the function of pedagogy not be restricted to traditional sources such as families, schools, and churches, Langman highlights the increasing role played by mass media and the culture industry to tout consumption and various forms of packaged fantasies as a means of distracting individuals from their own subjugation. Simultaneously, mass media socially constructs events and gives them meanings and interpretations aligned with hegemony. Reality is depicted in highly biased and one-sided ways that thwart critical thought and appeal to "common sense." The contemporary version of social character according to Langman and Ryan (2009) is the *carnival character*, whose principal means of coping and escaping is linking self-esteem with various forms of privatized hedonism. They further elaborate:

> Privatized hedonism can be thought of as an ideological justification for a complex pattern of global consumption in which consumers pursue a variety of themed or simulated experiences provided by the culture industries. These include mass mediated carnival cultures, theme parks and resorts, and the rapidly growing travel industry that provides guided tours or ocean cruises which provide simulated, themed environments. (p. 482)

These sources of satisfaction are meant to make up for the loss of satisfaction individuals previously derived from their working life. They are also intended to cushion individuals from feelings of anxiety and powerlessness through distraction.

Escapism enables individuals to avoid seeing themselves as responsible for their own subjugation as this would be accompanied by feelings of shame and the risk of social sanctions. Lacking confidence in their own ability to determine what is and is not real and feeling perplexed in the face of contradictory information, people defer to the powerful and those upheld as authorities or experts. Harkening back to Aristotelean logic, Langman (2015) explains that those who adopt authoritarian styles of thought tend to see the world in dualist, black or white terms. They also utilize defenses such as denial, splitting, and projection. Denial is the foundational defense as it is aimed at rejecting the reality of anything that may threaten one's sense of self or worldview. It is little wonder then that individuals in denial seek whenever possible to cut themselves off from information from the external world. And so they end up being ill-informed about world events, knowing little about their own government and who runs it, preferring to let others make decisions that are "best for them," and tending to be easily swayed by stereotypes and simplistic explanations as the means of understanding and alleviating their fears.

In concluding, Langman (2015) makes clear that an appreciation of the emotional basis of acquiring an identity as well as the role of identity in mediating between hegemonic forces at the cultural level and the individual, is not intended to replace social, economic, and political determinism with psychological determinism. Rather, it is to recognize an important element of Gramsci's (1971) work that sees culture as the contested terrain in which hegemonic struggles are enacted as the illusions and self-serving lies of the dominant ideology are exposed. This is all intended to prevent counter-hegemonic discourses and opposition. To overcome the power of hegemony, popular culture, business propaganda, religious and political rhetoric must all be submitted to critical examination. The false promises of private hedonism must be contested and exposed as dangerous distractions from genuinely problematic social realities. And the failures of capitalism revealed in multiple contradictions encountered in everyday life must be acknowledged. All these provide the path to liberation.

Mystification: Negotiating the Politics of Experience

To fully understanding the process of mystification we must get to the very core of how it operates, at the level of experience. This perspective is provided in the work of R. D. Laing (1960, 1967) in what he calls the social phenomenological approach. Laing (1967) asserts that despite its invisibility, only one's experience is apodictically evident. Our very sense of being present in the world as real, alive, whole, and temporally continuous (what Laing, 1960 calls ontological security) rests on the self-validating data of experience. Thus, our very psyche is our experience. He writes, "The experience of oneself and others is primary and self-validating. It exists prior to the scientific or philosophical difficulties about how such experience is possible or how it is to be explained" (p. 23). However, because Laing bases phenomenology in the social, its true field is what he calls *interexperience*, or how persons relate their experience of others to others' experience of their behavior.

In our relations with one another, we seek some degree of mutual understanding regarding our experiences of and with others. Because experience is invisible, we have only individuals' behavior, which is a function of their experience, as data to achieve that understanding. The same thing can be said for how individuals often attempt to come to some self-understanding. In this case, as well, they often look to their behavior and then make inferences about what motivated or caused their behavior. In both instances, however, there is always a degree of ambiguity or uncertainty about what specific experiences lie behind our or others' behavior. It is precisely that ambiguity and uncertainty that opens a space for the process of mystification to occur, especially when the degree of ambiguity causes a heightened level of anxiety. At such times, individuals desire an expedient means of eliminating discomfort. Like the earlier discussion of the role of recognition in the formation of our sense of identity, the ways in which others, especially powerful others, respond to our behavior and thus to our experience can have a significant impact on whether we trust and take ownership of it. Our interdependence makes mystification possible because it also makes it possible for others to negate our experience. Paralleling ideas put forward by Sartre (1953), Laing (1967) sees human agency as enabling human beings to act on their own or others' experience either by confirming, validating, or supporting it or by denying, undermining, or invalidating it. The destruction of experience gives rise to heightened states of alienation and deprives us of our humanity.

For Laing, mystification cannot traditionally be understood as an intrapsychic defense mechanism. Its occurrence within a social context makes it what he calls a *transpersonal* defense as it entails the action of one person on another. Like intrapsychic defenses, it may seem to operate like a mechanism with a force and will of its own, but this is a form of reification. Mystification is something that people do to themselves or others, even if it occurs with a certain degree of automaticity. It is an act of violence on that which provides individuals with a sense of ontological security. It is also a form of exploitation or oppression sanctioned within society. Laing (1967) writes, "We act on our experience at the behest of the others, just as we learn how to behave in compliance with them. We are taught what to experience and what not to experience, as we are taught what movements to make and what sounds to emit" (p. 37).

He also makes clear that much of this teaching is based on the dominant ideology within society. It assigns to certain individuals a greater degree of authority that sanctions their exercising power over the experience of others. However, exploitation must not be seen as such. It is typically disguised as a form of benevolence, something done in the best interests of the exploited. Because of this, the targets of mystification are led to feel one with their oppressors and a sense of gratitude for what is being done for them, accompanied by feeling that it is bad or irrational to rebel.

Though Laing (1967) often described the dynamics of mystification within the context of families, he understood that its primary function was to maintain the status quo within a system, to keep stereotyped and rigid patterns going, and to undermine any efforts to disrupt them. This often involves having to recognize the presence of conflicts and contradictions but then proceeding to obscure or distort what they are about. Since the underlying conflict remains, mystification ultimately fails, and threats to the system persist. Because the goal of mystification is to confuse, befuddle, and mask individuals' experience, it does not aim to ignore actual events as that would more readily expose the deception at work. Rather, it operates at the level of framing and interpreting what is going on. While the "facts" in question are apparent and readily observable, what remains vague or subject to question are their causes, consequences, and meaning. When the circumstances in question arouse uncomfortable emotions, fear, and insecurity, soothing, calming and even anesthetizing explanations are readily seized upon. When those same explanations carry the authority of ideological apparatuses and of institutions that have codified, defended, and propagated them, the exploited are even more easily seduced and the status quo is maintained.

Laing offers examples of how mystification might operate from his work with families and with individuals diagnosed with schizophrenia. One form is confirming the content of another person's experience but not the modality by which they experience. Instead, the modality is dismissed or mislabeled as manufactured by their imagination, or based in misperception or a state of confusion. "You weren't being treated unfairly. You're just being overly sensitive or acting overly privileged." Another is to confirm the content of another's experience but then replace whatever reasons they might have for what happened with attributions or meanings provided by the exploiter. For example, one might assert, "I know you thought the reason for losing your job was because the company wanted to make more money, but it's all this foreign competition from cheap labor that has depressed sales." A particularly powerful form of mystification occurs within a system with differential power in which the exploiter has been accorded the right to determine the experience of another who correspondingly is under the obligation to experience or not experience matters accordingly. Frequently, little heed is given to the experience of the victims of oppression, under the pretense that unlike their oppressors they are unable to fully fathom or comprehend the economic or political complexities at work.

Mystification attacks the very core of our humanity, our sense of being real and alive. In doing so, it touches upon human beings' deepest fear because the negation of their experience undermines the basis upon which their sense of being depends. However, it simultaneously deflects from the damage it inflicts by employing denial or distraction. By professing benevolence as one's motive, what looks like violence is framed as care and concern. By employing clever misdirection, the source of threat to individuals' being is attributed to someone or something else. And so, paradoxically, while mystification is intended to deal with fear, it acts to quickly stifle and salve it before it can give rise to either opposition or critical reflection. The exercise of power by the exploiters operates on the experience of the oppressed to ensure that it serves the needs and directives of the dominant ideology, using whatever means at hand: persuasion, deterrence, or coercion. The overall message is what you see is not what you see, what you think is not what you think, what you feel is not what you feel, *and* because that is so you will have to rely on the powerful to tell you what you see, think, and feel. The motives of the oppressed are discounted, trivialized, or villainized—at a terrible cost. As Laing observed, in its extreme form mystification leads to madness. It is also well known to be an essential tool in the practice of torture.

The Problem of the Ego Revisited— Once Again

The effectiveness of mystification is inextricably connected to the totalizing impact of hegemony on consciousness. While the effects of mystification on the oppressed have been the major subject of focus, it is essential to appreciate that oppressors also fall under the spell of mystification. In other words, though they are actively engaged in obfuscation and invalidation, they generally have little awareness of this and would be troubled or offended to be accused of it if confronted. The neoliberal lens through which all experience is processed and constructed is taken for granted by everyone. We are confronted by its version of truth no matter where we look. In this sense, mystification can be represented as a more sinister version of what is called Indra's net. In its original meaning, this image is used to capture the interconnectedness and unity of all things. It is imagined as a net with a multi-faceted jewel at every nexus, which then reflects every other jewel embroidered in the net. In like manner, mystification succeeds because we are trapped in a net of illusion, where no matter where we look and what we look at we see the same ideologically manufactured image of the world reflected back at us. A constant force is exerted upon us to surrender to these illusions, to comply with their dictates, and to resist any temptation to cast them off.

In this sense, hegemony is sustained by mere inertia. It works so effectively because it sets in motion a process whereby individuals irresistibly propound and reproduce it in actions they take every day. Each time individuals choose to act in accordance with hegemony, they regard their actions as proof of its reality and then become living examples of its reality in the eyes of others. Each choice becomes part of an ever-increasing, well-grooved path of least resistance. Hegemony becomes an indispensable tool for how to get by in life even if it means barely getting by because the alternative is failure, disaster, and realization of one's worst fears. What individuals fail to see is that mystification is a self-fulfilling prophecy at work. Hegemony is not inevitable or irresistible; there are alternatives.

Pride is also at work, although it seems at times hard to detect when the targets of oppression are so demeaned and belittled. The relational function of hegemony helps to clarify this. Though the oppressed may experience a lack of respect, worth, and empowerment, these feelings go unacknowledged by their oppressors. Instead mystification is employed to secure the loyalty of the oppressed by cultivating their identification with the social, political and economic power, and prestige connected to the status quo. Their sense of identity becomes so utterly bound up with promised idealized images of wealth, status, and success offered to all who subscribe to hegemony that the threat of sacrificing these beliefs and values is painful and frightening. Identifying with models and exemplars held up for them to emulate offers them vicarious feelings of worth and power. By the same token, those who enjoy power and prestige cling desperately to hegemony, often falling prey to mystification themselves to forestall any attacks on their sense of self. By elevating hegemony to an unquestionable status, individuals can at the same time elevate themselves. But what results is a fragile and empty narcissism precisely because it is propped up by so many illusions.

And what keeps the entire process going is insecurity. Mystification simultaneously stirs insecurity by eating away at the very foundation of one's sense of being, one's experience, while simultaneously offering a means of restoring security in the form of some ideologically prescribed solution. In a society where more is always better, in which desires are insatiable, individuals' psyches are colonized by needs and wishes that perpetuate the cycle of consumption that aggrandizes the wealthy and further impoverishes the disadvantaged. The true reasons for one's suffering are consistently mystified when drowned out by a plethora of socially sanctioned panaceas offering temporary relief, while at the same time conveying messages that stoke one's underlying emptiness and the fear that comes with it. The fear and the panacea work together to keep the oppressed in bondage to the powerful, who alone are portrayed as capable of providing any hope of relief for their anguish.

Neoliberal Hegemony

It is the consensus of many (Brown, 2006; Giroux, 2008; Harvey, 2005; Joseph, 2018) that the current hegemony is neoliberalism. As might be suggested by its name, neoliberalism has some relationship to the older tradition of liberalism while also differing from it (Thorsen, 2010). Thus, some examination of liberalism is necessary to provide context. Classical liberalism has its roots in the work of John Locke and Adam Smith and espoused a view extolling personal sovereignty and religious toleration. It also took a minimalist view of the state, whose role essentially was to ensure public order and a laissez-faire economic policy. Over time, different versions of liberalism evolved. For example, subsequent thinkers such as John Stuart Mill, John Dewey, and John Rawls argued for more active involvement of the state in economic policies in order to supply essential goods and services to all citizens and, when necessary, redistribute wealth and power to avoid inequities. The economic policies of John Maynard Keynes ascribe to this view. According to Gray (1995), all forms of liberalism have the following in common:

- Individualism, or the moral primacy of the person over the collective
- Egalitarianism, or according all persons the same moral status irrespective of legal or political order
- Universalism, or asserting a moral unity of human beings, with historical and cultural differences being of secondary importance
- Meliorism, or the belief in the improvability of all political and social institutions

While the foundations of neoliberalism can be traced back to liberalism, neoliberalism constitutes a distinct ideology by redefining liberalism and adopting a more right-wing or laissez-faire position regarding economic policy. In his history of neoliberalism, Harvey (2005) traces a substantial turn toward it in the economic crisis of the 1970s. He is among those who regard neoliberalism not as a rejuvenation of liberalism but as a distinct economic theory. For example, Harvey cites examples of the implementation of a neoliberal ideology in autocratic societies such as China and Chile, which held no liberal views. Meanwhile, in more democratic countries, Ronald Reagan and Margaret Thatcher played instrumental roles in the move toward neoliberalism while implementing policies undermining egalitarian principles. The crises at that time were seen as posing threats to the capitalist social order and exposing problems with capitalism that needed correction. One area critiqued by neoliberal thinkers was the Keynesian approach to economics. Among the critics of this view, who advanced a neoliberal political and economic philosophy, were Friedrich von Hayek (1944) and Milton Friedman (1980). For example, Friedman adopted a form of consequentialist neoliberalism in which he advocated for deregulation, privatization, and radical tax cuts based on his belief that these policies would have beneficial economic consequences by creating wealth and maximizing individual freedom to choose.

Whereas neoliberalism was imposed in some places by force (by the military in Chile and, financially, through the International Monetary Fund in Mozambique and the Philippines), consent of the governed by what would appear to be democratic means had to be secured in places like the United States and United Kingdom. Harvey (2005) utilizes Gramsci's concept of common sense to explain this transition. As noted previously, common sense must be rooted in long-standing regional and national traditions in order to win consent while masking underlying realities embedded in the ideology being advocated. An example in the case of neoliberalism was the resonance that "freedom" had in countries like the United States and United Kingdom. It was craftily utilized by the elite to win over the masses while in fact diminishing the agency of the masses and expanding their own. Freedom to choose was framed as providing individuals with a seemingly endless array of consumer goods and extolling the opportunities afforded by capitalism to free oneself from social constraints. At the same time, "bringing freedom" to people suffering under the tyranny of a despot was justification for war in Iraq (a war actually waged in the interests of greed). Working together, the state, corporations, and mass media—assisted by the rise of numerous conservative think-tanks—devised the images, the language, and the propaganda necessary to solidify neoliberalism as the new lens from which to see the world.

What then is neoliberalism? While arguing that there are different understandings regarding it, Thorsen (2010) proposes that certain central features can be identified. Combining his definition with the perspectives offered by Harvey (2006) and Sandel (2012), the following key elements of a neoliberalism can be offered:

- Human well-being can best be achieved by enabling individuals to utilize their entrepreneurial freedoms and skills in order to act out of their rational self-interest.
- Free markets and trade enable human beings to utilize their creative potential in entrepreneurial pursuits and, as a result, lead to a greater degree of individual liberty.
- The sole legitimate purpose of the state is to safeguard individual and, particularly, commercial liberty and strong private property rights, and establish and protect an institutional framework that promotes free markets and free trade.
- Anything and anyone can be commodified through processes such as privatization and deregulation, including what were once considered social goods such as education, prison, social welfare, and healthcare.
- Where such markets do not exist, the state should seek to establish them.
- Establishment by the state of means such as military, defense, police, and legal structures and processes will ensure, if force by necessary, the proper functioning of markets.
- Leaving markets and trade free of interference will lead to a greater degree of individual liberty and well-being and a more efficient allocation of resources.
- A laissez-faire policy must be adopted, such that the state should not intervene unless absolutely necessary in established markets or restrict the process of commodification because it is incapable of possessing the necessary knowledge to make changes or adjustments to the market and so risks creating adverse consequences such as limiting individual choice or decreasing efficiency.
- Corporations have a legitimate role in telling the state what to do regarding legislation and regulation to enhance profits and market expansion.
- Greed performs a positive function in promoting social and common good.

It is important to look beyond these common features of neoliberalism in order to discern the problematic deeper assumptions behind them and the destructive underlying image of the human being on which it is based. This closer look begins to reveal areas subject to critique and the numerous ways in which neoliberal ideology has proven to be harmful to human well-being. As the current hegemony, neoliberalism's overt assertions are more fantasy than fact and operate to conceal their actual function of protecting the few who benefit from them from the many who suffer from them. The skyrocketing inequality referenced earlier (Kohler et al., 2017)—in which the gap between the über-wealthy and the rest of society continues to grow—and the many well documented adverse consequences of this inequality (Wilkinson & Pickett, 2009) provide ample evidence of how neoliberalism has failed by its own proclaimed standards. Adopting a public health approach, Joseph (2018) makes a convincing case that neoliberal policies are the precondition of a host of negative effects that stretch all the way to jeopardizing our planetary survival. Capitalism continues to prey upon victims of disasters (Klein, 2008) and economic crises like those of the 1970s in order to use privatization to dismantle democracy, commodify social services, and eliminate public goods—for example, the privatization of the public school system in New Orleans after Hurricane Katrina (Saltman, 2007).

One feature of neoliberalism that reflects its roots in classical liberalism is its emphasis on the individual. However, it has exaggerated the centrality and reality of the individual at the expense of the collective and social. In doing so, it justifies the transformation of human beings by the elite into a means to accumulate profit, accompanied by indifference to their welfare and failure to provide them with a means of sharing in the wealth they help to generate. As Walzer (1990) explains, liberal political theory regards persons as "...radically isolated individuals, rational egotists, and existential agents, men and women protected and divided by their inalienable rights" (p. 7). He further elaborates,

> The members of liberal society share no political or religious traditions; they can only tell one story about themselves and that is the story of *ex nihilio* [*sic*] creation, which begins in the state of nature, or the original position. Each individual imagines himself absolutely free, unencumbered, and on his own—and enters society, accepting its obligations, only in order to minimize his risks. His goal is security...And as he imagines himself, so he *really is*. (pp. 7–8, italics in original).

As Walzer asserts, this view of the individual is a radical one that assigns the person ultimate ontological status at the expense of all else.

This extreme position leaves individuals free to choose simply by virtue of the right to do so, with the objective of securing maximum security and advantage to themselves. These choices are not bound by any external criteria or moral principles, but instead are guided solely by individuals' subjective and selfish interests and desires.

This overblown, and ultimately untenable and unsustainable, selfish, and competitive understanding of human beings, fully endorsed and fostered by neoliberalism, has taken on the quality of a bizarre caricature. This is particularly evident in its utter neglect of the ways in which humans are inextricably interwoven in patterns of relationship, networks of power, and a range of communities that provide them with meaning and purpose. Not only does it render the social and communal invisible, but it regards them as superfluous. Thus, as LaMothe (2015) laments, it undermines and damages the social–communal myths, narratives, and rituals essential to creating a shared vision, identity, and sense of meaning and purpose among members of society. Trust and the mutual recognition essential to the sustaining bonds that social networks provide is seriously eroded, and a sense of compassion for our fellow beings is fatally weakened. Such is the communitarian critique of neoliberal ideology but, as Walzer (1990) cautions, this does not negate data that support this ideology or the appeal that this way of understanding has for people. Moreover, those who benefit from neoliberalism employ multiple forms of mystification to produce support for its individualistic policies and stifle dissent.

The political uses of such understandings of the person by capitalist ideology criticized by Critical Psychology (Nightingale & Cromby, 2001; Small, 2005; Parker, 2007) continue to remain relevant. As Thorsen (2010) explains, this individualism forms the basis of what is considered moral virtue in neoliberalism. Good persons are those who can gain access to markets and engage them as a competent actor who is willing to accept the risks that come with such participation and to adjust to the ongoing changes involved in their participation. They are solely responsible for the consequences of their freely made decisions and choices. The existence of inequalities and obvious social injustice in this system is morally acceptable when explained as the result of decisions individuals make freely. As a result, individuals who claim that the state should regulate the market to ameliorate and correct for people who suffer as a result of these "freely made" decisions are regarded as morally depraved or suffering from some personal or psychological disorder. Because they are autonomous, discrete entities, individuals are falsely believed to make up something called "society," which has no tangible or valid existence in itself. Instead, it is every person for him- or herself. Individuals must be willing to compete with others for the things they need and desire, and in doing so either secure or fail to attain personal happiness.

The transformation of persons into both consumer and commodity, while presumably under the aegis of defending their subjectivity and freedom, achieves the exact opposite. The only freedom permitted individuals is the private exercise of pursuing self-interest in the pursuit of happiness through consumption. People are what they buy and what they possess. In order to be successful by virtue of the wealth, status, and privilege they have attained, individuals must be willing to compete with others for the things they need and want. It is a dog-eat-dog world. Those who fail to join the fray are castigated as not acting rationally or responsibly. This extreme version of self-responsibility so central to neoliberalism is indispensable to its political and economic agenda.

In this endorsement of an unbridled meritocracy, winners deserve the good things they fought for and losers deserve their horrible lot. Their failings are due to personal reasons or pathology, which then exempts society or the state from any obligation to intervene, assist in aiding them, or redress inequality. Social problems are framed as private concerns. The meaning of freedom thus assumes a negative connotation in terms of being untrammeled by limitations or by interference from the state or other forms of authority. Its positive meaning as the power both individually and collectively to engage in democratic deliberation and participation and to exert influence on the social, economic, and political conditions that impact one's life has no room in neoliberalism. Democracy is equated with the existence of formal rights to private property and to pursue one's entrepreneurial interests in the market rather than in the principle of sharing power and governance (Brown, 2006).

This decline of recognizing individuals as possessing equality and substantive citizenship in a democracy and its substitution of the governed citizen as entrepreneur and consumer can be understood from the lens of Foucault's work. Brown (2006) and Rose (1998) shed additional light on the political functions served by neoliberalism's view of the person. Neoliberalism is understood as a political rationality. A political rationality consists of ways and means utilized by political authorities to produce certain desired effects while avoiding unwanted ones, to determine the objectives toward which governmental rule should be addressed, and to establish the scope of political authority and the legitimate methods used to produce the types of citizens desired. The goal is to exercise authority over individuals from a distance by disseminating vocabularies and norms sanctioned by experts—particularly psychologists and members of other psy disciplines—to be utilized by individuals to understand themselves, life, and ideals worthy of pursuit. This represents a move away from technologies of power employed to shape conduct in order to produce desired effects and avoid unwanted ones. These are replaced with technologies of the self, which are practices and strategies used by individuals to represent themselves and to judge and conduct themselves. The self in neoliberal societies is an historical and cultural artifact suited to its underlying assumptions and values.

Rose (1998) sees in neoliberalism the creation of an enterprise culture and the establishment of a certain image of human beings appropriate to such a culture. In a sense, persons are entrepreneurs of themselves going about the project of becoming whole and striving to be the persons they want to be by seeking to maximize their own powers, happiness, and quality of life. This is achieved by instrumentalizing their autonomy in the assembling of a lifestyle by freely choosing from a world of goods provided by the market. All problems encountered in day-to-day life are manageable by virtue of being matters resolved by working on one's self and acquiring the tools from the marketplace to become more efficient, more efficacious, and thus more successful. Problems are merely private, and thus conveniently abstracted from the concerns of the state and located instead in the market. Health is not a personal right but a commodity. Students and prisoners are no longer the responsibility of the state but commodities traded in the pursuit of corporate profit. Experts assume increased status and power in assisting individuals in their pursuit of personal fulfillment in what is solely construed as one's earthly life. Rose writes, "The guidance of selves is no longer dependent on the authority of religion or traditional morality; it has been allocated to 'experts of subjectivity' who transfigure existential questions about the purpose of life and the meaning of suffering into technical questions of the most effective ways of managing malfunction and improving the 'quality of life'" (p. 151).

The free market and the elevation of entrepreneurial pursuit under neoliberalism is not restricted to the economic sphere, as the "market" assumes essentially the status of an absolute. What is in truth nothing more than a construct, an invention derived from the thinking of the advocates of capitalism, is not only reified but deified. It is depicted as an autonomous, self-regulated entity that defines how and why things happen, an irresistible force with a logic of its own to which human beings must comply (Esposito & Perez, 2014). All aspects of life are shaped by market rationality such that its principles dictate what is valuable, right, and desirable. Individuals must thus align their attitudes, values, and behaviors to fit market demands, and failure to do so is condemned as a form of personal deviance and understood as the reason for individuals' misfortune. Even government itself must pattern itself on a corporate model, with sound governance evaluated in terms of criteria such as good management, productivity, and profitability. This transformation serves ultimately to dangerously undermine participatory democracy (Ayers & Saad-Filho, 2015; Brown, 2006).

Enterprise culture thus forges notions of personhood in ways that align governmentality, and institutional and human technologies in the creation and fostering of the enterprising self, and an ethical understanding that upholds the market as the absolute against which to measure what is right, proper, and healthy. Rose (1998) elaborates, "Neoliberalism is thus more than a phenomenon at the level of political philosophy. It constitutes a mentality of government, a conception of how authorities should use their powers in order to improve national well-being, the ends they should seek, the evils they should avoid, the means they should use, and, crucially, the nature of the persons upon whom they must act" (p. 153). However, as Rose also observes, despite the power of neoliberal hegemony, there exist counter-discourses and counter-hegemonies. The excesses and abuses of neoliberalism create contradictions and conflicts that often painfully expose its fallacies. However, in order to seize upon these contradictions and conflicts and the alternatives that they suggest, we must be prepared to detect the multiple ways in which mystification is employed to thwart critique, discourage reflection, and defeat dissent. We must be willing to fully attend to and experience the scope and depth of suffering that is inflicted by the oppression generated by neoliberalism. And so, it is to this topic that we turn next.

Chapter 7

The Mystification of Suffering

Suffering in and out of Frame

The groundwork has been laid for turning to a key assertion of this book—that neoliberal ideology currently plays a major role not only in inflicting suffering on the oppressed but also in the mystification of the very suffering it has created. The chief means by which neoliberalism inflicts this suffering is in its creation of ever-expanding economic inequality and the range of adverse physical, psychological, and social consequences that have been associated with it (Joseph, 2017; Wilkinson & Pickett, 2009). In fashioning a world based on consumerism as the solution to all of life's problems, neoliberalism has commodified every facet of human life, including human beings themselves (Giroux, 2008). The measure by which the "morality" of actions is determined is based on profit and personal gain—establishing and sustaining a contemporary caste system of winners and losers, the privileged and everyone else. The use of force, both brutal and subtle, is freely applied to maintain the status quo, but at the same time sustains big business by pouring billions into corporations that profit from death and destruction (Chomsky, 1999; Joseph, 2017).

However, the harm done by neoliberalism cannot be fully comprehended by restricting one's focus to its direct material and psychological consequences. This damage is compounded and exacerbated by its utilization of mystification to either render those consequences invisible to both perpetrators of oppression and their victims or to produce a state of doubt and confusion in their minds powerful enough to distort the reality of the suffering it has created. These effects have one primary aim and that is to maintain the hold that neoliberal ideology has on people's minds and lives and to thus ensure that its hegemony continues. The enduring success of the powerful to maintain this hegemony is based upon their ability to exploit and oppress others to their benefit while simultaneously employing various forms of mystification to disavow their involvement in these actions and disguise the destructive consequences that they have.

The process of mystification utilizes the propensity for human beings to engage in self-deception. Since self-deception is most likely to be used in circumstances that are perceived as posing a threat to individuals' existence and being outside of their control, as well as in states of heightened alienation, the creation of these conditions is constantly employed by the powerful to foster mystification. As will be seen, various techniques and tools derived from neoliberal ideology are used to inculcate and enforce illusions designed to mystify and confuse the oppressed, including language, myth, metaphor, and disabling double binds. Most prominent in their machinations is the creation of fear. The degree to which fear has become a central part of daily life and a means by which the powerful exert control to achieve their purposes is observed by Furedi (2005):

> The term "politics of fear" contains the implication that politicians self-consciously manipulate people's anxieties in order to realize their objectives. There is little doubt that they do regard fear as an important resource for gaining a hearing for their message. Scare tactics can sometimes work to undermine opponents and to gain the acquiescence of the electorate. However, as we shall see, the politics of fear is not simply about the manipulation of public opinion. It exists as a force in its own right. Nevertheless, the political elites, public figures, sections of the media, and campaigners are directly culpable for using fear to promote their agenda. (p. 123)

As argued previously, what we call the unconscious (which has long been held to be essential to explaining self-deception) is actually a discrete altered state of consciousness that is triggered by the types of situations noted above. The experience of alienation—the sense that one has lost touch with themselves, others, and what they once believed to be real—is an indispensable means for fostering self-deception and mystification. In alienation, individuals experience themselves falling under the control of robotic-like processes intended to restore a sense of stability and safety that seem to operate with a will of their own. In such states, they lapse into a passive stance in which they are far more likely to surrender their agency to someone or something else. This passivity is also cemented by virtue of having entered a dissociative state in which it seems to individuals as though they are disconnected from and standing outside of themselves. They assume a detached posture, watching things as they happen to them. In this state of mind, it is much easier to relinquish control and submit to an external authority. Moreover, in dissociation there is a temporary suspension of the critical factor so that whatever is experienced is taken at face value and not subjected to analysis or judgment. This fosters a heightened degree of suggestibility and a tendency to process experiences in a concrete and literal manner. The harms caused by such uncritical acceptance of the language and metaphors utilized by neoliberalism will be described below.

All these elements are likewise evidenced in the process of mystification and serve to make it more effective in causing individuals to question their lived experience and so undermine the very basis for their establishing what is and is not real. This state of consciousness makes it difficult to see through the socially generated illusions being used to obscure what is actually happening. Mystification might be regarded as serving the same purposes as self-deception, but that would only be partially true because that would restrict the level of analysis to the individual. Mystification is a *social process* that utilizes ideology to manipulate the thoughts, feelings, and behaviors of individuals to define what is real, what is not, what events mean, and what is possible or not possible for human beings to do. The primary aim of mystification is a political one, the maintenance of hegemony. Mystification shares with self-deception the aim of alleviating the distress, fear, and sense of disintegration triggered by disturbing experiences that challenge one's sense of identity and worldview.

In other words, like self-deception it is called upon to deal with the suffering that inevitably follows the experience of loss. The irony is that it is the very ideology that mystification seeks to maintain that is the cause of that suffering. In other words, embedded in the process of mystification is a paradox very similar to one described by Bakan (1968) in his analysis of the stress response and defense mechanisms. The very thing intended to alleviate suffering and redress some wrong is the actual root of the problem and thus causes even greater suffering. Mystification offers no guidance or relief to the sufferer. It is an egregious abuse of power used to justify and so deny or disguise the oppression and injustice inflicted by the very ideology it seeks to keep hidden and protect.

And why is awareness of the suffering attributable to that ideology so threatening? Because should it become an object of awareness of both the victims and the perpetrators of oppression, it would stand as incontrovertible testimony to death and destruction inflicted by that ideology. That same awareness would clearly expose the ever-present contradictions embedded in neoliberalism that give rise to suffering. The unveiling of these contradictions and the willingness to sit with the suffering caused by them, as observed by Friere (1970), constitutes the essential first step in the development of critical consciousness. It enables the oppressed to give a name to what is happening to them and what they are experiencing. Giving a name to their suffering reframes it into a problem that is capable of critical examination and eventually of change. It is a valuable insight that can then be translated into transformative action in the process of praxis.

Nonetheless, certain obstacles must be faced and contended with in order for this process of liberation to unfold. The most significant of these is how fear and the destabilization of identity and worldview routinely employed to enforce hegemony can stymie the awakening of all parties involved in oppression. As Manders (2006) observes, "Relying on common sense wisdom in everyday life does grave injury to a specific and centrally human characteristic: *the potentiality for critical thought*" (p. 90, italics in original). The success of illusions manufactured by hegemony depends upon how effectively they mystify suffering. And so vast resources and energies are devoted to inhibiting critical examination of those illusions and the suffering that they cause. Looking again at Manders' analysis, it is not that those exposed to mystification do not think, but rather that efforts have been made to ensure that they do not think very deeply or for very long.

Langman (2015) concurs, noting that an abundant array of diversions is provided by the government, mass media, and the entertainment industry to keep any and all serious issues buried. Massive amounts of money are spent by the public relations industry and advertisers to disseminate false and misleading information geared toward activating fear or other powerful emotions. This thwarts critical thought and serves to manufacture consent (Chomsky, 2002), resulting in people being generally ill-informed, uncurious, and more easily duped by the cleverly fashioned truisms of "common sense." It is thus little wonder that when the contradictions within neoliberalism emerge, they often go neglected or cause little disturbance to individuals in their day-to-day lives. It is only by actively and consistently engaging in the process of demythologizing the reality presented to us by neoliberal hegemony and deconstructing its master narratives and central metaphors that the illusions woven by mystification can be undone.

The most basic and primal form in which mystification is practiced is denial. This means rendering invisible any evidence potentially contrary to the version of reality portrayed by hegemony and keeping competing views hidden. Neoliberal hegemony capitalizes on the human need for control and fear of the unknown in order to wield its power to establish reality and reckon what is true and what it not. These proclivities make it easier for various ideological apparatuses to filter out unpleasant facts that would otherwise cause individuals to question the core assumptions of the self-identity that has been crafted within them. Rather than recognize their dissatisfaction and disappointment, they are coaxed to hold fast to the comforting panaceas that have been supplied to keep their minds at ease. Prominent among those unpleasant facts that must be blocked from awareness are their own unhappiness and how many of their fellow human beings are suffering at the hands of neoliberalism. As thinkers like Chomsky (1999, 2002) have made amply clear, the corporate news media, the public relations industry, and the government constitute a formidable force behind the dissemination of "necessary illusions" used to form proper opinions, portray an approved version of reality, and manufacture consent for the agenda and goals of the elite.

The transformation of citizens into passive, uncritical consumers makes the provision of news or other forms of information dictated more by market-driven considerations than the desire to create a knowledgeable public. Before being presented for consumption, versions of events have been sanitized and very carefully crafted to exclude any substantive consideration of the many genuinely pressing issues that impact the lives of millions of individuals. What was once considered journalism has for the most part been substituted by either a form of entertainment aimed at selling products or carefully disguised propaganda aimed at selling government- or corporate-approved messages. No matter where they turn, individuals are bombarded by evocative images and overly dramatized narratives designed to stifle awareness, peddle commodities, and bolster support for the status quo. The mass media has increasingly become complicit with government and corporate interests, in large part because the distinction between them has become essentially blurred if not non-existent. The umbrage taken by journalists at increasingly being accused of reporting fake news is in many cases laughable when considering how much of their attention is given to matters of no great import and how scrupulously they avoid matters of substance and concern. The term "reality television" has become a pathetic oxymoron given the often bizarre and often improbable content of such programs. And yet, sadly, for many this has become their understanding of reality.

A powerful form of mystification of suffering practiced by mass media is essentially rendering it invisible and so non-existent. The ersatz world depicted in mass media intentionally omits serious examination of the plight of groups that have been marginalized, isolated, and ostracized not only from mainstream society but from the attention and awareness of those who do not share their abysmal circumstances. The oppressed have been excluded and, as social exclusion theory (Byrne, 2002) reveals, it is a multidimensional process in which the poor and dispossessed are shut out from social, economic, political, and cultural systems that provide individuals with integration within society. Often the separation is spatial, in which the excluded have been banished to places that daily besiege them with a host of detrimental and unhealthy conditions.

This exclusion thus does not merely inflict upon them a wide range of negative consequences but also ensures that their trials and tribulations go unacknowledged. Consequently, the ideology responsible for their exclusion remains hidden. It is hard to imagine today, for example, anything like the powerful photographs taken during the Great Depression by Dorothea Lange, which not only humanized those whose lives were touched by them but which captured the very real suffering they were undergoing. Likewise, the televising on the day after Thanksgiving in 1960 of a documentary like *Harvest of Shame* by eminent journalist Edward R. Murrow, which poignantly described the plight of migrant workers, would be utterly rejected by today's mass media. The powerful know that the most direct way in which to mystify suffering is essentially to make it disappear.

However, despite their best efforts, the powerful cannot always succeed in their campaign to keep tragic events and the suffering they cause out of sight. When such circumstances arise, the process of mystification is still very much in evidence. Neoliberal ideology is then employed to frame the event in order to once more minimize or disguise the suffering caused and obscure the causes for it. Lakoff (2002, 2004) describes frames as mental structures that shape the way in which we see the world. These frames constitute what is regarded as common sense. They are part of what he calls the cognitive unconscious, and people generally become aware of them indirectly through the language they use to describe their experiences. The use of frames to deal with a major tragic event is examined by Eric Klinenberg (2002) in his social autopsy of the heat wave in Chicago that led to an death figure of 739 above the norm.

This disaster unveiled evidence for what Klinenberg calls the social and political production of deprivation and suffering. These contributing factors included the higher death rates of isolated elderly individuals and African Americans living in degraded and dangerous neighborhoods, changes in city and social services due to privatization, and the ineffective mobilization of the city's response to the emergency. As the failures of the city's administration became more evident, it engaged in forms of distancing and denial that provide useful examples of how mystification can be used to define, frame, and ultimately disguise suffering, in this case caused by a disaster.

Klinenberg borrows from the work of sociologist Stanley Cohen (2001) and his examination of ways in which a society can deal with atrocities and suffering. Cohen describes different types of denial frequently used, each of which shed valuable light on the forms that mystification can take. The first is literal denial in which unwanted facts or information are outright denied. Hegemonically biased versions of history are an example of this, in which events pertinent to entire groups that have been the targets of atrocities have been deliberately omitted. The next is interpretive denial in which a fact is not denied but given a different meaning consistent with the dominant ideological frame. For example, individuals who are protesting oppression are labeled members of a group seeking to subvert the government. A third form is implicatory denial or the denial of responsibility by those in power for adverse consequences of an event. An example of this was defining the Chicago heat wave disaster as a "unique meteorological event" over which the city had no control, thus absolving it of any responsibility for the deaths that occurred.

There is also denial of voice or the silencing of anyone who might report damaging or unwanted information. This is evidenced in the power of government to control what information is provided or to censor information it considers unfavorable or dangerous. We rarely hear directly from the victims of oppression their own stories and narratives that graphically and genuinely convey their suffering. Denial of public record is the exercise of the power of the government to define the official version of an event. An example of this is the substantial discrepancy between the "official" death count in Puerto Rico of 64 deaths related to Hurricane Maria and the findings of researchers in the *New England Journal of Medicine* of between 4,645 and 5,740 deaths there (making the death toll three times worse than Hurricane Katrina in New Orleans). Finally, there is a form of denial practiced through euphemism and the renaming of events in accord with the dominant narrative, which illustrates the powerful use of language to frame suffering in such a way as to mystify it (e.g., innocent individuals killed in military action called collateral damage or describing older adults dying in a heat wave as obstinate recluses who refused help even when it was offered to them).

One final example of framing of disasters that illustrates mystification is constructing them as "spectacles." Gotham (2007) provides an examination of this in the case of Hurricane Katrina. The establishment of a consumer culture preoccupied with selling products and the expanded role of the entertainment industry in defining reality both play prominent roles in portraying tragic or disturbing events as spectacles. These events that frequently are the cause of considerable suffering are cast using superficial, brief, and overly dramatized depictions that are detached from social life and so possess a quality of unreality. They are often staged in a calculated manner in order to increase corporate profits through boosting viewership. Reporting is also used to convey government- and corporate-sanctioned messages that typically minimize their responsibility for either contributing to the disaster or providing aid or restitution to its victims. Thus, sociopolitical imperatives dictate the shape and manner in which the event is portrayed and hence structure how it is to be interpreted and understood.

Gotham (2007) writes, "Spectacles consist of hegemonic ideologies and spectacular images—for example, promotional rhetoric, corporate advertising and dramatic displays—that seek to distract and seduce people using the mechanisms of leisure, consumption and entertainment" (p. 95). In his analysis of Hurricane Katrina, Gotham discusses the work of French theorist Guy Debord (1994), who saw in the expansion of mass media and the culture industry their increasing use in defining and shaping life while obscuring the alienating effects of capitalism. Media's presentation of events, even as important and consequential as these, as fragmented, ephemeral, and discontinuous makes individuals mere spectators of their lives and distracts them from problems that merit their attention and concern. Beneath the hype and sleek veneer, the harsh reality of human suffering remains.

The Happiness Imperative

Such neglect of suffering is reinforced by one of the most prominent and powerful of the myths and narratives advanced by neoliberalism. This is the elevation of happiness as the primary goal of life and as the preeminent measure of well-being. If you are suffering, so the message goes, there must be something wrong with you—something that can be corrected by buying something. Neoliberalism's intent is to create a society in which individuals can freely pursue their self-interest free from all obstacles and impediments. This has become the foundation for a highly materialistic culture aimed toward the acquisition of happiness, which is the measure of one's success and well-being. This is supported by the image of the person advanced by neoliberalism. As Greene (2008) observes, this image consists of the utilitarian view of individualism that casts human beings as essentially hedonistic (and hence competitive, greedy, and self-interested) and the expressive view that places a high value on uniqueness and authenticity acquired through realization of one's potential with as little interference from others as possible. It is thus little surprise that, along with life and liberty, the pursuit of happiness has occupied a central place in the United States as a "God-given right."

But the imperative of happiness has a dark side, particularly as it allows no room for the inevitability of suffering. As noted in an earlier chapter, suffering is sometimes framed as antithetic to the pursuit of happiness. The state of suffering is seen as an indication of personal failure, imperfection, or non-compliance with social norms. Such is the case when neoliberalism asserts that the required circumstances have been provided to all individuals to attain happiness if they apply themselves to the task and strive to achieve the life that has been prescribed by those in authority. Never mind that making happiness something acquired by effort is inherently self-defeating. As Watts (1951) sagely observed, it is impossible to experience pleasure without its contrasting state of pain. And as Frankl (1967) asserts, pleasure can never be achieved as a goal because it is the byproduct of the pursuit of a goal that has a more substantial meaning and value.

Nonetheless it is not difficult to sell individuals on the need for happiness. Neoliberalism simply capitalizes on the human inclination to avoid or deny suffering. When in the throes of distress, those who are afflicted typically desire help and will readily seize upon any solution that offers the promise of relief. Yet the promised cure ultimately fails to provide the happiness one seeks. Whatever relief it offers is temporary, leaving a longing that can be exploited again and again (Cushman, 1990; Gruba-McCallister, 2007). The actual agenda behind these false solutions is to have people move away as quickly as possible from the experience of suffering and thus prevent them from discerning the actual reasons behind it. Valuable insights that could lead to resistance and the pursuit of true liberation are thus lost.

By portraying suffering as contrary to the natural state of affairs, or a sign of evil or wrong-doing (Moulyn, 1982), neoliberal ideology seeks to deprive both victims and perpetrators exposure to the evils and deficiencies that can be found in the status quo. Instead, it frames life's necessary disappointments and inconveniences in such a way as to encourage those experiencing them to resign themselves to the current state of affairs. An example of how the elevation of happiness as life's ultimate goal can be employed as a means of keeping the populace content in order to maintain the social order is astutely portrayed in the dystopic novel by Aldous Huxley (1932), *Brave New World*. In the world that he depicts, no effort is spared to create the illusion of perfection, and individuals are afforded a whole array of convenient panaceas to deal with whatever might trouble them. Anticipating the role of psychopharmaceuticals in enforcing social control and complacency, he describes the widespread use of soma to anesthetize characters from the slightest hint of unpleasantness.

In a poignant scene, the characters of Henry and Lenina are flying above the Crematorium where their fellow men and women meet their end when they outlive their usefulness. As they watch a column of hot air that once was a human life ascend from a chimney, Henry observes: "It was some human being finally and definitely disappearing. Going up in a squirt of hot gas. It would be curious to know who it was...Anyhow...there's one thing we can be certain of; whoever he may have been, he was happy when he was alive. Everybody's happy now." To which Lenina echoes, "Yes, everybody's happy now." Here we have a depiction of a scene that would ordinarily arouse some sadness about the passing of a life, but that feeling would pose a threat to the image of an ideal world central to a utopian society. And so, a message that has been repeatedly drummed into them (as it has been to people in our own times) becomes the automatic response they must make whenever anything might remind them of something as disturbing as human mortality. But, as Huxley makes clear, a death-denying world must inevitably become a life-denying one as well.

In the spirit of modernity from which it descended, neoliberalism publicly proclaims its goal of abolishing suffering by devoting considerable resources to finding cures to all manner of diseases, by promising success and wealth to any and all who will devote themselves to making use of all the opportunities afforded to them, and by manufacturing commodities guaranteeing those who acquire them the attainment of their fondest dreams. It all sounds so very comforting and reassuring, but there are dangerous strings attached. Happiness is not merely a promise made by the powerful that they will make everything right. It is also an obligation placed on every individual. They must comply with the requirements put forth by the neoliberal agenda if they intend to be counted among the rich and successful. And any failure on their part to do so becomes the sole reason for their unhappiness.

Evidence for the ultimate failure of the pursuit for happiness can be found in the research discussed previously on the materialistic value orientation or MVO (Kasser & Kanner, 2004). Individuals with a high MVO have been found to report a higher number of experiences, behaviors, and feelings connected with a diminished quality of life. They tend to be more insecure and have lower self-esteem. Similarly, Prilleltensky (2012) describes the failures of a materialistic society that extols happiness as the most important goal worth pursuing:

> Contemporary culture, media and the devotion to commercialism can most definitely erode flourishing (Sloan, 1996). The push to fulfill our lives through consumerism, competition, and immediate gratification is pernicious. Research amply demonstrates that the immediate gratification of buying a new car vanishes rather quickly. If you are going to spend money, research says, do so on experiences and not on material goods (Rath & Harter, 2010). Television shows that exalt celebrity life styles while increasing our sense of relative deprivation are injurious to our mental health (Fiske, 2011). The best prevention against these distorted constructions of love and life is to limit exposure. (p. 14)

The cultural imperative to be happy is critiqued by Ahmed (2010), who sees happiness as a promise dangled before individuals in order to manipulate their consciousness, align it with the dominant ideology, and direct them to make certain choices in life while avoiding others. The correct choices are those that are in accord with the values and beliefs approved by the powerful and privileged. True happiness is attainable only by conforming with what has been mandated by neoliberalism as morally valuable. As a result, individuals' happiness becomes conditional on making others happy—those who are considered authorities and whose prescriptions and directives must be obeyed. Ahmed also describes *happiness scripts* that play an integral role in governance of the subordinated and marginalized. These scripts are used to justify oppression and refute the role it plays in causing unhappiness. Those who fail to make correct choices and to live their lives in accord with the mandates of the status quo have placed themselves in their subjugated and unfavorable position. Their suffering is an inevitable and justified consequence of their failure. This framing of their suffering simultaneously undermines any resistance they might mount against their oppressors.

Chapman (2013) picks up on the work of Ahmed (2010) and expands its application to perpetrators of oppression. Those involved in oppression can be understood as occupying a continuum described by Kierkegaard (1941) in his treatment of despair, in which he observes that as consciousness increases so, too, does despair. Kierkegaard believed that most individuals are unconscious of being in despair and so would be both surprised and upset should anyone point out to them the contrary. Likewise. most people are not aware of their complicity in oppression. As Chapman observes, these individuals would find awareness of their complicity to be a deeply troubling experience. He writes:

> Acknowledging complicity in oppression provokes uncertainty, painful feelings, and a destabilization of identity. However difficult such experiences are, they are essential to politicized ethicality and accountability. I advocate that people journey with pain, uncertainty, and identity destabilization when implicating themselves in oppression, to cultivate a "troubled consciousness"....Implicating oneself in oppression requires measuring oneself by one's impact on oppressed peoples. This causes uncertainty and pain, and destabilizes one's sense of oneself as coherently moral. (p. 182)

Resistance to the suffering they feel upon recognizing the suffering they have caused others is more than just the product of some intrapsychic defense. Chapman acknowledges another form of the mystification of suffering in his proposal of a discursive force he calls *compulsory sound-mindedness.* He derives this idea in part from the happiness scripts described by Ahmed (2010). This discursive force pathologizes and deprecates any experiences that depart from contentment or the requirement that one be reasonable, as mandated by liberal individualism. A consistent theme within neoliberal ideology is that human beings need to conduct themselves in a rational manner. This means employing an instrumental form of reason and objectively seeking out means to achieve their goals and so maximize their self-interest and thus their happiness. Individuals who do not behave in such a manner are generally deemed as deficient or disordered. Any suffering they experience they have brought upon themselves.

Compulsory sound-mindedness thus prevents individuals from recognizing the essential link between the personal and political by rendering experiences evoked by one's involvement in oppression as worthless, unhealthy, and necessitating prompt resolution. The suffering that perpetrators legitimately feel upon discovery of the harm they have caused others is devalued, leading individuals to find ways to deny and retreat from it. The forms of unreason framed as falling outside of rational liberal individualism are identified by Chapman (2013). They include:

> ...such experiences, which are normatively psychologized and framed as useless, immobilizing, and best avoided. This obscures their part in ethical and political journeys. For my purposes, unreason includes: unhappy emotional experiences including anxiety and guilt; not-knowing or uncertainty; an unmoored sense of self, particularly when questioning one's morality; and a sense of self that incorporates others' presence. (p. 185)

While such experiences can clearly be frightening and unpleasant, as Chapman observes, they are in truth normal human responses to the discovery not only that one's fellow human beings are suffering unjustly but that one's actions have in some way contributed to this suffering. It is for this reason that Chapman emphasizes that the mystification not only of the suffering of the victims but also of the perpetrators steers individuals away from experiences that are politically and ethically important. As a result, it also steers them away from their accountability and the opportunity to journey with their uncertainty and painful emotions to effect a personal transformation with the potential to move them toward a deeper sense of justice and compassion.

For those who lie on the opposite end of the continuum of consciousness and openly and deliberately collude with and engage in oppression, similar patterns of mystification can be observed, but they are employed in the service of an extreme form of narcissism. Kierkegaard (1941) describes the most extreme forms of despair as "demonic," which fits with the previously discussed characterization of such individuals as demonstrating a malignant form of narcissism (Fromm, 1964; Peck, 1983). Unlike the case of individuals whose complicity is more unwitting, what is at stake for these narcissistic individuals is ensuring that the suffering of the oppressed and their role in it remains hidden or disguised in order to maintain their image of being unquestionably good, morally upright, and devoted to living the right kind of life. The work of M. Scott Peck (1983) on evil, described earlier, provides a useful framework for understanding such individuals. For them nothing less than perfection is acceptable in order to maintain their inflated self-image. The admission of guilt or involvement in moral wrongs inflicted often on the most vulnerable would be highly threatening to their self-image and cast doubt on their worldview, in which they feel utterly confirmed. Any form of troubled consciousness would be utterly intolerable and so is rejected or salved with the clever rationalizations so conveniently provided by the ideology they unswerving subscribe to. Their material success and attainment of power and prestige not only provide irrefutable validation of their moral rectitude and their justifiable claim to the happiness they have achieved, but also justification for the contempt they hold for those who occupy the lower rungs of society. Just as Peck asserts, their very refusal to admit to imperfection and journey with their suffering and the suffering of others only facilitates their proclivity to do harm to others they look down upon and then proceed to blame for their pain and misfortune.

Paralyzing Paradoxes and Damning Double-Binds

As this examination of the mystification of suffering continues, some of the other core assumptions of neoliberal ideology will be examined in order to elucidate the ways in which they discount or distort the toxic and pernicious effects they have on both the oppressed and the privileged. These cornerstones of neoliberalism are touted as integral elements of common sense and universal wisdom beyond doubt or question. In actuality, they function as potent legitimizing myths whose purpose is to assert the preeminence of the ruling ideology, secure loyalty to its dictates, and stifle dissent. Sidanius and Pratto (1999) describe legitimizing myths as the ideologies, stereotypes, values, and beliefs that bond people by virtue of providing intellectual and moral justification for traditions and the practices that establish the social hierarchy and the distribution of social value within it. These assumptions can also be conceptualized as the frames proposed by Lakoff (2002, 2004). Associated with these frames are language and metaphors functioning on an unconscious level that are used by individuals to guide their behaviors, formulate their goals, and act in accordance with values for how to conduct their lives. To achieve social change, Lakoff argues that we must challenge the persistent myths embedded in these frames and become aware of how we are manipulated by the language derived from them.

Because these myths and frames are human fabrications and social constructions, not objective facts and revealed truths, their actual origin is kept hidden to escape examination. This is achieved by means of mystification's inhibition of critical thought and the constriction of individuals' awareness and attention to only those issues and concerns approved by neoliberal ideology. The symbolic-meaning system espoused by neoliberalism is the principal means by which it maintains and reproduces power and domination. The efficacy of neoliberalism's language and metaphors in shaping consciousness is enhanced by establishing conditions in which they are understood literally. Both Fromm (1960) and Watts (1951, 1968) raised alarm about the power of language to enmesh individuals into fantasies that they then project on the world. This process fosters a perilous sense of alienation in which words become concretized labels that take the place of lived experience. Similarly, Joseph (2017) writes:

> Overall, political language by its very nature imposes an associative mental framework that, if reinforced properly, can narrow one's thoughts about social issues. Through this process, people lose focus on other possible factors or viewpoints. Political language also exploits our innate tendency to be superficial, shortsighted, and fragmented....Language, therefore, beyond being our main tool to learn and communicate, can also function as a tool for social control by strategically imposing or restricting ideas, values, and biases through associative influence. (p. 34)

Failing to see beyond the dazzling and distracting images manufactured by neoliberalism leads us to commit the Fallacy of Misplaced Concreteness. The map is repeatedly confused with the territory. As will be illustrated, at best it can be misguided to take words and metaphors literally and at worst it can be fatal.

In addition to using the reification of constructs and the hypostatization of the status quo to confuse and deceive, one other form of mystification makes individuals more vulnerable to falling under the spell of the illusions promulgated by neoliberalism. The meaning and relevance of paradox in relation to self-deception and the experience of alienation was discussed earlier. There is a long tradition of the benevolent and potentially health-promoting use of paradox to temporarily immobilize the intellect and discursive thought in order to expose the fictions that ensnare us and foster a direct and immediate encounter with our experience in the moment. An excellent example is the *koan*, or a statement that takes a dialectical and nonsensical form used by Zen teachers to help students achieve insight or *satori*. However, there is also a destructive form of this method in which incongruous messages and contradictory demands are simultaneously conveyed to individuals in order to ensnare them in a seemingly insoluble dilemma and drive them into a mental blind alley where they feel perplexed, immobilized, and helpless.

This type of paradox has been described as a pathogenic or schizophenogenic double-bind (Bateson et al., 1956) because of its proposed relationship to the development of certain serious forms of mental disorder. In this context, it is used to describe a persistent pattern of communication in a relationship that often involves a power differential between those who pose the paradoxical messages and the recipient. The contradictory demands being issued are enforced by some form of overt or implied punishment, and escape from the situation is not permitted. Not only does this dangerous double-bind stymie conventional logic and render a person's intellect incapable of comprehending the situation, it also creates a disabling and painful state of frustration, fear, and befuddlement. According to Laing (1969), a significant impact of the impossible and incongruous demands posed in this double bind is the mystification of the experience of the recipient, who soon loses touch with reality and retreats from such painful relationships to seek a measure of safety.

A more benign form of this type of double-bind can be used to induce a hypnotic trance (Erickson, Rossi, & Rossi, 1976) and thus utilize the potential for dissociation to facilitate healing and positive change. Similarly, Frankl (1967) has employed the therapeutic technique of paradoxical directives to help patients achieve a healthy sense of detachment from their symptoms. However, in the case of the harmful form of double-bind, the experience of derealization and depersonalization created in individuals is intended to undermine their confidence in their experience and stir fears that they are losing their grip on themselves and reality. This not only impairs their ability to discriminate between the contrary messages being conveyed and to resist the conflicting demands being made of them, but again establishes a state of alienation in which the literal processing of language and metaphor can be more effectively employed to manipulate their behavior, feelings, and actions.

Each of these assumptions made by neoliberalism will be examined here—the preeminence of the market; the emphasis on the person as an autonomous, hedonistic, and self-regulating individual; freedom as liberty or the ability to be unrestricted in rationally pursuing one's self-interest; and the responsibility individuals bear for pursuing opportunities offered to them and for the consequences if they fail to so. All have embedded within them troubling contradictions and incongruous demands that actually function in the service of mystification. These contradictions can be described by utilizing polar dimensions that have been described previously: the individual versus the collective, good/right versus evil/wrong, and control versus no control. All of these constitute issues pivotal to human life. Moreover, these contradictions are framed in ways to obscure the difference between inescapable and self-chosen suffering. As has been discussed, this confusion becomes the basis for even greater suffering.

Unfortunately, due to the proclivity, noted by Fromm (1960), of individuals being socialized to rely upon an Aristotelean either/or form of logic, they are ill-equipped to deal with these paradoxes. This form of logic fails utterly in comprehending the experience of paradox. The ambiguity that inevitably accompanies encounters with the existential dichotomies that cannot be resolved in a straightforward manner is experienced as threatening and thus something to be avoided. The result is that the underlying fallacies that arise when trying to respond to these issues in an extreme and one-sided fashion go unidentified, and those ensnared in the binds created by neoliberalism's portrayal of reality experience themselves as damned no matter what they do. And it is in precisely this way that that are confused, confounded, disempowered, and left vulnerable to the illusions that enslave them.

The Myth of the Market

No construct occupies a more central place in neoliberal ideology than the market. It is a metaphor central to the neoliberal worldview that colors all aspects of life. The market is cast in pseudo-scientific, objective terms as a natural, self-regulating entity that operates independently of human beings. It is asserted to be the driving force behind everything that occurs. It is governed by fixed and immutable laws. Hence the caution that it must remain "free" of all interference by government in order to unfold in accordance with its own laws and, in so doing, bring about maximum benefits. Likewise, given the implacable nature of the way in which the market operates and the inflexibility of its rules, human attempts to intervene in its process are not only futile but indicate irrationality and deviance in need of correction. Thus, it is expected that individuals conform to and comply with market demands and accept the consequences if they fail to do so.

The rules and regularities by which it operates are called market rationality, which defines reality and governs all aspects of life, not merely the economic sphere. As Thorsen (2010) observes, this market rationality also implies a market morality. The merit and soundness of all human actions are determined by the degree to which they are in accord with what the market deems to be rational, desirable, or acceptable. To align one's actions with the market is the highest good.

As Marx (1978) foresaw in his concept of commodity fetishism, the primacy of the market has resulted in the commodification of all facets of life. Human beings, as well as the relations between them, are framed in terms of financial transactions and thus often measured in terms of personal gain and loss. Life is devoted to producing and consuming. The goal of life is using one's powers and creativity to better oneself by accumulating wealth and acquiring goods advertised as indispensable to one's well-being. Energies must be diligently focused on working upon oneself as one would seek to improve a product. In this manner, individuals are assured that they can achieve their goals and fully realize their potential. As Soelle (2001) observes, under neoliberalism the ego is cast as motivated solely by enlightened self-interest. What this really means is that it is consuming ego, shaped by corporate and government propaganda to always be greedy for new things and to constantly search for the seemingly endless options and choices offered by the "temples of consumption." Our preoccupation is with having rather than with being, but the more we have the less we are. We see others as means to satisfy our craving for more or as assets to be tapped into or manipulated in our drive toward success.

Rose (1998) describes a similar transformation in neoliberalism's creation of an enterprise culture, which has been accompanied by forging an image of the human being to support it. Human beings as subjective and autonomous individuals are instructed to strive for fulfillment, excellence, and achievement. They are encouraged to make a "project" of themselves and "work" on every aspect of their lives in order to maximize their powers, fulfill their desires, and achieve happiness. Consumerism plays a central role in this process. Rose writes, "These objectives are to be achieved by instrumentalizing autonomy, and promising to promote it. Consumers are constituted as actors seeking to maximize their 'quality of life' by assembling a 'life style' through acts of choice in a world of goods. Each commodity is imbued with a 'personal meaning,' a glow cast back upon those who purchase it, illuminating the kind of person they are, or want to be" (p. 162). Throughout these analyses, the poisonous influence of the market in colonizing the human psyche with nagging desires that enslave them and enrich others is clearly displayed. So, too, is the devastating impact of commodification on the objectification of human beings, the very basis of oppression and the suffering it causes. The logic of the market makes it easier to inflict suffering and to deny it, given that you are dealing with things and not people. Such is the logic that justifies obscene levels of inequality, rampant greed, and callous disregard for the health of people and the well-being of our planet.

The power of the market expressed as metaphor can also be seen in the way in which it colors virtually every aspect of our lives. As Lakoff (2002, 2004) observes, so much of the language we use in everyday life is derived from market rationality and commodification. For example, he provides an extensive treatment about how morality under neoliberalism is basically associated with metaphors connected to financial transactions. A few examples help to illustrate this: talk of profiting from experience, the costs of a bad decision, owing someone who has done something good for them, retribution as paying someone back, or canceling a debt by doing a good deed. Lakoff believes that an understanding of the system of moral concepts that characterizes a society is important because political perspectives of considerable consequence are derived from them. This is because these moral metaphors provide answers to two critical questions that guide how society is structured and governed: What is a good person and what is a good society. For neoliberalism, the market is an essential part of the answer to those questions and so plays a central role in shaping persons and organizing society.

In a similar vein, Manders (2006) investigates how evidence for hegemony and mystification under neoliberalism can be found in common parlance and popular adages that make up common sense. Citing the work of Lakoff, he sees how core assumptions like the market become so fixed within our culture that they operate on an unconscious level while saturating individuals' values and worldview. Again, Manders provides a number of examples of how common sense reflects the prominence of the market: "Time is money, making something of oneself, laboring under false pretenses, selling oneself short, everything has a price, you get what you pay for." Clearly, when everyday discourse abounds in such references, the work of the mystification of suffering utilizing market rationality is made much easier.

This same language and associated metaphors are used to frame suffering and how it should be dealt with. In the calculus of the market, suffering becomes minimized, trivialized, privatized, and sanitized. It can be reduced to a problem whose impact can be calculated in dollars and cents, a form of some inefficiency or poor business practice, a threat to the status quo that must be expunged, a matter of personal distress or concern that can only be satisfactorily treated by the purchase of some product. As Esposito and Perez (2014) argue, the dominant frame employed by neoliberalism to characterize suffering is based upon the commodification of mental health (as well as physical health). Using this framework, attention is paradoxically deflected away from the material and social conditions created by the market that cause impairment and distress by ascribing the causes instead to individuals. It is used to convince those same individuals that the very same market is the only source from which they can acquire solutions to and relief from those problems. Deviance, moral censure, or some form of pathology is attributed to individuals who fail to accept the demands of the market or to rationally participate in the market to pursue their self-interest. Such individuals are criticized and punished for not demonstrating the characteristics associated with being well adjusted, rational, self-reliant, responsible, and productive. By failing to compete with others for what they desire, they have abdicated any right to complain or label the negative consequences they suffer as forms of injustice or inequality. Because it is required that everyone engages in the market by freely making choices from the options it offers, individuals alone bear responsibility for the consequences of those choices—good and bad.

This formulation mystifies suffering in several ways. The first, as Brown (2006) describes, is depoliticizing problems by interpreting them as individual and private matters. This either denies or disguises the role played by social, political, and economic factors in causing suffering (including those manufactured by the market itself). Suffering is indicative of some personal failure in adapting to the one force that constitutes reality—the market. However, this assertion poses a conundrum for the sufferer and utilizes it to sow seeds of confusion and doubt that impair his or her uncovering of the deception that is being perpetrated. On the one hand, it is an impersonal force beyond the control of individuals that is behind everything that happens. However, at the same time when that same force favors some and punishes others, it is assumed that these outcomes were achieved through their respective personal efforts and were thus subject to their control.

The prevalent strategy of blaming the victim is once more at work. There is no question that the force we call gravity is utterly impartial in its application to wealthy or poor, powerful or powerless. Yet this stands in stark contrast to the unquestionable partiality shown by the "natural" force called the market. The second form of mystification is when neoliberalism proceeds to advance market solutions as the sole means of removing the problems created by the market. This poses another set of paradoxes. One presents the market as both benevolent and harmful at the same time. The other tells those who suffer that help can only come from outside of them, but it's their responsibility to take control and enact their role as consumers in order to acquire it.

These dynamics are all at work in medicalization and the commodification of health and illness. The literature on medicalization describes how increasingly human problems that are justifiable reactions to adversity and unhealthy physical and social environments have been defined as medical problems and labeled as illnesses (Aho, 2008; Boggs, 2015; Conrad & Barker, 2010; Jacobs & Cohen, 2010). Depression, anxiety, and other psychological reactions associated with attempts at coping are natural responses to the loss, adversity, and trauma that are produced by oppressive social arrangements and practices. However, in the medicalization advanced by the neoliberal worldview, these experiences are labeled as irrational, unnatural, pathological, and unwanted. In invalidating these experiences, those in power endeavor to obliterate awareness of the injustice responsible for them. In the same breath, this suffering is attributed to impersonal material causes independent of context, combined with some innate biological vulnerability or imperfection within persons, *and* to their poor choices and irresponsibility.

At the same time, individuals both have and do not have control over why they are suffering. Little wonder that their suffering is only amplified by the impossible bind into which they are placed. They must work harder at becoming a productive member of society and pursue the happy and fulfilling life that the free market offers to all who are willing to submit to its demands. Simultaneously, they must place themselves in the hands of powerful others by purchasing solutions (drugs, medical treatment, psychotherapy, expert advice, and motivational speakers) to the anxiety, depression, and host of other ills having a material basis that stand in the way of attaining wealth and success. These solutions, of course, boost the profits of the industries that benefit from supposedly alleviating the very suffering they often are responsible for creating. In their treatment of the commodification of mental health Esposito and Perez (2014) point to the example of the growing use of prescription drugs, while Boggs (2015) provides an extensive exposé of how the health care industry has derived immense profits from obesity, addictions, and the stigmatization of normal problems such as shyness. Even as increasing amounts of money are spent on these medical "solutions," the overall health of individuals continues to decline.

This medicalization of increasing areas of life is now one of the primary means by which neoliberalism mystifies the suffering that arises from the oppression it has created. The same veneer of scientific objectivity and value neutrality evidenced in the myth of the market is part of the justification used to reduce human ills to biological malfunctions requiring market-based interventions. This is summarized by Speed, Moncrief, and Rapley (2014) in their work on de-medicalizing misery:

> ...the neurochemical society we currently inhabit acts to banish suffering by representing it as a condition arising from bodily dysfunction that needs fixing, rather than a social problem that needs redressing. The voice of the sufferer is silenced by virtue of being translated into the language of mental pathology, and the context of the sufferer, including the cause of the suffering, is written out of the story. It is in this sense that the medicalizing of misery has been said to act as a form of social control that bolsters and perpetuates the current social system (Conrad, 1992). By silencing expressions of disaffection and diverting

attention from the social conditions that contribute to the genesis of misery and madness, the mental health industry helps to ensure that the inadequacies of the current social structures and institutions remain unchallenged. (p. xiv)

A most effective way of obscuring the very real and concrete suffering of individuals at the hands of oppression is to transform it into an abstraction by means of a diagnostic label or category. That label then serves to intervene between persons seeking compassion and restitution for the injuries they have suffered and those who believe themselves to be working on their behalf. The individual is conveniently circumscribed by some condition or syndrome and their affliction is abstracted from the adverse conditions that have led to their troubles. As Miller (2005) observes, "By avoiding the pain and suffering of the patient and relegating them to an epiphenomenon, the biomedical model in psychiatry and psychology offers a theoretical firewall against the intrusion of social, economic, political, and moral factors into the treatment room... Unfortunately, rather than helping the client in this situation, the institution or practitioner 'redoubles' the patient's suffering by denying its existence" (p. 311). The ever-growing numbers of diagnoses in the Diagnostic and Statistical Manual are neither syndromes nor illnesses, but rather an unsettling and inexcusable catalogue of the many forms of suffering attributable to inequality and injustice. Despite the countless resources and tireless efforts to find a biological cause for schizophrenia, research has found the one strong contributing factor to be an early history of trauma and abuse (Williams, 2012). The same can be said of so many other so-called illnesses treated with drugs that boost the profits of the pharmaceutical industry.

This portrayal of the market conflates the social and the natural. It is a manifestation of the positivistic philosophy that emphasizes objectivity, reductionism, materialism, and the rise of instrumental reason extensively critiqued by Critical Theory (Held, 1980). Assigning the market the status of an actual objective entity operating by fixed physical laws commits the Fallacy of Misplaced Concreteness. *There is not a natural force called the market.* The market actually is a construct fabricated by thinkers who advance capitalist theory. Using the pretense of natural science to reify the market is nothing more than a ploy to disguise the ways in which this myth is used to oppress the subaltern class to the advantage of the powerful elite.

Further, as many have revealed, there is no free market (Chang, 2010; Joseph, 2017). There are always some rules and restrictions that set limits on its operations and the touted freedom of choice that individuals are told they possess. Examples include things like child labor laws or the prohibition of trade of certain things, such as illegal drugs. Further, history is filled with cases in which the market is manipulated to the advantage of the wealthy and detriment of everyone else. However, when those manipulations lead to financial crises that cause all manner of harms to those being exploited and reap huge benefits for the powerful, the impersonal workings of market are conveniently blamed. "Nothing could be done; it's all part of the market correcting itself." In this still another neoliberal illusion, we are again faced with a vexing contradiction. When suffering that afflicts large numbers of oppressed and marginalized groups arises from the inexorable and immutable lawful workings of the market, no human actor can be held accountable. But when members of those same groups, heedless of their needs, act as individuals in ways contrary to the requirements of a market and suffer adverse consequences, they are to blame.

It is not merely the reification of the market that is worthy of condemnation but, ultimately, its deification. In an act of shameless idolatry, neoliberalism has elevated the market to the status of an absolute. Like some deity, it is made to appear as though it impartially metes out rewards and punishments to individuals in accord with whether they obey its commandments. The success of the favored is deserved, just as is the punishment of those less fortunate. The myth of the market, as we have seen, comes with its own version of morality used to disguise its actual immorality. But a serious examination of the situation reveals that the market constitutes what Tillich (1957) calls a preliminary concern, a false and ultimately disappointing absolute. It demands the total surrender of individuals to its claims while promising total fulfillment. But those who make the commitment soon learn that they have been seduced by a false idol. The never-ending promises of commodities, options, choices, and opportunities to provide fulfillment fail one by one, leaving the seeker as empty as he or she was at the start (Gruba-McCallister, 2007).

The Individual—Asocial, Alienated, Abandoned, and Accused

A second myth closely entwined with the myth of the market is the characterization of the person as the consuming ego, the enterprising self—sovereign, autonomous, and unfettered by tradition and history. This extreme emphasis on individualism, as noted in the previous chapter, is an enduring part of the legacy of liberalism. Pivotal thinkers like Adam Smith and John Locke put forward the fundamental assumption that human beings are inherently self-interested, competitive, greedy, and acquisitive. They assert that in their natural state human beings are individuals that come prior to society. They possess natural rights and the freedom to enter into agreements with others in order to pursue personal profit by buying and selling as they please. The individual is thus the only legitimate focus of concern and analysis and society is nothing more than an aggregate of individuals, each seeking their own goals and pursuing their own endeavors. By pursuing their own profit and well-being, it is asserted that they are essentially doing something good for society.

However, serious contradictions between their espoused values and theory and their actual thought and practices, by now familiar in neoliberal ideology, can be found in these liberal thinkers (Kaufman, 2003). John Locke, for instance, was an investor in the transatlantic slave trade, advocated for enclosures that drove poor people from their land, and favored colonialism. It was the expectation of thinkers like Locke that individuals would respect each other's rights to life, liberty, and property. As a result, society needed to be protected from those who were not capable of using their reason and demonstrating such respect. This logic was cynically used to justify the domination and enslavement of members of inferior groups such as indigenous peoples and Africans.

This extreme version of individualism is a social construction that reflects the Western social, political, and economic context from which it arises (Kirkmayer, 2007). It is a juridical concept on which questions of moral agency, responsibility, and blame pivot. But, most important, it is a version of selfhood that has achieved ascendance because it provides the foundation for the dominance and legitimacy of neoliberal ideology (Greene, 2008). Contemporary theorists continue to advance arguments aimed at validating this view of the person. A prominent example is *social dominance theory* (SDT) by Sidanius and Pratto (1999). SDT asserts that human beings are predisposed by nature to have a drive toward domination, which then gives rise to group-based hierarchies of power. This sets up conditions leading to conflict between groups for control and dominance. In order to deal with these conflicts and maintain a certain degree of social stability, consensus on ideologies that assert the superiority of one group over others is necessary. Such ideologies promote and maintain group inequality, which then leads to discrimination, racism and other forms of oppression. By situating the causal factors for oppression in an evolutionary trait in human beings, SDT advances a dangerous form of determinism in which oppression is an inevitable, albeit undesirable, consequence. If we oppress others and treat them as less than, we are just doing what comes naturally and little can be done to change this. However, in his cogent critique of SDT, Joseph (2017) exposes it as just another social mythology. Similar to the reification of the market, the ascribing of inequality and oppression to natural forces over which we ultimately have no control neglects the far more powerful influence of sociocultural, political, and economic factors. And that neglect serves very important social and political functions.

This asociality of the individual has been exposed as not only implausible but also a means of advancing the hegemonic hold of neoliberalism. Critical Psychology has been among the most vocal of these critics, as has been discussed in previous chapters. Nightingale and Cromby (2001) observe that the isolation of individuals from society results in two consequences: creating unhappiness and leading people to believe that their suffering is the result of their own inadequacy. The extreme version of individualism in neoliberalism has been accompanied by a growing emphasis on the private over the public. The literal and figurative barriers erected between individuals by neoliberalism, as noted earlier, have banished those deemed as deviant, inferior, and undesirable from the public sphere and have left them, isolated and abandoned, to suffer. Yet a significant cause of their suffering is being cut off and separated, so they are unable to satisfy the basic needs rooted in their societal nature. By excluding them from sources of social capital, their sense of alienation and the suffering that comes with it are exacerbated. Ample research has established that social support and social cohesion are protective factors in promoting well-being (Marmot & Wilkinson, 2006).

The very insistence by neoliberalism on "being your own person" and "looking out for number one" is, again, riddled with contradictions and conflicting messages. At the same time that individuals are told to look to themselves to chart their course in life and to make choices that serve their self-interest, the standards by which they are told to measure their success and the exemplars held out to them to emulate are presented as existing outside of them. As Sampson (1989) explains in his critique of the contemporary view of the self-reliant, autonomous self, culture is not a mere instrumental way in which individuals fulfill their needs but is indispensable to understanding what it means to be a person and what their needs are. What it means for individuals to act rationally, exercise their agency, and advance their interests can only be discovered contextually and by means of engaging in a shared and communal process with others (Sandel, 1982). These things take on different meanings at different times and in different places.

As research on social determinants of health has established (Marmot & Wilkinson, 2006; Wilkinson & Pickett, 2009), knowing where one stands in the social order depends on the process of social comparison. This gives rise to higher levels of stress associated with feelings of shame, anger, and inferiority in societies with high levels of inequality and has been found to have a wide range of adverse health outcomes. Similarly, Prilleltensky (2012) cites research on upward and downward social comparisons in contemporary society exercising a strong degree of impact on reported happiness. Even the acquisition of the products promoted by our consumer society is not principally due to the much-touted motive of self-interest. As Joseph (2017) observes, "The materially obsessed consumer behavior we see today is really less about a given item's purpose and more about what that item means in terms of societal bonding. In effect, mere wants have been artificially turned into emotionally demanded needs by the drive for social inclusion" (p. 25).

In looking at the second consequence noted by Nightingale and Cromby (2001), another set of contradictions and incongruous demands aimed at mystifying suffering are found in neoliberalism's depiction of freedom and responsibility. By misconstruing the meaning of these ideas in order to justify neoliberalism, they become tools wielded to mystify suffering. Freedom is certainly highly extolled by neoliberal ideology, but a close examination reveals that this version of freedom is actually a much-skewed understanding of choice and a narrow and constricted form of freedom. Human agency is restricted to something exercised in reaction to a set of options or choices provided by the market for purposes of advancing one's private pursuits and achieving happiness. In other words, agency understood as true self-determination and the ability to generate one's own alternatives is contradicted by the requirement that individuals must ultimately make their actions conform to the irresistible laws of the market. The degree to which one's actions can clearly be seen as an exercise of one's capacity for reflection and reason or as actual forms of self-expression is much diminished in this version of freedom.

As ultimate power is assigned to the market, in the final analysis persons have only two choices—to surrender to market demands and be rewarded accordingly or to resist market demands and be punished accordingly. When the only real choices available to individuals are dictated by the market, freedom becomes illusory. Persons are once again caught in another version of the double-bind (Erickson, Rossi, & Rossi, 1976), in which only the illusion of choice is posed by presenting alternatives designed intentionally to lead to one expected or required outcome. "Do you want to buy Product A, Product B, or Product C?" The point, in other words, is that one way another you must look to consumption as the sole means to fulfill your desires or to allay your pain.

The view of freedom permitted individuals by neoliberalism is essentially a negative one, or what is called freedom from. Freedom is cast as liberty from the coercion of the state or other individuals regarding how persons choose to use their private property, pursue happiness, or exercise their rights. According to market rationality, only this form of freedom will enable individuals to maximize their material well-being. Just as in the case of the need to protect a free market from tampering, leaving individuals unhampered and free of interference will provide them with the same chance to be wealthy and successful if they have the desire and ability to work hard and make the most of the opportunities provided to them. This, of course, is the myth of the American Dream, an extolling of meritocracy based on effort rather than providing individuals access to a good life based on need.

But, here again, we are presented with an illusion intended to veil oppression and suffering. The praise given to equal rights possessed by all members of society that accompanies this definition of freedom as liberty actually makes the error of, first, assuming that everyone in society actually is accorded the same rights and, second, that merely assigning rights to individuals satisfies the requirement of social justice. From a procedural view of justice, the existence of substantial and egregious inequalities arising from neoliberal ideology essentially exposes the widespread unfair distribution of rights. This is rationalized as not all citizens deserve equal treatment because such equality of outcome will encourage laziness and irresponsibility and undermine achievement and enterprise. This is still another fallacious fundamental assumption of meritocracy used to justify inequities in power and wealth.

This preoccupation with rights to the exclusion of opportunities and resources fosters individualistic explanations of suffering as deserved. It removes individuals from the contexts that have been found to exert a profound influence on whether they are accorded rights or provided with the necessary opportunities and resources to realize those rights. By placing the burden for success or failure on the individual, meritocracy accepts that some people are freer, happier, and more privileged than others because they have somehow secured and effectively made use of the resources and opportunities that enabled them to achieve success. At the same time, neglect is shown in the ways in which a significant segment of society is seriously hampered by physical, economic, and political constraints that dramatically limit their choices and make them unable to realize their possibilities— circumstances they did not choose and that often are beyond their control.

The most flagrant example of this is poverty—a condition that ,for the most part, people neither choose nor create for themselves. The argument against the neoliberal explanation for poverty has previously been described in the work of Rank (2004). As he observes, "Where egregious conditions are beyond the control of the individuals directly affected, all members of the community must share in the responsibility and alleviation of those circumstances" (p. 153). Barry (2005) also underlines the point that in order to achieve social justice the fair distribution of opportunities and resources must be built upon the foundation provided by the assigning of liberal rights to all individuals. Several other examples help to solidify this argument. Increasingly obesity has become a problem among the poor (Compton & Shim, 2015). A common argument made against such individuals is based on ascribing an exaggerated view of personal responsibility to them. In this view, these individuals are to blame for their condition due to willfully engaging in unhealthy eating habits or lacking discipline. However, for most of these individuals it is their social and economic circumstances that contribute to their obesity. Many live in food deserts where there is little or no access to affordable and healthy food choices. Also, food insecurity and the stress of dealing with living in impoverished circumstances play a notable role in obesity.

Another instructive example provided by Klinenberg (2002) is how the privatization and commodification of what were once government-provided social and human services is unfairly used to hold people accountable for their suffering. This transformation of citizen into consumer is a central element of neoliberal ideology. During the heatwave of 1995 the City of Chicago had already engaged in substantial efforts to deliver city services using a model based on business and the private sector. This also included outsourcing services to private organizations. The model was one in which city residents were expected to be informed and smart shoppers of what city services were offered and where they were made available. As Klinenberg observed, this system rewarded those individuals who already possessed power and the social and cultural capital to access and navigate these systems, while at the same time punishing those who did not. Many of those who died during the heat wave did not have access to the information provided by the city regarding cooling centers and other services and also did not have the means or the resources to get to the cooling centers or services even if they were aware of them. They also were members of groups that lacked the skills and knowledge necessary to profit from the guidance and instructions provided on how to deal with the emergency. Despite this, city officials accused these individuals, a number of whom died, of not taking responsibility for their well-being and failing to take appropriate action to protect themselves.

The impact on African Americans in the United States of being deprived of the critical opportunities necessary to achieve success and partake of the benefits afforded to the privileged is described by Glaude (2016). The persistence of racial perspectives that white people are valued more than other people form the worldviews of members of society in ways that perpetuate inequalities and discrimination. They locate problems in the "bad" people subjected to inequality and discrimination and thus deflect attention away from the ways in which the powerful and the privileged maintain inequality. One way in which this occurs is by means of what Glaude calls *opportunity hoarding*. What he means by this is that discrimination may be perpetuated by the way in which individuals live their lives in areas that seem to have nothing to do with race. African Americans do not generally move in the same social circles as white Americans and as a result do not benefit from the social connections, support, and other benefits that favor white Americans. People often believe in meritocracy because they would like to think that they are masters of their destiny, but opportunity hoarding reveals that our ascribing to extreme individualism blinds us to the ways in which the social networks in which we move perpetuate inequality.

On the flip side, Glaude (2016) also talks about *opportunity deserts* in which many African Americans live. These are the impoverished and disadvantaged communities, both urban and rural, in which they find themselves trapped. These communities lack the social and educational opportunities needed to better their lives but have a heightened level of police surveillance, which increases their likelihood of becoming part of the criminal justice system. Faced with the lack of choices, people in these communities often succumb to the harsh limits imposed on them and lose hope. The privileged often maintain an ignorance that such places exist, which privatizes the suffering of African Americans. Glaude concludes his discussion of opportunity deserts by again describing how they function to mystify suffering:

> Whatever bad things are happening in opportunity deserts, it is not the concern of the state or of Americans who don't live there, beyond questions of their own safety and protection. They see it as an issue of individual behavior and bad choice. People who live in opportunity deserts, Americans think, have done something to deserve to be there. Social misery, understood in this sense, is a private affair. Somehow, people absurdly believe—and they have done so for much of our history—that black social misery is the result of hundreds of thousands of unrelated bad individual decisions by black people all across this country. (pp. 23–24)

One additional frequently employed form of mystification of suffering contributing to oppression is *the responsibility trap*. Exaggerated notions of responsibility continue to employ the following processes: locating problems in people, not in their contexts; blaming the victim; over-emphasizing the scope and impact of personal choice while neglecting the impact of other causal factors that are more prominent; setting up confusing situations that offer people the illusion of choice; being dismissive of suffering that results from what looks like a free choice by regarding it as deserved; and depriving individuals of compassion and needed assistance. Blaming people for their suffering has a long history. As theologian Elaine Pagels (1988) reveals, questions of free will, responsibility, sin, and whether human beings are capable of morally governing themselves were debated by the early Christian Church not merely as theological issues but in terms of how people should best be governed. For many years, the status of a Christian was one of being a rebel and non-conformist. Many different forms of Christianity developed after the death of Jesus. This all changed with the adoption of Christianity by the Emperor Constantine and its institution as the official religion of the Roman Empire. This altered political and social situation led to adopting the ideas of

Augustine, which asserted that human beings were corrupt by nature and inclined by original sin to do evil.

In Augustine's view, suffering was a legitimate punishment for human sinfulness, in particular the prideful attempt by human beings to assert their autonomy and show disobedience to the sovereign authority of God. This sinful proclivity, according to Augustine, carried with it troubling political implications. If left unchecked, humans' lust for willful power and their giving way to fleshly desires would lead to chaos, lawlessness, and a host of other ills. At a time when disparate groups calling themselves Christian held different beliefs and subscribed to different practices and views of authority, uniformity and order had to be asserted. The designation of Christianity as the state religion provided the opportunity to impose imperial rule and a newly established church hierarchy on those who would call themselves Christian. Augustine's theory provided the moral justification for the use of constraint, force, and fear by authorities to secure unquestioning obedience to the state and the Church. However, as Pagels (1988) points out, this rationale would not be as successful as it was without appealing on some level to people's need to find some explanation for their suffering. By ascribing their affliction to their own misdeeds, people gained some way of understanding suffering while also placing its occurrence within the operation of a divine law that made it seem to follow some predictable pattern. Thus, their suffering was not capricious but in some way within human control.

The political uses of the belief in the inherent evil of the human being continue to this day. This can be found in the important research done by Lakoff (2002, 2004). His impressive work illustrates that the distinctions between conservative beliefs and policies versus liberal ones can be explained based on their utilizing two different models of the family. The *strict father model* characteristic of the conservative worldview also undergirds a great deal of neoliberal ideology, including the free market, the centrality of self-interest, and the pursuit of wealth. In this model, children are born bad due to their being hedonistic and only wanting to do what feels good. This requires a strong and strict father who can protect the family from the dangerous world and teach children the difference between right and wrong. Such instruction requires the use of punishment to curb the willfulness of children. Learning such discipline is necessary in order to become prosperous and successful.

However, in some instances individuals do not learn these lessons and thus do not develop the self-discipline needed to do right and avoid wrong. For individuals like this, the negative consequences they suffer are deserved as they are self-inflicted. As a result, no efforts should be made to protect them or provide them with assistance with the problems they are seen to have created. This is a view characteristic of neoconservative ideology. Brown (2006) observes that despite neoliberalism and neoconservatism being distinct political rationalities, they have nonetheless converged in contemporary U.S. society to justify the economic and political order.

As in the case of the neoliberal framing of freedom, its insistence in holding people overly responsible for their choices and their consequences poses painful paradoxes that not only confuse but demoralize the oppressed and stigmatize them with unmerited moral condemnation. It also provides still another harmful version of the mystification of suffering. Baker and Newnes (2005) critique assumptions underlying the concept of moral responsibility and how power construes it as an internal attribute to evoke guilt and shame among youth who have failed to conform to the expectations and norms of those in authority. They write:

> One might infer, then, that in order to be judged to have taken responsibility, what people must do is simply what the system wants....The subtext of the phrase taking responsibility is thus "do what I as the more powerful persons expect of you." The apparent desire to get someone to take responsibility (or to do what they are told) can thus be more about conformity or punishment than helping them to lead a more fulfilling life. (p. 34)

As this quote illustrates, those receiving these messages are caught on the horns of a dilemma by being told to change their behavior and attitude, while, at the same time, being told that they cannot do so. They are exhorted to take the initiative in solving their own problems and avoiding dependency, while often being required to take some psychopharmaceutical agent or adhering to some treatment regimen for a disease over which they have no control.

A similar responsibility trap is described by Brown and Baker (2013) for those seeking mental health services. They argue that personal responsibility is urged upon mental health clients more than ever before. This again stands in stark contrast to the increasing emphasis placed on the biological basis for these disorders. Likewise, it comes at a time when access to services for mental health problems is decreasing, in part based on the belief among neoliberal politicians that such individuals need to take more responsibility for their actions and their care rather than have the government take care of them. In other words, they are undeserving of government services. This framework is increasingly leading to a punitive, and even brutal, attitude toward and treatment of mental health patients. The claim by professionals of the necessity of their assuming personal responsibility is sometimes used to deflect them from much-needed services or deny them treatment because they are unmotivated, non-compliant, or manipulative. Under even worse conditions, it gives rise to "neoliberal penalty," in which the perceived failure of self-control and responsibility on the part of individuals lead to them being treated as culpable for their behaviors and attitudes and deserving of criminal sanction.

This has given rise to the penal system becoming the new mental health care system. Brown and Baker (2013) see the growing influence of neoliberalism on health care policy as culminating in a punitive approach to those in society who are deemed as failing to fully participate in the expectation that they behave in an autonomous, productive, and responsible manner. At the same time, it adopts a consumer-driven model in which care for the suffering is structured using a business model and accordingly provided with strict attention to cost, outcome, and efficiency. Health considerations ultimately are nothing more than pretense as compassion and care take a back seat to profit and social control. Once more mystification is employed to craft a market-driven rationalization to disguise a calculated and callous response to market-manufactured misery.

Chapter 8

The Demystification of Suffering: Undoing Illusions and Pursuing Liberation

Three Steps from Disillusionment to Liberation

Pain, disappointment, frustration, confusion, and dread are among the feelings that accompany the experience of becoming disillusioned. Often such moments are the boundary experiences described by Jaspers (1984), in which the once familiar world we lived in and long-held beliefs we had about ourselves are radically challenged. Thus unanchored, we may fall into a state of alienation in which we feel estranged from ourselves and sense that we are no longer at home in the world. The temptation to frantically strive to restore things to the way they were before soon follows on the heels of shock at being so uprooted. At times we may be able to stitch the shattered shards of our worldview and self-concept back together. But we soon learn that there can be no going back when the next wave of challenges undoes the precarious solution we have crafted. Eventually, the loss we dread can no longer be denied and we are faced with either sinking deeper into an abyss or courageously finding our way forward.

We must grieve the loss and, guided by the values of compassion and justice, integrate the lessons they teach us into a more expansive understanding of ourselves, others, and life. We come to recognize that the suffering that once terrified us can in time free us and others. Without this positive potential embedded in acknowledging the suffering we share with our fellow human beings, all hope would be lost and life would be rendered meaningless.

We must not underestimate the perils posed by suffering to lead to even greater and more destructive suffering. Regrettably, the anguish caused by oppression does not stop with the material and psychological harms caused by the abuse of power by one group at the expense of another. The ideological bases of those oppressive practices pervade the consciousness of oppressors and the oppressed alike. Its beliefs and values become as familiar and unnoticed as the very air we breathe. Thus, it is no surprise that mystification ensnares everyone in a web of deceptions that are so persistent and persuasive that they seem beyond question. As a consequence, there is a second layer of suffering in which the adverse consequences of oppression are denied through invalidating the experience of its victims and assuaging the conscience of the perpetrators. By blocking the confrontation with the morally reprehensible consequences of oppression, mystification stymies the awakening of compassion for the afflicted. The call to question the status quo is unheeded. The potential of an open acceptance of suffering to expose the illusions that sustain injustice is left unrealized. In the process everyone loses, and the spiral of oppression continues to unfold.

Disillusionment is painful and disorienting, but it nevertheless remains an essential prelude to personal transformation and collective liberation. To avoid losing this opportunity for change on an individual and collective level, three critical steps must be taken. This chapter will be devoted to describing these three steps and how they perform an essential role in putting an end to the multiple ways in which oppression afflicts all of us. These three steps are the *naming, claiming, and reframing of suffering.* As I outline these steps, certain parallels will be noted with the first three of the Noble Truths articulated by the Buddha and described in the Introduction. Once more, the insights of the Buddha many years ago continue to ring true today.

Before any meaningful change can occur, there must first be clarity regarding what is in need of change. What exactly is the problem? Though the various ways in which oppression causes suffering may seem to be obvious, it is sad that all too often this is not the case. In previous chapters it has been illustrated that neoliberal ideology has been employed to deceive victims of oppression into regarding their suffering as due to their own deficiencies and irresponsibility, attributable to some illness or psychiatric condition in need of correction, or the inevitable consequence of natural forces over which no one has any control. That same ideology convinces oppressors that the harms they perpetrate are justifiable punishment for the wrongdoings of the victims, corrective actions directed at restoring victims to their place in the social hierarchy, or natural outcomes of the inherently competitive and self-serving nature of human beings. Considering this, it is essential that all those involved in the process of oppression know what is actually occurring. Those who are being oppressed need to know that this is what is happening to them, and those who are engaging in oppression must likewise know this is what they are doing. In other words, they need to *name it*, to freely and openly see it for what it is. Our blindness to the prevalence of suffering is the most dangerous manifestation of the workings of mystification.

Friere (1970) observes that this very act of *naming* is a form of praxis in which the causes of oppression are critically recognized and, through this insight, the world is transformed. He writes, "To exist, humanly, is to *name* the world, to change it. Once named, the world in its turn reappears to the namers as a problem and requires of them a new *naming*. Human beings are not built in silence, but in word, in work, in action reflection" (p. 88, italics in original). The oppressed are often silenced and deprived of the ability to name the world. However, speaking to their experience reverses the forces of dehumanization and lets them bring what has been hidden out in the open. Once what is obstructing their vision is removed, a new word that more truly captures their experience can be spoken. Then the world is no longer seen or understood as it had been before. A new vision has been disclosed to the oppressed.

The naming of a problem enables individuals to achieve some distance from it and so reflect upon it. This reflection does not merely deepen understanding; it also allows for the consideration of alternatives—new names. "The pain I feel is not my fault and not a natural consequence of some economic cycle. It is because I am being exploited and excluded." Thus, reclaiming the right of victims of oppression to speak is essential to empowering them and enabling them to take possession of their experience and their lives. The same process can enable oppressors to deal with the painful, but necessary, emotions that accompany realization of their complicity in a manner that enables them to embrace the political and personal significance of this realization (Chapman, 2013).

However, as implied by the attainment of critical distance in the process of naming, once suffering attributable to oppression is named, mere identification of the problem is not enough. Very often even facing one's suffering—no matter what its cause—evokes resistance. At first encounter, people are typically not inclined to consider that journeying with the suffering and seeing where it may lead them is worth the costs that come with it. So long as any experience is dismissed as incapable of ownership, human beings cannot experience being whole. The problem of alienation remains, and the vicious cycle generated by the fact that what is resisted persists ensures that avoidance of necessary suffering creates suffering that could have been avoided.

Thus, upon naming this suffering, individuals must sit with it and let it be. They must *claim* it. This willingness to let all the negative feelings, memories, and realizations make their presence known brings an intensity that stirs up apprehension that it may be too much to bear. For this reason, the process of naming, claiming, and reframing cannot be embarked on in isolation but rather must be conducted in solidarity with others (Friere, 1970). Human beings must reclaim their essential societal nature, which has been negated by neoliberalism's extreme emphasis on individualism. One cannot genuinely work for his or her own liberation without simultaneously, in an act of compassion, extending that work to their fellow human beings.

The attainment of critical consciousness is a joint process in which dialogue is central (Friere, 1970). Dialogue lies at the very heart of Friere's theory of co-intentional education as a pedagogy for the oppressed. Exposing the ideological foundation upon which oppressive practices rest is called demythologizing. What is presented by the powerful as a fixed, and thus unchangeable, reality is seen instead as a historical reality capable of change because the world in actuality unfolds as a ceaseless process. With illusions thus exposed, the experience of suffering can be seen with fresh eyes and removed from the dominant context that frames it in terms consistent with hegemony. The workings of oppression are revealed. Critical consciousness provides the means by which the meaning and purposes of suffering are *reframed*.

Co-intentional education occurs by means of dialogue in which the subjectivity and agency of the participants are affirmed and respected. This allows for the participants to meet and work cooperatively on shared problems. By raising questions regarding the myth that has been uncovered, they are able to freely communicate and mutually deliberate with one another. Through a combination of reflection and action that constitutes praxis, these conditions facilitate the participants coming to a critical grasp of the ways in which they participate in and with the world they live in. The distortion and obfuscation used to exercise power over them is critically examined, as is the role that participants may play in their own oppression. What follows is the creation of an alternative vision of the world that becomes the basis for efforts on behalf of transformation.

With the three steps to liberation briefly laid out, the remainder of the chapter will be devoted to fleshing out and expanding on each of them. Perspectives and concepts from previous chapters are drawn upon to offer clear and complete guidelines of how to move from disillusionment to liberation. These guidelines are directed to both individuals who have been victimized by oppression as well as those who wish to work in solidarity with them to undo the harm inflicted by mystification and to promote the critical consciousness necessary to effect genuine social change.

Some Things Can't Be Fixed or Helped

It may seem odd and counterproductive to embark on an examination of the need to identify and reject illusions that sustain oppressive structures and practices by considering things that cannot be changed. This would seem to play directly into the prevalent ideological propaganda that the status quo is the product of natural laws incapable of change. However, careful scrutiny of the ways in which this justification for oppression is used is a valuable exercise. It exposes the presence of certain contradictions embedded within this assumption that create confusion and reveals other common illusions asserted by neoliberalism that stand in the way of liberation. This confusion takes advantage of the often-encountered misunderstanding that exists in the minds of people regarding the difference between the two forms of suffering that have been described earlier. This helps to explain why this particular form of mystification is so successful in undermining identification of suffering capable of change and, subsequently, constructive action to eliminate it.

To reiterate, a significant cause of self-created suffering, which makes up the greater portion of human misery, originates in choices and actions taken by human beings aimed at trying to rid themselves of suffering that is inevitable because it is inherent to the human condition. Though self-created suffering is the only form of suffering capable of being avoided, it nonetheless often appears as though this fact is completely lost to individuals based on their belief that all suffering is evil and should be eliminated. They rigidly hold fast to the belief that they have a right to a pain-free life. Neoliberalism eagerly seizes upon this mistaken belief as it readily serves a number of its purposes. And it is precisely the ways in which this innate aversion to pain is exploited by neoliberalism to manipulate the oppressed and gain advantages for the powerful that should alert us to why the failure to accurately make this distinction is so dangerous and in need of exposure. The sad reality is that the tighter people hold on to that illusion, the greater the suffering they inflict upon themselves. Often their resistance to squarely facing life's inevitable distressing circumstances is more painful and detrimental than the suffering they are trying to evade.

This paradox of "suffering because we are suffering" provides stark and incontrovertible evidence of how failure to correctly discern between these two forms of suffering and how best to deal with each of them ends up being a self-defeating approach. What can and cannot be changed? What kind of control do we have over what happens? How do we respond to these events? When must we suffer and when do we unnecessarily inflict suffering on ourselves and others? These questions admittedly do not always lend themselves to simple and straightforward answers. There is no question that their ambiguity contributes to the confusion and misjudgment that people often demonstrate in attempting to deal with them. Nevertheless, no matter how much ambiguity they pose it is pivotal that we take them seriously. Such serious consideration offers hope of finding a way to deal in a compassionate manner with the inevitable disappointment that comes when our hope of being free of suffering is proven to be false and, conversely, restoring justice when we realize we have been unfairly subjected to wrongdoing.

The very belief that one can have or even deserves a pain-free life is perhaps the most dangerous of all illusions because it is bound to be repeatedly disappointed and so bring greater suffering on its heels. However, this does not prevent the ideological uses of this illusion to keep the oppressed under thumb and render them passive and consenting to their subjugation. Part of its destructive power is the way in which it encourages people to devote a disproportionate amount of their time and energy on doing all they can to put an end to the woes that have no cure or answer. This preoccupation with inescapable suffering, and the anxiety that accompanies it, is cultivated by neoliberalism defining instances of it as fixable for the right price or by doing as one is told.

This duplicitous characterization is then followed by the marketing of a veritable plethora of solutions that can be purchased, the dispensing of all kinds of advice by "highly qualified" experts, or the admonitions of people of power and prestige to "buck up" or "tough it out." One by one these promises, panaceas, and prescriptions in time prove false, but the search does not end and only grows more desperate. Mounting resistance to life's necessary losses not only does not alter the fact that they have occurred, but, ironically, it also results in human beings stubbornly holding fast to the very suffering they want to avoid. So long as the resistance remains, so too does the suffering, such that it feels as though it will never end.

The truth is that the pain following the losses that make up the fleeting process of life is likewise transient. If this process is allowed to unfold without interference, the suffering experienced is temporary. As the Buddha observed, we all grow old and eventually succumb to illness. The process of aging and the course of an illness are both composed of a series of events, each with a beginning and an end—the ultimate end being death. While this does not offer complete consolation, we can at least be assured that in time even the darkest episodes in our lives will come to an end. However, when human beings resist these inevitable losses and take desperate measures to reassert control by trying to fix things that cannot be fixed or find a solution that does not exist, nothing is gained and even more is lost. Not only do they not evade the discomfort and fears that accompany loss, but their refusal to accept them prolongs their suffering. This distinction between temporary and prolonged suffering is an important one that parallels inescapable and self-created suffering. Knowing how to distinguish between them exposes the ways in which neoliberal ideology attempts to conflate them, and thus is essential to attaining well-being and establishing justice.

The importance of this difference is a point astutely made by a Russian sage who attracted adherents based on his teachings about methods to achieve full awakening—George Gurdjieff. He begins his analysis of the problem by first providing an insightful observation of the vicious cycle created by resisting unavoidable suffering, which quoted here by one of his followers, Ouspensky (1941):

> Another thing that people must sacrifice *is their suffering*. It is very difficult also to sacrifice one's suffering. A man will renounce any pleasures you like but he will not give up his suffering. Man is made in such a way that he is never so much attached to anything as he is to his suffering….Nothing can be attained without suffering but at the same time one must begin by sacrificing suffering. (p. 274, italics in the original)

One is immediately struck by the provocative way in which Gurdjieff highlights what initially sounds like blatant contradictions. How can it be that human beings are attached to suffering? This is clearly contrary to what we often assume to be their hedonistic nature. Though human beings are typically portrayed as powerfully motivated to seek pleasure, upon closer consideration we can begin to identify times in which they actually behave in a very contrary fashion.

There are large numbers of people, for example, who persist in engaging in certain addictive forms of behavior despite the many harmful consequences they have for themselves and others. Or, in a more positive context, some individuals may renounce pleasure and engage in difficult and demanding forms of discipline in order to achieve mastery of some skill or develop some talent. How are we to understand this "attachment to suffering"? In addition, Gurdjieff poses a second paradox: While suffering is necessary to attain awakening, at the same time such suffering must be sacrificed. How can suffering be necessary and unnecessary to awakening?   Once more these conundrums can only be resolved by understanding that Gurdjieff is describing two different forms of suffering.

In recognition of this, Gurdjieff goes on to explain this distinction, "And work consists in subjecting oneself voluntarily to temporary suffering in order to be free of eternal suffering. But people are afraid of suffering. They want pleasure, at once and forever" (Ouspensky, 1941, p. 274). Gurdjieff asserts that not only do we need to correctly discern between the two forms of suffering, but we must then respond to them very differently in order to foster our transformation. Temporary suffering may arouse dread, frustration, and fear and it may at times seem unbearable, but it will eventually pass. However, it is the loss of control that is far more vexing than the unpleasantness caused us. The human need for control far exceeds the human need for happiness. As Kierkegaard (1936) observed, the "pleasure" humans want at once and forever is, in truth, the desire to always have things their way. And so until they are willing to believe that what they regard as vital and indispensable can be sacrificed, anyone or anything that tries to take this away will be opposed with all their might.

It is only our response to suffering that can transform it into something eternal, or what Kierkegaard (1941) called "the sickness unto death." This is because in rejecting the suffering that comes with being human, we continually engage in rejecting ourselves and life itself. We become trapped into a never-ceasing spiral of self-deception and self-defeat as there is nothing more futile than trying to be other than who we are or making life conform to our desires. There can be no darker point in one's life than this. If we instead freely engage in the ceaseless unfolding of our lives, we discover that our anguish is as fleeting as our joy and happiness. In accord with the Buddha's doctrine of *anicca*, everything is temporary (Rahula, 1974). As the quote by Alan Watts in the Introduction asserts, we come to realize that we must suffer for our pleasures. Suffering is comingled with pleasure because we are fallible, finite, and mortal beings. Franz Kafka (1958) expresses this point eloquently:

> We too must suffer all the suffering around us. What each of us possesses is not a body but a process of growth and it conducts us through every pain, in this form or that....In this process there is no place for justice, but no place either for dread of suffering or for the interpretation of suffering as merit. (p. 241)

Kafka's observation reflects his appreciation for the inescapable suffering that is rooted not merely in our physical being but also in our engagement in an unfolding process of growth that has its share of pain. We are all on a trajectory of development in which the collapse and disintegration of one step or level is required for movement to the next (Dabrowski, 1964, 1967). That brings inevitable losses and disappointments. Moreover, this pain is not a matter of justice, as Kafka observes. There is no court or law or authority that one can appeal to for relief or recourse regarding inescapable suffering. Likewise, it is meaningless to interpret this type of suffering as something one deserves or has earned. These ills are not ones that anyone merits based upon his or her actions or violation of some moral code. All are subject to them, no matter their station or desert. This, unfortunately, does not mean that these meanings are not ascribed to the experience of suffering in ways that are mystifying and oppressive.

Seeing suffering as punishment for wrongdoing is a viewpoint that has had an enduring hold on human beings—again, in part because it first offers a way of making sense of something that might otherwise defy reason and then by providing some illusory sense of restoring control over an uncontrollable situation (Pagels, 1988). However, in the current ideology this tactic of blaming the victim ensures confusion and mistaken thinking regarding what is just and deserved. When individuals have had little or nothing to do with the injuries and injustices committed against them, they need to exempt themselves of responsibility. The responsibility must be squarely placed where it belongs. This enables the victims to acknowledge that they have been victimized. They can then proceed to critically examine the oppressive processes at work in order to resist and remove them. This is something that can be helped. At the same time, it is essential that the oppressed recognize that there is a host of other afflictions that no amount of working for justice will alleviate or remove because these afflictions are interwoven with our humanity. Looking for help for these things often leads to individuals undergoing even greater exploitation, discrimination, and domination.

Interpreting inescapable suffering as right or wrong is not only misguided but harmful. If it becomes the focus of their concern, the oppressed become more vulnerable to the constant barrage of social messages that deceive them into looking for fairness where it cannot be found. These same messages are intended to make the oppressed less able to see unfairness when it is staring them in the face—in other words, they mystify their suffering. A lack of a ready explanation for their pain and unhappiness creates a great deal of anxiety for people. They are quick to seek out an answer or solution. When repeatedly told that they are expected to be responsible, the oppressed will adopt a judgmental perspective and castigate themselves as weak and vulnerable for getting sick, not achieving success, or repeatedly finding themselves on the losing end—when in fact they are not at fault. Conversely, when the exploitation and subjugation that gives rise to illness, disability, deprivation, and abject poverty is rendered invisible, they will fail to pass the judgment due their oppressors and passively accept their abject state as "just part of life."

Discerning the difference between inescapable and self-created suffering is pivotal not merely to liberation but to living a healthy life. As Kafka asserts, there are indeed times when we must suspend all judgment, dispense with the expectations and demands we so frequently place on life, and simply subject ourselves voluntarily to suffering despite our fear. This is not suffering that we wished upon ourselves, created, or earned. If we freely meet this suffering, in time it will pass. But, more important,, being present to that suffering without judgment enables us to hear the important messages it has to convey that otherwise would go unheeded. In some experiences of inescapable suffering, there are embedded valuable insights into the purpose and meaning of life.

As Kierkegaard (1948) asserts in *The Gospel of Suffering*, when we assimilate this suffering into our inmost being, we demonstrate our willingness to learn and grow from it. We come to an appreciation of how powerful identifications associated with our ego have limited us and constricted our consciousness in damaging ways. This makes it possible for us to relinquish these identifications and come to a fuller awareness of ourselves. In other forms of inescapable suffering, the role played by harmful illusions rooted in the dominant ideology are revealed. By avoiding the ways in which judgment causes us to become trapped in our distress and indignation at being victimized, we can use the opportunity offered by disillusionment to cease self-recrimination and instead channel anger into constructive action aimed at restoring justice.

This is what Gurdjieff means by sacrificing our suffering. What we are in fact sacrificing is an illusion that once seemed so very important to us. A belief considered to be beyond doubt is exposed and shown to be false. And the majority of those illusions have been placed in us in the service of the powerful. There can be no question that the truth *can* sometimes be a source of great suffering, but that does not change that it can also set us free. The workings of self-deception and mystification must be undone if there is any hope of becoming unshackled from lies that exact a heavy price from us. This means becoming aware of the ways in which fear has been wielded by ourselves or others as an instrument of oppression. It means becoming alert to the ways in which threats designed to tap into something we thought to be essential to our happiness and self-esteem trigger extreme measures to reassert control and preserve the status quo. What may look like our being in control is often actually allowing others to control us.

Once again, the ego is our undoing. What lies at the core of the ego is our selfish insistence that life comply with our demands and expectations. But life is singularly indifferent to our preferences. For human beings, each disappointment is experienced as a "kind of death" because of their powerful identification with some illusion. Only once we are willing to make the sacrifice, painful and frightening though it may be, do we see the light at the end of the tunnel. We realize that submitting ourselves to temporary suffering spares us of plunging into a far deeper and seemingly unending despair. In putting an end to our resistance to necessary suffering, we let go of the self-created suffering this resistance creates and sustains.

The Power of Acceptance to Promote Compassion and Justice

Disillusionment offers us the genuine opportunity to remove harmful obstacles to our growth and to pursue liberation for ourselves and others. For this to occur, however, we must adopt a compassionate attitude toward ourselves that openly acknowledges our pain without also seeking to either shove it out of our awareness or frantically trying to "fix it." Our ability to meet our own suffering correspondingly enables us to meet it in others. This makes fostering compassion a critical first step in pursuing justice. This echoes the assertion made by Williams (2008) that compassion is the moral foundation of social justice. Dass and Gorman (1985) make clear in their in-depth examination of service that while the knee-jerk response of fear to loss and pain is inevitable, it must eventually be dissolved by means of the suspension of judgment in order to allow compassion to unfold.

This dispassionate attentiveness to whatever we are experiencing in the moment—no matter how positive or negative—expands consciousness of ourselves, others, and the world. This allows for an integration of experiences that deepens our self-acceptance and self-understanding. As our appreciation for what it means to be human grows, it breaks down the barriers that we place between ourselves and others. The shared experience of suffering that comes with loss enables us to feel a deeper connection to our fellow human beings. We recognize our shared dreams and our common plight. We realize that despite seeming differences, we are at a deeper level interconnected. This makes it more possible for us to be moved by the pain of others and to feel a sense of responsibility for offering comfort and, where possible, removing the cause of their anguish. As Nouwen (1972) writes, "For a compassionate man nothing human is alien: no joy and no sorrow, no way of living and no way of dying" (p. 41).

This attitude of acceptance and suspension of judgment brings not only the power to transform our understanding of ourselves in growth-promoting ways. It also connects us with the immense suffering created by oppression and arouses a sense of injustice that can lead to constructive action. Given this, the cultivation of this attitude is an important step in demystifying suffering and promoting liberation. It is thus no surprise that this attitude has been understood as essential to the healing process as well as to achieving an elevated state of spiritual consciousness in diverse contemplative and meditative traditions. These traditions have been pursued for centuries not merely to attain enlightenment but to foster compassion and justice for all beings. The association between bringing an open and accepting attitude to painful and frightening experiences and well-being is based on the realization that disowning any facet of our humanity detracts from personal wholeness and sows seeds of discord within persons as well as between them. The connection between suffering and a sense of alienation, separation, and isolation was discussed in a previous chapter along with its adverse effects. Refusing to accept that there will always be times when things don't go our way or when life will not conform with our expectations ultimately places us at odds with ourselves, others, and life itself. So long as these fractures and splits remain unhealed, we cannot know peace or experience wholeness.

Through acceptance we find a way of moving past resistance and instead fully surrender to an experience of suffering that can expand our awareness rather than constrict it. This is described powerfully by Carl Jung (1933) when speaking to the centrality of acceptance to the healing relationship. Nonetheless, in doing so he highlights how passing judgment can give rise to oppression, which makes his insight equally valuable to those who seek to work for justice. He writes:

> We cannot change anything unless we accept it. Condemnation does not liberate, it oppresses. I am the oppressor of the person I condemn, not his friend or his fellow-sufferer. I do not in the least mean to say that we must never pass judgment in the cases of persons whom we desire to help and improve. But if the doctor wishes to help a human being he must be able to accept him as he is. And he can do this in reality only when he has already seen and accepted himself as he is. (pp. 234–235)

The concept of *passive volition* was noted in Chapter Five and called a form of consciousness in which we abandon ourselves to a process and let it unfold of its own accord. It was also described as an attitude of openness, acceptance, and receptivity in which individuals become completely absorbed in the object of their awareness. Passive volition is being introduced here again to establish the role it must play in the naming and claiming of suffering as steps toward enhancing awareness of oppression and promoting liberation. It provides a means of approaching experience that establishes a direct and immediate way of knowing the object of our awareness. Its non-interfering, non-controlling stance enables persons to abandon themselves to a process by willingly consenting to fully participate in it. Once again, examples of times when this might occur include being moved by some powerful work of art, engaging effortlessly in some athletic activity, or being swept up in a powerful spiritual experience.

In addition, when exercising passive volition individuals can temporarily suspend their judgment or evaluation of their experience and permit what is being experienced to reveal itself to them without being contaminated by expectations and preconceptions. This is very unlike our typical way of knowing and being in the world, described by Wilber (1977) as discursive knowledge. Our reliance on discursive thought is based on the dominance of the modern paradigm, with its emphasis on objectivity, quantification, and materialism. The objects of our awareness are labeled using language and classified into mutually exclusive categories. The relation between knower and known in discursive thought is a dualistic one in which the goal is to manipulate and achieve control over the object of awareness.

The direct knowledge fostered by passive volition leads to a more intimate and direct contact with experience that is unobscured by words and uncontaminated by categories. This approach to knowing is a central principle of phenomenological philosophy, sometimes referred to as *bracketing* (Spinelli, 2014). After engaging in a process of identifying the kinds of assumptions and preconceptions that typically bias our thought process, we temporarily set them aside or place them in brackets so that they do not color and distort our examination of our experience. The hope is that this will allow something essential about the object of our awareness to freely emerge and reveal itself to us.

The work of ending oppression and restoring justice requires the unveiling and undoing of harmful illusions whose purpose it is to ensure that the status quo goes unchallenged and unchanged, and to secure consent to our oppression. The fabric of these illusions that color our everyday experience is made up of ready-made explanations for why things are the way they are and soothing lies that are designed to allay our fears in the short term. A good deal of discursive thought—rooted as it is in language, categories, and metaphors derived from the dominant ideology, functions to enslave us—and it does this so thoroughly that it takes considerable effort and commitment to realize the impact of ideology on our experience. Some of the biases and preconceptions that contaminate and distort our experience have their origins in individuals, as described in the earlier discussion of the filtering function of consciousness and its role in self-deception. However, based on Fromm's (1941) analysis of the formation of social character and its serving as a type of internalized hegemony (Langman & Ryan, 2009), most of these biases are inculcated by means of socialization.

Passive volition and direct knowing are valuable tools that enable people to detect and unpack ideological biases that distort and obfuscate the experience of suffering so that it can be correctly named and seen for what it is. With the first step accomplished and the problem accurately identified, it can be followed by the second step of suspending judgment and refraining from labeling suffering in ways that provoke and maintain resistance to it. People can then accept or claim it rather than deny or disown it.

Based on this, it is no surprise that the practice of passive volition has been viewed as posing a threat to the status quo. Awakened individuals have historically been among the most vocal and sharpest critics of oppression and injustice (Fox, 1972, 1995; Huxley, 1944; Rakoczy, 2006). Neoliberal ideology is steeped in the same materialist, positivist, objective biases that undergird discursive thought. Early on, Critical Theory identified the rise of instrumental reason as closely associated with capitalism. Like discursive thought, instrumental reason employs a means–end rationality in which the goal of knowledge is to achieve control or manipulate the objects of knowledge for certain purposes or to achieve certain goals. Though this seemingly positivistic orientation is adopted by neoliberalism, this is a mere pretense of objectivity used to hide the working of ideological values and assumptions aimed at domination and dehumanization.

A good example of this bias is how educational institutions seek to foster discursive ways of knowing compatible with the neoliberal paradigm and to discourage more direct ways of knowing (Gruba-McCallister, 2002). Friere (1970) calls this dominant model the *banking approach* to education. Teachers are considered authority figures and possessors of truth. Their function is to dispense this knowledge to students, who are expected to be passive, adaptable, and compliant receptacles. This knowledge is to be simply received and internalized uncritically and later repeated back to teachers in order to receive approval in the form of passing grades. So it is that the process of education rests on an essentially oppressive relationship, and educational institutions play a pivotal role in inculcating the dominant ideology.

An exploration of the ways in which passive volition and direct knowledge can facilitate healing and a higher degree of well-being will help to further explain the positive role they play in the naming, claiming, and reframing of suffering. In an earlier discussion of freedom, it was noted that human beings do not have unlimited choices and complete control. The exercise of freedom is always situated within certain limitations or givens. Some of these givens are universal as they make up inherent features of the human condition. Others are unique to individuals as they consist of the specific facts that make up their life—for example, when and where they were born, their heredity, and the pattern of choices they have made in the past. These givens are called "thrownness" by Heidegger (1927/1978) and destiny by May

(1981). Though these givens curtail certain possibilities and confront us with some fixed conditions, without them true freedom is not possible. May writes:

> Destiny and freedom form a paradox, a dialectical relationship. By this I mean they are opposites that need each other...Out of the encountering of the forces of destiny come our possibilities, our opportunities. In the engaging of destiny our freedom is born, just as with the coming of the light the day overcomes night. Destiny...is not to be thought of as a ball and chain that afflict human beings. (p. 95)

Our essential nature as social beings makes the interdependent relationship between destiny and freedom inevitable. The choices we make unavoidably have consequences for others as well as ourselves, and the consequences can stretch across time. This is illustrated in another given called *historicity*. This refers the particular historical circumstances into which every human being is born. In reflecting on these circumstances it becomes clear that countless choices made by an unimaginable number of individuals whom we have never met and who will never know us come together to form the social, political, economic, and cultural situation that we enter into and that exercises a profound influence on our lives and our life chances. The extreme inequality of conditions that fashions a contemporary form of extreme injustice is unfortunately a set of givens that many individuals must contend with. The origins of this inequality stretch back over many years and involve the actions of many people. The cultivation of hope for individuals suffering the impact of inequality does not lie in the past actions and decisions that created this injustice, but in working toward compassion and justice today in order to remove injustice from the future.

Inevitable suffering is part of our destiny. This means that the physical and psychological harms caused by oppression are among the givens. We may wish otherwise and look for any number of ways to evade or fix this suffering but will soon learn that none exist. And so what remains is the necessity of accepting the tribulations one naturally experiences when oppressed and using this awareness as an impetus to discover, resist, and remove the reasons for them. This raises a point made by May (1981)—that individuals can make different responses to their destiny, including cooperating with, acknowledging, confronting, challenging, and rebelling against it. However, on one point he is clear; refusing to accept one's destiny is a destructive form of pride. One danger is people making the exceptional claim that rules that apply to everyone else do not apply to them. Another is that rejecting destiny means rejecting the freedom inextricably connected to it. That freedom, as will be noted below, is indispensable to responding to one's givens in a way that promotes growth rather than greater suffering.

It is not uncommon, for example, for persons in psychotherapy to present with the expectation and belief that they have the power to alter their thrownness or that they should have been provided with a different and more favorable set of givens. They often express a sense of outrage and frustration about the hand they have been dealt in life. Rather than recognize the options and opportunities available to them, they see themselves as plagued by a series of bad breaks or as constantly thwarted by circumstances that seem to always conspire against them. This passive and helpless stance is described as the *fate maneuver* (Binswanger, 1963).

While there is some legitimacy in persons feeling angry and unhappy about the unfortunate and hurtful circumstances in their lives, this does not legitimize their insistent claim that such things should not have happened or that somehow they or someone else should magically make their life what they want it to be. Because these events exist in the past, they are beyond control. Dwelling upon these injuries and disappointments serves only to exaggerate the amount of importance and influence ascribed to them and essentially creates a festering wound that never heals. This saps the energies needed to move forward with one's life despite the pain of these losses. The fate maneuver is thus a form of self-created suffering in which individuals try very hard to change things they cannot change, while adamantly avoiding making changes that are possible. By focusing on things that defy their need for control, such individuals feel an increasingly diminished sense of agency and relinquish responsibility for making choices and decisions that remain open to them. This stance also gives rise to their blaming others or impersonal forces for their circumstances. This, too, poses a paradox. While giving the appearance that they want to regain control over their lives, these individuals are instead firmly ensconced in a passive and helpless posture due to their inability to let go of the belief that they are victims of circumstances.

In the matter of those who have experienced oppression, this raises some pertinent issues. They can clearly make the legitimate claim that they were born in unjust circumstances that have had a progressively detrimental impact on their lives. They have been treated unfairly and continue to find themselves with very limited options for improving their situation. As a result, dismissing their feelings and legitimate grievances about the things over which they had no control would show a lack of understanding and compassion. Likewise, underestimating the very real obstacles and limitations that they still must contend with in order to assume more control would show a lack of appreciation for their lived experience. However, those who wish to promote justice and work for liberation, whether the oppressed or their allies, must balance such understanding with an astute awareness of the danger posed by individuals organizing their identity around being a victim. For some who are oppressed this regrettably forms a central identification that, though damaging, nonetheless becomes the foundation for how they understand themselves and live their lives. It is one of the primary ways that help us understand why people consent to being oppressed

The development of internalized oppression is one of the most detrimental examples of this (David, 2014; Friere, 1970). By adopting a negative self-image based on the actions and judgments of oppressors, the oppressed assume a submissive stance and doubt their ability to exercise freedom, making their liberation less likely. By means of mystification, the oppressed come to see their suffering as their fate, something that will have to endure no matter what. Reframing past injuries as forms of injustice, unveiling the actual forces that caused those injuries, and facilitating the processing and integration of the negative feelings attached to those injuries help the oppressed move beyond victimhood. This paves the way for the oppressed not to lock themselves into a preoccupation with their painful past that undermines their ability to make sense of their suffering. Instead, they are enabled to construct an imagined future that is more just and channel their energies toward realizing that future. While the injustices they have experienced at the hands of the powerful are facts, they are not, contrary to the ideological message they often hear, their fate.

In order to break free of this pattern of victimization, individuals must understand that before they are able to exercise freedom in their lives they must first commit themselves to their thrownness. This means achieving an honest grasp of what things in their lives cannot be fixed or helped and accepting these things as beyond their direct control. They may indeed have had cold and uncaring parents, or have been born with some disabling condition, or have been subject to oppression. Investing immense effort toward denying or trying to alter these unchangeable facts just brings more misery and unhappiness. Once accepted, all these things can be experienced as painful losses which when they are grieved can be integrated into their self-understanding. This then allows them to move on with their lives. However, so long as they remain unbearable tragedies or unforgivable injuries, the suffering they cause is prolonged and compounded.

By forsaking the fate maneuver, individuals come to a clearer realization of what it is that they can change by taking direct control of a situation and what it is they cannot change but nevertheless choose to deal with more productively by assuming a different attitude. This ability to take a stand toward things over which we have no control and make meaning of them is frequently the highest form of freedom (Frankl, 1967).

It may seem odd to associate acceptance and passive volition with the idea of freedom. This is due once again to the workings of neoliberalism. Under its influence, individuals have an extremely skewed view of what freedom means. For most people, freedom is about asserting and imposing their will on the world and others, controlling things to make them align with their desires, and resisting any limitations placed on them. This more active stance is based on the value placed on the competition, assertiveness, independence, autonomy, and self-interest espoused by neoliberalism. The disastrous consequences of the extremes to which this view has been taken have been discussed previously.

This is not to say that this view of freedom does not have its place and utility. It is well suited to things over which individuals actually are able to exert some control and influence, to forms of suffering that can be eliminated through different choices. However, it casts the world solely into unequal relationships governed by power, manipulation, and control—relations in which there are winners and losers, masters and slaves. These are the very relationships on which oppression is based. Moreover, when this form of freedom is confronted by those things that cannot be controlled, it is utterly confounded and falls into disastrous patterns of self-defeat.

Using the term passive *volition* makes clear that a form of will is still operative. Adopting an open and permissive stance is a decision individuals make not to actively assert their personal will or impose their desires and wishes on others or on circumstances. Instead, they relinquish control and surrender to some higher purpose or good (Cole & Pargament 1999). They consent to being guided or governed by a power or principle bigger than they are and, in doing so, situate their desires, hopes, and concerns within a more expansive and inclusive framework. The exercise of passive volition is often practiced within spiritual disciplines based on the recognition of some absolute or transcendent order or reality to which human will must conform. From this perspective, the abandonment of the ego allows for the experience of union with this higher order. This is one of the key elements of an elevated state of consciousness.

Similarly, Heidegger (Barrett, 1964) proposed that truth is only possible as a freedom to let-be or the adoption of an openness that allows truth to be revealed. This permissive, respectful, and loving attitude stands in awe of what is described by Heidegger (von Eckartsberg & Valle, 1981) as one of two modes of thinking called *meditative* (which echoes once again freedom's centrality to meditative and contemplative forms of spiritual discipline). He contrasts this with the *calculative* mode, which is synonymous with what has been described earlier as instrumental reason. These descriptions make clear that acceptance is not an expression of resignation, helplessness, or complete passivity. It requires strength of mind and heart to abandon our powerful need for control because it signals a willingness to face up to life in all its joys and sorrows without exception. It is the willingness to recognize that there is much about life that one cannot directly control, paired with the realization that one can still choose what attitude or stand to take toward these givens—to accept or resist them.

One other example taken from a spiritual tradition is instructive regarding the importance of acceptance and passive volition as it pertains to action taken in pursuit of justice. Allowing our actions to be guided by justice is one example of submitting our personal desires to a higher moral principle. In addition, that same detachment must be exercised regarding what the outcomes of our actions will be. This addresses one of the great dangers of social action taken on behalf of opposing or ending oppression. It is not uncommon to be daunted by the magnitude of the issues that one must grapple with. This may prove so intimidating that we fail to take any action at all because we don't even know where to begin our efforts.

Similarly, we may be so committed to making a difference that failure to do so leads to discouragement and abandonment of the cause. In these situations, we are once more either underestimating or exaggerating the degree of power we have to effect change and letting our expectations color what we judge to be success or failure. The Taoist principle of *wu wei*, or action without action, can provide some valuable guidance. Parallels between Heidegger's freedom to let-be and Taoist thought were drawn by von Eckartsberg and Valle (1981) based on their both assuming a non-interfering observation of the ever-unfolding flow of events.

The contradictory nature of *wu wei* is intended to challenge our accustomed way of thinking of action as a direct, assertive way of exercising control over a situation. A more passive form of control, a letting be or surrendering of oneself to a process lies at the heart of *wu wei*. The image of water is often used to represent the unfolding of effortless action—for example, observing how water in a river meets obstacles by going around or over them. Nonetheless, the power of this process of water merely brushing up against rocks over time can be witnessed in the shaping of natural wonders such as the Grand Canyon. Legault (2006) writes about how principles of Taoism can be used to productively engage in social activism. The principle of *wu wei* occupies a central place in his view of activism as he notes that we must let right action and acting out of duty to a higher principle arise of their own accord and then take the appropriate steps when they do so.

In order to let right action arise of its own accord, we must engage in an open and contemplative attitude of stillness and centeredness. The term vocation is based on "being called." To hear the call of duty to higher principles central to compassionate service, we must learn to still our minds and disengage ourselves from our own personal wishes and desires. We must get our ego out of the way because otherwise we are acting in compliance with our personal attachment and desires. Legault (2006) writes, "Our egos keep us clinging to our expectations....I believe that ego is among the chief ills that keeps us from living happily and accomplishing our work as activists. Ego prevents us from making the choices and decisions required of us to be successful in our cause" (p. 281).

Relinquishing desire does not mean relinquishing a passion for compassion and justice. When we allow passion to arise spontaneously in the face of suffering and oppression, it informs right action and guides how we extend service to others. "The *wu wei* of activism is about accepting things as they come. This includes our passionate—and yes, sometimes burning—desire to make change in the world. To fight this passion and the outrage it spawns would also go against the flow of things" (Legault, 2006, p. 141). Preoccupation with success or failure can often paralyze any social action or other forms of service, particularly because failure and setback are not unexpected. However, fear of failure and expectation of success are again rooted in our egos. The principle of *wu wei* frees us from these obstacles and enables us to be open to unforeseen consequences, both positive and negative, which we then accept as a natural part of the process of change. We accept things, come what may, and do not try to control a process that we can only facilitate through our detached participation in it. We become what St. Francis of Assisi describes as "instruments of peace." Finally, *wu wei* enables us to be gentle with ourselves with respect to expectations we have about our own effectiveness as social change agents. We learn to balance our actions between too much or too little effort. We adopt patience and trust in a process of change as it unfolds, seemingly of its own accord. We rest comfortable in our confidence that along with setbacks and failures there will also be successes, no matter how seemingly small.

The Painful Truth about Neoliberalism

Encounters with the necessity and inescapability of suffering, though sometimes taken to be a grim and undesirable truth, offer another advantage in demystifying suffering and encouraging action in opposition to oppression. They provide a potent challenge to the pretensions of neoliberalism and can weaken its grip on the consciousness of those under its sway. They provide irrefutable evidence that negates the claim that the aim of life, maximum happiness, is attainable. They belie all attempts to elevate the ego as an absolute. The tragic triad of our mortality, finitude, and fallibility validate the Buddha's assertion that life is suffering. There are persistent "problems" that cannot be fixed by all the power at neoliberalism's disposal. There are things that cannot be helped by fancy and expensive commodities, the latest cures, smooth-talking politicians, and smug experts with impressive credentials. One persuasive way to illustrate how our obsession with fixing things and misplacing our faith in science and technology to overcome the major maladies afflicting humans is to critically examine the example of the prevalent obsession in our society with finding cures.

Every year immense amounts of time, effort, and resources are poured into research devoted to finding cures for the major causes of death and disability. There is a veritable army of individuals working for a host of organizations that make ceaseless pleas for contributions to put an end to almost any disease one might imagine. Advertisements seek to convince millions of people that they suffer from a malady that can be either improved or cured by a drug or medical procedure that brings billions of dollars of profits to the drug and health care industry. While a number of those committed to this cause might be genuine in their desire to serve humanity, much of this effort is misguided. Even worse, it is often motivated more by economic gain and the craving for fame and acclaim.

A very cogent and convincing critique of efforts aimed at eliminating disease is made by James Fries (Fries, 1980, 2005; Fries & Crapo, 1981). He observes the shift in major causes of death away from infectious diseases at the turn of the 20th century to what are now chronic diseases—in particular coronary heart disease, cancer, and cardiovascular disease. The treatment of chronic diseases makes up 75% of health care costs in the United States (McDaniel & deGruy, 2014). These elevated costs are due in part to a greater number of older adults. However, another neglected factor is people developing symptoms related to these diseases early in life and experiencing impaired health for an extended period of time due to living longer. This results in a wide range of health care expenses. Fries also presents statistical data illustrating that while progress has been made in recent years in decreasing premature death and expanding the human lifespan, there is a limit to what further gains can be made. The lifespan of human beings is finite because of the development of some disease or other that ultimately causes death.

The crux of Fries' argument, however, is that the previously mentioned three major causes of death ultimately have their basis in an inevitable natural process. They are diseases of aging. As individuals grow older, for example, the process of atherosclerosis and the loss of organ reserve give rise to biological changes that are incremental and universal. These changes are then reflected in the progressive development of chronic diseases over individuals' lifespan. At some point these changes cross a clinical threshold and manifest as clinical symptoms. What has become alarming in recent years is that over time, these clinical symptoms are appearing earlier and earlier in the lifespan. As a result, people suffer the adverse consequences of these diseases for a longer period of time with an associated decline in their well-being and quality of life and a corresponding increase in health care costs.

In light of these diseases being a product of aging, unlike the case of infectious diseases, the likelihood of finding cures for chronic diseases is quite slim. There is no cure for aging. It is, as the Buddha observed so long ago, a source of suffering that is inevitable. However, as Fries also points out, in addition to the role played by these incremental biological changes, a combination of behavioral, social, and environmental factors has been found to accelerate the deleterious course of these progressive diseases. These factors include diet, levels of physical activity, exposure to environmental toxins, and environmental stress. Signs of atherosclerosis are now starting to be found in individuals in their teenage years (something that is not natural but attributable to behavioral, social, and environmental causes). These factors are not effectively or adequately addressed by the current biological determinism and dualistic view of mind and body central to the medical model. There is no drug, no medical procedure, and no "cure" that medicine can offer to eliminate or ameliorate these contributing factors. And so, even as the search for a cure goes on and the health care and drug companies reap increasing profits, people are getting sicker and sicker.

Millions of persons are experiencing a much longer period of morbidity or individual impairment and distress. This diminished quality of life is preventable if we are willing to question the sacred assumptions on which the medical model is based and willing to stop profiting by people's misery. What Fries argues for is that more attention and a greater devotion of resources be placed on the compression of morbidity, such that individuals develop symptoms much later in life—at a time when these changes would happen more naturally in the absence of avoidable risk factors. This could be achieved by the creation and implementation of wide-ranging prevention programs directed at removing or ameliorating the behavioral, social, and environmental risk factors for chronic disease (see also Albee, 1982, 1990).

As we have seen in the previous discussion of the social determinants of health and the rise of medicalization, however, there are powerful economic and political forces responsible for the presence of those risk factors because they benefit the wealthy and the powerful. Under neoliberalism virtually all the money spent on health care is devoted to treating disease after the fact—although prevention has been demonstrated to be more cost effective as well as more efficacious in enhancing the quality of individuals' lives (Prilleltensky, 2012). It is no surprise, therefore, that despite so much money being spent on providing this form of care, the health care outcomes that result are not commensurate with this expenditure (Nordal, 2012).

The sad truth is that this is one instance of many showing that the powerful and privileged would rather sacrifice human lives than forsake the neoliberal myths from which they so richly benefit. This pattern of false promises and invented fears illustrated in the futile promise of cures where none can be found has been employed in waging wars for profit, defeating efforts aimed at sensible gun control laws, and passing unjust legislation designed to fill prisons run for profit. Only when the immense and unnecessary suffering caused by these injustices is recognized clearly for what it is and allowed to deeply trouble those who come to this recognition will the destructive lies of neoliberalism be exposed. These are the painful truths that can stir compassion and inspire the end of oppression and the restoration of justice.

You Don't Have to Go It Alone

The preceding discussion of the three steps moving from disillusionment to liberation may seem to imply that they occur solely on the level of the individual, but this cannot be the case if there is to be any hope for real change. Actually, regarding this process as a matter solely of personal responsibility exposes one of the most destructive assumptions of neoliberal hegemony—its extreme view of individualism. Critical Psychology has been an outspoken critic of this viewpoint. It has also highlighted the adverse effects of the adoption of this view by psychology and others who claim they are committed to promoting well-being. We have seen how the depiction of human beings as autonomous, independent, bounded, and self-reliant exerts pressure on them to conform to such expectations. Those who fail to comply with these neoliberal values are labeled deviant or disordered (Esposito & Perez, 2014). To the contrary, this rejection of the societal nature of human beings as something that distinguishes them from all other species is the actual distortion and a cause of a host of problems. It results in "worldless" individuals and ultimately contributes to dehumanization by failing to acknowledge the vital relationship that exists between human beings to the world and others (Schraube & Osterkamp, 2013).

There is no facet of human experience that can be abstracted from the social context in which individuals live. Their thoughts, beliefs, values, and actions are grounded within a complex web of relationships. Nonetheless, while social circumstances play a significant role in shaping human beings, Critical Psychology balances this with a strong affirmation of human agency and subjectivity that enables human beings to affirm, produce, or transform the conditions under which they live. Rather than situating agency solely within individuals, it offers an expanded view of agency that is defined as mediating between the individual and society. It allows individuals to gain control over their life conditions in cooperation with others who seek to do likewise.

The crippling impact that the extreme version of individualism asserted by neoliberalism has had, and the many ways in which it has contributed to the creation and maintenance of oppression, must be among the most important illusions to be exposed and abandoned in the pursuit of liberation. As noted above, demystification is the beginning of a process that brings individuals to the realization that there is a great deal of suffering for which they are not responsible. It also reveals that, contrary to hegemonic assertions, the onus does not fall solely on them to ameliorate their suffering or fix their problems. However, to leave the matter at that is not enough to help individuals throw off the shackles of neoliberal ideology. Long accustomed to experiencing themselves as isolated, separated, abandoned, and at odds with their fellow human beings, the prospect of being-with others or joining together collectively to resolve shared problems will feel foreign and frightening. Recognizing the dangers posed to the status quo if the many undergoing oppression come to realize their common plight and shared enemy, the ruling elite devises multiple strategies designed to defeat a shared consciousness, such as class consciousness, and to turn fragmented groups against one another. The potential for the suffering shared by the oppressed to promote solidarity, mutual understanding, and care for one another will, once again, require that this suffering be named, claimed, and reframed

Many thinkers make democracy a condition for social justice (Friere, 1970; Nussbaum, 2006; Sen, 1999; Young, 1990). This upholding of the value of democracy is based on recognition of the essentially social nature of human beings. This insight can be found in the work of John Dewey (1916), who saw that democracy was more than just a form of government, but a means by which human beings lived in community with others. He saw it as the ultimate ethical ideal of humanity, writing,

> A democracy is more than a form of government; it is primarily a mode of associated living, of conjoint communicated experience. The extension in space of the number of individuals who participate in an interest so that each has to refer his own action to that of others, and to consider the action of others to give point and direction to his own, is equivalent to the breaking down of those barriers of class, race, and national territory

which kept men from perceiving the full import of their activity. (p. 87)

Democracy depends upon the establishment and maintenance of a more egalitarian relationship between members of a society that allows for true cooperation and collaboration. A hierarchy that privileges one form of knowledge or way of being to the exclusion of all others and accords one group with possession of power and privilege is clearly anti-democratic and opens the way for abuses of power and other forms of injustice. This harkens back to the importance of dialogue to liberation asserted by Friere (1970).

Dialogue is a mode of relating in which the agency and humanity of all participants is recognized, allowing for mutual respect, trust, faith, concern, and openness. This breaks down the barriers fueled by fear, suspicion, antagonism, and competition fostered by neoliberalism. As participants embrace their interdependence with others, they realize that all their actions have societal as well as personal consequences. Accompanying this is a realization that meeting one's needs and coming to terms with the demands of life requires cooperation with others. Determining the conditions of one's life can never be done independently and can only be fully realized together with others in a way in which the agency and dignity of all is respected.

The role of democracy in this process is to ensure that all members of society have the right and opportunity to participate in public discussion, deliberation, and decision-making through institutions made available for this and to thus decide collectively the goals and rules that will guide their actions (Young, 1990). This process respects self-determination as a cornerstone of freedom, while also making possible decisions that are more likely to promote just outcomes because dialogue encourages full and equal participation and maximizes the contribution of knowledge and perspectives that lead to the development of sound and inclusive social policy.

Critical Psychology (Osterkamp, 2009; Schraube & Osterkamp, 2013) has made valuable and needed contributions to the need to correct the extant view of the relationship between individual and society in order to expose the damaging influence of capitalism. Neoliberal ideology paradoxically so exaggerates the power of the individual that it subsequently leads to the formation of a shallow and fragile narcissism, while at the same time casting the environment as posing demands to which individuals must passively adapt. The result is what is described as *restrictive agency.* Important psychological functions that influence human behavior—such as motivations, thoughts and emotions—are described within neoliberal ideology as the result of passively putting up or coming to terms with external environmental conditions.

This viewpoint is then extended to the necessity for persons to adjust to prevailing power relations and exercise freedom only within the limits of what is permitted by authorities. This depiction is not an objective statement of facts derived through scientific study but is due to individuals living under historical conditions characterized by the antagonistic class relations of capitalist society. Thus, asserting one's agency in opposition to the power structure risks exposing oneself to conflict with those in authority. The result is that individuals have little choice but to accept the oppressive conditions under which they live and see it as the only channel by means of which to secure their own immediate advantage while evading punishment or censure.

Despite believing that this submission will secure benefits and meet their needs, individuals experience various undesirable consequences as well. Acting in a way that accepts societal restrictions demonstrates complicity with prevailing power relations. It also confirms and reinforces dependency. This is accompanied by suffering that is rooted not merely in not having one's needs met but being deprived of the means of meeting those needs due to dependency on others. This confirmation of dependency also elevates the importance of securing of short-term satisfaction over the possibility of achieving long-term goals and interests that are perceived as beyond one's control. Feeling at the mercy of others is an injury to individuals' sense of agency. With their capacity for either self-determination or cooperative pursuit of shared needs and interests thus undermined, individuals are willing to settle for whatever satisfaction they can secure, no matter how meager or insecure.

Another basic element of restrictive agency is that should individuals become aware of being complicit with existing power relations and engaging in competitive relations with others, they experience fulfilling their needs or achieving their goals as coming at the expense of others. This results in what Critical Psychology calls *guilt discourse.* There is an equating of the actions of these individuals with personal motivations that cast them as selfish and immoral. This equating of intention and action is a form of mystification because it veils the actual working of neoliberal ideology in individuals' engagement in restrictive agency. This experience is painful and based on either–or thinking in which one either is innocent and deserves rewards allotted by society or bad and deserving of recrimination. Thus, individuals seek to rid themselves of this guilt by projecting wrongdoing or immorality on others.

The production of guilt serves ideological purposes. It leads people to neglect the inherently complex and ambiguous nature of determining the grounds for one's actions. They fail to see the necessity of situating that process as a metasubjective one that involves others besides oneself. Causing people to focus on their guilt places excessive accountability on the individual and obscures the more significant role of ideology in forcing people to frame choices as win–lose situations. Finally, encouraging people to feel the need to win out over others every time they make a choice undermines the possibility of forming alliances with them and working with them to achieve critical consciousness and oppose oppression.

When people experience themselves as suffering from social causes due to the specific human vulnerability of dependency on others to fulfill their needs, they experience humiliation, shame, insecurity, and resentment. These feelings may cause them to retreat from communication and cooperation with others for fear of further injury. However, this means of resolving the situation serves only to confirm the very ideology responsible for their suffering—an ideology that denies their societal nature. Because that ideology has so thoroughly saturated their consciousness and because the costs of exposing it are so high, they cannot help but participate in it while also being afraid of recognizing this. Each time this occurs, the suffering remains mystified and thus not critically examined. Unjust power relations are normalized and justified. More than ever it is essential that individuals remain present to that suffering—whether it manifests itself as fear, shame, guilt, or anger—but also reach out to others. Restrictive conditions can only be overcome in communion and cooperation with others.

In opposition to restrictive agency and guilt discourse, Critical Psychology urges the adoption of *generalized agency* and *reason discourse*—both of which restore the interdependent relationship between human agency and societality. Generalized agency asserts the possibility for human beings to jointly determine the life conditions to which they are subjected and to engage together in critical reflection in order to grasp the conflicts and contradictions posed by neoliberalism. Interpreting one's actions as not solely motivated by personal responsibility is facilitated by engaging in reason discourse with others who are impacted by those actions. Generalized agency acknowledges that all individuals seeking to engage in a self-determined life and the pursuit of personal interests will in the process sometimes contribute to the oppression of others.

Through reason discourse there can be open communication with fellow human beings about how they also find themselves in similar circumstances and experiencing similar emotional reactions. This lifts the understanding achieved out of the narrow confines of restrictive agency and enhances the ability of those in dialogue to become aware of the ideological reasons for the ways in which they participate in these relations with others. Rather than stopping at the realization that one acts solely based on his or her own private interests, individuals utilize the human capacity to transcend the immediate situation and gain critical distance from their experience. This allows them to recognize how they may sometimes unwittingly negate others' subjectivity without immediately passing judgment upon themselves for this.

In the previous discussions of self-deception and mystification, suspension of the critical function and the subsequent tendency to adopt a narrow and overly literal state of consciousness were identified as playing an integral role in these processes. This uncritical stance is often combined with a preoccupation with locating reasons and causes for human action solely within isolated and bounded individuals who exist apart from others and independent of context. Methods such as traditional psychotherapy, unfortunately, often operate within this framework. Ironically, they extol the importance of making individuals more self-aware as a means of attaining insights that will resolve their suffering while neglecting the equal importance of making them socially aware. The "self" of which clients are being made aware is a highly constricted one and an artifact of the extreme individualism of neoliberal ideology. The "reasons" uncovered thus more often than not lead individuals to blame themselves while hiding and excusing the larger role played by ideology. Small (2005) proposes a greater emphasis be placed on the development of "outsight," or a deepened awareness of the role that material conditions and power relations play in causing distress and harm. This puts the degree of responsibility of individuals in perspective and results in a realistic grasp of what is and is not under their direct control.

Critical Psychology helps to resolve this shortcoming by providing the conceptual tools to recognize the societal reality of one's own and others' actions. While seeking to discern the reasons and grounds for their own actions, individuals also accept and seek to understand the reasons and grounds for the actions of others. Placing actions within the multiple contexts in which they occur and which influence them, may present individuals with a more complex and ambiguous picture of how choices are made. It also exposes the harmful misconceptions spawned by an overly simplistic approach. It enables all involved in dialogue to move past judgment and condemnation. It breaks down isolation and antagonism and promotes mutual respect and trust. Ultimately, this encourages a more compassionate stance as well as one that moves people beyond focusing solely on their own suffering and connecting with the suffering of others. The ground has been laid for people to work together for justice.

As the ravages of neoliberalism continue unabated, the circumstances of human beings who seek to live a life of decency and be treated with dignity and respect continue to worsen. Oppression does not only continue to devastate lives and destroy the environment on which our survival depends but extends its deadly reach into ever more areas of life. The growing magnitude of morally indefensible degrees of inequality and disproportionate distribution of power and privilege add more and more individuals to those who are marginalized, exploited, dominated, damaged, and excluded. Suffering that is unnecessary and unquestionably unjust mounts each day. That suffering can be intimidating, terrifying, and overwhelming—these are reactions we must accept. But what we cannot accept is that suffering goes unheeded and unattended. It can be something that bonds us and that urges us to take action to launch meaningful opposition if we take care not to make the mistake of facing and opposing it alone. As the Labor Party leader in the United Kingdom, Jeremy Corbyn constantly seeks to remind his followers, "We are the many; they are the few." To his encouraging observation, I would add that we have the two most powerful forces for good on our side—justice and compassion. Let us together take up these banners and turn the tides of oppression.

References

Ahmed, S. (2010). *The promise of happiness.* Durham, NC: Duke University Press.

Aho, K. (2008). Medicalizing mental health: A phenomenological alternative. *Journal of Medical Humanities, 29,* 243–259.

Albee, G. W. (1982). Preventing psychopathology and promoting human potential. *American Psychologist, 37*(9), 1043–1050.

Albee, G. W. (1990). The futility of psychotherapy. *Journal of Mind and Behavior, 11,* 369–374.

Antonovsky, A. (1987). *Unraveling the mystery of health.* San Francisco, CA: Jossey-Bass.

Assagioli, R. (1965). *Psychosynthesis: A manual of principles and techniques.* New York, NY: The Viking Press.

Augoustinos, M. (1999). Ideology, false consciousness and psychology. *Theory & Psychology, 9* (3), 295–312.

Ayers, A. J., & Saad-Filho, A. (2015). Democracy against neoliberalism: Paradoxes, limitations, transcendence. *Critical Sociology, 41*(4–5), 597-618.

Bakan, D. (1968). *Disease, pain, and sacrifice: Toward a psychology of suffering.* Chicago, IL: Beacon Press.

Baker, E., & Newnes, C. (2005). The discourse of responsibility. In C. Newnes & N. Radcliffe (Eds.), *Making and breaking children's lies* (pp. 30–39). Ross-on-Rye, UK: PCCS Books, Ltd.

Bandura, A. (1997). *Self-efficacy: The exercise of control.* New York, NY: W. H. Freeman.

Barrett, W. (1964). *What is existentialism?* New York, NY: Grove Press.

Barry B. (2005). *Why social justice matters.* Cambridge, MA: Polity Press.

Bateson, G., Jackson, D. D., Haley, J., & Weakland, J. H. (1956). Toward a theory of schizophrenia. *Behavioral Science, 1,* 251–264.

Beauchamp, D. E. (2003). Public health as social justice. In R. Hofrichter (Ed.), *Health and social justice: Politics, ideology, and inequity in the distribution of disease* (pp. 267–284). San Francisco, CA: Jossey-Bass.

Becker, E. (1973). *The denial of death.* New York, NY: Simon & Schuster.

Bentham, J. (1988). *The principles of morals and legislation.* Amherst, NY: Prometheus Books.

Biglan, A. (2015). *The nurture effect.* Oakland, CA: New Harbinger Publications, Inc.

Binswanger, L. (1963). *Being-in-the-world* (J. Needleman, Trans.). New York, NY: Basic Books.

Boggs, C. (2015). The medicalized society. *Critical Sociology, 4*(3), 517–535.

Bourdieu. P. (1998). *On television.* (P. Pankhurst Ferguson, Trans.). New York, NY: The New Press.

Brinton, C. (1931). Equality. *Encyclopedia of the social sciences* (Vol. 5). New York, NY: Macmillan.

Bronfenbrenner, U. (1979). *The ecology of human development: Experiments by nature and design.* Cambridge, MA: Harvard University Press.

Bronfenbrenner, U. (1989). Ecological systems theory. *Annals of Child Development, 6,* 187–249.

Brown, W. (2006). American nightmare: Neoliberalism, neoconservatism, and de-demoncratization. *Political Theory, 34*(6), 690-714.

Brown, B., & Baker, S. (2013). *Responsible citizens.* London, UK: Anthem Press.

Brown, W. (2006). American nightmare: Neoliberalism, neoconservatism, and de-democratization. *Political Theory, 34*(6), 690–714.

Burr, V., & Dick, P. (2017). Social constructionism. In B. Gough (Ed.), *The Palgrave handbook of critical social psychology* (pp. 59–80). London, UK: PalgraveMacmillan.

Byrne, D. (2002). *Social exclusion.* Buckingham, UK: Open University Press.

Calhoun, L. G., & Tedeschi, R. G. (1999). *Facilitating posttraumatic growth: A clinician's guide.* Mahwah, NJ: Lawrence Erlbaum.

Cassell, E. J. (1991). *The nature of suffering and the goals of medicine.* New York, NY: Oxford University Press.

Cassell, E, J. (1999). Diagnosing suffering: A perspective. *Annals of Internal Medicine, 131*(7), 531–534.

Chang, H. (2010). *Twenty-three things they don't tell you about capitalism.* New York, NY: Bloomsbury Press.

Chapman, C. (2013). Cultivating a troubled consciousness: Compulsory sound-mindedness and complicity in oppression. *Health, Culture and Society, 5*(1), 182-198.

Chetty, R., Grusky, D., Hell, M., Hendren, N., Manduka, R., & Narang, J. (2017). The fading American dream: Trends in absolute income mobility since 1940. *Science, 356,* 398–406.

Chomsky, N. (1999). *Profit over people: Neoliberalism and global order.* New York, NY: Seven Stories Press.

Chomsky, N. (2002). *Media control: The spectacular achievements of propaganda* (2nd ed.). New York, NY: Seven Stories Press.

Cohen, L. (2003). *A consumer's republic: The politics of mass consumption in post-war America.* New York, NY: Alfred A. Knopf.

Cohen, S. (2001). *States of denial: Knowing about atrocities and suffering.* Cambridge, MA: Polity Press.

Cole, B. S., & Pargament, K. I. (1999). Spiritual surrender: A paradoxical path to control. In W. M. Miller (Ed.), *Integrating spirituality into treatment: Resources for practitioners* (pp. 179–198). Washington, DC: American Psychological Association.

Combs, A. (2002). *The radiance of being: Understanding the grand integral vision; living the integral life* (2nd ed.). St Paul, MN: Paragon House.

Combs, A. (2009). *Consciousness explained better: Toward an integral understanding of the multifaceted nature of consciousness.* St. Paul, MN: Paragon House.

Compton, M. T., & Shim, R. S. (Eds.). (2015). *The social determinants of mental health.* Washington, DC: American Psychiatric Publishing.

Conrad, P., & Barker, K. K. (2010). The social construction of illness: Key insights and policy implications. *Journal of Health and Social Behavior, 51*(5), 67–79.

Crabtree, A. (1993). *From Mesmer to Freud: Magnetic sleep and the roots of psychological healing.* New Haven, CT: Yale University Press.

Crocker, D. A. (1992). Functioning and capability: The foundations of Sen's and Nussbaum's development ethic. *Political Theory, 20*(4), 584–612.

Csikszentmihalyi, M. (1999). If we are so rich, why aren't we happy? *American Psychologist, 54*, 821–827.

Cudd, A. (2006). *Analyzing oppression.* New York, NY: Oxford University Press.

Cushman, P. (1990). Why the self is empty: Toward a historically situated psychology. *American Psychologist, 45*(5), 599–611.

Cutter, S. L. (2006). (Ed.). *Hazards, vulnerability, and environmental justice.* London, UK: Earthscan.

Dabrowski, K. (1964). *Positive disintegration.* London, UK: Little, Brown.

Dabrowski, K. (1967). *Personality shaping through positive disintegration.* Boston, MA: Little, Brown.

Dass, R., & Gorman, R. (1985). *How can I help?: Stories and reflections on service.* New York, NY: Alfred A. Knopf.

David, E. J. R. (Ed.). (2014). *Internalized oppression: The psychology of marginalized groups.* New York, NY: Springer Publishing Company.

David, E. J. R., & Derthick, A. E. (2014). What is internalized oppression, and so what? In E. J. R. David (Ed.), *Internalized oppression: The psychology of marginalized groups* (pp. 1–30). New York, NY: Springer Publishing Company.

Day, K., Rickett, B., & Woolhouse, M. (2014). Class dismissed: Putting social class on the critical psychological agenda. *Social and Personality Psychology Compass, 8*(8), 397–407.

Debord, G. (1994). *The society of the spectacle* (D. Nicholson-Smith, Trans.). New York, NY: Zone Press.

Deikman, A. (1976). Bimodal consciousness and the mystic experience. In P. R. Lee, R. E. Ornstein, D. Galin, A. Deikman, & C. Tart, *Symposium on consciousness* (pp. 67–88). New York, NY: Penguin Books.

Deutsch, M. (2006). A framework for thinking about oppression and its change. *Social Justice Research, 19*(1), 7–41.

Dewey, J. (1916). *Democracy and education.* New York, NY: The Free Press.

DiMaggio, A. R. (2015). Class sub-conscious: Hegemony, false consciousness, and the development of political and economic policy attitudes. *Critical Sociology, 41*(3), 493–516.

Du Bois, W. E. B. (1969). *The souls of black folk.* New York, NY: New American Library.

Ellenberger, H. F. (1970). *The discovery of the unconscious: The history and evolution of dynamic psychiatry.* New York, NY: Basic Books.

Engels, F. (1892/1943). *The condition of the working class in England in 1844* (F. K. Wischnewetzky, Trans.). London, UK: George Allen and Unwin.

Erickson, E. (1950). *Childhood and society.* New York, NY: Norton

Erickson, M. H., Rossi, E. L., & Rossi, S. I. (1976). Hypnotic realities. New York, NY: John Wiley and Sons.

Esposito, L., & Perez, F. M. (2014). Neoliberalism and the commodification of mental health. *Humanity & Society, 38*(4), 414–442.

Evans, G. W. (2004). The environment of childhood poverty. *American Psychologist, 59*(2), 77–92.

Evans, G. W., & Cassells, R. C. (2014). Childhood poverty, cumulative risk exposure, and mental health in emerging adults. *Clinical Psychological Science, 2*(3), 287–296.

Fanon, F. (1963). *The wretched of the earth* (C. Farrington, Trans.). New York, NY: Grove Press.

Fanon, F. (1967). *Black skin, White masks* (C. Farrington, Trans.). New York, NY: Grove Press.

Foreman, M. D. (2010). *A guide to integral psychotherapy: Complexity, integration, and spirituality in practice.* Albany, NY: State University of New York Press.

Foucault, M. (1999/1975). *Discipline and punishment: The birth of the prison* (A. Sheridan, Trans.). New York, NY: Vintage/Random House.

Fox, M. (1972). *On becoming a musical, mystical bear: Spirituality American style.* New York, NY: Paulist Press.

Fox, M. (1995). *Wrestling with the prophets: Essays on creation spirituality and everyday life.* San Francisco, CA: HarperCollins.

Frank, A. W. (2001). Can we research suffering? *Qualitative Health Research, 11*(3), 353–362.

Frankena, W. K. (1962). The concept of social justice. In R. B. Brandt (Ed.), *Social justice* (pp. 1–29). Englewood Cliffs, NJ: Prentice-Hall.

Frankl, V. E. (1953). *The doctor and the soul: From psychotherapy to logotherapy* (R. & C. Winston, Trans.). New York, NY: Bantam.

Frankl, V. E. (1959). *Man's search for meaning.* New York, NY: Simon & Schuster.

Frankl, V. E. (1967). *Psychotherapy and existentialism: Selected papers on logotherapy.* New York, NY: Simon & Schuster.

Fraser, N. (1997). *Justice interruptus: Critical reflections on the "postsocialist" condition.* New York, NY: Routledge.

Freud, S. (1920). *A general introduction to psychoanalysis.* New York, NY: Washington Square Press.

Freud, S. (1959). A case of successful treatment with hypnotism: With some remarks on the origins of hysterical symptoms through counterwill. In *Collected papers, Volume Five,* (pp. 32–46). New York, NY: Basic Books.

Freud, S. (1961). *Beyond the pleasure principle.* New York, NY: W. W. Norton.

Friedman, M. (1980). *Free to choose.* New York, NY: Harcourt Brace Jovanovich.

Friere, P. (1970). *Pedagogy of the oppressed.* New York, NY: Herder and Herder.

Fries, J. F. (1980). Aging, natural death, and the compression of morbidity. *New England Journal of Medicine, 303,* 130–135.

Fries, J. F. (2005). The compression of morbidity. *The Milbank Quarterly, 83*(4), 801–823.

Fries, J. F., & Crapo, L. M. (1981). *Vitality and aging: Implications of the rectangular curve.* San Francisco, CA: W. H. Freeman.

Fromm, E. (1941). *Escape from freedom.* New York, NY: Henry Holt.

Fromm, E. (1947). *Man for himself: An inquiry into the psychology of ethics.* New York, NY: Holt, Rinehart, & Winston.

Fromm, E. (1955). *The sane society.* Greenwich, CT: Fawcett Publications, Inc.

Fromm, E. (1960). Psychoanalysis and Zen Buddhism. In D. T. Suzuki, E. Fromm, & R. DeMartino, *Zen Buddhism and psychoanalysis* (pp. 77–141). New York, NY: Grove Press.

Fromm, E. (1964). *The heart of man: Its genius for good and evil.* New York, NY: Harper & Row.

Fromm, E. (1976). *To have or to be?* New York, NY: Harper & Row.

Fromm, E. (1986). *For the love of life* (R. & R. Kimber, Trans.). New York, NY: The Free Press.

Furedi, F. (2005). *Politics of fear.* New York, NY: Continuum.

Galton, F. (1892). *Hereditary genius: An inquiry into its laws and consequences.* London, UK: Macmillan.

Garcia-Remeu, A. P., & Tart, C. T. (2013). Altered states of consciousness and transpersonal psychology. In H. L. Friedman & G. Hartelius, (Eds.), *The Wiley-Blackwell handbook of transpersonal psychology* (pp. 121–140). Chichester, UK: John Wiley & Sons.

Gewirth, A. (1962). Political justice. In R. B. Brandt (Ed.), *Social justice* (pp. 119-169). Englewood Cliffs, NJ: Prentice-Hall.

Gibson, J. (2015). A relational approach to suffering: A reappraisal of suffering in the helping relationship. *Journal of Humanistic Psychology, 55*(1), 1–20.

Giroux, H. A. (2008). *Against the terror of neoliberalism: Politics beyond the age of greed.* Boulder, CO: Paradigm Publisher.

Glaude Jr., E. S. (2016). *Democracy in black: How race still enslaves the American soul.* New York, NY: Crown Publishing.

Goldberg, C. (1995). The daimonic development of the malevolent personality. *Journal of Humanistic Psychology, 35*(3), 7–36.

Goldberg, C., & Crespo, V. (2003). Suffering and personal agency. *International Journal of Psychotherapy, 8*(2), 85–93.

Goldstein, K. (1963). *The organism: A holistic approach to biology from pathological data in man.* Boston, MA: Beacon.

Goleman, D. (1985). *Vital lies, simple truths: The psychology of self-deception.* New York, NY: Simon and Schuster.

Goodman, D. J. (2001). *Promoting diversity and social justice: Educating people from privileged groups.* Thousand Oaks, CA: Sage.

Goodman, I. A., Liang, B., Helms, J. E., Latta, R. E., Sparks, E., & Weintraub, S. R. (2004). Training counseling psychologists as social justice agents: Feminist and multicultural principles in action. *The Counseling Psychologist, 32,* 793–837.

Gotham, K. F. (2007). Critical theory and Katrina: Disaster, spectacle and immanent critique. *City, 11*(1), 81–99.

Gramsci, A. (1971). *Selections from the prison notebooks* (Q. Hoare & G. Nowell Smith, Trans.). New York, NY: International Publishers.

Gray, J. (1995). *Liberalism* (2nd ed.). Buckingham, UK: Open University Press.

Green, E., & Green, A. (1978). *Beyond biofeedback.* New York, NY: Delacorte Press.

Greene, T. W. (2008). Three ideologies of individualism: Toward assimilating a theory of individualisms and their consequences. *Critical Sociology, 34*(1), 117–137.

Greenwald, A. (1980). The totalitarian ego: Fabrication and revision of personal history. *American Psychologist, 35*(7), 603–618.

Grossman, D. (1995). *On killing: The psychological cost of learning to kill in war and society.* New York, NY: Little, Brown & Company.

Gruba-McCallister, F. P. (1992). Becoming self through suffering: The Irenaean theodicy and advanced development. *Advanced Development, 4,* 49–58.

Gruba-McCallister, F. P. (1993). The imp of the reverse: A phenomenology of the unconscious. *Journal of Religion and Health, 32*(2), 107–120.

Gruba-McCallister, F. P. (2002). Education through compassion: The cultivation of the prophetic contemplative. In J. Mills (Ed.), *A pedagogy of becoming* (pp. 73–92). New York, NY: Rodopi Press.

Gruba-McCallister, F. P. (2007). Narcissism and the empty self: To have or to be. *The Journal of Individual Psychology, 63*(2), 182–192.

Gruba-McCallister, F. P., & Levington, C. (1995). Suffering and transcendence in human experience. *Review of Existential Psychology and Psychiatry, 22,* 99–115.

Hamilton, M. B. (1987). The elements of the concept of ideology. *Political Studies, 35,* 18–38.

Harris, L. T., & Fiske, S. (2006). Dehumanizing the lowest of the low: Neuroimaging responses to extreme out-groups. *Psychological Science, 17*(10), 847–853.

Harvey, D. (2005). *A brief history of neoliberalism.* New York, NY: Oxford University Press.

Harvey, J. (2000). Social privilege and moral subordination. *Journal of Social Philosophy, 31*(2), 177–188,

Harvey, J. (2010). Victims, resistance, and civilized oppression. *Journal of Social Philosophy, 41*(1), 13–27.

Hayek, F. A. (1944). *The road to serfdom.* London, UK: Routledge.

Hebblethwaite, B. (1976). *Evil, suffering and religion.* New York, NY: Hawthorne Books, Inc.

Heidegger, M. (1978). *Being and time* (J. Macquarrie & E. Robinson, Trans.). Oxford, UK: Basil Blackwell. (Original work published in 1927)

Held, D. (1980). *Introduction to critical theory: Horkheimer to Habermas.* Berkeley, CA: University of California Press.

Helsel, P. B. (2009). Simone Weil's passion mysticism: The paradox of chronic pain and the transformation of the cross. *Pastoral Psychology, 58,* 55-63.

Hick, J. (1989). *An interpretation of religion: Human responses to the transcendent.* New Haven, CT: Yale University Press.

Hick, J. (2007). *Evil and the God of love.* New York, NY: Palgrave MacMillan.

Hilgard, E. R. (1986). *Divided consciousness: Multiple controls in human thought and action.* New York, NY: Wiley.

Hofrichter, R. (2003). The politics of health inequities: Contested terrains. In R. Hofrichter (Ed.), *Health and social justice: Politics, ideology, and inequity in the distribution of disease* (pp. 1–56). San Francisco, CA: Jossey-Bass.

hooks, b. (2000). *Where we stand: Class matters.* New York, NY: Routledge.

Horkheimer, M., & Adorno, T. (1995). *Dialectic of enlightenment* (J. Cumming, Trans.). New York, NY: Herder & Herder. (Original work published in 1944)

Husserl, E. (1962). *Ideas: General introduction to pure phenomenology* (W. R. Boyce Gibson, Trans.). New York, NY: Collier Books.

Huxley, A. (1932). *Brave new world.* New York, NY: Bantam.

Huxley, A. (1944). *The perennial philosophy.* New York, NY: Harper.

Ingersoll, R. E., & Zeitler, D. M. (2010). *Integral psychotherapy: Inside out/outside in.* Albany, NY: State University of New York Press.

Isenberg, N. (2016). *White trash: The 400-year untold history of class in America.* New York, NY: Viking Press.

Jacobs, D. H. (1994). Environmental failure-oppression is the only cause of psychopathology. *Journal of Mind and Behavior, 15*(1–2), 1–18.

Jacobs, D. H., & Cohen, D. (2009). Does "psychological dysfunction" mean anything? A critical essay on pathology versus agency. *Journal of Humanistic Psychology, 50*(3), 312–334.

James, W. (1958). *The varieties of religious experience.* New York, NY: New American Library.

James, W. (1959)

James, W. (1981). *The principles of psychology.* Cambridge, MA: Harvard University Press. (Original work published in 1890)

Jaspers, K. (1984). *General psychopathology* (J. Hoenig & M. Hamilton, Trans.). Chicago, IL: University of Chicago Press.

Jensen, K., Vaish, A., & Schmidt, M. F. H. (2014). The emergence of human prosociality: With others through feeling, concerns, and norms. *Frontiers in Psychology, 5,* 1–16.

Joseph, P. (2018). *The new human rights movement: Reinventing the economy to end oppression.* Dallas, TX: BenBella Books, Inc.

Jost, J. T. (2006). The end of the end of ideology. *American Psychologist, 61*(7), 651–670.

Jost, J. T., & Amodio, D. M. (2012). Political ideology as motivated social cognition: Behavioral and neuroscientific evidence. *Motivation and emotion, 36,* 55–64.

Jung, C. G. (1933). *Modern man in search of a soul* (W. S. Dell & C. F. Baynes, Trans.). New York, NY: Harcourt Brace Jovanovich.

Kafka, F. (1958). *The complete Kafka.* New York, NY: Pocket Books.

Kafka, J. S. (1971). Ambiguity and individuation: A critique and reformulation of double-bind theory. *Archives of General Psychiatry, 25,* 232–239.

Kasser, T., & Kanner, A. D. (Eds.). (2004). *Psychology and consumer culture: The struggle for a good life in materialistic world.* Washington, DC: American Psychological Association.

Kasser, T., Ryan, R. M., Couchman, C. E., & Sheldon, K. M. (2004). Materialistic values: Their causes and consequences. In T. Kasser & A. D. Kanner (Eds.), *Psychology and consumer culture: The struggle for a good life in a materialistic world* (pp. 11–28). Washington, DC: American Psychological Association.

Kaufman, C. (2003). *Ideas for action: Relevant theory for radical change.* Cambridge, MA: South End Press.

Kierkegaard, S. (1936). *A Kierkegaard anthology* (R. Bretall, Ed.). New York, NY: Modern Library.

Kierkegaard, S. (1941). *The sickness unto death* (W. Kaufman, Trans.). Princeton, NJ: Princeton University Press.

Kierkegaard, S. (1948). *The gospel of suffering and the lilies of the field* (D. W. Swenson & L. M. Swenson, Trans.). Minneapolis, MN: Augsburg Publishing House.

Kierkegaard, S. (1980). *The concept of anxiety* (R. Thompte, Trans.). Princeton, NJ: Princeton University Press.

Kirkmayer, L. J. (2007). Psychotherapy and the cultural concept of the person. *Transcultural Psychiatry, 44*(2), 232–257.

Klein, N. (2008). *The shock doctrine: The rise of disaster capitalism.* New York, NY: Picador.

Kleinman, A. (1988). *The illness narratives: Suffering, healing and the human condition.* New York, NY: Basic Books.

Klinenberg, E. (2002). *Heat wave: A social autopsy of disaster in Chicago.* Chicago, IL: University of Chicago Press.

Koestler, A. (1967). *The ghost in the machine.* Chicago, IL: Henry Regnery.

Kohler, et al. (2017). Greater post-Neolithic wealth disparities in Eurasia than in North America and Mesoamerica. *Nature, 551,* 619–622.

Krieger, N. (2005). (Ed.). *Embodying inequality: Epidemiologic perspectives.* Amityville, NY: Baywood Publishing Company, Inc.

Krugman, P. (2007). *The conscience of a liberal.* New York, NY: W. W. Norton & Company.

Laing, R. D. (1960). *The divided self.* Middlesex, UK: Penguin Books.

Laing, R. D. (1967). *The politics of experience.* New York, NY: Pantheon Books.

Laing, R. D. (1969). *The politics of the family and other essays.* New York, NY: Vintage Books.

Laing, R. D. (1972). *Knots.* New York, NY: Vintage Books.

Lakoff, G. (2002). *Moral politics: How liberals and conservatives think* (2nd Ed.). Chicago, IL: The University of Chicago Press.

Lakoff, G. (2004). *Don't think of an elephant.* White River Junction, VT: Chelsea Green Publishing.

LaMothe, R. (2015). The colonizing realities of neoliberal capitalism. *Pastoral Psychology, 65,* 23–40.

Langman, L. (2015). Why is assent willing? Culture, character and consciousness. *Critical Sociology, 41*(3), 463–481.

Langman, L., & Ryan, M. (2009). Capitalism and the carnival character: The escape from reality. *Critical Sociology, 35*(4), 471–492.

Lasch, C. (1979). *The culture of narcissism: American life in an age of diminishing expectations.* New York, NY: Warner Books Inc.

Laski, M. (1968). *Ecstasy: A study of some secular and religious experiences.* New York, NY: Greenwood Press.

Lazarus, R. S., & Folkman, S. (1984). *Stress, appraisal, and coping.* New York, NY: Springer Publishing.

Legault, S. (2006). *Carry tiger to mountain: The tao of activism and leadership.* Vancouver, CA: Arsenal Pulp Press.

Lerner, M. (1986). *Surplus powerlessness.* Oakland, CA: The Institute for Labor and Mental Health.

Macionis, J. J. (2002). *Society: The basics.* (6th ed.). Upper Saddle River, NJ: Prentice-Hall.

Manders, D. W. (2006). *The hegemony of common sense: Wisdom and mystification in everyday life.* New York, NY: Peter Lang Publishing Inc.

Marmot, M., & Wilkinson, R. G. (Eds.) (2006). *Social determinants of health* (2nd ed.). Oxford, UK: Oxford University Press.

Marx, K., & Engels, F. (1932). *The German ideology.* New York, NY: Vintage Books. (Original work published 1845)

Marx, K. (1978). *The Marx and Engels reader.* New York, NY: Norton.

Maslow, A. H. (1971). *The farther reaches of human nature.* New York, NY: Viking Press.

May, R. (1958). Contributions of existential psychotherapy. In R. May, E. Angel, & H. E. Ellenberger (Eds.), *Existence* (pp. 37–91). Northvale, NJ: Jason Aronson.

May, R. (1981). *Freedom and destiny.* New York, NY: Dell Publishing Co.

McDonald, D. A., Walsh, R., & Shapiro, S. L. (2013). Meditation: Empirical research and future directions. In H. L. Friedman & G. Hartelius, (Eds.), *The Wiley-Blackwell handbook of transpersonal psychology* (pp. 433–458). Chichester, UK: John Wiley & Sons.

McDonald, S. H., & deGruy, F. V. (2014). An introduction to primary care and psychology. *American Psychologist, 69*(4), 325–331.

Mill, J. S. (1998). *Utilitarianism* (R. Crisp, Ed.). Oxford, UK: Oxford University Press. (Original work published 1861)

Miller, D. (1999). *Principles of social justice.* Cambridge, MA: Harvard University Press.

Miller, J. G. (1984). Culture and the development of everyday social explanation. *Journal of Personality and Social Psychology, 46,* 961–978.

Miller, R. B. (2005). Suffering in psychology: The demoralization of psychotherapeutic practice. *Journal of Psychotherapy Integration, 15*(3), 299–336.

Miller, R. B. (2013). Deny no evil, ignore no evil, reframe no evil: Psychology's moral agenda. In A. C. Bohart, B. S. Held, E. Mendelowitz, & K. J. Schneider (Eds.), *Humanity's dark side: Evil, destructive experience, and psychotherapy* (pp. 213–236). Washington, DC: American Psychological Association.

Morgan, D., & Wilkinson, I. (2001). The problem of suffering and the sociological task of theodicy. *European Journal of Social Theory, 4*(2), 199–214.

Mowrer, O. H. (1948). Learning theory and the neurotic paradox. *American Journal of Orthopsychiatry, 18,* 571-610.

Moulyn, A. (1982). *The meaning of suffering: An interpretation of human existence from the viewpoint of time.* Westport, CT: Greenwood Press.

Mullaly, B. (2010). *Challenging oppression and confronting privilege: A critical social work approach* (2nd Ed.). Don Mill, Ontario: Oxford University Press.

Nightingale, D. J., & Cromby, J. (2001). Critical psychology and the ideology of individualism. *Journal of Critical Psychology, Counseling and Psychotherapy, 1*(2), 117–128.

Nouwen, H. J. M. (1972). *The wounded healer: Ministry in contemporary society.* New York, NY: Image Books.

Nordal, K. C. (2012). Healthcare reform: Implications for independent practice. *Professional Psychology: Research and Practice, 43*(6), 535–544.

Nussbaum, M. C. (1992). Human functioning and social justice: In defense of Aristotelian essentialism. *Political Theory, 20*(2), 202–246.

Nussbaum, M. C. (2003). Capabilities as fundamental entitlements: Sen and social justice. *Feminist Economics, 9*(2-3), 33–59.

Nussbaum, M.C. (2004). Beyond the social contract: Capabilities and global justice. *Oxford Development Studies, 32*(1), 3–18.

Nussbaum, M. C. (2006). *Frontiers of justice: Disability, nationality, species membership.* Cambridge, MA: The Belknap Press of Harvard University Press.

O'Brien, D. T. (2014). An evolutionary model of the environmental conditions that shape the development of prosociality. *Evolutionary Psychology, 12*(2), 386–402.

Osterkamp, U. (1999). On psychology, ideology and individual's societal nature. *Theory & Psychology, 9*(3), 379–392.

Ouspensky, P. D. (1941). *In search of the miraculous.* New York, NY: Harcourt, Brace, and World.

Pagels, E. (1988). *Adam, Eve and the serpent.* New York, NY: Random House.

Parker, I. (2007). *Revolution in psychology: Alienation to emancipation.* London, UK: Pluto Press.

Paschall, M. J., & Fishbein, D. H. (2002). Executive cognitive function and aggression: A public health perspective. *Aggression and violent behavior, 7*(3), 215–235.

Peck, M. S. (1983). *People of the lie: The hope for healing human evil.* New York, NY: Simon & Schuster, Inc.

Polanyi, M. (1967). *The tacit dimension.* New York, NY: Doubleday.

Prilleltensky, I. (1989). Psychology and the status quo. *American Psychologist, 44*, 795–802.

Prilleltensky, I. (1997). Values, assumptions, and practices: Assessing the moral implications of psychological discourse and action. *American Psychologist, 52*(5), 517–535.

Prilleltensky, I. (2008). The role of power in wellness, oppression, and liberation: The promise of psychopolitical validity. *Journal of Community Psychology, 36*(2), 116–136.

Prilleltensky, I. (2012). Wellness as fairness. *American Journal of Community Psychology, 49*, 1–12.

Prilleltensky, I., & Gonick, L. (1996). Politics change, oppression remains: On the psychology and politics of oppression. *Political Psychology, 17*, 127–147.

Prilleltensky, I., & Nelson, G. (2002). *Doing psychology critically: Making a difference in diverse settings.* New York, NY: Palgrave Macmillan.

Prilleltensky, I., & Prilleltensky, O. (2006). *Promoting well-being: Linking personal, organizational, and community change.* Hoboken, NJ: John Wiley & Sons, Inc.

Putnam, R. (2000). *Bowling alone: The collapse and revival of American community.* New York, NY: Simon & Schuster.

Radley, A. (2004). Suffering. In M. Murray (Ed.), *Critical health psychology* (pp. 31–43). Houndmills, Basingstoke, Hampshire, UK: Palgrave Macmillan.

Rahula, W. (1974). *What the Buddha taught.* New York, NY: Grove Press.

Rakoczy, S. (2006). *Great mystics & social justice: Walking with the two feet of love.* New York, NY: Paulist Press.

Rand, A. (1964). *The virtue of selfishness.* New York, NY: Penguin Books.

Rank, M. R. (2004). *One nation, underprivileged: Why American poverty affects us all.* New York, NY: Oxford University Press.

Rawls, J. (1971). *A theory of justice.* Cambridge, MA: The Belknap Press of Harvard University Press.

Rawls, J. (2001). *Justice as fairness: A restatement* (E. Kelly, Ed.). Cambridge, MA: The Belknap Press of Harvard University Press.

Rehmann, J. (2013). *Theories of ideology: The powers of alienation and subjection.* Chicago, IL: Haymarket Books.

Rogers, A., & Pilgrim, D. (2003). *Mental health and inequality.* New York, NY: Palgrave Macmillan.

Rose, N. (1998). *Inventing our selves: Psychology, power, and personhood.* Cambridge, UK: Cambridge University Press.

Rose, S. M., & Hatzenbuehler, S. (2009). Embodying social class: The link between poverty, income equality and health. *International Social Work, 52*(4), 459-471.

Ruether, R. R. (1972). *Liberation theology: Human hope confronts Christian history and American power.* New York, NY: Paulist Press.

Ryan, W. (1971). *Blaming the victim.* New York, NY: Pantheon Books.

Saltman, K. J. (2007). Schooling in disaster capitalism: How the political right is using disaster to privatize public schooling. *Teacher Education Quarterly,* Spring 2007, 131–156.

Sampson, E. E. (1975). On justice as equality. *Journal of Social Issues, 31*(3), 45–64.

Sampson, E. E. (1985). The decentralization of identity: Toward a revised concept of personal and social order. *American Psychologist, 40*(11), 1203–1211.

Sampson, E. E. (1989). The challenge of social change for psychology: Globalization and psychology's theory of the person. *American Psychologist, 44*(6), 914–921.

Sandel, M. J. (1982). *Liberalism and the limits of justice.* Cambridge, UK: Cambridge University Press.

Sandel, M. J. (2012). *What money can't buy: The moral limits of markets.* New York, NY: Farrar, Straus and Giroux.

Sartre, J. P. (1953). *Being and nothingness* (H. Barnes, Trans.). New York, NY: Washington Square Press.

Scarry, E. (1985). *The body in pain: The making and unmaking of the world.* New York, NY: Oxford University Press.

Schacht, R. (1970). *Alienation.* Garden City, NY: Doubleday & Co.

Schor, J. B. (2004). *Born to buy: The commercialization and the new consumer culture.* New York, NY: Scribner.

Schraube, E., & Osterkamp, U. (2013). *Psychology from the standpoint of the subject: Selected writings of Klaus Holzkamp*. Houndmills, Basingstoke, Hampshire: UK: Palgrave Macmillan.

Seligman, M. E. P. (1975). *Helplessness: On depression, development, and death*. San Francisco, CA: W. H. Freeman.

Selye, H. (1974). *Stress without distress*. New York, NY: New American Library.

Selye, H. (1976). *The stress of life* (Revised ed.). New York, NY: McGraw-Hill.

Semega, J. L., Fontenot, K. R., & Kollar, M. A. (2017). *Income and poverty in the United States: 2016*. U. S. Department of Commerce.

Sen, A. (1999). *Development as freedom*. New York, NY: Anchor Books.

Sidanius, J., & Pratto, F. (1999). *Social dominance: An intergroup theory of social hierarchy and oppression*. Cambridge, UK: Cambridge University Press.

Silberman, S. (2015). *Neurotribes: The legacy of autism and the future of neurodiversity*. New York, NY: Penguin Books.

Small, D. (2005). *Power, interest and psychology: Elements of a social materialist understanding of distress*. Ross-on-Wye, UK: PCCS Books.

Smith, L. (2010). *Psychology, poverty, and the end of social exclusion: Putting our practice to work*. New York, NY: Teachers College Press.

Soelle, D. (1975). *Suffering* (E. R. Kalin, Trans.). Philadelphia, PA: Fortress Press.

Soelle, D. (2001). *The silent cry: Mysticism and resistance* (B. & M. Rumscheidt, Trans.). Minneapolis, MN: Fortress Press.

Solomon, R. C., & Murphy, M. C. (Eds.) (2000). *What is justice?: Classic and contemporary readings* (2nd Ed.). New York, NY: Oxford University Press.

Solomon, S., Greenberg, J., & Pyszczynski, T. (1991). A terror management theory of social behavior: The psychological function of self-esteem and cultural worldviews. In M. P. Zanna (Ed.), *Advances in experimental and social psychology* (Vol. 24, pp. 91–159). Orlando, FL: Academic Press.

Speed, E., Moncrieff, J., & Rapley, M. (Eds.) (2014). *De-medicalizing misery: Society, politics and the mental health industry*. New York, NY: Palgrave Macmillan.

Spinelli, E. (2014). *Practicing existential therapy: The relational world* (2nd ed.). London, UK: Sage.

Staub, E. (1989). *The roots of evil: The origins of genocide and other group violence*. Cambridge, UK: Cambridge University Press.

Sullivan, H. S. (1953). *The interpersonal theory of psychiatry*. New York, NY: Norton.

Sullivan, J. W. N. (1960). *Beethoven: His spiritual development*. New York, NY: Vintage Books.

Swanson, J. (2008). Recognition and redistribution: Rethinking culture and the economic. *Theory, Culture & Society, 22*, 87–118.

Teo, T. (1998). Prolegomenon to a contemporary psychology of liberation. *Theory & Psychology, 8*(4), 527–547.

Teo, T. (2015). Critical psychology: A geography of intellectual engagement and resistance. *American Psychologist, 70*(3), 243–254.

Thompson, N. (1997). *Anti-discriminatory practice* (2nd ed.). London, UK: Macmillan.

Thorsen, D. E. (2010). The neoliberal challenge: What is neoliberalism. *Contemporary Readings in Law and Social Justice, 11*(2), 118-214.

Tillich, P. (1952). *The courage to be.* New Haven, CT: Yale University Press.

Tillich, P. (1957). *The dynamics of faith.* New York, NY: Harper & Row.

von Eckhartsberg, R., & Valle, R. S. (1981), Heideggerian thinking and the Eastern mind. In R. S. Valle & R. von Eckhartsberg (Eds.), *The metaphors of consciousness* (pp. 287–311). New York, NY: Plenum Press.

Vlastos, G. (1962). Justice and equality. In R. B. Brandt (Ed.), *Social justice* (pp. 31–72). Englewood Cliffs, NJ: Prentice-Hall.

Wachtel, P. L. (1989). *The poverty of affluence: A psychological portrait of the American way of life.* Philadelphia, PA: New Society Publishers.

Walzer, M. (1990). The communitarian critique of liberalism. *Political Theory. 18*(1), 6–23.

Watts, A. W. (1951). *The wisdom of insecurity.* New York, NY: Vintage Books.

Watts, A. W. (1961). *Psychotherapy east and west.* New York, NY: Pantheon Books.

Watts, A. W. (1966). *The book: On the taboo against knowing who you are.* New York, NY: Collier Books.

Watts, A. W. (1968). *Does it matter?* New York, NY: Vintage Books.

Watts, A. W. (1972). *The supreme identity.* New York, NY: Vintage Books.

Wayment, H. A., & Bauer, J. J. (Eds.). (2008). *Transcending self-interest: Psychological explorations of the quiet ego.* Washington, DC: American Psychological Association.

Weber, M. (1930). *The Protestant ethic and the spirit of capitalism.* London, UK: Routledge.

Weil, S. (1952). *The need for roots* (A. Wills, Trans.). New York, NY: Harper & Row.

Weil, S. (1977). *Waiting on God* (2nd ed.) (E. Craufurd, Trans.). London, UK: HarperCollins.

Wickramasekera II, I. E. (2013). Hypnosis and transpersonal psychology: Answering the call within. In H. L. Friedman & G. Hartelius, (Eds.), *The Wiley-Blackwell handbook of transpersonal psychology* (pp. 492–511). Chichester, UK: John Wiley & Sons.

Wilber, K. (1977). *The spectrum of consciousness.* Wheaton, IL: Theosophical Publishing House.

Wilber, K. (1980). *The Atman project: A transpersonal view of human development.* Wheaton, IL: The Theosophical Publishing House.

Wilber, K. (1998). *The marriage of sense and soul: Integrating science and religion.* New York, NY: Random House.

Wilber, K. (2000). *Integral psychology: Consciousness, spirit, psychology, therapy.* Boston, MA: Shambhala Press.

Wilkinson, R., & Pickett, K. (2009). *The spirit level: Why greater equality makes societies stronger.* New York, NY: Bloomsbury Press.

Williams, C. R. (2008). Compassion, suffering and the self: A moral psychology of social justice. *Current Sociology, 56*(5), 5–24.

Williams, P. (2012). *Rethinking madness: Towards a paradigm shift in our understanding and treatment of psychosis.* San Francisco, CA: Sky's Edge Publishing.

Wineman, S. (1984). *The politics of human services.* Montreal, Canada: Black Rose Books.

Wright, E. O. (1994). *Interrogating inequality: Essays on class analysis, socialism, and Marxism.* New York, NY: Verso.

Yalom, I. D. (1980). *Existential psychotherapy.* New York, NY: Basic Books.

Young, I. M. (1990). *Justice and the politics of difference.* Princeton, NJ: Princeton University Press.

Youssef, H. A., & Fadi, S. A. (1996). Frantz Fanon and political psychiatry. *History of Psychiatry, 7,* 525–532.

Name Index

Subject Index

About the Author

Frank Gruba-McCallister, PhD, received his master's and doctoral degree in Clinical Psychology from Purdue University. He is currently retired after having taught for more than thirty-three years at the Illinois School of Professional Psychology-Chicago, Adler University, and the Chicago School of Professional Psychology-Chicago. He has been the recipient of numerous of awards for teaching. He also served in academic administration at all three schools. While the Vice-President of Academic Affairs at Adler, he oversaw the revision of all degree programs to support the newly adopted mission of the school to educate socially responsible practitioners. This included adding courses to the curriculum and a community service practicum that provided students with knowledge and skills to advance social justice. This innovation was recognized by the Clinical Psychology Doctoral program, which received the 2007 American Psychological Association's Board of Education Affairs Award for Innovative Practices in Graduate Education in Psychology, a prestigious and highly competitive honor. Dr. Gruba-McCallister also was one of the two developers of a Masters in Police Psychology program, which was the only program of its type in the United States. It was designed for uniformed and civilian employees of police departments and other law enforcement agencies and provided them with knowledge and methods in psychology that could be integrated into their work to better protect them against the stress and adverse impact of their work and provide more effective, sensitive and, community-oriented services to the people they serve. Prior to teaching, Dr. Gruba-McCallister provided clinical service primarily to individuals in a medical setting and in private practice. He continues his commitment to social justice through writing, advocacy, and political activism.